The Unity of the Bible

The Unity of the Bible

Exploring the Beauty and Structure of the Bible

Duane L. Christensen

Paulist Press
New York/Mahwah, N.J.

Cover design by Valerie Petro
Book design by Celine M. Allen

Library of Congress Cataloging-in-Publication Data

Christensen, Duane L., 1938–
   The unity of the Bible : exploring the beauty and structure of the Bible /
Duane L. Christensen.
      p. cm.
   ISBN 0-8091-4110-8 (alk. paper)
   1. Bible—Introductions. I. Title
   BS475.3 .C48 2003
   220.6'1—dc21

                                                          2003004705

Published by Paulist Press
997 Macarthur Boulevard
Mahwah, New Jersey 07430

www.paulistpress.com

Printed and bound in the
United States of America

Contents

To Dr. Ronald E. Cottle Sr.
President and Founder of Christian Life School of Theology
whose vision inspired me to write this book
in conjunction with my CLST course on
The Bible as a Whole

1

Origin and Formation of the Tanakh

To become familiar with the Bible as a whole is a challenge, for the Bible is a big book. For most of us, it is actually many books—a library of sixty-six books in the Christian tradition (not counting the Apocrypha). In one sense, this is true; but at the same time, it is also misleading, for the Bible is somehow *one book*—a single book from a single source. At least that is what we affirm in public worship when we say, "Here ends the reading from the Word of God" or "The Word of the Lord." Our goal in this book is to lay the foundation for achieving fluency in the knowledge and use of the Bible as a whole. To that end, we will explore its literary structure and contents as a single book—the "Word of God"—which is to be enjoyed as a remarkable work of art.

There are different ways to approach the Bible. In some sense, it is a bit like buying a car. We might simply take a long, loving look at it, which could be called the "aesthetic approach." When it comes to a Ferrari, that's about all most of us will ever do. A second approach is to take it for a "test drive," putting its teaching to work. This might be called the "functional approach," which is a useful way to experience its worth. A third approach might involve opening the hood and getting out the manual so as to discover how the car was built and what its inner characteristics are. As we become familiar with each part and how the parts function together, we begin to know the car in a special way. This is the "genetic approach," which we intend to apply to this study of the Bible. Our task is to "open the hood" and to discover how the Bible "was built," how its various parts function together to make an organic whole that continues to speak its time-honored message today, as it has in ages past.

The giant sequoia redwood tree begins as a tiny seed, lodged within a surprisingly small cone—much smaller than that of a pine tree. And so it is with the Bible. God's revelation in the pages of this book begins in the mysterious experience of the man Moses on Mount Sinai, more than three thousand years ago, when God gave him the Ten Commandments. Those commandments are the stipulations of a "treaty," or covenant relationship, that God established with his chosen people Israel. That simple beginning in the experience of a single man alone on a mountain with God is the "seed" from which the "giant sequoia" of God's revelation grew.

THE CANONICAL PROCESS IN TWO STAGES

The Bible we have today was formed in two stages within a historical process that extends more than a thousand years. The first stage extends from the time of Moses to Ezra (ca. 1200–400 B.C.E.), in the writing of the Tanakh—an acronym formed from the first letters of the Hebrew words for Law, Prophets, and Writings: *Torah* (TA), *Nevi'im* (NA), and *Kethuvim* (KH). The canonical process was completed in the apostolic era of the early Christian movement in a second stage of this historical process, which we designate here as the formation of the "Completed Tanakh" (ca. 50–100 C.E.). There was an initial period of time when the Hebrew Scriptures of ancient Israel were compiled in the approximate list and arrangement they have in the Standard Jewish Bible (Tanakh). And there was a second time-period when the Christian Scriptures (the "Apostolic Writings") were added to the Tanakh to form the Bible as the "Completed Tanakh."

To discover how the Bible we have today was formed, we need to examine closely each of these two major stages in the canonical process. Our goal is to see more clearly the nature of the Tanakh and the relation between these twenty-two books, as the books of the Hebrew Bible were numbered in antiquity, and the traditional twenty-seven books of the New Testament. The total number of books in the Completed Tanakh is thus forty-nine ($22 + 27 = 49 = 7^2$).

There is no detailed account in any of our sources as to how this happened. The story must be pieced together from evidence found in various sources as well as from a close reading of the biblical text itself. In both of the major stages in the canonical process of writing the First Testament (Tanakh) and the Second Testament (Apostolic Writings, commonly known as the New Testament), the motivating factor is a theological crisis within the ongoing community of faith. The writing of the scriptures is a response to these challenges.

In the first instance, the crisis is the destruction of the city of Jerusalem and the First Temple (Solomon's Temple) by Nebuchadnezzar, king of Babylon, in 586 B.C.E. This traumatic event and the great relocation of the population of the people of ancient Israel that followed (the Babylonian Exile) mark the end of an era. We move from the kingdom of ancient Israel to nascent Judaism and the role of a canonical text of sacred scripture around which life is organized in the era of the Second Temple (ca. 520–20 B.C.E.).

In the second instance, it is the crisis of Paul and others in the early Christian community, as they struggle with their understanding of eschatology and the destruction of the Third Temple (Herod's Temple) in the city of Jerusalem by the Romans in 70 C.E. The construction of the Third Temple began in the eighteenth year of King Herod's reign (20 B.C.E.). According to the Gospel of John (2:20), the building of that temple took forty-six years. Josephus tells us that final embellishments were being made to the Third Temple virtually to the time of the Great Revolt of the Jews against Rome (66–73 C.E.), when Titus and the Tenth Roman Legion Fretensis turned that magnificent structure into smoldering ruins in 70 C.E.

The destruction of the Temple in Jerusalem plays a major role in each of the two major stages in the canonical process. In the first instance, the destruction of the First Temple (Solomon's Temple, ca. 950–586 B.C.E.) and the Babylonian Exile that follows precipitate the formation of the Tanakh as the Word of God in the period of transition from the Neo-Babylonian Empire to the Persian Empire. In the second instance, it is the destruction of the Third Temple (Herod's Temple, 20 B.C.E.–70 C.E.) that culminates in the formation of the Completed Tanakh, with the addition of the Apostolic Writings in which Paul, Luke, Mark, and John play primary roles.

The crisis of the persecution of Christians by Nero after the burning of Rome (64 C.E.) and the events unfolding in Palestine in the Jewish revolt against Rome (66–73 C.E.), play a major role in the formation of the Apostolic Writings and the Completed Tanakh. The first Christians were Jews and as such they were part of a people (Israel) who had a set of highly revered scriptures. In this regard, it is interesting to read the words of Paul to Timothy:

> But you [Timothy], continue in what you have learned and have become convinced of, recalling...how from childhood you have known the holy scriptures, which can give you wisdom that leads to deliverance through trusting in Yeshua the Messiah. All scripture is God-breathed and is valuable. (2 Tim 3:14–16)

Christians did not take the Jewish Scriptures from the Jews—Christianity originated within Judaism. Jesus was a Jew and these were his scriptures; his disciples were Jews and these were their scriptures; the first Christians of Jerusalem were Jews and these were their scriptures. As my colleague John Miller puts it, "Christianity was born with a Bible in its cradle!"

THE CANONICAL PROCESS FROM MOSES TO EZRA

As Moses lived with the words of the Ten Commandments that God had given him, he gradually expanded those principles into what we call the "Torah"—the teaching of God in the form of laws and narrative. In recent years, scholars have discovered that the great collection of laws in the "Central Core" of Deuteronomy (chaps. 12—26) is an expansion of the Ten Commandments. The order of those commandments, as recorded in Deuteronomy 5:6–21, determines the order of the laws preserved in the Central Core. Moreover, the laws in Deuteronomy 12—26 were used to shape the narratives in the book of Genesis, and throughout the whole of what is sometimes called the "Primary History"—Genesis through 2 Kings in the Tanakh. This body of literature is also called the Torah (five books of Moses) and the Former Prophets (Joshua, Judges, 1–2 Samuel, and 1–2 Kings). Put in simple words, Deuteronomy functions as a bridge connecting the "Law and the Prophets" in the structure and content of the Tanakh.

Toward the end of the period of the monarchy in ancient Israel, King Josiah set out to repair the Temple in Jerusalem. As we learn in the story, which is told in detail in 2 Kings 22—23, the "book of the Torah" was found in the process of repairing the Temple. And "when the king heard the words of the book of the Torah, he rent his clothes" in consternation (2 Kgs 22:11) and immediately set out to lead the entire nation of Israel in a great renewal of their covenant with God, as recorded in the book of Deuteronomy. It is within this particular historical context that canonical activity led to the writing of a "first edition" of the Former Prophets. The religious reform in Jerusalem came to naught as Josiah was killed by the Egyptians in battle, when "Pharaoh Neco slew him at Megiddo...and [Josiah's] servants carried him dead in a chariot from Megiddo, and brought him to Jerusalem, and buried him in his own tomb" (2 Kgs 23:29–30). Things went from bad to worse from a political point of view until the city of Jerusalem itself, along with the Temple of Solomon, was destroyed by Nebuchadnezzar, king of Babylon, and the people of Israel were carried away in captivity (587–586 B.C.E.).

The canonical activity continued as the writing of the Former Prophets was updated to include these tragic events and complemented by the writing of the Latter Prophets (the books of Isaiah, Jeremiah, Ezekiel, and The Twelve [Lesser Prophets]). As we will see, these books emerge together as a single literary and canonical entity, in which Deuteronomy is the bridge tying together the Torah and two segments of the Prophets, as follows:

	Genesis	Exodus	
	Leviticus	Numbers	
	Deuteronomy		
Joshua	Judges	Isaiah	Jeremiah
Samuel	Kings	Ezekiel	The Twelve

The Primary History (Genesis through 2 Kings) was expanded to constitute "the Law and the Prophets." These in turn make up the first two divisions of the Tanakh.

The Former and the Latter Prophets were published together as literary complements in the context of the Babylonian Exile (ca. 587–538 B.C.E.). In chapter 3, we will show in detail how closely these two sections of the canon of the Tanakh are tied together to constitute a single literary and canonical entity—the Prophets (*Nevi'im*). In chapter 4, we will tell the story of how the third section of the canon emerged at this same time in the form of four books, which we will call the "Hagiographa." Other books (Esther, Daniel, Ezra, Nehemiah, and 1–2 Chronicles) were subsequently added to make up the Writings of the Tanakh.

The end result of this phase in the canonical process was the formation of a seventeen-book canon, which we call the "deuteronomic" canon because of the central role of the book of Deuteronomy in its literary structure:

Genesis	Exodus	Joshua	Judges
Leviticus	Numbers	Samuel	Kings
	Deuteronomy		
Isaiah	Jeremiah	Psalms	Proverbs
Ezekiel	The Twelve	Job	*Megilloth*

The term *Megilloth* here refers to the "Festal Scrolls," which originally numbered only four: Ruth, Song of Songs, Ecclesiastes, and Lamentations. In time, the book of Esther took its place as the fifth of these scrolls. More on this in chapter 4.

It is important to observe at this point that the "chiastic" relationship among the four groups of four books, which are structured around the book of Deuteronomy in the above diagram, also constitutes the four primary sections of the canon of the Tanakh:

Torah	Former Prophets
Latter Prophets	"Hagiographa"

Each of these four sections of the deuteronomic canon is composed of four parts, which are arranged in a chiasm (a:b::b:a). In short, the final shape of the Tanakh is determined at the outset:

Tanakh = Torah + Prophets (in two parts) + **Writings**

It should be remembered that we are a long way here from the modern concept of a "book" in which all of these sections are arranged together in sewn leaves between two covers. For hundreds of years the individual books of the Tanakh were written on scrolls. Eventually it was Christians who put the Greek translation of the Tanakh, the Septuagint, together with their Greek "New Testament" into the form of a codex made of parchment leaves, which were written on both sides and sewn together, to constitute the first true "books" of the Western world.

As time passed, additions were made to the canon of the Tanakh. The book of Esther became the fifth of the Festal Scrolls (*Megilloth*). And the book of Daniel took its place among the Writings as a bridge among the four "books" in the "Hagiographa" of the seventeen-book deuteronomic canon, the four Latter Prophets, and two groups of four "history books." The Former Prophets have their parallel in what we designate here as the "Chronicler's History," which is made up of four parts: Ezra, Nehemiah, 1 Chronicles, and 2 Chronicles.

One aspect of the role of the book of Daniel as a literary bridge in this structure may be outlined as follows:

Joshua	Judges	Isaiah	Jeremiah
Samuel	Kings	Ezekiel	The Twelve
	Daniel		
	Ezra	Nehemiah	
	1 Chronicles	2 Chronicles	

According to this structure, Daniel functions as a literary bridge connecting the Former Prophets, the Latter Prophets, and the still "Later Prophets," i.e., the Chronicler's History. In some circles, the book of

Daniel was treated as though it were a sixth Festal Scroll. At the
same time, it is closely related to Ezra and Nehemiah in a number of
ways; and it is also a work of narrative history, like the Former
Prophets. Though the book of Daniel functions as wisdom,
prophecy, and history, it also represents a unique literary genre as the
only example of full-blown apocalyptic literature in the canon of the
Tanakh. As the preceding diagram suggests, however, the most
important role of Daniel is that of prophet. Among many Christians
through the centuries, Daniel is considered to be one of the four so-
called "Major Prophets," as a sequel to the big three—Isaiah, Jeremiah, and Ezekiel. That's where the book is located in the order of
the books of the Bible in printed versions of the English Bible.

In the hands of Ezra, who is sometimes called a "second Moses"
in Jewish tradition, the canon of the Hebrew Scriptures was expanded
to form the twenty-two-book "pentateuchal" canon, which Josephus
subsequently described as consisting of five books of Moses, thirteen
prophets, and four "Hagiographa." It was this way of looking at the
structure of the Tanakh that influenced Paul and others responsible
for the structure of the canon of the Apostolic Writings (the New Testament). What had begun as an attempt to add a fifth section to the
Tanakh, corresponding to the Writings of the Hebrew Bible, gradually evolved into a forty-nine-book canon of sacred scripture. This
canon of the "Completed Tanakh" may be outlined in a concentric
structure as follows:

The Completed Tanakh—a Canon of 49 Books	*Genesis–Revelation*	
A Beginnings—creation and story of the patriarchs	Genesis	1
B Israel's History: Exodus→Eisodus (Entry)→Exile	Exodus–Kings	8
C Latter Prophets	Isaiah, Jeremiah, Ezekiel, and The Twelve	4
D Writings of the Tanakh	"Hagiographa," Daniel, Chronicler's History	9
X **New Torah**	Four Gospels and Acts	5
D´ Ecclesiastical Letters of Paul	Romans–2 Thessalonians	9
C´ Personal Letters of Paul	Timothy (2), Titus, Philemon	4
B´ Apostolic "History"—four "pillars"	Hebrews and 7 General Epistles	8
A´ "Final ending" and new creation	Revelation	1

In this diagram, the number of books in each category is given in the column at the far right. These numbers are balanced perfectly in an inverted pattern. If items A and B and A´ and B´ are combined, as they are in the very concept of the Primary History (Genesis through Kings), the balance is even more striking: $(9 + 4 + 9) + 5 + (9 + 4 + 9)$.

2

The Torah
From Creation to the Death of Moses

The Hebrew Bible (Tanakh) contains individual writings that go back to the time of Moses. But the Bible itself, as a collection of canonical (authoritative) texts in the religion of ancient Judaism, emerges in the wake of the destruction of Jerusalem and Solomon's Temple in 586 B.C.E. The first step in the canonical process culminates in the formation of the Torah, the first five books in the Hebrew Bible, which constitute the "canon within the canon"—the most authoritative section of the Tanakh.

Ancient Palestinian Judaism organized its life around the recitation of the Torah in public worship according to a pattern of prescribed readings (*parashot*) within a three-year cycle, which took the people through the whole of the Torah (the Pentateuch, the five books of Moses). Two such cycles were followed by a "sabbatical year," in which the entire book of Deuteronomy was presented at the Festival of Booths (see Deut 31:10–13). It is the renewal of the covenant God established with his people under Moses at Mount Sinai that constitutes the center of the canonical process. The stipulations of that covenant are summarized in the words of the Ten Commandments (Deut 5:6–21, cf. Exod 20:2–17).

BEGINNING OF CANON HISTORY: EXODUS THROUGH DEUTERONOMY

From the perspective of canon history, the Bible begins with the story of Moses and the establishment of Israel as God's chosen people.

10

That story is told in the books of Exodus through Deuteronomy, which are arranged in a chiastic structure as follows:

Exodus	Leviticus
Numbers	Deuteronomy

In this diagram, Exodus and Deuteronomy are structural pairs, along with Leviticus and Numbers. Moreover, the three "wilderness books" of Exodus through Numbers form a sub-unit of their own, for these three books are different from Deuteronomy in many ways.

The story of Israel as a national entity begins with the birth of Moses in Exodus 1 and ends with the death of Moses and the transition in leadership to his successor Joshua in Deuteronomy 34. At the same time, this "foundational story" takes place within a larger structural frame, which extends from creation to the eschaton. Within this narrative framework we find the nesting of parallel features, which may be outlined in an elaborate seven-part series of nested menorah patterns ("wheels within wheels"):

The Tanakh in a Menorah Pattern	*Torah/Prophets/Writings*
A Primeval History	Gen 1–11
B Patriarchs: Abraham, Isaac and Jacob	Gen12–36
C Joseph and his eleven brothers (esp. Judah)	Gen 37–50
X **Journey home—to the land of Canaan**	**Exod–Deut**
C´ Former Prophets	Joshua, Judges, 1–2 Samuel and 1–2 Kings
B´ Latter Prophets	Isaiah, Jeremiah, Ezekiel, and The Twelve
A´ Writings of the Tanakh	"Hagiographa" (4), Daniel, and Chronicler's History (4)

2nd Level Menorah: Journey to the Promised Land	*Exod–Deut*
A Birth of Moses—God's chosen leader for the people of Israel	Exod 1:1–22
B Moses is called to leadership—the Exodus	Exod 2:1–14:31
C *Song of Moses* at the crossing of the Red Sea	Exod 15:1–21
X **Journey from Egypt to the plains of Moab**	Exod 15:22–Deut 31:30
C´ *Song of Moses* in the plains of Moab	Deut 32:1–52
B´ Blessing of Moses and transfer of leadership—the Eisodus	Deut 33:1–29
A´ Death of Moses and transition of leadership to Joshua	Deut 34:1–12

3rd Level Menorah: God's Revelation at Mount Sinai	*Exod 15:22—Deut 31:30*
A Journey from the Red Sea to Mount Sinai	Exod 15:22—19:25
B Covenant Code—including the Ten Commandments	Exod 20:1—23:33
C Revelation at Sinai: Covenant with Israel made and broken	Exod 24:1—33:23
X **Journey through the wilderness to the plains of Moab**	Exod 34—Deut 5
C´ Revelation at Sinai: Preparation for covenant renewal	Deut 6:1—11:32
B´ Deuteronomic Code—built on the Ten Commandments	Deut 12:1—26:19
A´ Journey from Moab across the Jordan River (anticipated)	Deut 27:1—31:30

4th Level Menorah: From Sinai to the Plains of Moab	*Exod 34—Deut 5*
A Second giving of the Ten Commandments	Exod 34
B At Mount Sinai, "Moses finished the work" (40:33)	Exod 35:1—40:33
C The cloud and glory—God's tabernacling presence	Exod 40:34—Lev 27
X **Journey from Sinai to the plains of Moab**	Num 1—36
C´ The Eisodus into the Promised Land under Moses	Deut 1:1—3:22
B´ In the plains of Moab, Moses finished his work	Deut 3:23—4:49
A´ Theophany and covenant at Horeb—the Ten Commandments	Deut 5

5th Level Menorah: Forty Years in the Wilderness	*Num 1—36*
A Israel prepares to enter the Promised Land	1:1—10:36
B Journey from Mount Sinai to Kadesh in the wilderness of Paran	11:1—35
C Political rebellion on the part of Miriam and Aaron	12:1—16
X **Forty years on the edge of the Promised Land**	13:1—20:21
C´ Death of Aaron at Mount Hor (Miriam died at Kadesh [20:1])	20:22—29
B´ Journey from Kadesh to the plains of Moab	21:1—25:18
A´ Israel prepares to enter the Promised Land	26:1—36:13

6th Level Menorah: Rebellion in the Wilderness	*Num 13:1—20:21*
A Disaster at Kadesh—rebellion of the spies	13:1—14:45
B Laws on cultic matters—stoning narrative for violating the Sabbath	15:1—41
C Rebellion of Korah, Dathan, and Abiram—swallowed by the earth	16:1—33
X **Confirmation of Aaron as priestly leader**	16:34—17:13
C´ Levites are given the tithe as their tribal allotment	18:1—32
B´ Laws on matters of defilement—the red heifer	19:1—22
A´ Waters of Meribah and the "rebellion" of Moses	20:1—21

7th Level Menorah: Confirmation of Aaron's Priesthood	Num 16:34—17:13
A All Israel fled saying, "The earth will swallow us too!"	16:34-35
B Making of the bronze covering for the altar from rebels' censers	16:36-40
C Rebellion of the congregation—God decides to "consume them"	16:41-45
X **Moses commands Aaron to make atonement for the people**	16:46
C´ Aaron takes incense in a censer and stays the plague	16:47-50
B´ Test of the rods—Aaron's rod blooms to end the murmuring	17:1-12
A´ The Israelites are afraid: "Are we all to perish?"	17:13

The story of Moses as founder of the religion of ancient Israel is the structural center of a menorah pattern that embraces the whole of the Tanakh. The stories in the Primeval History (Genesis 1—11), from Adam to Abram, are set over against the Writings of the Tanakh. And the story of the Fathers (Abraham, Isaac, Jacob, and his twelve sons) is set over against the Latter Prophets (Isaiah, Jeremiah, Ezekiel, and the Book of the Twelve [Lesser Prophets]). The story of Joseph and his brothers, with particular interest in Judah in Genesis 37—50, anticipates the story of the Former Prophets (Joshua through 2 Kings). Joseph (through his sons Ephraim and Manasseh) and Judah dominate the story of the nation of Israel in the Promised Land in the Former Prophets, as their eponymous ancestors do in the narrative of Genesis. And in the structural center of the Tanakh as a whole we find the epic story of Israel's journey home, from slavery in the land of Egypt.

In one sense, Exodus through Deuteronomy is the story of Moses as leader of ancient Israel—from his birth in Egypt to his death in Moab, on the eve of the entry into the Promised Land (the Eisodus) under Joshua. It is the story of the Exodus from Egypt on the part of the "children of Israel," who move from bondage in Egypt to become a special people in a covenant relationship with God that was established in the wilderness. That covenant, which is based on the Ten Commandments Moses receives from God on Mount Sinai, includes a code of law (Exod 20:23—23:33, the Covenant Code) upon which the people of Israel are to order their lives in the Promised Land. The work that Moses accomplishes in this epic journey includes the construction of a center of worship known as the Tabernacle where the glory of God is made present. The experience of deliverance from bondage is the grounds for celebration as witnessed by the inclusion of two "Songs of Moses" (Exod 15 and Deut 32).

The primary focus is not the story of Moses, as such. Moses is simply the leader God chooses to lay a foundation on which to build. The goal of the epic journey of the children of Israel is to experience the presence of God in an established covenant relationship. God himself is the subject of this story.

GENESIS WITHIN THE CANONICAL PROCESS

Though the books of Exodus through Deuteronomy are the beginning of the canonical process from a historical point of view, they constitute the second chapter of God's story in human history so far as the Tanakh is concerned. The first chapter is the book of Genesis, which takes its place within a larger literary context of the Primary History, which may be outlined in a nested series of three menorah patterns:

The Primary History in a Menorah Pattern	*Gen–2 Kgs*
A Primeval History: From covenant of Noah to that of Abraham	Gen 1–11
B Land promise given to Abraham, Isaac, and Jacob	Gen 12–50
C Egypt judged–plagues and institution of Passover	Exod 1:1–12:36
X **Exodus and Eisodus–battle camp at Gilgal**	Exod 12:37–Josh 4
C´ Canaan conquered–observance of Passover	Josh 5–12
B´ Land promise fulfilled–allotment of the Promised Land	Josh 13–24
A´ "Special History": Israel as the people of the covenant	Judg–2 Kgs

2nd Level Menorah: Exodus and Eisodus	*Exod 12:37–Josh 4:24*
A The Exodus from Egypt–crossing the Red Sea	Exod 12:37–14:31
B Song of Moses at the crossing of the Sea	Exod 15:1–21
C Wilderness wandering	Exod 15:22–18:27
X **God establishes the covenant at Mount Sinai**	Exod 19:1–Num 10:10

C´	Wilderness wandering and transfer of leadership	Num 10:11–Deut 31:30
B´	Song of Moses in Moab; blessing and death of Moses	Deut 32–34
A´	The Eisodus (entry)—crossing the Jordan River	Josh 1–4

3rd Level Menorah: Covenant at Sinai		*Exod 19:1–Num 10:10*
A	Covenant ratified and regulated	Exod 19:1–24:18
B	Tabernacle planned	Exod 25:1–31:18
C	Covenant broken—incident with the golden calf	Exod 32:1-35
X	**Theophany on Sinai: The promised presence**	Exod 33:1-23
C´	Covenant renewed	Exod 34:1-35
B´	Tabernacle built	Exod 35:1–40:38
A´	Covenant regulations	Lev 1:1–Num 10:10

Though it is proper to think of the Torah as a literary unit within the Bible (i.e., the Pentateuch), it is also important to remember that it is an integral part of all that follows—in both testaments. The book of Deuteronomy, in particular, functions as a bridge connecting the Torah with the Prophets (both Former Prophets and Latter Prophets).

In the above structure, Genesis 1—11 forms the introduction to what some call the Hexateuch (Genesis through Joshua), as well as to what we call here the "Special History" of Israel as the people of the covenant in the Promised Land (Judges through 2 Kings). As the introduction to the Bible as a whole, Genesis 1—11 is a remarkable work of literary art that cannot be reduced to any single structure. One of the more useful readings may be outlined as follows:

The Primeval History in a Menorah Pattern		*Gen 1—11*
A	Adam and Eve—the story of creation	1:1–3:21
B	Expulsion from the Garden of Eden	3:22–4:26
C	Generations of Adam and sons	5:1-32
X	**Noah and the flood—a new creation**	6:1–9:29
C´	Generations of Noah and sons	10:1-32
B´	Dispersion—the story of the Tower of Babel	11:1-9
A´	Abram and Sarai—beginning of a new story	11:10-32

The opening account of the Creation Story (Genesis 1—4), which includes the account of Adam and his three sons (Cain, Abel, and Seth), is set over against the dispersion of human beings among the groups of antiquity in the story of the Tower of Babel. This latter story is preceded by the account of Noah and his three sons: Shem, Ham, and Japheth (Gen 10—11). Within this structure we find a reference to Enoch, a man who "walked with God" (Gen 5:22, 24), and the elaborate story of Noah who also "walked with God" (Gen 6:9). These are the only two individuals in Genesis whose relationship with God is described in this terminology.

A major shift occurs as we move from chapter 11 to chapter 12 in Genesis. In Genesis 1—11, the story deals with the human race as a whole. In Genesis 12, the story narrows its focus to a single man and his family in the person of Abra(ha)m. The content of the story that follows in the Abraham cycle may be outlined in a series of three nested menorah patterns:

The Abram/Abraham Narrative Cycle in Genesis	Gen 11:27—22:24
A Genealogy of Terah (Abraham's father)	11:27-32
B Start of Abram's spiritual odyssey (Abraham's call)	12:1-5
C Building of altars in the Promised Land (at Shechem)	12:6-9
X **Abram/Abraham among foreign peoples**	12:10—21:34
C´ Building of an altar on Mount Moriah to sacrifice Isaac	22:1-9
B´ Climax of Abraham's spiritual odyssey (the *Akedah*)	22:10-19
A´ Genealogy of Nahor (Abraham's brother)	22:20-24

2nd Level Menorah: Abra(ha)m among Foreign Peoples	Gen 12:10—21:34
A Sarai's ordeal in a foreign palace; Abram and Lot part	12:10—13:18
B Abram comes to the rescue of Sodom and Lot	14:1-24
C Covenant of sacrifice with Abram (and Sarai)	15:1-21
X **Covenant of circumcision with Abraham (name changed)**	16:1—17:27
C´ A son promised to Abraham and Sarah	18:1-15
B´ Abraham comes to the rescue of Sodom and Lot	18:16—19:38
A´ Sarah's ordeal in a foreign palace; Abraham and Ishmael part	20:1—21:34

3rd Level Menorah: Covenant of Circumcision	Gen 16—17
A Hagar (with Ishmael) driven out of Abram's house	16:1–10
B Birth of Ishmael announced by an angel	16:11–16
C Yahweh speaks: "I will make my covenant between you and me"	17:1–2
X **Abram's name changed to Abraham—"father of many nations"**	17:3–8
C´ Elohim speaks: "Every male among you shall be circumcised"	17:9–14
B´ Birth of Isaac announced by God	17:15–19
A´ Ishmael included in the covenant of circumcision	17:20–27

This structure presents the life story of Abraham, describing his journeys and places of worship, promises from and covenants with God, dealings with other peoples in the region, and domestic life. The focus of attention is the all-important question of an heir to Abraham through whom God's covenant promise is to be implemented—and the status of his two sons, Ishmael and Isaac. In the center of this structure, the names of Abram and Sarai are changed to Abraham and Sarah, and the rite of circumcision is instituted as a sign of God's covenant with his chosen people.

The second major cycle in the Genesis narrative, which focuses on the person of Jacob, the grandson of Abraham, extends from the death of Abraham to the death of his son Isaac in Genesis 25—35. The Jacob cycle deals with the episodes in the life of Isaac's younger son Jacob (Israel) in relation to his twin brother Esau (Edom). Before Jacob's birth, God reveals to his mother Rebekah that she has "two nations in her womb" and "the elder shall serve the younger" (Gen 25:23). Eventually Jacob and Esau are reconciled; but in the twenty years that intervene, much happens to set the stage for what follows. In the course of seven years, Jacob (Israel) has eleven sons and a daughter (Dinah) who are born in Paddan-aram in Mesopotamia. Another son, Benjamin, is born later in the land of Canaan, after Jacob's ordeal at the Jabbok River (Genesis 32), during which his name is changed to Israel. Benjamin's mother Rachel dies in childbirth and is buried near Bethlehem (Gen 35:18–20). The content of this narrative cycle may be outlined in a series of three nested menorah patterns:

The Jacob/Israel Narrative Cycle in a Menorah Pattern	*Gen 25:7—35:29*
A Death of Abraham (at 175 years of age) and Ishmael (at 137 years of age)	25:7-18
B Rebekah's struggle in childbirth, birth of Jacob and Esau	25:19-34
C Interlude: Rebekah in a foreign palace; pact with foreigners	26:1-35
X **Conflict between Jacob and Esau**	27:1-33:20
C´ Interlude: Dinah in a foreign palace; pact with foreigners	34:1-31
B´ Rachel's struggle in childbirth, birth of Benjamin	35:1-26
A´ Death of Isaac (at 180 years of age)	35:27-29

2nd Level Menorah: Conflict between Jacob and Esau	*Gen 27—33*
A Isaac blesses Jacob and Esau—Esau plans to kill Jacob	27:1-46
B Jacob fears Esau and flees to Mesopotamia	28:1-9
C Jacob encounters angels of God at Bethel—Jacob's dream	28:10-22
X **Jacob spends twenty years in Haran with his uncle Laban**	29:1—31:55
C´ Jacob encounters angels of God at Mahanaim	32:1-2
B´ Jacob fears Esau and tries to appease him—Jacob wrestles with God	32:3-32
A´ Jacob and Esau meet after twenty years—their conflict is resolved	33:1-20

3rd Level Menorah: Jacob's Twenty Years in Haran	*Gen 29—31*
A Jacob arrives at Haran—he meets Rachel at the well	29:1-14
B Jacob marries Laban's daughters Leah and Rachel	29:15-30
C Jacob's wife Leah (and concubines) are fertile: ten sons	29:31—30:24
X **Birth of Joseph to Rachel—"May Yahweh add another"**	30:25-26
C´ Jacob's flocks are fertile at the expense of Laban	30:27-43
B´ Jacob leaves Haran with family and flocks—covenant with Laban	31:1-54
A´ Laban returns to Haran	31:55

As the reader moves more deeply into the center of the nested menorah patterns, the focus narrows to the conflict between Jacob and Esau, and then to Jacob's twenty years in Haran during which eleven of his twelve sons (the tribes of Israel) are born. At the center, the focus is on the birth of Joseph whose name is interpreted as a foreshadowing of the coming birth of his younger brother Benjamin—the only one of the twelve to be born in the Promised Land.

The third major narrative cycle in Genesis 12—50, which is often referred to as the Joseph Story (Gen 37—50), may also be outlined in a menorah pattern within a menorah pattern:

Story of Jacob's Twelve Sons (Israel) in a Menorah Pattern	*Gen 37—50*
A Joseph and his brothers; Jacob and Joseph part company	37:1-36
B Interlude: Story of Judah and Tamar—Joseph not present	38:1-30
C Reversal: Joseph guilty—Potiphar's wife innocent	39:1-23
X **Joseph and his brothers in Egypt**	40:1—47:27
C´ Reversal: Ephraim firstborn—Manasseh secondborn	47:28—48:22
B´ Interlude: Blessing Jacob—Joseph nominally present	49:1-28
A´ Joseph and his brothers; Jacob and Joseph part company (in death)	49:29—50:26

2nd Level Menorah: Joseph and His Brothers in Egypt	*Gen 40:1—47:27*
A Joseph a hero in Egypt	40:1—41:57
B Joseph's brothers make two trips to Egypt in search of food	42:1—43:34
C Final test: Joseph detains Benjamin	44:1-17
X **Judah's speech: "(Keep me) in place of the boy"**	44:18-34
C´ Conclusion of the test: Joseph reveals himself	45:1-28
B´ The story of the migration to Egypt is told twice	46:1—47:12
A´ Joseph a hero in Egypt	47:13-27

In this literary unit the focus of attention is on the twelve sons of Jacob (Israel). Judah plays a primary role in the story, particularly in his remarkable speech at the structural center (Gen 44:18–34). Joseph is not presented as a patriarch together with Abraham, Isaac, and Jacob. He is merely one of the twelve sons of Jacob/Israel and the father of two Israelite tribes, Ephraim and Manasseh, which produce some of Israel's most important leaders (Joshua, Gideon, and Samuel) in the era from Moses to David.

Properly speaking, the story of Joseph is not a story about Joseph alone, but about all twelve sons of Jacob. Moreover, as the above structure suggests, it is the speech of Joseph's brother Judah that stands at the structural center of this concluding segment in the book of Genesis. A scion of the tribe of Judah, in the person of

David, will take center stage at a later point in the unfolding drama
of the Bible. It is interesting to note that it is Judah who suggests
that his younger brother Joseph be sold into slavery in the first place
(Gen 37:26–28). He apparently learns his lesson well; for this time,
when his youngest brother Benjamin faces a similar fate, Judah vol-
unteers to take his place in slavery (Gen 44:33).

Many students of the Bible have puzzled over the placing of the
story of Judah and Tamar in Genesis 38 after the first chapter in the so-
called Joseph Story. One of the reasons becomes evident in the
structural design of the whole. The birth of the twins, Perez and
Zerah, to Judah through his daughter-in-law Tamar is significant
because King David comes from the line of Perez (cf. Ruth 4:18–
22). Like the story of Tamar in Genesis 38, the story of Ruth also
turns on the theme of the levirate obligation in the law of Deuteronomy 25:5–10. In the "Deathbed Blessing of Jacob" in Genesis 49,
which makes up the corresponding section in the above structural
design, Judah plays a dominant role in ways that foreshadow, once
again, the kingdom of David to come:

> The scepter shall not depart from Judah
>   nor the ruler's staff from between his feet;
> Until tribute comes to him and the obedience of the peoples is his.
> Binding his foal to the vine and his donkey's colt to the choice
>   vine;
> He washes his garments in wine and his robe in the blood of grapes;
> His eyes are darker than wine
>   and his teeth whiter than milk. (Gen 49:10–12)

The imagery of this poem appears again in a much later context,
where another scion of David (and Judah) makes his "triumphal
entry" into the city of Jerusalem—with Zion's king "coming, sitting
on a donkey's colt" (John 12:15; see also Matt 21:5 and Zech 9:9).
This event sets the stage for the institution of the "Lord's Supper"
and its "blood of grapes" that washes garments stained in sin to
make them whiter than snow.

The structure of the book of Genesis as a whole reinforces this conclusion, as careful study of the figure of Isaac within the concentric literary structure of Genesis reveals:

The Book of Genesis in Five Parts	Gen 1–50
A Primeval History—from Adam to Abram	1:1–11:32
B Abram/Abraham cycle (with Sarai/Sarah)	12:1–25:11
X **Ishmael and Isaac—promised sons of God's covenant**	16:1–35:29
B´ Jacob/Israel (and Esau/Edom) cycle	25:19–49:33
A´ "Special History" (foreshadowed); focus on Joseph and Judah	37:1–50:26

The story of Isaac within the book of Genesis is not a narrative cycle like that of Abram/Abraham and Jacob/Israel. It is contained within the body of these two adjoining narrative cycles and is closely connected with the story of his elder half-brother Ishmael. The story of Ishmael may be outlined in a menorah pattern as follows:

The Story of Ishmael in a Menorah Pattern	Gen 16:1–25:18
A Birth of Ishmael to Hagar, Sarai's maid	16:1-16
B Covenant of circumcision includes Ishmael	17:1-27
C Abraham and the birth of Isaac—Ishmael is sent away	18:1–21:34
X **The *Akedah*—in which tradition includes Ishmael**	22:1-19
C´ Abraham after the *Akedah*—buried by Isaac and Ishmael	22:20–25:11
B´ Descendants of Ishmael	25:12-16
A´ Death of Ishmael at 137 years of age	25:17-18

Ishmael plays a peculiar role in the Bible, along with Hagar his mother, who enjoys the distinction of being the only woman in Genesis 12—50 to whom God communicates directly on two occasions. In the first instance, the angel of Yahweh tells her to return to her mistress Sarai and submit to her, for Hagar's descendants through Ishmael will be so numerous "that they cannot be numbered for multitude" (16:10). In the second instance, the angel of God shows Hagar water in the wilderness and informs her once again that God will make Ishmael into "a great nation" (21:18).

Ishmael is included in the covenant of circumcision that God establishes with his father Abraham (17:25–26). And the names of his twelve sons are listed in the order of their birth (25:13–15). Jewish tradition suggests that Abraham's wife Keturah is in fact Hagar, which would make her six sons brothers of Ishmael (25:1–2). Nonetheless, the biblical text is clear that Isaac is Abraham's primary heir and his other sons are sent away. In the story of the *Akedah* (binding of Isaac), Jewish tradition places Ishmael in that scene, along with Eliezer of Damascus (15:2), for the two young men that Abraham leaves with his donkey as he and his son Isaac ascend Mount Moriah are identified as Abraham's two prior heirs— Eliezer and Ishmael. Muslim tradition goes much further, for there it is Ishmael who is the intended sacrificial victim and not Isaac.

Within the concentric structure of Genesis as a whole, the disturbing story of the *Akedah* (the binding of Isaac) in Genesis 22 functions as both the concluding episode in the Abraham narrative cycle and as a center within the center of the book of Genesis. The story of Isaac may also be outlined in a menorah pattern with the *Akedah* at its center as follows:

Isaac the Promised Son of God's Covenant	Gen 18–35
A Birth of Isaac, as promised by "angels"	18:1–15; 21:1–7
B Abraham's two sons—story of Isaac and Ishmael	21:8–21
C Abraham and Abimelech—Abraham's sojourn in Philistia	21:22–34
X **The *Akedah*—the binding of Isaac (testing of Abraham)**	22:1–19
C´ Isaac and Abimelech—Isaac's sojourn with the Philistines	26:1–33
B´ Isaac's two sons—story of Jacob and Esau	26:34–35:27
A´ Death of Isaac at 180 years of age	35:28–29

The specific boundaries in this concentric structural design are difficult to delineate because of the presence of material that belongs to other narrative structures. These blocks of material include the story of Abraham and Sarah (Gen 18:16—21:34), the genealogy of Nahor (Gen 22:20–24), the concluding stories about Abraham and Sarah after the *Akedah* (Gen 23:1—25:11), a genealogy of Ishmael (25:12–18), and an introduction to the rivalry between Jacob and Esau (Gen 25:19–27).

In the story of the *Akedah*, Abraham is commanded by God to sacrifice his "only son" Isaac (Gen 22:2) as a burnt offering on Mount Moriah, which is subsequently identified with the Temple Mount in Jerusalem. This story has profound ties to the sacrificial death of another "only (begotten) son" on Golgotha ("place of the skull"), outside the city walls in ancient Jerusalem many centuries later, as a number of the early church fathers saw so clearly. In patristic theology, Isaac is presented as an example of the perfect sacrifice that foreshadows the crucified Christ.

GENESIS 1—11 AS INTRODUCTION TO THE BIBLE

As in other works of literary art, there is more than one way to outline Genesis 1—11. We have already examined a menorah pattern with the story of Noah and the flood at the center (see page 15 above). The fact that the outer frame in that structure moves from the story of Adam and Eve (Gen 1:1—3:21) to a brief introduction of Abram and Sarai (Gen 11:29–31) suggests that Genesis 1—11 functions as the introduction to the Abraham narrative cycle in Genesis 12—22.

Genesis 1—11 also functions as the introduction to more distant texts within the Tanakh, particularly within the Writings, as careful reflection on the details of the following menorah pattern suggests:

The Primeval History in a Menorah Pattern	*Gen 1—11*
A Story of Creation (ending with Adam's three sons)	1:1–4:26
B From Adam to Noah: Enoch ("walked with God"–5:22)	5:1–32
C Sons of God take daughters of *ha'adam* as wives	6:1–2
X **Yahweh speaks—a "riddle in the middle"**	6:3
C´ Sons of God and daughters of *ha'adam* breed giants	6:4
B´ Story of Noah (who "walked with God"–6:9)	6:5–9:29
A´ Story of Dispersion (starting with Noah's three sons)	10:1–11:32

When Yahweh says, "My spirit shall not abide in *ha'adam* forever… their days shall be one hundred and twenty years" (6:3), the meaning is not at all clear. It is possible to interpret the text as a limit

of one hundred and twenty years, and then God will send final judgment in the Great Flood. At the same time, the curious word
beshaggam in the middle of this verse has at least two meanings. Of
the two most obvious possibilities, the traditional rendering "in that
also" *ha'adam* is flesh (i.e., mortal) is followed by most translators,
ancient and modern. That same word, however, may also be translated "because of their going astray," with the variant reading, which
appears in some Hebrew manuscripts. The only difference between
the two readings is the length of the vowel in the final syllable of the
word *beshaggam*. The reading with a long *a* (*beshaggām*) presents
the justification for God's judgment. At the same time, however, the
reference to a limitation of one hundred and twenty years calls attention to the two references to the death of Moses in Deuteronomy
31:2 and 34:7 at the age of 120. Moses died because he was a hundred and twenty years old—but he did not die because he was physi-
cally worn out. "His eye was not dim, nor his natural force abated"
(Deut 34:7, KJV). He died because he reached the limit God had set
for him, namely the limit of one hundred and twenty years, which is
anticipated in the "riddle in the middle" of Genesis 6:3.

It is possible to interpret the reference to the "sons of God" in
Gen 6:1–4 in relation to the story of Job, where "the sons of God
came to present themselves before the Lord, and Satan came also
among them" (Job 1:6).

READING THE FIVE BOOKS OF MOSES FROM THE CENTER

The concentric structure of the book of Genesis is outlined above in
five parts. Another way of looking at its concentric structure is to
outline the book in a nested menorah pattern with its focus on Isaac
blessing his two sons, Jacob and Esau.

The Book of Genesis in a Menorah Pattern	Gen 1–50
A Primeval History	1:1–11:32
B Abram/Abraham narrative cycle	12:1–25:18
C Jacob and Esau—Isaac seeks refuge in Philistia (Gerar)	25:19–26:34

X	**Isaac blesses Jacob and Esau**	27:1–28:4
C´	Jacob and Esau—Jacob seeks refuge in Paddan-aram	28:5–9
B´	Jacob/Israel and Esau/Edom narrative cycle	28:10–36:43
A´	"Special History" (foreshadowed): Focus on Joseph and Judah	37:1–50:26

2nd Level Menorah: Isaac Blesses Jacob and Esau		*Gen 27:1–28:4*
A	Isaac's request—that Esau bring him "savory food"	27:1-4
B	Rebekah instructs Jacob and assists him in deceiving Isaac	27:5-26
C	Isaac blesses Jacob, thinking he is blessing Esau	27:27-29
X	**Esau brings "savory food" to receive Isaac's blessing**	27:30-38
C´	Isaac blesses Esau (inverting words of Jacob's blessing)	27:39-40
B´	Rebekah instructs Jacob to flee Esau's wrath	27:41-45
A´	Isaac's request—that Jacob take a wife in Paddan-aram	27:46—28:4

The first level menorah pattern in this structure focuses on the blessing of both Jacob and Esau, which they receive from their father Isaac. The two blessings appear at the structural center of the book of Genesis, framing the account of the arrival of Esau with the savory food his father had requested (Gen 27:30–38). In the center of this passage we find the words of Isaac who is trembling violently as he tells Esau that he has just blessed another in his place—"and he shall be blessed" (27:33). The words spoken cannot be retracted. Isaac manages to bless his son Esau as well, but the very words contain an inversion of the blessing already given to Jacob (cf. 27:28 and 27:39).

The concentric structures of the Abram/Abraham and Jacob/Israel narrative cycles are outlined above. The two cycles include parallel accounts of the ages of the patriarchs Abraham and Isaac at the point of their deaths (Gen 25:7 and 35:28), which introduces an important matter of the mysterious numbers in the Bible, for these two numbers are part of a larger numerical design.

Ancestor	*Age at Death*			*Sum of Digits*
Abraham	175	=	7×5^2	$7 + 5 + 5 = 17$
Isaac	180	=	5×6^2	$5 + 6 + 6 = 17$
Jacob	147	=	3×7^2	$3 + 7 + 7 = 17$
(Israel)	64	=	1×8^2	$1 + 8 + 8 = 17$

Moreover, the numerical value of the Hebrew word "Israel" (ישראל) is 64.

$$(י = 10) + (ש = 21) + (ר = 20) + (א = 1) + (ל = 12) = 64$$

Rashi, the medieval Jewish scholar, calculates that Jacob was 63 years of age when he left home. Jacob spent 20 years in Laban's house in Haran, serving Laban 14 years for his two wives, Rachel and Leah, and another 6 years for Laban's flocks. Thus, the total number of years Jacob lived with his father Isaac and his uncle Laban is 63 + 20 = 83. And since he died at 147, he lived 64 years in another "home." Jacob's name was changed to "Israel" at the Jabbok River in his wrestling match with an angel. The next day he entered the Promised Land as "Israel." If these calculations are correct, the life span of "Israel" is 64 years, and the genealogy of the four "generations" of patriarchs converges on "Israel," whose age at death fits the formula in question: 1 x 8 x 8 = 64.

The Book of Exodus

On one level, the narrative in Exodus through Deuteronomy is the story of Moses as the paradigm of leadership in ancient Israel. Joshua continues this pattern of leadership, which is taken up by those who follow him as "judges" in ancient Israel. As the last of the judges, the prophet Samuel inaugurates a new pattern of leadership in the division of power between the prophet and the king (the "Samuel Compromise"). Moses prefigures the roles of both prophet and king in Israel, as leader par excellence.

The story of God's redemptive activity with the people of Israel begins with the book of Exodus, which may be outlined in a nested menorah pattern as follows:

The Book of Exodus in a Menorah Pattern	Exod 1—40
A God delivers the people from Egypt—pillars of cloud and fire	1:1–15:19
B Journey to Sinai with God's provision in the wilderness	15:20–17:16
C Jethro's visit—Moses organizes the judicial leadership	18:1–27
X **Threefold theophany on Sinai—God reveals himself**	19:1–24:14

C′	Moses spends forty days on the mountain with God	24:15-18
B′	The building of the Tabernacle at Mount Sinai	25:1–40:33
A′	Yahweh's glory fills the Tabernacle—the cloud and the fire	40:34-38

2nd Level Menorah: Threefold Theophany on Mount Sinai		Exod 19:1–24:14
A	God's invitation for Israel to be "a kingdom of priests"	19:1-6
B	Theophany: Moses brings the people out to meet God	19:7-25
C	Giving of the Ten Commandments (orally)	20:1-17
X	**Theophany: Moses meets God in thick darkness**	20:18-21
C′	Giving of the Covenant Code (orally)	20:22–23:33
B′	Theophany: Moses brings the leadership to "see" God	24:1-11
A′	Invitation for Moses to receive the gift of the stone tablets	24:12-14

The outermost frame in this structure focuses on the image of the numinous cloud and fire, in which Yahweh guides the people of Israel in their epic journey from slavery in Egypt to the Promised Land. After Pharaoh finally lets the people go, God leads them through the wilderness with a pillar of cloud by day and a pillar of fire by night (Exod 13:21–22). Exodus concludes with the cloud covering the tent of meeting and the glory of Yahweh filling the Tabernacle that Moses erects at Mount Sinai (Exod 40:34–38). The cloud and the glory are present when Moses ascends the mountain in the theophany at the center of the book of Exodus (24:13–18). Moses spends forty days and forty nights in the cloud and "the appearance of the glory of Yahweh is like a devouring fire on the top of mountain in the sight of the people of Israel" (24:17).

The focus of attention in this reading of the book of Exodus from the center is on a threefold theophany at Mount Sinai. There God reveals himself to Moses "in thick darkness" (20:21)—along with the Ten Commandments (20:1–17) and the Covenant Code (21:1—24:18), which are given to Moses orally. In the second frame, Moses leads the people of Israel on their journey from the Red Sea to Mount Sinai (15:22—18:27). On this journey God supplies the people with bread and water in the wilderness (16:1–17:7). The second frame concludes with a detailed account of the work that God instructs Moses to do at Mount Sinai—the building of the Tabernacle (25:1—40:33).

The story of the Exodus from Egypt with Moses as leader, which we find in Exodus 1—15, may be outlined in another menorah pattern:

Emergence of Moses as Leader in Israel	*Exod 1:1—15:19*
A Call and naming of Moses—to draw the people through the waters	1:1—4:31
B Contest with Pharaoh—"Yahweh hardened Pharaoh's heart"	5:1—11:10
C The first Passover and the feast of unleavened bread	12:1–28
X **Yahweh smites the firstborn in the land of Egypt**	12:29–42
C´ Instructions for observing Passover in the future	12:43–51
B´ Consecration of the firstborn in Israel	13:1–16
A´ The sea-crossing—Moses draws the people through the waters	13:17—15:19

When Pharoah's daughter discovers the infant Moses in an "ark" (*tebah*, a term used earlier for Noah's ark) floating in the Nile River, she unwittingly plays the role of a prophet—for the name "Moses" actually means "one who draws (the people) through the waters" (2:10). The crossing of the Red Sea is the fulfillment of the prophecy inherent in the name of Moses. The focus of attention in this literary unit is on the institution of Passover, which is the most important of the festivals observed by God's people through the ages. Yeshua the Messiah will add depth to this imagery in time to come, as he becomes the Passover lamb who is at the same time the great high priest who offers that sacrifice. He is also both a new Moses and the long awaited "son of David," the king of Israel.

This section on the journey of the people of Israel from the crossing of the sea to Mount Sinai may also be outlined in a menorah pattern:

Journey from the Sea-Crossing to Rephidim	*Exod 15:20—17:16*
A Miriam's song—beginning of the wars of Yahweh	15:20–21
B Marah—bitter water made sweet ["I am Yahweh who heals"]	15:22–27
C Journey from Elim to the wilderness of Sin—no food	16:1–3
X **God's provision in the wilderness: Manna and quail**	16:4–36
C´ Journey from the wilderness of Sin to Rephidim—no water	17:1
B´ Massah and Meribah—water from the rock	17:2–7
A´ Joshua and the war against Amalek [Yahweh's enemy]	17:8–16

The outer frame in this literary structure opens with a brief reference, on the part of Miriam, to Yahweh as a Divine Warrior who "has triumphed gloriously; the horse and his rider he has thrown into the sea" (15:21). It concludes with the account of the initial battle in the wars of Yahweh, which is fought under the leadership of Joshua, against the Amalekites who subsequently become the traditional enemies of Yahweh (17:8–16). This literary unit begins and ends with fragments from the most ancient war songs in the Tanakh (15:21 and 17:16).

The account of the journey from the Red Sea to Mount Sinai is framed by parallel stories in which Yahweh produces water for his people in the wilderness—at Marah (15:22–26) and at Massah and Meribah (17:2–7). The journey is in two stages, which highlight the primary needs of God's people: food (15:27—16:3) and water (17:1). The focus of attention in the literary unit as a whole is on God's miraculous provision of daily bread in the morning ("manna") and meat ("quails") in the evening (16:4–36). The provision of manna continues until the beginning of the second phase of the wars of Yahweh, when Joshua establishes the battle camp at Gilgal and the people observe the first Passover in the Promised Land (Josh 5:12).

The story of the war with Amalek in 17:8–16 concludes the previous structure and functions as the beginning of another menorah pattern, which focuses on God's revelation of himself to Moses and Joshua:

From the War with Amalek to the Covenant at Mount Sinai	*Exod 17:8–24:14*
A Joshua and the war with Amalek	17:8-16
B Jethro's visit—Moses follows his advice in judicial organization	18:1-27
C Theophany at Mount Sinai—Yahweh reveals himself	19:1-25
X **The Ten Commandments and the Covenant Code**	20:1-23:33
C´ Moses writes Yahweh's words and ratifies the covenant	24:1-8
B´ Moses with Aaron, Nadab, Abihu, and 70 elders on Mount Sinai	24:9-11
A´ Joshua with Moses on Mount Sinai	24:12-14

The focus of attention here is on the giving of the Ten Commandments (20:1–17) and the expansion of these principles in the detailed laws of the Covenant Code (20:22—23:33). In the innermost frame of this concentric structure we find specific reference to Moses writing the "book of the covenant," which he reads "in the hearing of the people" (24:4–7). This constitutes the initial step in the canonical process that ultimately produces the Torah as we now have it.

The goal of the journey to Mount Sinai is the establishment of God's covenant with his chosen people and the building of the Tabernacle, which constitutes the location of his presence in the midst of that people. The story of the building of the Tabernacle may be outlined in a nested menorah pattern as follows:

The Building of the Tabernacle at Mount Sinai	Exod 25—40
A The tabernacle complex designed	25:1–31:11
B The Sabbath law	31:12–17
C The two tablets of the covenant	31:18
X **The covenant with Yahweh broken and renewed**	32:1–34:28
C′ The shining face of Moses–with the two tablets (34:29)	34:29–35
B′ Sabbath regulations	35:1–3
A′ The tabernacle complex constructed	35:4–40:38

2nd Level Menorah: The Covenant Broken and Renewed	Exod 32:1–34:28
A Breaking of the covenant–the golden calf/two tablets shattered	32:1–35
B Yahweh speaks: I will not go with this "stiff-necked people"	33:1–6
C Moses experiences Yahweh's presence in the Tent of Meeting	33:7–11a
X **Joshua did not depart from the Tent of Meeting**	33:11b
C′ Moses will experience Yahweh's presence in the future	33:12–16
B′ Yahweh speaks: I will show you a glimpse of my glory	33:17–23
A′ Renewal of the covenant–with two new tablets of stone	34:1–28

The lengthy accounts of the design of the Tabernacle (25:1—31:11) and its subsequent construction and dedication (35:4—40:38) function as a literary frame around the story of the breaking and renewal of God's covenant in the incident of the golden calf (Exod 32—33). As we have already seen, we are dealing here with the structural center of the Primary History as a whole. Moreover, the structure highlights the principle of the "riddle in the middle" with its brief reference to Joshua who "did not depart from the tent" (33:11b). This brief note anticipates the transfer of leadership from

Moses to Joshua in Deuteronomy 31—34 and the Eisodus into the Promised Land in the book of Joshua within the Former Prophets. The book of Exodus concludes with the account of the erection of the Tabernacle and installation of its equipment (40:1–33) and the appearance of the glory of Yahweh, which fills the Tabernacle. This sets the stage for the book of Leviticus.

The Book of Leviticus

According to the anthropologist Mary Douglas, the governing principle in the organization of Leviticus as a whole is the architectural design of the Tabernacle (*Leviticus as Literature*, Oxford University Press, 1999).

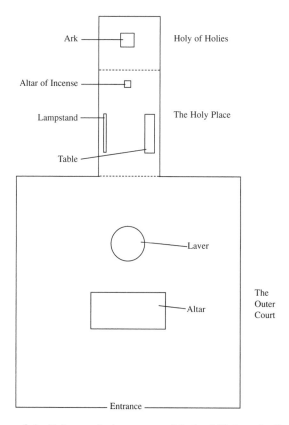

Furnishings of the Tabernacle (courtesy of Oxford University Press)

The entrance to the Tabernacle complex opens to a large outer court measuring fifty by fifty cubits, which has near its center the large altar for sacrificial offerings and the laver used by the priests to wash themselves. A screen separates the Tabernacle from the outer court. Beyond the screen are two rooms, the first of which is the Holy Place measuring twenty by ten cubits that contains the lampstand, the table for the bread of the presence, and the altar of incense. A second screen separates this room from the Holy of Holies, which measures 2¹/2 by 2¹/2 cubits. The ark is located beneath the shadowing protective wings of two cherubim. The content of the twenty-seven chapters of Leviticus is projected on this grand plan of the Tabernacle as follows:

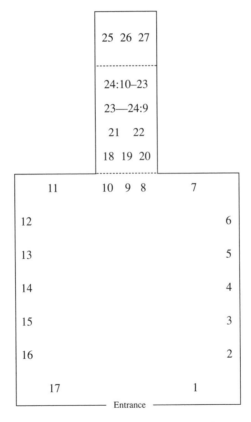

Inside the House/Book of God (courtesy of Oxford University Press)

Reading Leviticus in terms of the architectural design of the Tabernacle suggests that the function of the book is to bring us into the Holy Place to encounter God. To bridge the gap between finite and sinful human beings and an infinite and holy God, three things are required:

1. we must bring sacrificial offerings (chaps. 1—7)
2. we need a priest to mediate on our behalf (chaps. 8—10)
3. an expiatory process must eliminate impurity at all levels (chaps. 11—16)

The first seven chapters of Leviticus take the reader from the entrance of the Tabernacle to the first of two narrative screens (10:1–7 and 24:10–23). The sacrificial offerings of Leviticus 1—7 are offered on the altar in the outer court. The first screen of the Tabernacle includes the fire narrative in which Nadab and Abihu, the sons of Aaron, are consumed by Yahweh's fire (10:1–2). The way of purification continues in the outer court of the Tabernacle (chaps. 11—16), as worshipers make their way symbolically back to the entrance of the Tabernacle. The ritual of the Day of Atonement provides the purification of the sanctuary itself (chap. 16), which enables the worshiper to pass through the screen from the outer court to the Holy Place (chaps. 17—24). Here we find the central chapter of the book, with its instructions for the life of moral and ritual holiness (chap. 19). Holiness in daily life is explored further in chapters 20—24, which reach their climax in the stoning narrative of 24:10–23. This episode of punishment for blasphemy (a violation of the third commandment) constitutes the second screen, which separates the Holy Place (chaps. 17—24) from the Holy of Holies (chaps. 25—27). Within the Holy of Holies we find the covenant stipulations, including the blessings and curses (chap. 26). On either side of this pivotal chapter, we find proclamations of liberty—in person-to-person obligations (25:2–55) and in debts to Yahweh (with religious vows, 27:1–33).

Jewish tradition divides Leviticus into ten *parashot* (weekly readings), the first of which may be outlined in a menorah pattern:

Parashah 24: Sacrificial Instructions Directed to the Laity   *Lev 1:1—6:7*

A The burnt offering—a sacrifice of praise; completely burned   1:1–17

B   The cereal offering—unburned portion is consumed by the priests   2:1–16

C   The well-being (peace) offering—a covenant meal   3:1–16

X   **Warning: "You may eat neither suet (fat) nor blood"**   3:17

C´   The purification (sin) offering—efficacious only for unwitting sin   4:1–35

B´   The graduated purification (sin) offering—so that all may participate   5:1–13

A´ The reparation (guilt) offering—for offenses requiring restitution   5:14—6:7

Since the suet (fat) and the blood of sacrificial animals belong to Yahweh, they must be consumed by fire on the altar. With this principle in the center, five types of offerings are delineated. On one side, the offerings progress from those that are consumed in their entirety on the altar (burnt offerings, chap. 1), to those that are consumed by the priests alone (cereal offerings, chap. 2), to those consumed by the entire worshiping community in a covenant meal ("peace" offerings, chap. 3). On the other side, we find a progression of offerings designed to deal with impurity caused by unwitting sins. There is no prescribed offering to deal with deliberate disobedience by violating the stipulations of the covenant agreement, for sacrifice is not a magical means of atonement. It is an act of worship.

The second of the weekly readings (*Parashah* 25), which concerns the same offerings from the perspective of priestly instructions and elaboration of priestly prerogatives, may be outlined in a menorah pattern as follows:

Parashah 25: Sacrifices with Priestly Tasks and Prerogatives   *Lev 6:8—8:36*

A Burnt offering—a perpetual fire shall be kept burning on the altar   6:8–13

B   Cereal offering and the high priests' daily cereal offering   6:14–23

C   Purification (sin) offering—eaten by priests   6:24–29

X   **Warning: Offerings on the Day of Atonement cannot be eaten**   6:30

C´   Reparation (guilt) offering and priestly dues from the holy offerings   7:1–10

B´   Well-being (peace) offering and the priestly dues from them   7:11–37

A´ Consecration of the priests—in the matter of ordination sacrifices   8:1–36

In the structural center of this menorah pattern we find a warning with regard to purification (sin) offerings on the annual Day of Atonement. Any offering from which blood is brought into the Tent of Meeting to make atonement in the Holy Place cannot be eaten— "it shall be burned with fire" (6:30). The concluding section in this menorah pattern, which deals with priestly ordination, may be explored in another menorah pattern:

The Ordination of the Priests	*Lev 8*
A The congregation is assembled at the door of the Tent of Meeting	8:1–9
B The ceremony of anointment—the Tabernacle, its altar, and Aaron	8:10–13
C Offering the bull of the sin offering for the priests	8:14–17
X **Offering the ram of the burnt offering**	8:18–21
C´ Offering the ram of ordination	8:22–29
B´ The priests and their garments are consecrated with anointing oil	8:30
A´ Aaron and his sons serve at the door of the Tent of Meeting seven days	8:31–36

This ceremony of ordination fulfills what Moses was commanded to do in Exodus 29:4–6. In preparation for this ceremony, the entire congregation assembles at the door of the Tent of Meeting (8:1–9). At the conclusion of the ceremony, Aaron and his sons take their place at the door of the Tent of Meeting. They boil the meat of the sacrificial offering "at the door of the tent of meeting, and there eat it and the bread that is in the basket of ordination offerings" (8:31, RSV). Aaron and his sons remain at the door of the Tent of Meeting for seven days performing what Yahweh commanded through Moses (8:36). The structural center of this literary unit focuses on "the ram of the burnt offering," which enables Aaron and his sons to perform their duties on behalf of the congregation in holiness.

The service of ordination in Leviticus 8 sets the stage for the commencement of Aaron's high priesthood, which is developed in another menorah patten—in *Parashah* 26 (chaps. 9—11):

Parashah 26: 1st Screen—Denying Entrance to the Holy Place	*Lev 9—11*
A Ordination service: Aaron offers a sin offering and a burnt offering	9:1–14
B Aaron presents the people's offerings (as instructed in chaps. 1–7)	9:15–21
C Aaron blesses the people and Yahweh's fire consumes the offering	9:22–24

X   Nadab and Abihu offer unholy fire/consumed by Yahweh's fire   10:1–7

C´   Yahweh commands Aaron to be holy when entering the Tabernacle   10:8–11

B´   Aaron defends Eleazar and Ithamar for not eating the priestly portions 10:12–20

A´ Diet laws (and addendum: priests must decide what is clean and unclean)   11:1–47

The focus of attention here is on what Mary Douglas calls the first
of two narrative screens that correspond to the curtains at the
entrance to the Holy Place and the Holy of Holies. In Jewish tradition, *Parashah* 26 is called *Shemini* ("Eight")—a reference to the
eighth day, following the seven-day ordination ceremony (8:33). On
that day something mysterious happened. Two of Aaron's sons,
Nadab and Abihu, offered "unholy fire" before Yahweh—"and fire
came forth from the presence of Yahweh and devoured them, and
they died before Yahweh" (10:2). The passage displays the familiar
qualities of the "riddle in the middle" in that the biblical text does
not specify precisely what their sin was in presenting this "unholy
fire." At any rate, as Mary Douglas observes, the progression of
movement into the Tent of Meeting symbolically is interrupted
sharply by this brief narrative. Readers must remain in the outer
court of the Tabernacle and make their way back to its entrance
once again. While doing so, they must purge themselves of all
impurity. Only then can their high priest take them inside the Holy
Place where they will find the path to ritual and moral holiness in
Leviticus 19. The rich symbolism here takes on deeper meaning in
relation to Yeshua the Messiah (Jesus Christ) in Hebrews 9:11—
10:18.

The task of purgation on the way to holiness is explored in
another menorah pattern that includes three weekly portions in the
lectionary cycle of readings from the Torah (*Parashot* 27–29). The
next eleven chapters of Leviticus, which take the reader back to the
door of the Tent of Meeting and from there into the Holy Place, may
be outlined in a nested menorah pattern as follows:

Parashot 27–29: Removing Impurity to Enter the Holy Place   *Lev 12—18*

A   Purification of a woman after childbirth   12:1–8

B	"Leprosy" and purification after "leprosy"	13:1—14:57
C	Purification in the loss of vital fluids—male and female	15:1-33
X	**The Day of Atonement**	16:1-34
C´	The slaughter and consumption of meat	17:1-16
B´	As a holy people, Israel must not follow pagan practices	18:1-5
A´	Illicit sexual practices	18:6-30

2nd Level Menorah: The Day of Atonement	*Lev 16*
A Setting: Yahweh speaks to Moses after the death of Nadab and Abihu	16:1
B Precautions and provisions—putting on vestments and ritual washing	16:2-5
C Purgation ritual—Aaron offers a bull and a goat as sin offerings	16:6-19
X **The scapegoat ritual—2nd goat released in "a solitary land"**	16:20-22a
C´ The altar sacrifices—Aaron offers burnt offerings	16:22b-25
B´ Purification of the high priest's assistants	16:26-28
A´ The date is fixed for all time—the 10th day of the 7th month	16:29-34

The structure of the nested menorah pattern here moves from the death of Nadab and Abihu (10:1–7), in the center of the previous menorah pattern to the institution of the Day of Atonement (chap. 16), which begins with a specific reference to that earlier event (16:1). The nested concentric structure converges on the scapegoat ritual, in which Aaron imparts the sin of the people to a goat that is released in the wilderness (16:20–22a). The outermost frame concerns purification in sexual matters (12:1–8 and 18:6–30). The second frame presents a lengthy section on "leprosy" and its purification (chaps. 13—14), which is set over against a much shorter passage that enjoins Israel to be a holy people by not following pagan practices (18:1–5). The third frame opens with a chapter on purification from contamination from bodily discharges (chap. 15), and continues with another chapter on contamination from taking improperly prepared foods into the body (chap. 17). Between these two chapters stands the account of the Day of Atonement, which is explored in a second-level menorah pattern.

Within the above menorah pattern, Leviticus 15 displays a menorah pattern of its own, as the following outline of its contents shows:

Purification in the Loss of Vital Fluids—Male and Female	*Lev 15*
A Yahweh tells Moses and Aaron to instruct the people of Israel	15:1-2a
B Abnormal male discharges	15:2b-15
C Normal male discharges	15:16-17
X **Marital intercourse**	15:18
C´ Normal female discharges	15:19-24
B´ Abnormal female discharges	15:25-30
A´ Consequences for the sanctuary and for the people of Israel	15:31-33

Both contaminating and normal bodily discharges of the two sexes are carefully arranged in a concentric pattern, with a single verse on the union of the two sexes in the center.

In the final four weekly readings of Leviticus (*Parashot* 30–33), we find a menorah pattern that highlights the central teaching of Leviticus:

Parashot 30–33: From the Holy Place to the Holy of Holies	*Lev 19—27*
A Inside the Holy Place—ritual and moral holiness	19:1-37
B Penalties for Molek worship, necromacy, and sexual offences	20:1-27
C Restrictions placed on priests to guard against ritual defilement	21:1—22:33
X **The holiness calendar**	23:1-44
C´ Oil for the lampstand and bread for the Table of Presence	24:1-9
B´ The case of blasphemy	24:10-23
A´ Inside the Holy of Holies: Liberation in the covenant relationship	25:1—27:34

2nd Level Menorah: The Holiness Calendar	*Lev 23*
A Yahweh instructs Moses on the appointed feasts	23:1-2
B Sabbath—the 7th day is a sabbath of solemn rest	23:3
C Summary: "These are the appointed feasts of Yahweh"	23:4
X **Spring and fall festivals—leave gleanings for the poor**	23:5-36
C´ Summary: "These are the appointed feasts of Yahweh"	23:37-38
B´ Sukkot—"You shall dwell in booths for seven days" [15 Tishri]	23:39-43
A´ Moses instructs the people on the appointed feasts	23:44

3rd Level Menorah: Spring and Fall Festivals—Leave Gleanings	*Lev 23:5—36*
A Festival of Passover and Unleavened Bread [14–15 Nisan]	23:5-8
B Wave offering [day after last Sabbath of Unleavened Bread]	23:9-14
C Festival of Weeks (Pentecost)—50 days after wave offering	23:15-21
X **Leave gleanings for the poor when you reap the harvest**	23:22
C´ Festival of trumpets (New Year) [1 Tishri]	23:23-25
B´ Day of Atonement—"a sabbath of solemn rest" [10 Tishri]	23:26-32
A´ Festival of Booths—seven-day festival [15–22 Tishri]	23:33-36

The outer frame here opens with a chapter on ritual and moral holiness (Leviticus 19), which Mary Douglas describes as the central chapter of the entire book of Leviticus. From an architectural point of view, this is the goal worshipers are seeking as they move from the outer court of the Tabernacle into the Holy Place within the Tent of Meeting. That chapter is set over against the concluding three chapters (Lev 25—27), which correspond to "The Holy of Holies." The second narrative screen in 24:10–23 forms the barrier between these two places.

The concluding section of Leviticus consists of two weekly readings (*Parashot* 32–33), which may be outlined in a menorah pattern:

Parashot 32–33: Liberation in the Covenant Relationship	*Lev 25—27*
A Sinai opening: "Yahweh spoke to Moses *on Mount Sinai*, saying"	25:1
B The sabbatical year—"of solemn rest for the land"	25:2-7
C Proclamation of liberty in person-to-person obligations (Jubilee)	25:8-55
X **Covenant stipulations with blessings and curses/*on Mount Sinai***	26:1-46
C´ Proclamation of liberty in debts to Yahweh (with religious vows)	27:1-29
B´ The tithe is holy to Yahweh, it shall not be redeemed	27:30-33
A´ Sinai ending: "The commandments Yahweh gave *on Mount Sinai*"	27:34

The beginning, middle, and end of this concentric unit are marked by repetition of the phrase "on Mount Sinai," as Mary Douglas has noted. The second frame moves from a brief section on the sabbatical year in Israel (25:2–7), to another on the holiness of the tithe

(27:30–33). The innermost frame focuses on the theme of liberty. On the one hand, it is liberty in person-to-person obligations in terms of the year of Jubilee (25:8–55). On the other, it is liberty in relation to obligations owed to Yahweh himself in terms of religious vows (27:1–29). The center of this concluding section focuses on the blessings and the curses of the covenant God has established with his people (chap. 26).

Even though Leviticus enjoys a peculiar architectural design, which represents the physical structure of the Tabernacle in ancient Israel, the book as a whole can still be outlined in a nested menorah pattern as well:

The Book of Leviticus in a Menorah Pattern	*Lev 1—27*
A In the outer court: The way to holiness for God's people	1:1—10:20
B In the outer court: The way of purification	11:1—17:16
C Inside the Tabernacle (the Holy Place): The way of holiness	18:1-30
X **The life of moral and ritual holiness**	19:1-37
C´ Inside the Tabernacle (the Holy Place): The way of holiness	20:1—22:33
B´ Moving toward the Holy of Holies: Holiness in daily life	23:1—24:22
A´ Inside the Holy of Holies: Liberation in the covenant relationship	25:1—27:34

2nd Level Menorah: The Life of Moral and Ritual Holiness	*Lev 19*
A Keynote: "You shall be holy; for I Yahweh your God am holy"	19:1-2
B Honor your parents, keep the Sabbath, and do not turn to idols	19:3-4
C Offer sacrifices as God has instructed or be cut off	19:5-8
X **Ten commandments on living a holy life**	19:9-32
C´ Love your neighbor (i.e., the sojourner) as yourself	19:33-34
B´ Do nothing wrong in your dealings in human society	19:35-36
A´ Summation: "You shall observe all my statutes...I am Yahweh"	19:37

As we move more deeply into the structural center of Leviticus in chapter 19, we find an interesting reflection on the Ten Commandments. The outermost frame highlights the central message of the book as a whole, namely a summons to live a life of moral and ritual holiness (19:2 and 19:37). The second frame focuses on four specific commandments in the familiar pattern of three plus one, with modifications of Commandments 1–5 arranged in three parts (19:3–4), which are set over against a summary of Commandments 6–10 (19:35–36). The innermost frame highlights the two primary dimensions in the original Ten Commandments—the vertical dimension in terms of our relationship to God (19:5–8), and the horizontal dimension in terms of our relationship to fellow human beings (19:33–34). And in the structural center we find a listing of specific commandments. This listing is arranged in ten parts by repetition of the refrain, "I am Yahweh (your God)." These "ten commandments," which constitute the guide to living a holy life, may be summarized as follows:

Ten Commandments for Holy Living in the Book of Leviticus	*Lev 19:9–32*
1. When you harvest the land, leave gleanings for the poor	19:9–10
2. Do not steal, deal falsely, lie, or swear falsely by Yahweh's name	19:11–12
3. Show love to your neighbor, especially those who are handicapped	19:13–14
4. Do no injustice in judgment—show no partiality and do not slander	19:15–16
5. No hatred, vengeance, or grudges—"Love your neighbor as yourself"	19:17–18
6. No illicit mixtures—in livestock, agriculture, and sexual matters	19:19–25
7. Do not eat blood, do not participate in the occult pagan practices	19:26–28
8. No harlotry, keep Yahweh's sabbaths, reverence God's sanctuary	19:29–30
9. Do not turn to mediums or wizards	19:31
10. Show honor to the elderly and fear God	19:32

The book of Leviticus is much more than a handbook for the Levites in ancient Israel to follow in outmoded ritual practice. Yeshua the Messiah (Jesus Christ) was quite correct when he concluded his summary of the demands of the Torah with the simple statement, "You shall love your neighbor as yourself" (Matt 19:19). He was quoting Leviticus 19:18, which stands in the structural center of the list of "ten commandments" in the book of Leviticus.

The Book of Numbers

For an outline of the book of Numbers in a series of nested menorah patterns, see Section A above ("Beginning of Canon History: Exodus through Deuteronomy"). Mary Douglas outlines the book of Numbers in thirteen parts, which alternate between Story and Law in a series of "parallel rungs" in what she calls "the book in a ring" (Mary Douglas, *In the Wilderness: The Doctrine of Defilement in the Book of Numbers* [JSOT Supplement Series 158. Sheffield, UK: Sheffield Academic Press, 1993], p. 118).

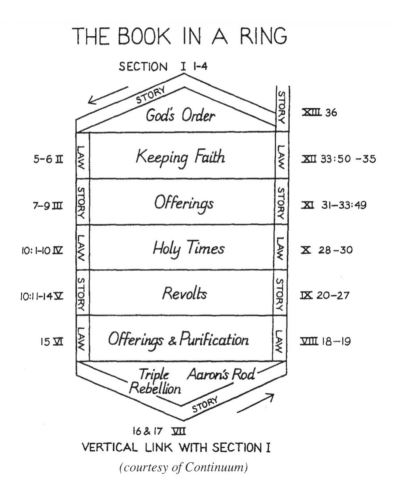

(courtesy of Continuum)

The concentric structure observed by Mary Douglas may also be outlined in a nested menorah pattern as follows:

The Book of Numbers in a Menorah Pattern	Num 1—36
A Story: Census of the 12 tribes, heirs to land and danger of encroachment	1:1—4:49
B Law: Keeping faith and breaking faith	5:1—6:27
C Story: Gifts to Yahweh and Yahweh's gifts to Aaron	7:1—8:26
X **Forty years in the wilderness—from Sinai to the plains of Moab**	9:1—30:16
C´ Story: Defeat of Midianite kings, booty purified; summary of journey	31:1—33:49
B´ Law: Destroy images, partition the Promised Land, cities of refuge	33:50—35:34
A´ Story: The sons of Joseph and the land [encroachment]	36:1-13

2nd Level Menorah: From the Wilderness of Sinai to the Plains of Moab	Num 9—30
A Law: Passover; blowing trumpets and appointed feasts	9:1—10:10
B Story: The Wilderness of Paran	10:11—14:45
C Law: Offerings for priests, guilt, and innocence	15:1-40
X **Story: Encroachment punished, 12 rods subject to Aaron's rod**	16:1—17:13
C´ Law: Offerings for priests, cleansing from blood	18:1—19:22
B´ Story: The Wilderness of Zin	20:1—27:23
A´ Law: Appointed feasts [including trumpets] and women's vows	28:1—30:16

The book of Numbers begins and ends with lengthy sections that present the people of Israel preparing to enter the Promised Land. In the first instance, they depart from Mount Sinai but fail to enter the land in spite of the guiding presence of Yahweh's cloud leading them day by day (Num 10:33–34). Their journey from Sinai to Kadesh-barnea is filled with complaining and even outright rebellion on the part of Aaron and Miriam who are jealous of their brother Moses (chaps. 11—12). When spies are sent into the land of Canaan, they bring back a discouraging report and the people refuse to enter the land (chap. 13). In spite of intercessory prayer on their behalf by Moses (chap. 14), the people of Israel are forced to spend forty years on the edge of the Promised Land. Eventually they launch out from Kadesh-barnea and make their way around Edom to the plains of Moab (chap. 21). There the first phase of the wars of Yahweh is

completed with the conquest of the two Amorite kings, Sihon and
Og. The tribes of Reuben, Gad, and half of Manasseh now possess
their own land and the stage is set for another chapter in God's story.
Preparations resume to enter the Promised Land; but this time the
journey will take place under new leadership. A second census of the
people marks the beginning of the second lengthy section (chaps.
26—36) in which plans are made to enter the Promised Land by way
of the Jordan Valley north of the Dead Sea.

Though there is a great deal of merit in the arguments of Mary
Douglas to see Numbers in the structural form of a "book in a ring,"
her model appears a bit forced in regards to the alternating sections
on law throughout the book as a whole. A more useful portrayal of
the structure of the book of Numbers emerges from reflection on the
boundaries of the *parashot* (weekly portions in the lectionary cycle),
which suggests that the book is divided into three major parts: 1:1—
12:16 (*Parashot* 34–36), 13:1—25:9 (*Parashot* 37–40), and 25:10—
36:13 (*Parashot* 41–43).

Parashot 34–36: Preparing to Enter the Promised Land	*Num 1:1—12:16*
A Military census and arrangement of the wilderness camp	1:1–2:34
B Census of the Levites	3:1–4:49
C Purification of the camp	5:1–6:27
X **Offerings from tribal leaders and consecration of the Levites**	7:1–8:26
C´ Second observance of Passover (at Sinai)–the journey begins	9:1–23
B´ Instructions on blowing trumpets to signal Israel is on the march	10:1–10
A´ The trek from Sinai to Kadesh	10:11–12:16

Parashot 37–40: From an "Unholy War" to the Wars of Yahweh	*Num 13:1—25:9*
A The reconnaissance of Canaan and Israel's unholy war	13:1–14:45
B Cultic regulations	15:1–41
C Encroachment on the part of Korah, Dathan, Abiram, and On	16:1–50
X **Aaron's budding rod—shows special status of his priesthood**	17:1–12
C´ Responsibility of Aaronic priesthood and other Levites	18:1–32
B´ Purification from contamination by a corpse	19:1–22
A´ The trek from Kadesh to Shittim and the wars of Yahweh	20:1–25:9

Parashot 41–43: Preparing for Life in the Promised Land   *Num 25:10—36:13*

A	From sin at Peor to Zelophehad's daughters (inheritance rights)	25:10–27:11
B	Joshua commissioned to succeed Moses for Eisodus into Cisjordan	27:12–23
C	Cultic calendar for life in the land [+ addendum on vows]	28:1–30:16
X	**Holy war vs. Midian—cleansing the contamination of Peor**	**31:1–54**
C´	Allotment of land in Transjordan	32:1–42
B´	The trek from Egypt to the Jordan for Eisodus into Cisjordan	33:1–35:34
A´	Heiresses must marry within their clan (Zelophehad's daughters)	36:1–13

In this reading, the focus of attention in the first two menorah patterns (*Parashot* 34–40) is on the consecration of the Levites and the special status of the priesthood of Aaron within the tribe of Levi. The focus on the holy war against Midian in the third section (*Parashot* 41–43) sets the stage for the presentation of the "wars of Yahweh," which follows—i.e., the actual Eisodus into the Promised Land under Moses and Joshua.

It is instructive to outline Numbers in terms of nested menorah patterns that focus attention on the narrative (story) sections, and the journey from Sinai to the plains of Moab in particular:

The Book of Numbers in a Menorah Pattern   *Num 1—36*

A	The people of God prepare to enter the Promised Land	1:1–10:10
B	Journey from Sinai to Kadesh-barnea	10:11–12:16
C	The reconnaissance of Canaan and Israel's unholy war	13:1–14:45
X	**Encroachment on the Tabernacle—special status of Aaron**	**15:1–19:22**
C´	Planned detour through Edom	20:1–21
B´	Journey from Kadesh-barnea to the plains of Moab	20:22–25:18
A´	The people of God prepare to enter the Promised Land	26:1–36:13

2nd Level Menorah: Encroachment on the Tabernacle   *Num 15:1—19:22*

A	Cultic regulation	15:1–41
B	Revolts against Moses—Korah, Dathan, Abiram, and On	16:1–40
C	People rebel against Moses and Aaron; God sends a plague	16:41–50
X	**Aaron's budding rod—shows special status of his priesthood**	**17:1–11**

C´   People complain: "We are perishing, we are lost"   17:12–13
B´   Responsibility of Aaronic priesthood and other Levites   18:1–32
A´ Rites for purifying a person who is defiled by a corpse   19:1–22

In this reading, the two major sections on laws become a framework around the second-level menorah pattern (chaps. 15—19), which is spelled out in greater detail. The content of the other sections in the primary menorah structure may also be explored in menorah patterns.

The opening section of the book of Numbers, which concerns the organization of the wilderness camp for the journey to the Promised Land, may be outlined in a nested menorah pattern as follows:

The People of God Prepare to Enter the Promised Land	Num 1:1—10:10
A Military census in the wilderness of Sinai (excluding Levi)	1:1–54
B The arrangement of the camp (excluding Levites)	2:1–34
C Census of the Levites	3:1—4:49
X **Purification of the camp**	5:1—6:27
C´ Offerings from tribal leaders and consecration of Levites	7:1—8:26
B´ Second observance of Passover (at Sinai)—the journey begins	9:1–23
A´ Instructions for blowing trumpets to signal Israel is on the march	10:1–10

The outermost frame here opens with a military census of the tribes of Israel, except for Levi (1:1–54). It concludes with a brief section on the blowing of special trumpets by "the sons of Aaron, the priests," to signal that the people of Israel are on the march (10:1–10). The second frame opens with an account of the arrangement of the tribes symmetrically around the Tent of Meeting, or Tabernacle (see diagram on next page).

It concludes with an observance of Passover, after which the journey from Mount Sinai to the Promised Land begins (9:1–23). The innermost frame focuses on the Levites, who are first numbered in a census of their own (3:1—4:49), and then consecrated after tribal leaders present their offerings and dedicate the altar (7:1—8:26). In the center we find a section on the purification of

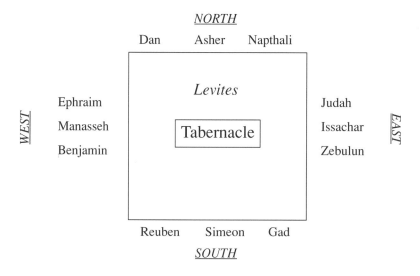

Arrangement of Tribes around the Tent of Meeting

the camp (5:1—6:27), which is explored in detail in a second-level menorah pattern as follows:

2nd Level Menorah: Purification of the Camp	*Num 5—6*
A Sanctity of the Tabernacle—excluding those who are impure	5:1–4
B Case law: Breaking faith when there is no next of kin	5:5–10
C Case of a woman suspected of adultery—the facts of the case	5:11–14
X **The ritual ordeal to determine guilt or innocence**	5:15–28
C´ Case of a woman suspected of adultery—presumptive subscript	5:29–31
B´ Case law: The Nazirite vow—for innocent contamination by a corpse	6:1–21
A´ Aaronic benediction: "May Yahweh bless you and keep you"	6:22–27

This nested menorah pattern converges on the curious case of a ritual ordeal to determine the guilt or innocence of a woman suspected of adultery (5:15–28). If the principle of the "riddle in the middle" applies, one wonders if there is symbolic meaning here. Is Israel herself to be taken as the woman in question, in terms of her covenant relationship with Yahweh?

The account of Israel's journey from Sinai to Transjordan may also be outlined in a nested menorah pattern as follows:

The Journey from Sinai to Transjordan	Num 10:11—22:1
A From Sinai to Kadesh	10:11—12:16
B The reconnaissance of Canaan and Israel's unholy war	13:1—14:45
C Cultic regulations	15:1-41
X **Encroachment on the Tabernacle—special status of Aaron**	16:1—18:32
C´ Purification from contamination by a corpse	19:1-22
B´ Planned detour through Edom—to get to the Promised Land	20:1-21
A´ From Kadesh to the plains of Moab	20:22—22:1

The outermost frame in this reading moves from Sinai to Kadesh, on the one hand (10:11—12:16), and from Kadesh to the plains of Moab, on the other (20:22—22:1). The second frame opens with the account of the sending of twelve spies to spy out to the land of Canaan, their bad report, and Israel's subsequent abortive attempt to enter the land of Canaan (13:1—14:45). It continues with their unsuccessful request to pass through the land of Edom on route to the Promised Land (20:1–21). The innermost frame consists of two parallel chapters on matters of cultic regulation (15:1–41 and 19:1–22). The middle section in this menorah pattern, which is also the structural center of the book of Numbers as a whole, takes up the matter of encroachment on the part of priestly rivals and the special status of Aaron within the Levitical priesthood (16:1—18:32). This section is explored in detail as a "wheel within a wheel"—another menorah pattern:

2nd Level Menorah: Encroachment on the Tabernacle	Num 16—18
A Revolts against Moses—Korah, Dathan, Abiram, and On	16:1-40
B People rebel against Moses and Aaron	16:41-45
C Aaron takes incense in a censer and stays the plague	16:46-50
X **Test of the rods—one from each of the twelve tribes**	17:1-7
C´ Aaron's rod buds and produces ripe almonds	17:8-11
B´ People complain: "We are perishing, we are lost"	17:12-13
A´ Laws on provisioning the cult	18:1-32

The miracle of the budding of Aaron's rod sets him apart as God's chosen leader in the priestly establishment (17:1–7). It is interesting to note how similar the structural center of Numbers is to that of Deuteronomy (Deut 18:1–8). Both passages are concerned with provisioning the cultic establishment and the priority of Levitical priests descended from Aaron.

The third major major section in Numbers may also be outlined in a nested menorah pattern:

The People of God Prepare to Enter the Promised Land	Num 26–36
A Second military census—of the new generation of warriors	26:1–65
B The law of succession in inheritance	27:1–11
C The succession of Moses by Joshua	27:12–23
X **Calendar of public sacrifices + an addendum on vows**	28:1–30:16
C´ The war against Midian	31:1–54
B´ The settlement of Transjordan	32:1–42
A´ Trek from Egypt to the Jordan River for the Eisodus into Canaan	33:1–36:13

A second military census, taken in the plains of Moab (26:1–65), is set over against a summation of the trek from Egypt to the Jordan River in forty-two stages (33:1–56). That journey, which began at Ramses (in Egypt, on the day after the original Passover celebration), took the Israelites to Mount Nebo, where Moses died. The text continues with a presentation of ideal boundaries of the Promised Land (34:1–29) and division of that land, including plans for Levitical cities and cities of asylum (35:1–34). The law of succession in inheritance (27:1–11) is set over against the actual inheritance of the land in Transjordan by the tribes of Reuben, Gad, and half of the tribe of Manasseh (32:1–42). The innermost frame moves from the succession of Joshua as Moses' successor (27:12–23) to an account of the war against Midian in which Eleazar, the son and successor of Aaron, plays a dominant role in the distribution of booty (31:1–54).

In the middle of the above menorah pattern, we find a detailed presentation of the calendar of public sacrifices for life in the Promised Land, which may be outlined in another menorah pattern:

2nd Level Menorah: The Cultic Calendar for Life in the Land	Num 28–30
A Public offerings—daily, sabbath, and new moon	28:1-15
B Paschal sacrifice and Unleavened Bread and the Feast of Weeks	28:16-31
C *Rosh Hashanah*—1st day of the seventh month	29:1-6
X **Day of Atonement—10th day of the seventh month**	29:7-11
C´ Festival of *Sukkot* (Booths)—15th to the 21st of the seventh month	29:12-34
B´ Sacrifices on the 8th day of *Sukkot*	29:35-38
A´ Private offerings may be presented as well + addendum on vows	29:39–30:16

The concentric structure of Numbers 28:1—29:40 converges on the
high holy days of the fall festival, and on the tenth day of Tishri in
particular—the Day of Atonement (29:7–11).

The Book of Numbers and the "Book of the Wars of Yahweh"

The Book of the Wars of Yahweh is mentioned only once in the Bible—
in Numbers 21:14, where it is cited to settle a boundary dispute shortly
before the conquest of the Amorite kingdom of Sihon. The document
in question was not a "book" as such, at least in the way we think about
books today. It was a scroll, or perhaps merely a familiar oral tradition—for no copy of this document has ever been found.

The narrator cited *The Book of the Wars of Yahweh* primarily
because it placed the boundary of Moab at the Arnon River.
Though the Hebrew text is difficult to interpret, it may be rendered
as follows:

> The Benefactor (i.e., Yahweh) has come in a storm;
> Yea, he has come to the wadis of the Arnon.
> He marched through the wadis;
> He marched, he turned aside—to the seat of Ar;
> He leaned toward the border of Moab.

Because of archaic features, the Hebrew text was subsequently misread with resultant confusion in the ancient versions and modern
translations.

The picture presented in this poem is that of the Divine Warrior (Yahweh) poised on the edge of the Promised Land, before the most celebrated battles of the Eisodus into the Promised Land. He has come in the whirlwind with his hosts to the sources of the Arnon River in Transjordan. He marches through the wadi valleys, turning aside to settle affairs with Moab before marching on against the two Amorite kings to the north, and then across the Jordan River to the battle camp at Gilgal and the conquest of the land of Canaan in Cisjordan. The picture is indeed a fitting one for the *incipit* (opening phrase in an old text) of a narrative poem entitled *The Book of the Wars of Yahweh.*

The wars of Yahweh were commemorated in ancient Israel in public worship, in some ways somewhat parallel to what Christian communities have done with the Eucharist, which is a symbolic portrayal of the death of the Messiah Yeshua (Jesus Christ). The people of ancient Israel remembered the wars of Yahweh as the primary salvational event in their history. These wars have two phases: the Exodus from Egypt and the Eisodus (Entry) into the Promised Land. The Eisodus takes place in two parts—under Moses in Transjordan and Joshua in Cisjordan.

The primary battles of the Exodus from Egypt focus on the defeat of Pharaoh at the crossing of the Red Sea (Exod 14—15) and the defeat of the Amalekites on the way to Mount Sinai (Exod 17:8–15). They also include the defeat the king of Arad (Num 21:1–3) and the Midianites (Num 31). The defeat of the two Amorite kings, Sihon and Og, whose land was occupied by the Transjordanian tribes of Reuben, Gad, and Manasseh (east) belongs to first phase of the Eisodus into the Promised Land.

It should be noted that Joshua is presented as the military commander in Israel under Moses' leadership as early as the battle against the Amalekites in Exodus 17:8–13. Thus it is also possible to consider all of the battles from the crossing of the Red Sea to the crossing of the Jordan River as the first phase of the Eisodus into the Promised Land. The second phase of the Eisodus takes place after the death of Moses, as Joshua becomes the instrument of Yahweh in the conquest of the land of the Canaanites (Cisjordan) recorded in Joshua 1—12.

To some extent, the Eisodus continues in Judges and 1 Samuel. David completes the conquest of the whole of the Promised Land when he establishes the Davidic Empire. Though it is useful to think of David's achievement as an extension of the wars of Yahweh, *The Book of the Wars of Yahweh* appears to have focused specifically on the mighty acts of God in the days of Moses and Joshua.

The Book of Deuteronomy

Deuteronomy may be outlined in a four-part series of nested menorah patterns:

The Book of Deuteronomy in a Menorah Pattern	*Deut 1—34*
A Eisodus into the Promised Land under Moses	1:1—3:22
B Covenant at Horeb—Moses and the Ten Words	3:23—7:11
C Life in the Promised Land—the great peroration	7:12—11:25
X **Moses proclaims the Torah: Covenant stipulations**	11:26—26:19
C´ Covenant renewal at Shechem in the Promised Land	27:1—29:9
B´ Appeal for covenant loyalty in the Promised Land	29:10—30:20
A´ Eisodus into the Promised Land under Joshua (anticipated)	31:1—34:12

2nd Level Menorah: Covenant Stipulations and Worship	*Deut 11:26—26:19*
A Covenant renewal in convocation	11:26-32
B Public worship at the central sanctuary and in local towns	12:1—14:21
C Laws on human affairs in relation to God	14:22—16:17
X **Laws on leadership and authority—executive and judicial**	16:18—21:9
C´ Laws on human affairs in relation to others	21:10—25:19
B´ Public worship at the central sanctuary and in local towns	26:1-15
A´ Mutual covenant commitments between Yahweh and Israel	26:16-19

3rd Level Menorah: Laws on Leadership and Authority	*Deut 16:18—21:9*
A You shall appoint judges and officials in your towns	16:18-20
B Do not erect an *asherah* or sacred pillar beside Yahweh's altar	16:21-22

C	Do not sacrifice a blemished animal to Yahweh	17:1
X	**Laws on leadership—judicial, political, and priestly**	17:2—19:19
C´	*Lex talionis* is intended as a deterrent to false witnesses	19:20-21
B´	Humanitarian concerns: holy war—deferments and limits	20:1-20
A´	Unsolved murder—role of elders and judges	21:1-9

4th Level Menorah: Laws on Leadership		*Deut 17:2—19:19*
A	Law on idolatry within the gates of local towns in the land	17:2-7
B	Law concerning the central tribunal	17:8-13
C	Law of the king	17:14-20
X	**Law of the Levites—endowment of the clergy**	18:1-8
C´	Law of the prophets	18:9-22
B´	Laws concerning the cities of asylum—manslaughter	19:1-13
A´	Laws on encroachment and witnesses in court	19:14-19

The outer frame in this structure opens with a review of the first phase of the Eisodus into the Promised Land, in which Moses leads the people in conquering the Amorite kingdoms of Sihon and Og (Deut 1:1—3:22). It continues with the transfer of leadership to Joshua (31:1—34:12), who will lead the people in part two of the Eisodus—the conquest of Canaan west of the Jordan River. The second frame moves from the establishment of the covenant at Mount Horeb, including the giving of the Ten Commandments (3:23—7:11), to an appeal for covenant loyalty in time to come (29:10—30:20). The innermost frame opens with a moving sermon on keeping God's commandments as a requisite for continued life in the Promised Land (7:12—11:25) and closes with a description of prescribed worship and covenant renewal in the future (29:10—30:20). And in the structural center we find the Deuteronomic Code of Law, in which the laws are structured according to the order of the Ten Commandments (11:26—25:19).

As one moves more deeply into the nested menorah patterns in Deuteronomy, the focus centers on laws concerning leadership and authority, both civic and religious. At the very center of Deuteronomy we find the brief law of the Levites (18:1-8), who were probably the ones responsible for the transmission of this legal corpus in ancient Israel. On either side of this law we find the pivotal laws on the king and the prophets, which play a dominant role in shaping the content of much of the Former Prophets—especially 1 and 2 Kings.

The menorah pattern is a dominant structure in Deuteronomy. At the same time, it is important to note that the book is also structured in a concentric design in terms of the eleven weekly portions in the lectionary cycle of *parashot*—the readings from Deuteronomy in Jewish worship, as observed in synagogue tradition to the present day. These eleven readings may be outlined in a menorah pattern as follows:

The Eleven Readings (Parashot) *in a Menorah Pattern*	Readings	Deut 1—34
A Eisodus into the Promised Land under Moses	#1	1:1—3:22
B Essence of the covenant—Moses and the Ten Words	#2	3:23—7:11
C Life in the Promised Land—the great peroration	#3	7:12—11:25
X **Central Core: The Deuteronomic Code**	#4-6	11:26—25:19
C´ Public worship and covenant renewal in the Promised Land	#7	26:1—29:9
B´ Appeal for covenant loyalty	#8	29:10—30:20
A´ Anticipation of Eisodus into the Promised Land under Joshua	#9-11	31:1—34:12

Each of these sections of Deuteronomy may be explored further in terms of menorah patterns (i.e., "wheels within a wheel").

The first of the weekly readings in Deuteronomy (*Parashah* 44) may be outlined in a series of nested menorah patterns as follows:

Reading 1: *Eisodus into the Promised Land under Moses*	Deut 1:1—3:22
A Summons to enter the Promised Land	1:1-8
B Organization of the people for life in the land	1:9-18
C Israel's unholy war—failure to enter the Promised Land	1:19-2:1
X **March of conquest from Mount Seir to the Promised Land**	2:2-25
C´ Yahweh's Holy War—conquest of Sihon and Og in Transjordan	2:26-3:11
B´ Distribution of the land in Transjordan	3:12-17
A´ Summons to take possession of the Promised Land	3:18-22

2nd Level Menorah: The March from Seir to the Promised Land	Deut 2:2—25
A Summons to journey northward (to the land beyond Edom)	2:2–3
B You are to pass through the territory of the children of Esau	2:4
C Summons not to contend with the children of Esau	2:5–6
X **A look back at what God has already done in Transjordan**	2:7–16
C´ Summons not to contend with the children of Lot (Moab and Ammon)	2:17–21
B´ The children of Esau dispossessed the Horites in times past	2:22
A´ Summons to cross the Arnon Valley and to battle against Sihon	2:23–25

3rd Level Menorah: A Look Back at What God Has Already Done	Deut 2:7–16
A A look backward: God's provision for 40 years in the wilderness	2:7
B Travel notice—we went from Seir to the wilderness of Moab	2:8
C Moab belongs to the sons of Lot (who dispossessed the Emim)	2:9
X **Rephaim lived there in times past (Moab calls them Emim)**	2:10–11
C´ Seir belongs to the sons of Esau who dispossessed the Horites	2:12
B´ Travel notice—we crossed the Zered Valley	2:13–14a
A´ A look backward: A generation of warriors dead	2:14b–16

The wars of Yahweh are in two parts: the Exodus from Egypt and
the Eisodus into the Promised Land. The Eisodus in turn is in two
phases: the conquest of Transjordan under Moses and the conquest
of Cisjordan (the so-called "West Bank") under Joshua. The focus of
interest here is on the Eisodus under Moses, in anticipation of what
is yet to come under Joshua. Phase one of the Eisodus begins with
Yahweh's march of conquest from Mount Seir in Edom to the
Promised Land north of the Arnon Valley in Transjordan. As one
moves more deeply into the concentric menorah patterns in Reading
1 (Deut 1:1—3:22), it becomes increasingly clear that what has
already been achieved by Edom, Moab, and Ammon is considered to
be part of the Eisodus in the broadest sense. These members of the
extended family of God's people, as it were, have already dispos-
sessed the Horites and the Emim in Transjordan. These former
inhabitants of the land are considered to be among the Rephaim,
who are as "tall as the Anakim"—i.e., a legendary race of giants.

The second of the weekly readings (*Parashah* 45) may be outlined in a menorah pattern within a menorah pattern:

Reading 2: Essence of the Covenant—Moses and the Ten Words	*Deut 3:23—7:11*
A Transition from Moses to Joshua—"crossing over"	3:23–29
B Exhortation to keep the Torah—focus on Commandments 1 and 2	4:1–40
C Transition and introduction to the Ten Words of the Torah	4:41–49
X **Theophany and covenant at Horeb—giving of the Ten Words**	5:1–22
C´ God's desire is for us to fear him by keeping the Torah	5:23—6:3
B´ Sermonic elaboration of Commandments 1 and 2	6:4–25
A´ The practice of holiness in the land by keeping the Torah	7:1–11

2nd Level Menorah: Theophany and Covenant—the Ten Words	*Deut 5:1–22*
A Yahweh's covenant and theophany	5:1–5
B Monotheism—Commandments 1 through 3	5:6–11
C Fourth Commandment: Observe the Sabbath	5:12–14
X **Remember your deliverance from slavery in Egypt (Exodus)**	5:15
C´ Fifth Commandment: "Honor your father and your mother"	5:16
B´ Morality—Commandments 6 through 10	5:17–21
A´ Yahweh's theophany and covenant	5:22

The focus of attention here is on God's revelation to Moses on Mount Sinai and the covenant he established with Israel at that time, a covenant that centers on the Ten Commandments (the Ten Words). The first four commandments deal with the vertical relationship between human beings and God within the concept of monotheism and proper worship. The last six of the Ten Commandments deal with the horizontal relationship between human beings themselves within the general concept of morality:

A. Our Relationship to God
   (5:12-15)

B. Our Relationship to Others
   (5:16-21)

1. No other gods allowed
2. No images allowed
3. No misuse of Yahweh's name allowed
4. Observe the Sabbath
5. Honor your father and your mother
6. Do not kill
7. Do not commit adultery
8. Do not steal

9. Do not bear false witness

10. Do not covet what belongs to your neighbor

These commandments are the stipulations of the covenant relationship between God and his people.

God's desire for his people is explored in greater depth in the following menorah pattern:

God's Desire Is that We Fear Him by Keeping the Torah	*Deut 5:23—6:3*
A Yahweh spoke to us on the mountain from the midst of the fire	5:23-24
B People address Moses: The fire will consume us, be our mediator	5:25-27
C Yahweh's speech: I hear what the people have said	5:28
X **Would that they would fear me by keeping my commandments**	5:29-30
C´ Yahweh's speech: Let me tell you the commandments	5:31
B´ Moses says to the people: Do what Yahweh has commanded	5:32—6:1
A´ That you may fear Yahweh by keeping his commandments	6:2-3

The moral life God demands is explored in another menorah pattern:

The Practice of Holiness in the Land by Keeping the Torah	*Deut 6:4—7:11*
A The great commandment: Love Yahweh your God	6:4-9
B Remember to fear Yahweh, for he is a jealous God	6:10-15
C Be careful to keep the commandments	6:16-19
X **Tell your children of the Exodus from Egypt**	6:20-22
C´ Yahweh will preserve us, if we keep his commandments	6:23-25
B´ Destroy your enemies, for you are a holy people	7:1-10
A´ Summary: Keep Yahweh's commandments	7:11

The third weekly reading (*Parashah* 46) in Deuteronomy may be outlined in a menorah pattern within a menorah pattern:

Reading 3: Life in the Promised Land—Great Commandment	*Deut 7:12—11:25*
A You will be blessed above all the peoples if you obey	7:12-26
B Remember the lessons from the wanderings in the wilderness	8:1-20
C Hear, O Israel, you are about to cross the Jordan River	9:1-29

X	**At that time Yahweh spoke the Ten Words**	10:1–7
C´	At that time Yahweh set apart the tribe of Levi	10:8–11
B´	Love God and remember what he did for you in the wilderness	10:12–11:9
A´	If you love God, you will possess the Promised Land	11:10–25

2nd Level Menorah: At That Time Yahweh Spoke the Ten Words	*Deut 10:1–7*
A Moses is told to replace the stone tablets and make an ark to hold them	10:1
B God promises to write the words again on the tablets	10:2
C Moses makes the ark, takes the tablets, and goes up the mountain	10:3
X **Yahweh writes the Ten Words and gives them to Moses**	10:4
C´ Moses goes down the mountain	10:5a
B´ Moses puts the tablets in the ark he has made	10:5b
A´ Israel journeys on, Aaron dies and is replaced by Eleazar	10:6–7

Once again, the focus of attention is on keeping the Ten Commandments that Moses received from God on Mount Sinai. That point is
reiterated within Reading 3 in two more menorah patterns:

Love God and Remember What He Did for You in the Wilderness	*Deut 10:12–11:9*
A God requires that you love him by keeping his commandments	10:12–13
B God chose you and your children above all peoples	10:14–15
C Circumcise the foreskins of your hearts—love the resident alien	10:16–19
X **Love Yahweh your God by keeping his commandments**	10:20–11:1
C´ Your children do not know what God did in the Exodus	11:2–4
B´ Your eyes have seen what God did for you in the wilderness	11:5–7
A´ Keep the commandments that you may live in the land	11:8–9

If You Love God You Will Possess the Promised Land	*Deut 11:10–25*
A The land you are entering is not like the land of Egypt	11:10
B Yahweh is the one who takes care of the land your are entering	11:11–12
C If you obey these commandments, God will bless you in the land	11:13–15
X **Keep "these my words" before you; do not serve other gods**	11:16–19
C´ Keep these commandments before you and remain in the land	11:20–21
B´ If you keep this commandment, Yahweh will drive the nations out	11:22–23
A´ All of the land on which your foot treads will be yours	11:24–25

The laws of Israel's covenant with Yahweh in Readings 4 through 6 (Deut 11:26—25:19) touch on virtually every aspect of a person's life in ancient Israel. At first glance, the contents appear to be arranged in a somewhat random order—particularly in Deuteronomy 19—25. The key to understanding the arrangement of these laws is to note that they appear in the order of the Ten Commandments of 5:6–21 and that they form a community or expansion of these summary laws as follows:

Commandment		*Section in Deut 11—25*	
Introduction		11:26-32	covenant renewal in convocation
1-2	no other gods but Yahweh	12:1–13:18	worship at the central sanctuary
3	taking God's name in vain	14:1-21	a holy people in relation to God
4	keeping the Sabbath holy	14:22—16:17	cult and society in sacred rhythm
5	parental respect	16:18–18:22	leadership and authority in Israel
6	homicide	19:1—21:9	murder, justice, and war
7	adultery	21:10–24:4	marriage, family, sex, and mixtures
8-10	theft, false testimony, and coveting	24:5—25:16	humanitarian concerns
Addendum		25:17-19	remember to hate the Amalekites

Another way of looking at the overall structure of what is often called the "Central Core" is to outline its content in a menorah pattern, which includes Deuteronomy 26, as follows:

The Central Core of Deuteronomy in a Menorah Pattern	*Deut 11:26—26:19*
A Covenant renewal in convocation	11:26-32
B Public worship at the central sanctuary and in local towns	12:1—14:21
C Laws on human affairs in relation to God	14:22—16:17
X **Laws on leadership and authority—executive and judicial**	16:18—21:9
C´ Laws on human affairs in relation to others	21:10—25:19
B´ Public worship at the central sanctuary and in local towns	26:1-15
A´ Mutual covenant commitments between Yahweh and Israel	26:16-19

2nd Level Menorah (Reading 5): Laws on Leadership and Authority Deut 16:18—21:9

A	You shall appoint judges and officials in your towns	16:18-20
B	Laws on matters pertaining to God—improper worship	16:21—17:1
C	Law on witnesses—when a person worships another god	17:2-7
X	**Laws on leadership: king, priests, and prophets**	17:8—19:13
C´	Laws on encroachment and witnesses in court	19:14-21
B´	Humanitarian concerns: Holy war—deferments and limits	20:1-20
A´	Unsolved murder—the role of elders and judges	21:1-9

3rd Level: Laws on Leadership—King, Priests, and Prophets   Deut 17:8—19:13

A	Law concerning the central tribunal	17:8-13
B	Law of the king	17:14-20
C	Levites have no territorial inheritance—Yahweh is their inheritance	18:1-2
X	**The priests' portion comes from the sacrifices and firstfruits**	18:3-4
C´	Local Levites are free to minister at the central sanctuary	18:5-8
B´	Law of the prophets	18:9-22
A´	Laws concerning the cities of asylum—manslaughter	19:1-13

The laws in Reading 5 (16:18—21:9), which occupy the central position in the concentric structural design of Deuteronomy as a whole, focus attention on matters of leadership and authority in ancient Israel, namely on laws pertaining to judges, officials, the king, Levitical priests, prophets, and judicial courts. The fact that this reading is found at the second level in the nested menorah patterns shows that the Central Core (Deut 12—26) is carefully integrated into its larger literary context. This conclusion is substantiated by the observation that chapter 26 is in fact the first section of Reading 7 (Deut 26:1—29:9).

The laws in Reading 4 (*Parashah* 47) may be outlined in a nested menorah pattern as follows:

Reading 4: Laws on Human Affairs in Relation to God   Deut 11:26—16:17

A	Covenant renewal under Moses in Moab and Joshua in Shechem	11:26-32
B	Laws that ensure exclusive worship of Yahweh—no idolatry	12:1—13:18

C	Do not gash yourself (blood implied), for you are a holy people	14:1-2
X	**What you may eat of land, water, and winged animals**	14:3-21a
C´	You are holy; do not boil a kid in its mother's milk (blood implied)	14:21b
B´	Periodic duties—tithes, protection of the poor, firstborn	14:22—15:23
A´	Pilgrimage festivals to the central sanctuary in the Promised Land	16:1-17

2nd Level: What You May Eat of Land, Water, and Winged Animals	Deut 14:3—21a	
A	Do not eat any abominable thing	14:3
B	Land animals: Eat those with divided hooves that chew the cud	14:4-6
C	Do not eat certain animals that merely appear to chew the cud	14:7
X	**Do not eat swine—it parts the hoof but does not chew the cud**	14:8
C´	Water animals: Eat only those that have fins and scales	14:9-10
B´	Winged animals: All clean birds and winged things you may eat	14:11-20
A´	Do not eat anything that dies of itself—give that to the resident alien	14:21a

The outermost frame in the concentric structure of Reading 4 focuses on matters of worship at the central sanctuary in the Promised Land—in terms of covenant renewal at Shechem (11:26–32) and the three pilgrimage festivals to the central sanctuary (16:1–17). The second frame takes up the matter of idolatry and proper worship at the central sanctuary (12:1—13:18) and the periodic duties demanded of the worshiping community (14:22—15:23). The innermost frame consists of two brief laws, both of which make implicit reference to illicit use of blood. On the one hand, we have the prohibition of pagan mourning customs that require drawing blood by gashing one-self (14:1–2); and, on the other hand, we have the peculiar prohibition of boiling a kid in its mother's milk (14:21b). This latter law is closely connected with the section at the center of this menorah pattern, which delineates what one may eat of land, water, and winged animals (14:3–21a). Jewish tradition has built the system of the kosher kitchen from this verse (cf. Exod 23:19; 34:26), in which meat and dairy products—including the utensils and dishes used to cook and eat them—are kept separate.

Casper Labuschagne has called attention to the fact that at eight days after the birth of the firstborn, the mother goat is still producing beestings, which are of a reddish color. As Labuschagne put it, "Modern science has taught us that this is due to the high concentration of albumen and globulin, proteins which occur in blood, and owing to the fact that to a greater or lesser extent beestings do contain actual blood" (*The Scriptures and the Scrolls*, ed. F. García Martínez. VTSup 49 [Leiden: Brill, 1992], pp. 6–17). The concentric structure shown here supports this conclusion in drawing attention to the parallel text in 14:1–2; both texts make implicit reference to forbidden practices involving blood. The two passages serve as a framework to set off the detailed account of what one may eat of land, water, and winged animals in 14:3–21a. At the structural center of this list we find the command not to eat swine (14:8), because that animal parts the hoof but does not chew the cud. Scholars continue to debate the reasoning behind this prohibition. Whatever the reason, the prohibition of eating pork is central in Jewish (and Muslim) cultures.

The two laws concerning illicit use of blood in this context (14: 1–2 and 21b) call attention to the laws concerning sacred and secular slaughter in ancient Israel (12:8–28), which may be outlined in a menorah pattern as follows:

Laws on Sacred and Secular Slaughter in Ancient Israel	Deut 12:8–28
A Worship Yahweh with your tithes and offerings at the central sanctuary	12:8–12
B *Take heed that you do not* offer sacrifices wherever you choose	12:13
C Offer sacrifices at the place God chooses	12:14a
X **Eat meat but pour out the blood on the ground**	12:14b–16
C´ Eat the tithe and offerings in the place God chooses	12:17–18
B´ *Take heed that you do not* forsake the Levite	12:19
A´ You may eat meat at home but not blood; pour out the blood properly	12:20–28

In the structural center of Reading 5 (*Parashah* 48, Deut 16:18— 21:9), which focuses on leadership and authority in ancient Israel, specific reference is made to the matter of sacrifices and the offering of firstfruits at the central sanctuary (18:3–4). The livelihood of the Levitical priests is dependent on these sacrificial offerings. Proper disposal of the blood is absolutely essential and holiness itself is at stake. That is the issue in 14:21 where the assertion is made that because "you are a people holy to Yahweh your God, 'You shall not boil a kid in its mother's milk.'" Life itself is in the blood (cf. Lev 17:11).

The forty-three laws in Reading 6 (*Parashah* 49, Deut 21:10—25:19) may also be outlined in a menorah pattern as follows:

Reading 6: Laws on Human Affairs in Relation to Others	Deut 21:10–25:19
A On marriage—with a woman captured in war	21:10-14
B Twelve laws on family, "true religion," and illicit mixtures	21:15–22:12
C Six laws on sexual misconduct	22:13-29
X **Prohibition of marrying one's father's wife**	22:30
C´ Seven laws on "true religion"	23:1-25
B´ Fifteen laws on marriage, war, and "true religion"	24:1–25:16
A´ On war—remember to hate the Amalekites	25:17-19

Since there are eleven weekly portions in the cycle of Torah readings in Deuteronomy, Reading 6 is also a structural center—the middle week in a sequence of eleven weeks. As such it illustrates the phenomenon of the "riddle in the middle" in a remarkable manner. In the center of this structure we find a curious law that prohibits a man from marrying his father's wife (22:30). This law functions as a literary bridge connecting two larger groups of laws on matters of social ethics (21:10—22:29 and 23:1–25). It is also parallel with a somewhat similar law prohibiting remarriage if one's former wife has remarried (24:1–4), which functions in the same manner connecting the laws of 23:1–25 and 24:5—25:19.

Calum Carmichael has demonstrated the close connection between the wording of the law in 22:30 and the narrative concerning Reuben and his father's concubine in Genesis 35:22 and 49:4. The law prohibiting a man from taking his father's wife includes the taking and possessing of his father's concubine. In other words, the law shapes the narrative, which focuses on Reuben's intercourse with Bilhah. In his discussion of what he calls the law on "a forbidden relationship with a father's wife," Carmichael says: "In the law, a man's wife is his skirt, and for a son to lie with her means that figuratively he has removed his father's covering and put it on himself. In a literal sense he uncovers his stepmother's nakedness, in a figurative sense, his father's" (*Law and Narrative in the Bible* [Ithaca: Cornell University Press, 1985], p. 222). This observation raises the fascinating question of the nature of the whole of Reading 6 in relation to narrative tradition elsewhere in the Hebrew Bible, and to the book of Genesis in particular. It appears that we have here the most extensive occurrence of the phenomenon of the "riddle in the middle" within a concentric literary structure of the Tanakh. A detailed discussion of this matter is beyond the scope of this introductory textbook. For purposes of illustration, a significant part of the data may be summarized in the following nested menorah pattern:

Laws that Shape Narratives in Genesis, Exodus, and Numbers		*Deut 24:6–25:19*
A Isaac and Ishmael: Millstone as pledge	Gen 21:9–12	Deut 24:6
B Sale of Joseph: Theft of a fellow Israelite	Gen 37:26–28	Deut 24:7
C Miriam's leprosy: Dealing with "leprosy"	Num 12:1–14	Deut 24:8–9
X **Stories of the Fathers in Genesis**		Deut 24:10–25:10
C´ Judah and Tamar: Immodest lady wrestler	Gen 38	Deut 25:11–12
B´ Joseph and Manna: Honest weights and measures	Gen 42–44, Ex 16	Deut 25:13–16
A´ Amalek's attack: "Remember to hate Amalek"	Exod 17:8–14	Deut 25:17–19

2nd Level: Stories of Abraham, Isaac, Jacob, Joseph, and Judah		*Deut 24:10–25:10*
A Finding a wife for Isaac: Distrained property	Gen 24 (and 15)	Deut 24:10–13
B Jacob and Laban: The hired servant	Gen 31:4–42	Deut 24:14–15
C Hamor and his son Shechem: Fathers and sons	Gen 34	Deut 24:16
X **Joseph in Egypt: Protecting the vulnerable**	Gen 37–47	Deut 24:17–22
C´ Joseph in Egypt: Limits on flogging	Gen 37–47	Deut 25:1–3
B´ Judah and Tamar: Unmuzzling the ox	Gen 38	Deut 25:4
A´ Judah and Tamar: Levirate marriage	Gen 38	Deut 25:5–10

For purposes of illustration, let us examine the text of Deut 24:10–13 in relation to the narratives in Genesis 15 and 24. The "pledge" (עבוֹט) in the law is Rebekah in Genesis 24, who is obtained as a wife for Isaac by an unnamed servant who is sent to obtain the "pledge from the house of Laban." Specific wording in this story carries the reader back to the earlier story of Abram in Genesis 15, when God "brought him outside" and blessed him. Then, "as the sun was going down" ... "when the sun had gone down ... on that day Yahweh made a covenant with Abram" (Gen 15:12–18). Here Rebekah, the עבוט in Genesis 24, is related to the "fathers" (אבות) of Genesis 15:15. Like Sarah before her, she is a "matriarch"—one of the "mothers of the Fathers," as it were, whose lineage through her son Esau includes the chiefs of Edom, one of whom takes center stage in another time and at another place within the biblical narrative—in the land of Uz. There Job lives to see "his sons, and his son's sons, four generations." Like his "brother" Abraham, Job "died, an old man, and full of days" (Job 42:16–17, cf. Gen 15:15).

The words in the law "that he may sleep in his garment" (24:13) take on fresh meaning in relation to the story in Genesis, where Isaac "took Rebekah and she became his wife" (Gen 24:67). In the Hebrew text, this same expression appears in Deuteronomy 21:11; 22:13; 23:1, and 24:1–5 (five times). Moreover, the words "he shall bless you" (Deut 24:13) become "and they blessed" in Genesis 24:60. They introduce the blessing pronounced by the men of Laban's house on Rebekah: "Our sister, may you become the mother of thousands of ten thousands, and may your descendants possess the gate of those who hate them!"

At this point, the reader is reminded of a similar blessing given to Abraham in times past. And the very next phrase in the law of Deuteronomy 24:13, "it shall be counted as righteousness," takes us back to the narrative of God's covenant with Abram in Genesis 15. God *brought him outside* and said, "Look toward heaven, and number the stars, if you are able ... so shall your descendants be" (Gen 15:5). And Abram believed God, who *reckoned it to him as righteousness* (Gen 15:6). A bit later in the narrative, "Yahweh said to Abram, 'Know of a surety that your descendants will be ... oppressed for four hundred years ... As for yourself, you shall go to your fathers in peace; you shall be buried in a good old age. And *they shall come back here in the fourth generation*'" (Gen 15: 12–18). This statement takes on new meaning in this reading, for that is what we just did in this reading of Genesis through the lens of the laws of Deuteronomy. The four generations are Abraham, Isaac, Jacob/Israel, and Jacob's twelve sons (the tribes of Israel), with the focus narrowing to the persons of Joseph (Deut 24:7, 17–22; 25:1–3, 13–16) and Judah (Deut 25:4–12) in that fourth generation. The moment the sale of Joseph by his brothers is first introduced in Deuteronomy 24:7 (in the law prohibiting a "theft" of a fellow Israelite) our attention is directed to Miriam's "leprosy" (Deut 24:8–9) in the era of the Exodus from Egypt. This is the "present," from the perspective of Deuteronomy. The next law (24:10–13) takes us back three generations to Isaac's quest for a wife in Genesis 24:1–67, which then takes us back still further, one more generation, to the original story of Abram. There the author already outlined all that was to follow in a brief prophecy, which concludes with the curious words "they will come back here in the fourth generation."

The content of Reading 7 (*Parashah* 50, Deut 26:1—29:9) may be outlined in the following nested menorah pattern:

Reading 7: Public Worship and Covenant Renewal	Deut 26:1—29:9
A Preview—two liturgies for worship in the Promised Land	26:1–15
B Mutual commitment between God and Israel in covenant renewal	26:16–19
C Shechem ceremony dramatizing Israel's covenant responsibilities	27:1–10
X **Curses and blessings—with threefold expansion of curses**	27:11—28:57
C´ Final curse: The complete reversal of Israel's history	28:58–68
B´ Summation: "These are the words of the covenant"	29:1
A´ Review—remembering the mighty acts of God in times past	29:2–9

2nd Level Menorah: Covenant Curses and Blessings	Deut 27:11—28:57
A Positioning of the tribes at Shechem and litany of curses	27:11–26
B Six covenant blessings (in three pairs)	28:1–6
C Promises expanding on the blessings	28:7–10
X **Threefold blessing: progeny, property (livestock), and produce**	28:11
C´ Promises expanding on the blessings	28:12–14
B´ Six covenant curses (in three pairs)	28:15–19
A´ Threefold expansion of the covenant curses	28:20–57

The first half of the outermost frame in this menorah pattern, with its two liturgies for use in the annual pilgrimage festivals (26:1–15), functions as a transitional passage. It ties together the stipulations of the covenant as spelled out in the laws of the Central Core (Deut 12—26) with the covenant ceremony that follows in 27:1—29:9 and the appeal for covenant loyalty in 29:10—30:20. A close reading of Deuteronomy 27—30 reveals a mixture of two covenant ceremonies: one on the plains of Moab, in the days of Moses, and another to be observed at Shechem under Joshua. It is useful here to anticipate the discussion to follow in Reading 8 (*Parashah* 51, Deut 29:10—30:20) by outlining the whole in a single concentric structure as follows:

Readings 7 and 8: Worshiping in a Covenant Community	*Deut 26—30*
A Public worship at the annual festivals in the Promised Land	26:1–19
B The covenant blessings and curses	27:1—28:68
X **Summation: "These are the words of the covenant"**	29:1
B´ The covenant is for future generations too	29:2–29
A´ The terms of the covenant are doable	30:1–20

The outermost frame opens with a brief summary of the nature of "true religion" in the Promised Land, in which the needs of "the Levite and the resident alien in your midst" are met (26:10–11). It concludes the assurance that "this commandment that I command you today is not too hard for you" (30:11). This instruction is not beyond your reach, it is doable. The words of the covenant are the words that Yahweh commanded Moses in the land of Moab, in addition to the covenant he made with them at Mount Sinai (29:1). The movement in the inner frame of the above structure is from an expanded description of future disasters in the wake of covenant violation (28:20–37) to the declaration that the terms of the covenant apply for future generations as well (29:13–14).

As we move more deeply into the center of the threefold expansion of the curses at the structural center of the initial menorah pattern (27:11—28:57), we find in the center a threefold blessing: progeny, property (in terms of livestock), and produce (28:11). This theme is developed in numerous ways throughout the extensive section on the covenant curses and blessings in Deuteronomy 27—28, which is illustrated in the outline of the second expansion of the curses in a nested menorah pattern:

Second Expansion of Curses: Oppression, Exile, and Slavery	*Deut 28:20–44*
A Triad of afflictions: Curse, confusion, and cumbrance	28:20–22
B Agricultural disaster (drought and hardened soil)	28:23–24
C War: Defeat leading to Israel becoming an object lesson	28:25–26
X **Physical and emotional oppression—undoing the blessing**	28:27–35
C´ War: Exile leading to Israel becoming an object lesson	28:36–37
B´ Agricultural disaster (crop-destroying pests)	28:38–42
A´ Economic collapse—impoverishment and debt	28:43–44

2nd Level Menorah: Physical and Emotional Oppression	*Deut 28:27–35*
A "Boils" of Egypt (sent from Yahweh)	28:27
B Madness and blindness	28:28–29a
C Oppressed and robbed all the days	28:29b
X **Undoing of the threefold blessing (in 28:4, 8, 11)**	28:30–31
C´ Oppressed and crushed all the days	28:32–33
B´ Madness from what one sees	28:34
A´ "Boils" (sent from Yahweh)	28:35

The detailed parallelism within this elaborate expansion of covenant curses has drawn comment from numerous scholars. The tedious listing of calamities displays unusual balance and symmetry, which converges on the undoing of the threefold blessing God has bestowed on his covenant people in progeny, property (livestock), and produce.

The eighth of the eleven weekly portions in the lectionary cycle of Torah readings from Deuteronomy is known as "Taking One's Stand," from its opening words in the Hebrew text. Individuals are invited to take their stand as obedient members of the covenant community. The covenant is intended not only for "those who are here with us standing today before Yahweh our God"; it is also "with those who are not here with us today" (29:15)—that is, for all future generations of God's people. The content of Reading 8 (*Parashah* 51, Deut 29:10—30:20) may be outlined in a menorah pattern as follows:

Reading 8: Appeal for Covenant Loyalty	*Deut 29:10—30:20*
A The covenant is binding on future generations too	29:10-15
B Those with reservations about keeping the covenant are warned	29:16-21
C Exile from the land for breaking the covenant foretold	29:22-28
X **Secret and revealed things: "Do all the words of this Torah"**	29:29
C´ Possibility of restoration—when you return, God will return	30:1-10
B´ God's commandments are doable	30:11-14
A´ The choice before you is between life and death—choose life	30:15-20

The center of this menorah pattern contains perhaps the most striking example of the principle of the "riddle in the middle" in the book of Deuteronomy. The words translated "to us and to our children" in 29:29 constitute the tenth (and final) example of the *Nequdoth* in the Torah. Each of the ten consonants of the Hebrew text has a special mark over it in the Leningrad Codex. The Aleppo Codex, however, has twelve dots rather than ten. These dots function as a form of commentary in shorthand, or homiletic notes to such a commentary, on the Hebrew text. The twelve dots in the Aleppo Codex may refer to the twelve tribes of Israel, which the scribe understood to be the meaning of the words "to us and to our children." The secret things belong to God; but God's revelation in "the words of this Torah" belongs to Israel. The ten dots in the Leningrad Codex may refer to the "Ten Words" (Ten Commandments), which are expanded into what eventually became the book of Deuteronomy as we now have it.

The scribe who added the *Nequdoth* was probably aware of the fact that the numerical value of the two words under the dots is 32 + 64 (= 2 x 32) = 96 (= 3 x 32). In terms of the usual association of the number 32 with the Hebrew word for "glory," כבוד, (20 + 2 + 6 + 4 = 32) in the numerical composition of Deuteronomy, this number is used to call attention to the glory of Yahweh. It is probably no coincidence that the numerical value of the Hebrew word ישראל, "Israel," is 64 (= 10 + 21 + 20 + 1 + 12). The glory of Israel is to be found in the Torah, which God entrusted to her (cf. Deut 4:5–8). The ten curious dots over ten successive letters in the Hebrew text stand for the "Ten Words," which are entrusted to Israel. And those words are "for us and for our children," that is, for all Israel. In short, the book of Deuteronomy has the title "these are the words," which are in essence an expansion of the original "Ten Words" (the Ten Commandments). The secret things belong to God, but the revealed things belong to us and to our children forever—namely, "to do all the words of this Torah." The *Nequdoth*, at least in·this instance, constitute a form of homiletical notes for the informed rabbi to teach the central message of Deuteronomy.

The "riddle in the middle" in 29:29 is followed immediately by a menorah pattern that reiterates the "great commandment," which plays such a prominent role in Reading 2 (Deut 3:23—7:11; see especially 6:4–9).

Possibility of Restoration: When You Return, God will Return	*Deut 30:1–10*
A Recall these words and return to Yahweh	30:1–2
B Yahweh will restore you and he will return	30:3
C Yahweh will bring you back to the land of your fathers	30:4–5
X **Love Yahweh your God with all you heart and with all your soul**	30:6–7
C´ You will return and heed the voice of Yahweh	30:8
B´ Yahweh will return to take delight in you	30:9
A´ You will heed Yahweh's voice when you return to him	30:10

The key word שׁוּב, "return," appears in seven clauses within this menorah pattern. Three of these occurrences are in the outermost frame, which focuses on the need to return to Yahweh at that point in the future when the terms of the covenant have been broken (30:1–2). The way "to return" is to obey Yahweh's voice (30:10). The second frame also contains three occurrences of the key Hebrew verbal root in parallel verses (30:3 and 9), which focus on the assurance that Yahweh will return to his people and that he will restore their fortunes after the captivity. The innermost frame has its focus on the fact that when the people return by obeying Yahweh (30:8), Yahweh will bring them back to the land of their fathers (30:4–5). And in the center we find a restatement of the "great commandment"

—"to love Yahweh your God with all your heart and with all your soul" (30:6–7).

The shift from the style of direct speech to that of narrative in Deuteronomy 31, and the disparate nature of its sub-units led Gerhard von Rad to conclude "that the material from chap. 31 onward does not in any way belong to Deuteronomy any longer, but belongs instead to the great historical work in which Deuteronomy was aborted as a literary unit" (*Deuteronomy: A Commentary*. The Old Testament Library [Philadelphia: Westminster, 1966], p. 188). It was von Rad's failure to observe the concentric structure of the text that led to his negative assessment that "the whole chapter contains the debris of traditions rather than a real advance in the narrative" (p. 190). This chapter is in fact closely connected to 3:23–28 and plays a foundational role in the structure of all that follows in Deuteronomy 32—34. A different conclusion from that of von Rad is suggested by the following outline of 3:23–29 and 31:1–30 in menorah patterns:

Transition from Moses to Joshua: "Crossing Over"	*Deut 3:23–29*
A Introduction to the dialogue: Moses seeks God's favor	3:23
B Moses offers praise for the privilege of "seeing" God's greatness	3:24
C Moses asks permission to cross over to "see" the land	3:25
X **Yahweh is "cross" with Moses**	3:26
C´ Moses is permitted to "see" the land but not to cross over	3:27
B´ Moses is to command Joshua to cross over to the land Moses "sees"	3:28
A´ Concluding travel notice: "We remained opposite Beth-peor"	3:29

Reading 9: From Moses to Joshua—Moses Prepares to Die	*Deut 31:1–30*
A Moses announces his departure and replacement by Joshua	31:1–6
B Moses appoints Joshua as his successor	31:7–8
C Torah to be read at the Feast of Booths to teach future generations	31:9–13
X **Theophany in the Tent of Meeting with Moses and Joshua**	31:14–18
C´ The writing of the Song as a witness to future generations	31:19–22
B´ Yahweh appoints Joshua to succeed Moses	31:23
A´ The Torah and Song are given as witnesses to future generations	31:24–30

Moses' request for permission to "cross over" into Cisjordan (3:23–25) is set over against Yahweh's command that Moses encourage

Joshua, who will "cross over before the people" (3:28). The center of this menorah pattern is marked by a whimsical sense of humor. Yahweh is "cross" with Moses in response to his request to "cross over" into Cisjordan (3:26). At the same time, Yahweh both denies and grants Moses' request to "see the good land that is beyond the Jordan" (3:25). Yahweh "did not listen" to Moses (3:26), and yet he did, for he commanded him to "go up to the top of the Pisgah (range)...and see with your eyes" (3:27). In Deuteronomy 31—34 Moses obeys this command and he sees from the top of Mount Nebo what no tourist today can possibly see: "All the land, the Gilead as far as Dan, and all of Naphtali, and all the land of Ephraim and Man-asseh, and all the land of Judah as far as the Western Sea, the Negev, and the Plain, that is, the valley of Jericho the city of palms, as far as Zoar" (34:1–3). In short, Moses "saw" all of the land, but he never set foot on any of it.

Gerhard von Rad was correct in his assessment that Deuteron-omy 31—34 is closely connected to the book of Joshua that follows. It should be noted, however, how closely the center of the menorah pattern in Deuteronomy 31:14–15 is related to a more distant text in Exodus 33:11, which also places Moses and Joshua together in the Tent of Meeting. That text adds the note that Moses' servant Joshua "did not depart from the tent." The larger concentric design of the whole of the Torah and the Former Prophets, in which this verse stands in the structural center of Exodus 33, is explored above in the section on "The Book of Exodus."

The final three weekly portions of Torah readings (Deut 31—34), which are read in the month of Tishri from Rosh Hashanah (1 Tishri) to *Simchat Torah* (23 Tishri), are shorter than the others, as the worshiping community moves into the high holy days of the Jewish calendar. The Ten Days of Repentance extend from Rosh Hashanah (1 Tishri) to Yom Kippur (Day of Atonement, 10 Tishri). The Festival of Booths (15–22 Tishri) follows them and sets the stage for *Simchat Torah*—the end of one cycle of readings from the Torah and the beginning of the next.

The content of Readings 9–11 (*Parashot* 52–54, Deut 31—34) may be outlined in nested menorah patterns in two different ways, depending on whether the focus of attention is on the Song of Moses (Deut 32) or the testamentary blessing of Moses (Deut 33). When the Song of Moses is the focus, the nested menorah pattern is as follows:

Readings 9–11: Anticipating the Eisodus into the Promised Land	Deut 31:1—34:12
A Moses' final provisions in view of his impending death	31:1-13
B Yahweh's charge to Moses and Joshua in the Tent of Meeting	31:14-23
C Moses gives the Torah to the Levitical priests	31:24-27
X **The Song of Moses within its narrative context**	31:28—32:45
C´ Moses commands the people to observe the Torah	32:46-47
B´ Yahweh commands Moses to climb Mount Nebo to "see" the land	32:48-52
A´ Moses' blessing, death, funeral, and necrology	33:1—34:12

2nd Level Menorah: The Song of Moses in its Narrative Context	Deut 31:28—32:45
A Moses gathers the leaders to hear the Song	31:28-30
B Yahweh's blessing of Israel in times past	32:1-14
C Israel's disloyalty—they forsook the one who made them	32:15-18
X **Yahweh's decision to punish Israel**	32:19-35
C´ Yahweh's loyalty—his plan to deliver Israel	32:36
B´ Yahweh's "vengeance"—punishment and salvation in the future	32:37-43
A´ Moses speaks all the words of this Song to the people	32:44-45

In this reading, the focus narrows to the issue of Yahweh's "vengeance"—his redemptive judgment on Israel. Yahweh himself decides to punish Israel for her disloyalty (32:19–35). But his anger has limits and he also shows mercy. He "redeems" the very people he "sold" (32:36–39).

The Song of Moses, which makes up the greater part of Reading 10 (Deut 32:1–52), may be outlined in a nested menorah pattern of its own as follows:

The Song of Moses	Deut 32:1–43
A Exordium: Yahweh's faithfulness and Israel's disloyalty	32:1-6
B Past: Yahweh's benefactions to Israel in times past	32:7-14

C	Israel's disloyalty—they forsook the one who made them	32:15-18
X	**Yahweh's decision to punish Israel**	32:19-35
C´	Yahweh's loyalty—his plan to deliver Israel	32:36
B´	Future: Yahweh will take vengeance on his enemies	32:37-42
A´	Coda: Celebration of Yahweh's deliverance of Israel	32:43

2nd Level Menorah: God's Decision to Punish Israel	*Deut 32:19-35*
A Yahweh's response: "I will hide my face from them"	32:19-21
B The fire of Yahweh's anger will consume the earth	32:22
C Yahweh's judgment: Bereavement and terror—for everyone	32:23-25
X **Yahweh's mercy: He chooses to limit Israel's punishment**	32:26-29
C´ Our God is not like other gods—he "sold" Israel	32:30-31
B´ The enemy will drink the cup of Yahweh's wrath	32:32-33
A´ Yahweh's decision: "To me belong vengeance and recompense"	32:34-35

In his study of the structure of the Song of Moses, Patrick Skehan argues persuasively that the poem as a whole divides naturally into three major parts (vv. 1–14, 15–29, and 30–43). Each of these three parts has twenty-three versets. The structure observed by Skehan is confirmed on more objective grounds in my commentary on Deuteronomy. That structure is more complex than Skehan realized, however, as shown by noting the major divisions within the first and third sections:

The Song of Moses in a Five-Part Concentric Structure	*Deut 32:1–43*
A God's justice and Israel's disloyalty	32:1-6
B God's blessing on Israel in times past	32:7-14
X **Israel's sin provokes God's punishment**	32:15-29
B´ God's decision to punish both Israel and her enemies	32:30-35
A´ God's "vengeance"—Israel is delivered	32:36-43

In this reading there are twenty-three versets in the center section (32:15–29), and twenty-three versets in each of the two frames around that center: the outer frame (32:1–6 + 36–43) and the inner (32:7–14 + 30–35). As we have already noted, there are also twenty-three versets in each of the three major parts of the Song of Moses

(32:1–14, 15–29, and 30–43). In the numerical composition of the book of Deuteronomy, the number 23 is associated with the word "glory," which indicates that this remarkable poem was written to the glory of Yahweh.

The primary message of Readings 9–11 (*Parashot* 52–54, Deut 31—34) shifts when the focus of attention moves to the testamentary blessing in chapter 33, as the following nested menorah pattern shows:

Readings 9–11: Anticipating the Eisodus into the Promised Land	Deut 31:1—34:12
A Moses' final charges to Joshua and to all Israel (and the Song)	31:1–32:47
B Moses commanded to ascend Mount Nebo to "see" the land	32:48–52
C First stanza of ancient hymn: Yahweh's protection and provision	33:1–5
X **Moses' testamentary blessing of the twelve tribes of Israel**	33:6–25
C´ Second stanza of ancient hymn: Israel's security and blessing	33:26–29
B´ Moses ascends Mount Nebo where he "sees" the Promised Land	34:1–4
A´ Transition of leadership from Moses to Joshua	34:5–12

2nd Level Menorah: Testamentary Blessing of the Twelve Tribes	Deut 33:6–25
A Reuben and Judah	33:6–7
B Levi—with the first apostrophe (and Simeon?)	33:8–11
C Benjamin	33:12
X **Joseph (Ephraim and Manasseh)**	33:13–17
C´ Zebulun and Issachar	33:18–19
B´ Gad—with the second apostrophe	33:20–21
A´ Dan, Naphtali, and Asher	33:22–25

The outermost frame in this menorah pattern moves from Moses' final charges to Joshua and the people of Israel (31:1—32:47) to the actual transition of leadership from Moses to Joshua (34:5–12). The words of 32:48–52, which look back to 3:27 and even further back to Numbers 27:12–14, are now fulfilled explicitly in 34:1–4 as Moses ascends Mount Nebo to "see" the Promised Land. Two stanzas of an ancient hymn of praise to Yahweh are used as the innermost frame to highlight the blessings bestowed on the tribes of Israel (33:6–25). As the reader moves more deeply into the center itself, the focus narrows to the tribe of Joseph (i.e., Ephraim and Manasseh).

At this point, it is useful to call the reader's attention to the earlier discussion of "Genesis 1—11 as Introduction to the Bible." Reading 11 (Deut 33—34), the final reading in the annual lectionary cycle of Torah readings (*Parashot* 54), takes place on *Simchat Torah*, the 23rd of Tishri. The concluding section of this reading may be outlined as follows:

A	Moses sees the whole of the land "with his *eyes*"	Deut 34:1-4
B	Death and burial of Moses—"no one *knows* where"	Deut 34:5-6
X	**Moses was 120 years old—"his *eye* was not dim"**	Deut 34:7-8
B´	Incomparability of Moses—"whom Yahweh *knew* face to face"	Deut 34:9-10
A´	Moses did great wonders "before *the eyes* of all Israel"	Deut 34:11-12

The first weekly portion (Gen 1:1—6:8), which is known as "In the beginning," actually commences on *Simchat Torah*, when the Torah scroll is re-rolled to its beginning. The second portion (Gen 6:9—11:32) is known as "Noah." When the content of these two readings is outlined in a menorah pattern, we have the following:

Parashot *1 and 2 in a Menorah Pattern*		*Gen 1—11*
A	Story of creation/dispersion [ending with three sons of Adam]	1:1–4:26
B	Enoch (who "walked with God")	5:1-32
C	Sons of God take daughters of *ha'adam* as wives	6:1-2
X	**Yahweh says: "He is flesh and his days shall be 120 years"**	6:3
C´	Sons of God and daughters of *ha'adam* breed giants in the land	6:4
B´	Noah (who "walked with God")	6:5–9:29
A´	Story of dispersion [beginning with three sons of Noah]	10:1—11:32

The center of this structure presents the phenomenon of the "riddle in the middle," as the hearer is startled by the sudden reference to what looks at first glance like what is normally called mythology. The "sons of God" marry "daughters of Adam" to produce the giants of old (the *Nephilim*). In addition to the two interpretations of the curious word *beshaggam* in the center of the center in this menorah pattern discussed above, a third reading is also possible. More than a century ago, Abraham Geiger cited both Josephus and Jerome in his arguments that the word *beshaggam* refers to Moses in terms of gematria—where the words משה ("Moses") and בשגם (*beshaggam*) are identical. Moreover, in the regular cycle of weekly readings from the Torah, the text of Deuteronomy 34:7 is read the week before—on *Simchat Torah* (which translates as "the joy of the Torah").

3

The Prophets
From Joshua to the Second Temple

The death of Moses sets the stage for part two of the Eisodus. "After
the death of Moses the *servant of Yahweh*, Yahweh said to Joshua
son of Nun, Moses' attendant: *My servant Moses* is dead. Prepare to
cross the Jordan, together with all this people, into the land that I am
about to give to you and to the children of Israel" (Josh 1:1–2). The
use of the phrase *children of Israel* here reminds the attentive reader
of the book of Exodus, where these same words appear twice—at
the beginning and end of the opening paragraph. In the first instance
the words refer to Jacob/Israel's twelve sons (Exod 1:1); and in the
second they refer to the people of Israel who were "fruitful and multiplied and filled the earth" (Exod 1:7). The children of Israel are
now ready to "subdue" the land and to "have dominion" over it (cf.
Gen 1:28). Joshua is the leader chosen by God to initiate the next
stage in God's process of creation—of a people who will become a
blessing to all the nations.

THE FORMER PROPHETS

The Torah plus the Former Prophets (i.e., Genesis through 2 Kings)
is often called the "Primary History." The book of Joshua functions
within the Primary History as a "bridge" connecting the five books
of Moses (the Torah) with the "Special History" of ancient Israel
(Judges through 2 Kings)—the story of the people of God's

covenant within their own land. Moses leads the people of Israel out of slavery in Egypt (the Exodus). The entry into the Promised Land (the Eisodus) is in two parts: the conquest of the Amorite kingdoms of Sihon and Og in Transjordan under Moses, and the conquest of the land west of the Jordan (Cisjordan) under Joshua.

The book of Joshua is the first book within the Former Prophets. As such, it stands within a larger structure, which may be outlined in a menorah pattern:

The Former Prophets in a Menorah Pattern	*Josh–2 Kgs*
A Taking the land under charismatic leadership	Josh
B Possessing the land under charismatic judges	Judg
C Possessing the land under charismatic kings (Saul and David)	1 Sam
X The kingdom of David established	2 Sam 1:1—2:4a
C´ Possessing the land under a dynastic king (David)	2 Sam
B´ Possessing the land under dynastic kings (Solomon to Ahab)	1 Kgs
A´ Loss of the land under monarchic leadership	2 Kgs

In terms of this concentric design, the establishment of the dynastic kingdom of David is the central theme of the Former Prophets. In many respects, the figure of Joshua foreshadows the figure of Josiah at the end of 2 Kings (chaps. 22—23), to form a literary framework around the Former Prophets as a whole.

At the same time, the figure of Joshua appears as part of a framing device within the Former Prophets to set the stage for the appearance of the prophet Elijah in 2 Kings 17:1. In Joshua 6:26, Joshua pronounces a curse, saying: "Cursed before Yahweh be the man that rises up and rebuilds this city, Jericho. At the cost of his first-born shall he lay its foundation, and at the cost of his youngest son shall he set up its gates." Much later we read that "Hiel of Bethel built Jericho. He laid its foundation at the cost of Abiram his first-born, and set up its gates at the cost of his youngest son Segub, according to the word of Yahweh, which he spoke by Joshua the son of Nun" (1 Kgs 16:34). The Former Prophets may be outlined in a nested menorah pattern with the story of Elijah in the center.

Menorah Pattern: The Former Prophets with Elijah in the Center	Josh–2 Kgs
A From the destruction of Jericho (Josh 6) to its rebuilding	Josh–1 Kgs 15:34
B Prophecy of Joshua fulfilled (see Josh 6:26)	1 Kgs 16:1–34
C The prophet Elijah is introduced	1 Kgs 17:1
X **The story of the prophet Elijah and King Ahab**	1 Kgs 17:2–19:18
C´ The prophet Elisha is introduced	1 Kgs 19:19–21
B´ Prophecy of Yahweh to Elijah about to be fulfilled	1 Kgs 20–2 Kgs 13
A´ From the death of Elisha to the destruction of Solomon's Temple	2 Kgs 14–25

2nd Level Menorah Pattern: The Story of Elijah and Ahab	1 Kgs 17:2–19:18
A God's threefold command to Elijah: "Go!…Go!…Go!"	17:2–19:8
B At the cave on Horeb: "What are you doing here, Elijah?"	19:9–10
C God is not present in the wind, the earthquake, and the fire	19:11–12a
X **Riddle in the middle: The "still small voice" of Yahweh**	19:12b
C´ Elijah wraps his face in his mantle and stands at the cave's entrance	19:13a
B´ At the cave on Horeb: "What are you doing here, Elijah?"	19:13b–14
A´ God's threefold command: "Go…anoint Hazael, Jehu, and Elisha	19:15–18

This concentric structure suggests that the appearance of the prophet
Elijah in the narrative of the Former Prophets marks the dawn of a
new era in the story of God's people. The person of Joshua functions
as a literary frame around all that happens from Joshua's prophecy
about Jericho (Josh 6:26) to the fulfillment of that prophecy at the
moment Elijah steps on stage. And the focus of the ensuing narrative
quickly converges on the mysterious theophany of Elijah on Mount
Horeb (Sinai).

The Book of Joshua

The book of Joshua is a record of Israel's appropriation of its inheritance through conflict and the loss of that land because of the breaking of the covenant God established with the people at Mount Sinai.
The epic story of the Exodus from Egypt under Moses and the Eisodus into the Promised Land under Moses and Joshua is sometimes

described as the "Wars of Yahweh" (cf. Num 21:14). The people of Israel commemorated these wars annually, when they gathered together for the spring Festival of Passover at Gilgal in the Jordan Valley. There they remembered what God did for them when he brought them out of the land of Egypt under the leadership of Moses (the Exodus) and into the Promised Land (the Eisodus) under Moses and then Joshua.

The primary battles of the Exodus are the defeat of Pharaoh and his armies at the crossing of the Red Sea (Exod 14—15), the defeat of the Amalekites (Exod 17:8–15), the defeat of the Midianites (Num 31), and the conquest of the two Amorite kings, Sihon and Og. The tribes of Reuben, Gad, and Manasseh (east) occupy the land of these two Amorite kings in what is usually called Transjordan (the eastern side of the Jordan River). The primary battles of the Eisodus under Joshua are the conquest of Jericho (Josh 6), Ai (Josh 7—8), and the rest of Cisjordan (west of the Jordan, Josh 9—12). The battles of the Exodus (under Moses) and the Eisodus (under Joshua) constitute the "Wars of Yahweh" (cf. Num 21:14).

The book of Joshua is in two major parts: the invasion and conquest of the land west of the Jordan River (Josh 1—12) and the distribution of the land to the twelve tribes (Josh 13—24), which may be outlined in a menorah pattern:

The Book of Joshua in a Menorah Pattern	Josh 1—24
A The Eisodus (Entry) into the Promised Land	1:1–5:15
B Conquest of the land west of the Jordan River	6:1–11:23
C Land conquered by Moses: kingdoms of Sihon and Og	12:1–6
X **Kings of the land conquered by Joshua—list of 31 kings**	12:7–24
C´ Parts of Canaan allotted but not yet conquered	13:1–7
B´ Allotment of the land (west) to the twelve tribes of Israel	13:8–21:45
A´ Joshua's "Exodus"—farewell address and covenant renewal	22:1–24:33

The first and last of these seven major sections of the book of Joshua are approximately the same in total length—presenting Joshua's "Eisodus" (entry into the Promised Land) as commander-in-chief of the tribes of Israel and his own "Exodus" (departure by way of death), which ends an era. In between these two sections are two others of approximately the same length—one that describes the conquests of Joshua west of the Jordan River (6:1—11:23) and another, which details the allotment of this same land to the individual tribes (13:8—21:45). The innermost frame contrasts the land conquered by Moses (12:1–6) with the land still remaining to be conquered (13:1–7).

Joshua is presented as a judge in Israel (Josh 17:14–18), before the period of the judges that follows. The tribe of Joseph (Ephraim and Manasseh) complains that they have received only one portion as their inheritance even though they are numerous (17:14). Joshua tells them to "clear ground there for yourselves in the land of the Perizzites and the Rephaim, since the hill country of Ephraim is too narrow for you" (17:15). The reader is invited to compare the role of Joshua with that of Deborah, the first among Israel's subsequent political leaders to be called a "prophet" (Judg 4:4), who is also numbered among the official judges.

The Book of Judges

The book of Judges is connected to the book of Joshua with the repetition of the account of the death of Joshua in Judges 2:8–9 in almost identical language to that of Joshua 24:29–30. The repetition invites the reader to look closely at the what lies between, which may be outlined in a menorah pattern:

Joshua's Death and Failure to Complete the Conquest	*Josh 24:29–Judg 2:9*
A Joshua dies at the age of 110 and is buried in Timnath-heres	Josh 24:29–31
B Joseph's bones are buried in Shechem and Eleazar is buried in Gibeah	Josh 24:32–33
C Judah and the other tribes fail to complete the conquest	Judg 1:1–36
X **Yahweh's angel speaks: "I will not drive them out before you"**	Judg 2:1–3
C´ The people weep—so they name the place "Bochim" (weeping)	Judg 2:4–5
B´ When Joshua dismisses the people, they go to their own inheritances	Judg 2:6–7
A´ Joshua dies at the age of 110 and is buried in Timnath-heres	Judg 2:8–9

The second frame opens with Joseph's bones finding a final resting place at Shechem, which becomes "an inheritance of the descendants of Joseph" (Josh 24:32). It includes the death of Aaron's son Eleazar who is buried at Gibeah, his inheritance "in the hill country of Ephraim" (24:33). The second half of this frame continues with Joshua's dismissal of the people who then go to their own inheritances (Judg 2:6–7). The innermost frame moves from an account of the failure of the individual tribes to complete the conquest (Judg 1) to an account of the people weeping in response to the message given by the angel of Yahweh (Judg 2:4–5). The speech of the angel, which is in the structural center (Judg 2:1–3), indicts the people of Israel for not doing what Yahweh has commanded them to do. In response to their disobedience, Yahweh will no longer drive the peoples of the land out before the Israelite forces. In short, the "Wars of Yahweh" (i.e., the Exodus from Egypt and the Eisodus into the Promised Land) have come to an end.

The office of judge in Israel is transitional, spanning the time from Moses and Joshua to Samuel, who anoints Saul and David as kings. Moses and Joshua are supreme leaders who function in executive, military, judicial, and religious roles. With the advent of kingship, however, something new appears—namely, a division of powers in which the king and the prophet share parallel responsibilities in leadership (the Samuel Compromise). Joshua foreshadows these developments by assuming specific roles that are later taken by those who are called prophets in ancient Israel.

The "Special History" of Israel begins in the book of Judges, which is closely connected to 1 and 2 Samuel and the establishment of David's dynastic kingship centered in Jerusalem. On the surface, the book of Judges appears to be a miscellaneous collection of independent stories about twelve political leaders in the days when "there was no king in Israel [and] all the people did what was right in their own eyes" (Judg 17:6 = 21:25). Close reading, however, reveals the fact that the leadership of David is already anticipated here, and that the proper role of the king's relationship to the Law and the Prophets in ancient Israel is presented at the outset in the story of Deborah and Barak. The central stories of Gideon and his son Abimelech and Jephthah and his unnamed daughter explore further matters pertaining to kingship in ancient Israel. Moreover, the stories of Samson reveal why the establishment of the monarchy is needed and set the stage for Samuel, the last of the judges and the first of the prophets in the classical sense of that office, which is defined over against the king.

The book of Judges may be outlined in a menorah pattern:

The Book of Judges in a Menorah Pattern	*Judg 1—21*
A Cycle of idolatry/oppression/deliverance: Othniel, Ehud, and Shamgar	1:1–3:31
B Deborah and Barak vs. Canaanites: Positive pattern of leadership	4:1–5:31
C Gideon and his son Abimelech: First steps toward monarchy	6:1–9:57
X **Tola (Ephraim) and Jair (Gilead): Reversal of the Eisodus**	10:1-6
C´ Jephthah and his daughter: First steps toward monarchy	10:7–12:15
B´ Samson against the Philistines: Negative pattern of leadership	13:1–16:31
A´ Micah's idolatry; rape and murder of the Levite's concubine	17:1–21:25

Following a brief discussion of Israel's failure to complete the conquest of Canaan (Judg 1), the book of Judges presents the cycle of idolatry, oppression, and deliverance (Judg 2), which is repeated again and again in the pages that follow. The cycle is illustrated first in the story of Othniel, son of Caleb's younger brother Kenaz, who delivers Israel out of the hands of King Cushan-rishathaim of Aram-naharaim who oppressed Israel for eight years (Judg 3:8). The stage is set for the more detailed stories of Deborah, Gideon, and Jephthah that follow in Judges 4—12.

It is important to note the geographical design reflected in the relationships between the twelve judges that appear in the above menorah pattern. The first judges to appear are the trio of Othniel, Ehud, and Shamgar (Judg 3:7–31)—three so-called "minor judges" —who are set over against Samson (Judg 13—16). In fact, the brief presentation of Shamgar gives only one specific fact about him: he "killed six hundred of the Philistines with an oxgoad" (Judg 3:31). This comment foreshadows the story of Samson who picked up "a

fresh jawbone of an ass . . . and with it killed a thousand (Philistines)"
(Judg 15:15). All four of these "judges" are located in the southern
part of the Promised Land and none of them have much to say about
the true nature of kingship or the kingship of David in particular.
This will come into clearer focus in the two other groups of four
judges: Deborah, who is set over against Ibzan, Elon, and Abdon as
judges in the northern part of the Promised Land; and Gideon, Tola,
Jair, and Jephthah, who are located in the central region. In fact, the
story of Jephthah goes out of its way to describe the fugitive warrior
in words that foreshadow the early career of King David: "Outlaws
collected around Jephthah and went raiding with him" (Judg 11:3,
cf. 1 Sam 22:2).

Though the story of Samson (Judg 13—16) is different from the
others, it is part of the same scheme in the manner in which his
exploit of killing a "young lion" in Judah with his bare hands at
Timnah among the Philistines is told. The riddle that emerges from
this event—about the honey taken from the carcass of the dead lion
(Judg 14:14)—is one of the keys to unraveling the meaning of this
remarkable story. The reference to the "bees" (deborim) in Judges
14:8 invites a comparison with the story of Deborah (her name
comes from the same Hebrew word). In her role as judge, Deborah
functions as one who dispenses justice and exercises the power to
lead the people of Israel in holy war (alongside Barak). Samson, on
the other hand, is a warlord only (perhaps one should say "a one
man army," since he does not command troops in battle). There is no
indication in the text that he ever served as "judge" in the sense of
one who dispenses justice. At the same time, it should be noted that
the reference to the young lion of Judah that Samson kills reminds
us of Jacob's blessing of the tribe of Judah in Genesis 49:9–10,
which foreshadows the kingdom of David to come. Samson personi-
fies one aspect of the Samuel Compromise—the warlord (nagid),
whereas Deborah embodies primarily the other aspect—that of the
prophet (nabi'). The ideal so far as political leadership in ancient
Israel is concerned is achieved when these two roles are exercised in
balance by two persons: the king and the prophet.

The Samuel Compromise: Parallel Roles of the Prophet and the King
[Picture used with permission—copyright Larry Gonick; all rights reserved]

The story of Gideon introduces the subject of kingship explicitly when the people ask him to "rule over us, you and your son and your grandson also" (Judg 8:22). It is Gideon's son Abimelech who actually becomes Israel's first king and rules in that capacity at Shechem for three years (9:22) until his assassination. It should be noted that the evils of kingship are explored subtly in the story of Jephthah who agrees to rule as Israel's "head" (i.e., military chief) but not as its "leader" in the sense of one who dispenses justice (Judg 11:4–11). Individual kings will cling tightly to their power, once they obtain it; and they will do great injustice in the land—particularly when they refuse to hear the word of Yahweh as delivered through his chosen prophets in times to come.

In the middle of the concentric structure of Judges we find a curious note about two otherwise unknown leaders in ancient Israel: Tola, from the hill country of Ephraim who "judged Israel for twenty-three years" (10:1–2), and Jair from Gilead who "judged Israel twenty-two years" (10:3). We also learn that Jair "had thirty sons who rode on thirty donkeys; and they had thirty towns, which are in the land of Gilead" (10:4). And that's all we know about these two men, other than their respective places of burial: Tola at Shamir and Jair at Kamon. What we have here is a striking example of the narrative principle of a "riddle in the middle." When we examine these two judges, along with the other six so-called minor judges, we discover two interesting facts. In the first place, we find a geographical pattern in the manner in which the eight minor judges are presented. We have three judges from the south (Judah and Benjamin) in the persons of Othniel, Ehud, and Eglon (3:7–31), which are set over against three judges from the north (Zebulun and Ephraim) in the persons of Ibzan, Elon, and Abdon. The two judges in the center of the book of Judges, Tola and Jair, are from the center of the country—and the geographical movement is from west to east, the reverse of the Eisodus (Entry into the Promised Land) under Joshua. We find here a subtle hint that a great reversal of the fortunes of ancient Israel has already begun, one that will eventually take the Israelites out of the Promised Land and back into bondage in a distant foreign land.

The second observation of note we can make from the literary structure of Judges is that the book is primarily the narrative story of four persons: Deborah, Gideon, Jephthah, and Samson. Together these stories tell us much about leadership in ancient Israel. The story of Gideon and his son Abimelech introduces the subject of kingship directly. Gideon is the first person who is actually asked to become a king in ancient Israel (8:22); and his son Abimelech is in fact the first king in Israel, a king who ruled for three years in Shechem (9:22). The story of Jephthah carries us further in its curious portrayal of leadership in which the one who exercises power perpetrates the most unjust deed recorded in the pages of scripture, the sacrifice of his beloved and only child—an unnamed virgin (Judg 11). Some details in that story carry us back to the story of the *Akedah* of Genesis 22, while others foreshadow the stories of both Saul (and his son Jonathan) and David in time to come.

The Books of First and Second Samuel

The books of 1 and 2 Samuel carry the subject of leadership in ancient Israel further, as David moves from the position of a charismatic warlord (*nagid*), like Jephthah before him, to become king (*melek*) of all Israel. Samuel is presented as the long-awaited "prophet like Moses" (Deut 34:10), and the first in a long line of such prophets whom canonical tradition divides into two groups in the Tanakh: the Former Prophets and the Latter Prophets.

1 and 2 Samuel in a Menorah Pattern	*1 Sam 1–2 Sam 24*
A Samuel as prophet (3:20) and judge (7:15); his farewell	1 Sam 1:1–15:35
B David becomes charismatic king of all Israel	1 Sam 16:1–2 Sam 5:25
C Transfer of ark to Jerusalem—Yahweh enthroned on it	2 Sam 6:1-19
X **David as *melek* (6:20) vs. *nagid* (6:21)—Michal's alienation**	2 Sam 6:20-23
C´ Nathan's oracle: David's "house" is blessed forever	2 Sam 7:1-29
B´ David's wars and rebellion from within and without	2 Sam 8:1–20:26
A´ David violates the Torah (Deut 21:22-23); David's farewell	21:1-24:25

The books of 1 and 2 Samuel introduce the subject of kingship in ancient Israel, as David moves from the position of a charismatic warlord (*nagid*), like Jephthah before him, to become the king (*melek*) of all Israel. In the curious episode about Michal's resentment for the manner in which David uncovered himself in dancing before Yahweh (2 Sam 6:20–23), Michal refers to him as "king (*melek*)." In his response, David refers to himself as "prince" (*nagid*). The enigmatic story, with its conclusion that "Michal the daughter of Saul had no child to the day of her death" (6:23) has the quality of a "riddle in the middle" of the two books of Samuel.

The outermost frame in this menorah pattern takes up two other terms of political leadership, with Samuel presented as prophet (*nabi'*, 1 Sam 3:20) and judge ("Samuel judged Israel all the days of his life," 1 Sam 7:15). In the second half of this frame, David is presented as a king guilty of violating the Torah of Moses (2 Sam 21:1–14). In the second frame, David becomes king of all Israel (1 Sam 16:1—2 Sam 5:25), but his rule ends in rebellion from within and without (2 Sam 8:1—20:26).

The Book of First Samuel

The book of 1 Samuel may be outlined in a menorah pattern:

The Book of First Samuel in a Menorah Pattern	*1 Sam 1—31*
A Samuel as prophet and Yahweh as king—enthroned on the ark	1:1–3:21
B Ark of the Covenant captured by the Philistines	4:1–5:12
C Ark of the Covenant returned and kept in Kiriath-jearim for 20 years	6:1–7:2
X **Samuel as judge of all Israel**	7:3-17
C´ People request a king—Saul delivers Israel from the Ammonites	8:1–12:25
B´ Saul as ruler—continued conflict with the Philistines	13:1–15:35
A´ David as God's choice to be king in Israel (i.e., "son of Saul")	16:1–31:13

Samuel is the towering figure in the transition to a new era. Like Samson, Samuel is dedicated to God as a Nazirite from birth; and he becomes the first true prophet in the historical sense of a person who occupies an office of leadership in ancient Israel alongside that of the king. He is also described as a judge in Israel (1 Sam 7:15). His circuit of judicial responsibility in the tribal lands of Benjamin and Ephraim is foreshadowed by the prophetess Deborah who judges Israel from beneath "the palm of Deborah" in the same geographical locality—"between Ramah and Bethel in the hill country of Ephraim" (Judg 4:5). Samuel judges Israel year by year as he makes his circuit journey "to Bethel, Gilgal, and Mizpah; and he judged Israel in all these places. Then he would come back to Ramah, for his home was there" (1 Sam 7:15–17).

Early in Samuel's career, the Philistines capture the Ark of the Covenant and destroy Shiloh, where the ark was located in the days of Eli, the priest who raised Samuel as a member of his family. The capture of the ark is seen as the moment the glory of God departs from Israel (1 Sam 4:21–22). That is the meaning of the name Ichabod, the son born to the wife of Phinehas, the son of Eli. Her final words before she dies in childbirth are, "The glory has departed from Israel, for the ark of God has been captured" (1 Sam 4:22). The anointing of Saul as king by the prophet Samuel brings rejoicing to the people of Israel (1 Sam 11:15); but it does not bring back the "glory of God." That moment comes later when King Solomon dedicates the newly built Temple in Jerusalem and the glory of Yahweh fills the house of Yahweh (1 Kings 8:11).

Political concepts in the early monarchy are explored in other ways in 1 Samuel, as the following series of menorah patterns reveals:

The Samuel Compromise	1 Sam 1—15
A Samuel called as prophet with Yahweh as king enthroned on the ark	1:1–4:1a
B Israel defeated by the Philistines who capture the ark	4:1b–22
C The ark troubles the Philistines and they return it to Israel	5:1–7:2
X **Saul becomes ruler of Israel together with Samuel**	7:3—12:25
C´ Saul begins war with the Philistines; Samuel rejects Saul	13:1-15a
B´ Saul wages war with the Philistines	13:15b—14:52
A´ Samuel rejects Saul as king for not destroying the Amalekites	15:1-35

2nd Level Menorah: Samuel and Saul Rule Israel Together	1 Sam 7:3—12:25
A Samuel as judge	7:3-17
B The people of Israel demand a king	8:1–22
C Saul as Israel's first "king" (nagid = permanent warlord)	9:1-27
X **Samuel as prophet (nabi') anoints Saul as "king" (nagid)**	10:1-8
C´ Saul among the prophets (nabi'im, 10:11; cf. 19:24)	10:9-16
B´ Saul proclaimed king; proves himself in war with the Ammonites	10:17—11:15
A´ Samuel as prophet [his speech concerns Saul as king (melek)]	12:1-25

The Samuel Compromise is achieved by dividing the office of judge in ancient Israel into two separate offices. The spiritual responsibility of discerning Yahweh's will and translating the implications of his cosmic rule into historical categories falls to the new office of the *nabi'* ("the one called"—i.e., the prophet). The political responsibility of carrying out the action required by this translation is assigned to the office of the *nagid*, or military commander. Thus begin the separation of powers in political philosophy generally and the tension-filled relationship between kings and prophets in the history of ancient Israel.

The manner in which David succeeds Saul as king in Israel is presented in a most interesting manner from a literary point of view, as the following outline of 1 Samuel 15—22 reveals:

The Story of David, Jonathan, and Saul	1 Sam 15—22
A Saul rejected as king; Samuel hews Agag in pieces before Yahweh	15:1–35
B David is anointed king and becomes Saul's armor-bearer	16:1–23
C David kills Goliath: "Whose son is this young man?" (17:55)	17:1–58
X **David becomes Saul's "son"**	18:1–20:42
C´ David obtains Goliath's sword from the priest Ahimelech in Nob	21:1–9
B´ David flees from Saul and takes refuge with King Achish of Gath	21:10–15
A´ David as a fugitive from Saul; Ahimelech finds refuge with David	22:1–23

2nd Level Menorah: David Becomes Saul's "Son"	1 Sam 18—20
A Jonathan (son of Saul) makes a covenant with David	18:1–9
B Saul tries to kill David with a spear—David enters Saul's army	18:10–16
C Saul promises David marriage to Merab for fighting Philistines	18:17–19
X **David marries Michal, Saul's younger daughter**	18:20–29
C´ David's success against the Philistines increases his fame	18:30
B´ Saul tries to kill David with a spear—David comes to Samuel	19:1–24
A´ Jonathan makes a covenant with the house of David (20:8, 16)	20:1–42

In like manner, the next stage of David's political rise to power may also be outlined in a menorah pattern within a menorah pattern:

David the "Son" of Saul Becomes Israel's Leader (Nagid)	1 Sam 23—30
A David consults Abiathar's ephod and saves the city of Keilah	23:1-13
B Saul remains in the Wilderness of Ziph trying to kill David	23:14
C Saul searches for David near Jeshimon—"Rock of Escape"	23:15-28
X **David the "son" of Saul will be the *nagid* in Israel**	23:29—26:25
C´ David takes refuge among the Philistines	27:1-12
B´ Saul consults Samuel's spirit about battle with the Philistines	28:1—29:11
A´ David consults Abiathar's ephod and avenges Ziklag	30:1-31

2nd Level Menorah: David Will Be the Nagid in Israel	1 Sam 23:29—26:25
A David spares Saul at Engedi: "See my father...*my son David*"	23:29—24:22
B Death of Samuel	25:1
C David, Nabal, and Abigail—Nabal plays the fool with David	25:2-23
X **Abigail's prophecy—David as *nagid* in Israel (v. 30)**	25:24-31
C´ Death of Nabal—David marries Abigail	25:32-43
B´ Loss of Michal, daughter of Saul—she is given to Palti as wife	25:44
A´ David spares Saul near Jeshimon—"*my son David*" (3 times)	26:1-25

The theological point to this story is that David is in fact the "son" of Saul by God's choice, for he is to succeed Saul as king in Israel. In short, what we have here is the concept of "kingship mediated through sonship."

The Book of Second Samuel

The book of 2 Samuel presents the establishment of the dynastic kingdom of "Israel" with the city of Jerusalem as its capital.

The Book of Second Samuel in a Menorah Pattern	2 Sam 1—24
A David becomes king of Judah	1:1—2:32
B David becomes the charismatic king of all Israel	3:1—7:29
C David completes the "conquest" of the Promised Land	8:1—10:19
X **David and Bathsheba: Solomon as "beloved" of Yahweh**	11:1—12:31
C´ David is unable to rule over his own "house"	13:1—20:26
B´ David's final deeds and his farewell address	21:1—24:17
A´ David purchases the site for the Temple in Jerusalem	24:18-25

In the structural center of 2 Samuel we find the familiar story of David and Bathsheba, and the naming of their second son Solomon as the "beloved of Yahweh" (Jedidiah). Solomon is chosen to succeed David and to build the Temple in Jerusalem. The theme of the Ark of the Covenant as a symbol of the presence of the glory of Yahweh is picked up once again, as David transfers it from its temporary lodging place in Kiriath-jearim to the Tabernacle he constructs in Jerusalem (2 Sam 6). Jerusalem is the new capital of Israel and the prophet Nathan affirms David's desire to build a dynastic temple there with the promise that God is building a permanent "house" of David by establishing the Davidic dynasty in Jerusalem. The second half of 2 Samuel focuses on David's show of kindness to Mephibosheth (or Meribbaal), grandson of Saul. The rebellions on the part of Absalom and Sheba that frame this central concern prepare the reader for the eventual breakup of the Davidic monarchy, which is postponed until the death of David's son Solomon and the establishment of the Northern Kingdom of Israel under Jeroboam I (1 Kgs 12).

The story of the transformation of the kingdom of Israel into the Davidic Empire may also be outlined in a menorah pattern within a menorah pattern:

David's Kingdom Becomes a Dynastic Empire	*2 Sam 1—10*
A David as king of Judah in Hebron	1:1–2:7
B Abner (Saul's cousin) opposes David—Joab murders Abner	2:8–3:39
C Jonathan's son Mephibosheth becomes lame; murder of Ish-bosheth	4:1-12
X **David's kingdom becomes a dynasty**	5:1–8:18
C´ Jonathan's son Mephibosheth is brought into David's household	9:1-13
B´ Hanun (king of the Ammonites) humiliates David's envoys	10:1-5
A´ David completes the "Conquest"—the Davidic Empire established	10:6-19

2nd Level Menorah: David's Kingdom Becomes a Dynasty	*2 Sam 5—8*
A David becomes king of all Israel and Judah	5:1-5
B David's house—Jerusalem becomes David's capital	5:6-25
C Transfer of the Ark of the Covenant to Jerusalem	6:1-15

X	**Saul's daughter Michal—despised David / spurned by David**	6:16–23
C´	David wishes to build a temple to house the ark and Nathan concurs	7:1–3
B´	David's "house" in Nathan's dynastic oracle—the Davidic dynasty	7:4–29
A´	David's wars—Yahweh gives victory to David wherever he goes	8:1–18

Saul's daughter Michal occupies a place of central importance in the literary structure of 1 and 2 Samuel. The brief story of her alienation from David occupies the center of the concentric structure of 2 Samuel 1—10. As we have already seen, it also occupies the center of the concentric structure of 1 and 2 Samuel as a whole. Moreover, the story of David's marriage to Michal in 1 Samuel 18:20–29 is in the structural center of 1 Samuel 15—22.

The most elaborate nesting of menorah patterns within menorah patterns in the two books of Samuel concerns the problems within David's family, from his adultery with Bathsheba to the rebellion of his son Absalom.

David's Sin and Its Consequences	*2 Sam 11—24*
A David commits adultery with Bathsheba, mother of Solomon	11:1–27
B Nathan's parable—Bathsheba's child dies, but Solomon is born	12:1–31
C David's son Amnon rapes Tamar and Absalom takes revenge	13:1—14:33
X **Rebellion of Absalom and David's flight to Transjordan**	15:1—20:22
C´ David sins in executing Saul's sons—Mephibosheth spared	21:1–14
B´ David's song and last words—looking backward in time	21:15—23:39
A´ David purchases land where the Temple will be built in Jerusalem	24:1–25

2nd Level Menorah: Absalom Revolts against David	*2 Sam 15—20*
A Absalom conspires to replace David as king in Hebron	15:1–12
B On leaving, David leaves ten concubines "to look after the house"	15:13–16
C David prepares to leave Jerusalem to Absalom's control	15:17–23
X **David flees and then returns to Jerusalem**	15:24—19:43
C´ Sheba conspires to remove Benjamin from David's kingdom	20:1–2
B´ On his return, David puts the ten concubines under house arrest	20:3
A´ Joab murders Amasa, regains his position, and quells the revolt	20:4–22

3rd Level Menorah: David's Flight and Return to Jerusalem	*2 Sam 15:24—19:43*
A David instructs Zadok and Abiathar to return with the ark to Jerusalem	15:24-29
B David mourns over his departure—"weeping as he went" (v. 30)	15:30-37
C Absalom usurps the throne while David is in flight	16:1-4
X **David's future is in the hands of Hushai**	16:5—17:29
C´ Absalom is defeated and dies at the hands of Joab	18:1-18
B´ David mourns Absalom's death	18:19-33
A´ David attempts to restore a divided and disorganized nation	19:1-43

4th Level Menorah: David's Future in the Hands of Hushai	*2 Sam 16:5—17:29*
A Curse of Shimei	16:5-13
B David arrives at camp near the Jordan weary	16:14
C Hushai seeks to give counsel to Absalom along with Ahithophel	16:15-19
X **Absalom rejects Ahithophel's counsel**	16:20—17:22
C´ Ahithophel commits suicide	17:23
B´ David encamped at Mahanaim and Absalom in Gilead	17:24-26
A´ Blessing of Shobi (Ammon), Machir (Lodebar), and Barzillai (Gilead)	17:27-29

5th Level Menorah: Absalom Rejects Ahithophel's Counsel	*2 Sam 16:20—17:22*
A Absalom asks Ahithophel for advice	16:20-22
B Ahithophel's counsel "was as if one consulted the oracle of God"	16:23
C Ahithophel's counsel: pursue David at once and kill only him	17:1-4
X **Absalom turns to Hushai for counsel**	17:5-6
C´ Hushai's counsel: David is "like a bear robbed of her cubs"	17:7-13
B´ Absalom decides Hushai's counsel is better than that of Ahithophel	17:14
A´ Hushai warns David to escape	17:15-22

Once again, the concentric literary structure of 2 Samuel 11—24 presents a somewhat enigmatic center. As one moves more deeply into the nested concentric structure, the focus of the story shifts from members of David's personal family to the wisdom of a professional advisor in the royal court. The story turns on the conflict between the counsel of Ahithophel and that of Hushai. When Absalom rejects Ahithophel and turns to Hushai, he seals his own fate as well as that of Ahithophel. Both men must die.

Another menorah pattern within a menorah pattern appears in 2 Samuel 16—21, which may be outlined as follows:

David's Army Defeats Absalom and Sheba	2 Sam 16—21
A Mephibosheth remains in Jerusalem thinking he will be king	16:1–4
B From David's flight before Absalom to death of Ahithophel	16:5–17:23
C Absalom replaces Joab with Amasa—Joab kills Absalom	17:24–19:12
X **David is a magnanimous conqueror**	19:13–20:5
C´ Joab murders Amasa and leaves him "wallowing in his blood"	20:6–13
B´ From Sheba's flight to his death at the hands of Joab	20:14–22
A´ David spares Mephibosheth when he appeases the Gibeonites	21:1–22

2nd Level Menorah: David Is a Magnanimous Conqueror	2 Sam 19:13—20:5
A Amasa's appointment is affirmed by David after Absalom's death	19:13–14
B David comes to the Jordan to meet the people of Judah at Gilgal	19:15
C David pardons Shimei	19:16–23
X **David brings Mephibosheth to "eat at his table"**	19:24–30
C´ David invites Barzillai to Jerusalem; Barzillai defers to Chimham	19:31–39
B´ David goes to Gilgal with Chimham, servant of Barzillai	19:40–43
A´ Revolt of Sheba—Amasa is summoned to pursue Sheba	20:1–5

The focus of this narrative structure is on Jonathan's son Mephibosheth, the grandson of Saul. David spurns Saul's daughter Michal, but he shows compassion on Mephibosheth.

The Books of First and Second Kings

The story in 1 Kings begins with the words, "David was old and advanced in years; and although they covered him with clothes, he could not get warm" (1 Kgs 1:1). The picture of a senile king whose life force is ebbing is the very opposite of the earlier description of the death of Moses. "When [Moses] died, his eye was not dim nor his natural force abated" (Deut 34:7; KJV). The book of 1 Kings ends with Jehoshaphat, a descendant of David, offering a feeble attempt to maintain fidelity to God's covenant with his chosen people: "he did what was right in the sight of Yahweh" (1 Kgs 22:43). That same text continues, however, with these words: "yet the high places were not taken away, and the people still sacrificed and offered incense on the high places."

When the books of 1 and 2 Kings are outlined in a menorah pattern, the major theme of the literary work emerges—the relation between the king and the prophet in ancient Israel.

Kings and Prophets from David to Josiah	*1 and 2 Kgs*
A The united monarchy under Solomon	1 Kgs 1:1–11:43
B The divided kingdom from Solomon to the prophet Elijah	1 Kgs 12:1–16:34
C Ministry of Elijah—to the repentance of Ahab	1 Kgs 17:1–21:29
X **True and false prophets and the death of Ahab**	1 Kgs 22:1-53
C´ Ministry of Elijah, Elisha, and "Jonah"—to death of Jehu	2 Kgs 1:1–10:36
B´ Judah and dissolution and exile of Northern Kingdom	2 Kgs 11:1–20:21
A´ Josiah's reformation; apostasy and destruction in Judah	2 Kgs 21:1–25:30

2nd Level Menorah: True and False Prophets—Death of Ahab	*1 Kgs 22*
A Jehoshaphat and Ahab—joint venture (Israel and Judah) against Aram	22:1-4
B Jehoshaphat and Ahab inquire of the prophets of Yahweh	22:5-6
C Micaiah the prophet is summoned by Jehoshaphat and Ahab	22:7-9
X **Prophetic conflict: Micaiah vs. Zedekiah (and 400 others)**	22:10-28
C´ Micaiah's prophecy fulfilled—Ahab mortally wounded in battle	22:29-36
B´ Fulfillment of Elijah's prophecy (21:19)—Ahab's death	22:37-38
A´ Ahab and Jehoshaphat—summary of their reigns	22:39-50

3rd Level Menorah: Source of the True Prophet's Authority	*1 Kgs 22:10-28*
A Prophecy of Zedekiah: "Go up . . . and triumph!"	22:10-12
B Micaiah repeats Zedekiah's words in sarcasm	22:13-15
C Ahab is angry: "Tell me nothing but the truth in Yahweh's name"	22:16-18
X **Source of Micaiah's authority—Yahweh's "heavenly court"**	22:19-22
C´ Yahweh puts a lying spirit in the mouth of Ahab's prophets	22:23
B´ Zedekiah strikes Micaiah in anger for challenging his message	22:24-27
A´ Prophecy of Micaiah: Ahab will not "return in peace"	22:28

In Solomon's reign, Israel enjoys splendor and opulence; but surface appearances are misleading. The journey ahead for Israel as a nation is downhill, and close reading of the biblical text reveals that Solomon himself is responsible for what happens. Solomon violates all three of the provisions in the "law of the king" in Deuteronomy: acquiring many horses, many wives, and silver and gold "in great quantity for himself" (Deut 17:16–17). But, more important, *there is not one single mention of a prophet of Yahweh alongside the king during King Solomon's reign.* The moment Solomon dies, however, the prophets return. Just before Solomon's death, his adversary Jeroboam encounters the prophet Ahijah on the road, who "laid hold of the new garment he was wearing and tore it into twelve pieces. He then said to Jeroboam: Take for yourself ten pieces; (for) Yahweh, the God of Israel... is about to tear the kingdom from the hand of Solomon, and (he) will give you ten tribes" (1 Kgs 11:30–31).

After Solomon's death, the pairing of prophets and kings is highlighted in both Israel and Judah in the book of 1 Kings: Ahijah and Jeroboam I (Israel), Shemaiah and Rehoboam (Judah), Jehu son of Hanani and Baasha (Judah). The structure of 2 Kings highlights the role of five key prophets who play major political roles in Israel: Elijah, Elisha, Elisha's disciple "Jonah" prior to the fall of Samaria, Isaiah (with King Hezekiah), and Huldah (with King Josiah) in Judah afterward.

As we move more deeply into the nested concentric structure of 1 and 2 Kings, it becomes increasingly clear that the central themes are the relationship between kings and prophets in Israel and Judah, prophetic conflict, and the authority of the true prophet. The pivotal story is that of the true prophet Micaiah in relation to the false prophet Zedekiah and two kings—Ahab in Israel and Jehoshaphat in Judah. The true prophet's word comes to pass because it comes directly from Yahweh's "heavenly court."

The Book of 1 Kings

Immediately after Solomon's death, his son Rehoboam confronts "Shemaiah the man of God" (1 Kgs 12:21–24) and the shared rule of prophet and king in both the Northern Kingdom and Judah returns, as the nested menorah patterns of 1 Kings reveal.

Kings and Prophets from David to Ahab	1 Kgs 1–22
A Death of David and the role of Nathan in Solomon's succession	1:1–2:46
B Kingdom of Solomon—no prophetic voice (cf. Deut 17:14-20)	3:1–11:40
C Death of Solomon and succession of Rehoboam in Jerusalem	11:41–43
X **Rehoboam and Jeroboam in conflict: Division of the monarchy**	12:1–14:31
C´ From Jeroboam I to Ahab in the Northern Kingdom of Israel	15:1–16:34
B´ Ahab and Elijah in the Northern Kingdom (cf. Deut 18:19-22)	17:1–21:29
A´ Prophetic conflict and the death of Ahab: Micaiah and Zedekiah	22:1-53

2nd Level Menorah: Conflict between Rehoboam and Jeroboam	1 Kgs 12–14
A Rehoboam goes to Shechem seeking divine legitimation of his rule	12:1-19
B Shemaiah confronts Rehoboam on authority to declare holy war	12:20-25
C Sin of Jeroboam—golden calves and a new cultic establishment	12:26-33
X **Parable on prophetic conflict: Two prophets and lion of Judah**	13:1-32
C´ Jeroboam's sin becomes the sin of the house of Jeroboam	13:33-34
B´ Jeroboam inquires of the prophet Ahijah about his son Abijah	14:1-20
A´ Rehoboam reigns over Judah	14:21-31

3rd Level Menorah: Conflict between Two Unnamed Prophets	1 Kgs 13:1-32
A The man of God from Judah speaks against Jeroboam's altar	13:1-2a
B Prophecy: "O altar, you will be desecrated by Josiah" (in the future)	13:2b-5
C The man of God jeopardizes his life because of a "lie"	13:6-22
X **Man of God from Judah is killed by the lion of Judah**	13:23-25
C´ The old prophet from Bethel (the liar) goes to retrieve the body	13:26-28
B´ Command: "Bury my bones beside his" (in grave found by Josiah)	13:29-31
A´ The old prophet speaks about the saying against the altar in Bethel	13:32

The focus of attention in this reading of the book of 1 Kings is one of the most fascinating stories in the Bible, a story that is perhaps the ultimate source of the figure of Aslan in *The Chronicles of Narnia* by C. S. Lewis. This profound story of prophetic conflict, in which an unnamed man of God from Judah is slain by a mysterious "lion

of Judah," is explored graphically by Gustav Doré in a remarkable
woodcut.

The Two Prophets and the "Lion of Judah" in 1 Kings 13
(*from* Artemus' Edition, The Dore Bible Gallery,
Philadelphia: Henry Artemus, page 39 [facing page])

The Book of 2 Kings

With the first verse of 2 Kings we enter a new chapter in the "Special History" of God's covenant people—the breakup of David's
empire and the loss of the land of Israel. The story begins with the

remark, "After the death of Ahab, Moab rebelled against Israel" (2 Kgs 1:1). This is the first mention of any member nation within David's empire breaking away. By the end of the book, not only is that empire gone, but Jerusalem itself is destroyed and the Temple of Solomon is in ruins. The only glimmer of hope remaining at that point in time is the fact that King Jehoiachin of Judah "put aside his prison clothes" in Babylon, and "every day of his life dined regularly in (King Evil-merodach's) presence. For his allowance, a regular allowance was given him by the king, a portion every day, as long as he lived" (2 Kgs 25:29–30). But the fact that Jehoiachin needed an "allowance" from his superior to get by is a long way from the glory of his predecessors David and Solomon. In fact, one could say that Jehoiachin is no longer a king at all, but merely a ward in the court of the king of Babylon.

As noted earlier, the stories of Elijah in the second half of 1 Kings are also the center of a larger concentric structural design that extends throughout the whole of the Former Prophets and beyond.

Outline of the Former Prophets with Elijah in the Center	*Josh—2 Kgs*
A From the destruction of Jericho (Joshua 6) to its rebuilding	Josh—1 Kgs 15:34
B Prophecy of Joshua fulfilled (see Josh 6:26)	1 Kgs 16:1–34
C Beginning of the story of Elijah	1 Kgs 17:1
X **The story of the prophet Elijah and King Ahab**	1 Kgs 17:2—19:18
C´ Beginning of the story of Elisha	1 Kgs 19:19–21
B´ Prophecy of Yahweh to Elijah about to be fulfilled	1 Kgs 20—2 Kgs 13
A´ From death of Elisha to the destruction of Solomon's Temple	2 Kgs 14—25

2nd Level Menorah: The Story of Elijah and Ahab	*1 Kgs 17:2—19:18*
A God's threefold command to Elijah: "Go!…Go!…Go!"	17:2—19:8
B At the cave on Horeb: "What are you doing here?"	19:9–10
C God is not present in the wind, the earthquake, and the fire	19:11–12a
X **Riddle in the middle: The "still small voice" of Yahweh**	19:12b
C´ Elijah wraps his face in his mantle and stands at the cave's entrance	19:13a
B´ At the cave on Horeb: "What are you doing here?"	19:13b–14
A´ God's threefold command: "Go…anoint Hazael, Jehu and Elisha	19:15–18

The center of this structure focuses on what happens on Mount Horeb when Elijah spends the night in the same cave Moses visited earlier when God covered him with his hand, allowing him to have a glimpse of his glory as it passed by (Exod 33:21–23). God's glory departed from Israel in the days of Samuel, when the Philistines captured the Ark of the Covenant.

In this story of Elijah, the prophet receives three commands from God, each of which is introduced with the imperative of the same Hebrew verb:

"Go from here and turn eastward,
    and hide yourself by the Wadi Cherith" (17:3)

"Go now to Zarephath, which belongs to Sidon, and live there"
    (17:9)

"Go present yourself to Ahab, I will send rain on the earth" (18:1)

The fourth occurrence of this same Hebrew word is in 19:15—"Go, return on your way to the wilderness of Damascus; when you arrive, you shall anoint Hazael as king over Aram. Also you shall anoint Jehu son of Nimshi as king over Israel; and you shall anoint Elisha son of Shaphat of Abel-meholah as prophet in your place." As God has given a threefold command to Elijah in the opening scenes of this narrative cycle, he also gives him a threefold command on the holy mountain. The curious thing to note, however, is the fact that Elijah does not seem to obey these three commands. Immediately after his experience on Mount Horeb, Elijah "threw his mantle over [Elisha]" (1 Kgs 19:19). When Elijah ascends to heaven, Elisha picks up this same mantle (2 Kgs 2:1–14). It is Elisha who fulfills the second command given to Elijah on Mount Horeb, when he is instrumental in Hazael's usurpation of the throne in Aram from Ben-hadad in Damascus (2 Kgs 8:7–15). It is an unnamed disciple of Elisha who anoints Jehu to be king in Israel; Jewish tradition identifies him as the prophet Jonah.

Elijah is unique within the Tanakh in that he does not die. Though Enoch shares this privilege in some respects, there is an important difference between the two. The text says, "Enoch walked with God; and he was not, for God took him" (Gen 5:24). The ascension of Elijah is different in that Elijah knows the nature of his imminent departure in advance (2 Kgs 2:1); and there is a witness to the event in the person of Elisha, who becomes Elijah's successor. Moreover, an expectation develops early in Jewish tradition that Elijah is coming back. The final words of the book of Malachi witness to this fact: "Behold, I will send you Elijah the prophet before the great and terrible day of Yahweh comes" (Mal 4:5).

In Jewish tradition, an extra plate is set at the table for the Passover Seder (the ceremonial dinner held on the first night of Passover) each year for Elijah. The children are encouraged to stay awake so that they may see him, for indeed Elijah will come, and he will drink his cup of wine; for Elijah lives! He not only did not die—he continues to be present. This concept is biblical, for the ministry of the prophet Elijah continues in his successors. That is the meaning of what took place on Mount Sinai (Horeb) in 1 Kings 19:11–13, the structural center of the Former Prophets as a body of canonical literature. The mysterious content of the message God communicates to Elijah in that "awesome silence" is spelled out in detail a few verses later in the form of a riddle. Elijah does fulfill those three commands—for he is present in the ministry of each one of his successors: Elisha, Jonah, and every other "prophet like Moses" that God chooses to carry on the work of Elijah. The narrative structure of this open-ended story may be diagrammed as follows:

A   Elijah as the prophet like Moses of Deuteronomy 18:18

B   Elisha as the first of the successors of the prophet Elijah

X   **Jonah and other canonical successors of Elijah in the Latter Prophets**

B´   Elijah's other successors and the one who is yet to come in Malachi 4:5

A´ Jesus Christ appears with Moses and Elijah on the Mount of Transfiguration

Jonah functions as a bridge connecting the Former Prophets and the Latter Prophets. He is the great reversal of "the prophet like Moses," in the sense that he demonstrates by his actions that he does not in fact fear Yahweh as he claims (Jonah 1:9). In the beginning of the book of Jonah, God tells the prophet: "Arise, go..." God once addressed similar words to Moses: "*Arise, go* on your journey at the head of the people, that they may go in and possess the land, which I swore to their fathers to give them" (Deut 10:11). Elisha is the first of the line of successors to the prophet Elijah. These successors are divided into two groups: the Former and the Latter Prophets. The Former Prophets are those who are chosen to be included in the narrative story that extends from the book of Joshua through 2 Kings. The Latter Prophets are those who are selected for another purpose: to examine their words in relation to the building, the destruction, and the future rebuilding of the Temple in Jerusalem that houses the glory of Yahweh in our midst.

Kings and Prophets from the Death of Ahab to the Exile	**2 Kgs 1–25**
A Elijah's ministry continues through Elisha and "Jonah"—Jehu's purge	1:1–10:36
B Athaliah and restoration under Joash—Temple repaired	11:1–12:21
C Wars with Aram and civil war—Judah's defeat; death of Elisha	13:1–14:22
X **Jeroboam II and the prophet Jonah: Expansion to the north**	14:23–29
C´ War with Assyria: Fall of Samaria—Israel's exile in Assyria	15:1–17:41
B´ Restoration (Hezekiah and Isaiah)—Jerusalem delivered from Assyria	18:1–20:21
A´ Josiah and Huldah restore David's kingdom—fall of Jerusalem and exile	21:1–25:30

In this reading of 2 Kings we discover an important theme that sets the stage for the study of the Latter Prophets. In spite of the dominant leitmotif of the dissolution of David's empire, which is suggested from the opening verse and completed by the end of the book, we find what appears to be the very opposite idea highlighted at the end of 2 Kings in the restoration of David's monarchy. The "empire of David" as a political entity is being separated from the "kingdom of David" as a spiritual reality. The political empire is fading away, but the "kingdom of David" lives on as the true successors of the prophet Elijah take their place alongside the kings in ancient Israel and beyond—in the world empires of Assyria, Babylon, and Persia.

    The most interesting feature of the concentric structure of 2 Kings is the brief passage at the center, which functions as a "riddle in the middle." The prophet Jonah appears by name for the first time in the Bible, and all that we are told about him is that he is the "servant" of Yahweh and "the son of Amittai, the prophet, who was from Gath-hepher" (2 Kgs 14:25). The reader's attention immediately shifts forward in the biblical text to the delightful story of "Jonah the son of Amittai" (Jonah 1:1) who takes his place alongside "the king of Nineveh" (Jonah 3:6) in the Latter Prophets.

THE LATTER PROPHETS

A major theme of the Pentateuch and the Former Prophets (the Primary History) is that of leadership in ancient Israel. The transition of leadership from the period of the Judges to the early monarchy in the kingdoms of Saul and David takes place in Samuel, the last of the judges and the first in the line of prophets who share their authority with a king. In the Latter Prophets, the theme of shared authority between prophet and king is combined with a second theme of equal importance, namely the Temple in Jerusalem, as the following diagram shows:

David/Nathan
Solomon's Temple Built in Jerusalem
Hezekiah/Isaiah
Josiah/Jeremiah
Solomon's Temple Destroyed
Jehoiachin/Ezekiel
Zerubbabel/The Twelve
Second Temple Built in Jerusalem
Messiah/Elijah

When Nebuchadnezzar destroys Solomon's Temple in 586 B.C.E., both Jeremiah and Ezekiel experience the trauma directly. Jeremiah lives through the destruction of Jerusalem and spends his final years in exile in Egypt, where he is taken against his own will ca. 582 B.C.E. (Jer 42—43). Ezekiel has been carried into captivity earlier, in

597 B.C.E., and is living in exile in Babylon when the Temple in Jerusalem is destroyed ten years later.

The two central prophetic books of Jeremiah and Ezekiel, which frame the actual destruction of the First Temple, are in turn framed by the books of the prophet Isaiah and The Twelve (Lesser Prophets). The prophet Isaiah is linked with King Hezekiah in the second half of the eighth century B.C.E. Isaiah and Hezekiah spearhead the first great religious reformation in ancient Israel. The Book of the Twelve emerges in the Exile and focuses its attention on the building of the Second Temple under Zerubbabel, the scion of David. The books of Haggai and Zechariah, in particular, are devoted to this vision, which results in the dedication of the rebuilt Temple in 515 B.C.E. and the projection of a larger hope for a more splendid restoration in the distant future (Zech 9—14). The book of Malachi concludes the Book of the Twelve (Lesser Prophets) with a vision of the coming Messiah, who will be preceded by the return of the prophet Elijah (Mal 4:5–6). It is this vision that sets the stage for the appearance of John the Baptist and Jesus, and the formation of the Completed Tanakh.

The concentric structural design of the Latter Prophets as a whole may be outlined in the broadest strokes as follows:

Structure of the Latter Prophets in Five Parts

A	Book of Isaiah	ca. 750–500 B.C.E.	Jerusalem and First Temple
B	Book of Jeremiah	ca. 620–580 B.C.E.	Exile → Egypt
X	Fall of Jerusalem and destruction of First Temple		Jer 52 = 2 Kings 24:18—25:30
B´	Book of Ezekiel	ca. 600–570 B.C.E.	Exile → Babylon
A´	Book of the Twelve	ca. 750–500 B.C.E.	Jerusalem and Second Temple

The ending of the Former Prophets is repeated in the structural center of the Latter Prophets. Neither Jeremiah nor Ezekiel is mentioned by name in the Former Prophets—a fact that is often noted with astonishment. There is nothing surprising in this, however, for the decision regarding the category to which each prophet is assigned is a canonical one, in the sense that it has been determined by a prior commitment to a larger structure of the canon as a whole. The only prophets that appear in both segments of the Prophets in the canon of the Tanakh are Jonah and Isaiah, for different reasons.

The prophets Jeremiah and Ezekiel are contemporaries. Both come from priestly families in or near the city of Jerusalem. Jeremiah was born in the Levitical town of Anathoth, the hometown of the prophetess Huldah, who was brought into the royal court in Jerusalem during the reign of Josiah (2 Kgs 22:14). Jeremiah is portrayed as one of the priestly descendants of Abiathar whom David established in Jerusalem as one of his two high priests. Ezekiel, on the other hand, is presumably a descendant of David's other high priest, Zadok (2 Sam 8:17). When Solomon becomes king, he deposes Abiathar from his office as priest (1 Kgs 2:27) in Jerusalem and establishes the Zadokites as the official priestly family in the First Temple until the time when Josiah brings Huldah and Jeremiah into the royal court in Jerusalem from nearby Anathoth. Ezekiel is among the priests in Jerusalem who are exiled to Babylon after the siege of Jerusalem in 597 B.C.E. (2 Kgs 24:16).

At first glance, the books of Jeremiah and Ezekiel are so different in literary form and style that it makes little sense to treat them as a single literary unit. In fact, the two prophets and their books are often the focus of sharp contrast. In terms of theology and literary style, the book of Jeremiah is similar to the book of Deuteronomy. The content and style of Ezekiel are similar to the content and style of the book of Leviticus. Nonetheless, the two books are connected by a lengthy quotation from 2 Kings that ties them together and functions as the structural center of the Latter Prophets as a whole.

The Latter Prophets in a Menorah Pattern	Isa—Mal
A Isaiah's memoirs—climaxed by the Day of Yahweh	Isa 1—12
B Judah and Israel among the nations	Isa 13—33
C Judgment on the nations and return of the redeemed to Zion	Isa 34—35
X **From Jonah and Isaiah to Jeremiah and Ezekiel**	[2 Kgs 14:25—25:30]
C´ Day of Yahweh against Judah and the nations	Zeph 1—3
B´ Rebuilding the Temple and restoration of Jerusalem and Judah	Hag 1:1—Zech 8:23
A´ Day of Yahweh—disputation on God's justice	Zech 9:1—Mal 4:6

2nd Level Menorah: From Former Prophets to Latter Prophets	*[2 Kgs 14—25]*
A Isaiah and Hezekiah: God's "vengeance" against Assyria	Isa 36:1—39:8
B Israel as Yahweh's servant among the nations	Isa 40:1—55:13
C Yahweh's great day of salvation is coming soon	Isa 56:1—66:24
X **Jeremiah–Ezekiel: destruction of Jerusalem and the Temple**	[2 Kgs 24:18–25:30]
C´ Declaration of Yahweh's love for Israel	Hosea
B´ Divine Warrior ("enemy from the north") vs. Israel and the nations	Joel–Obadiah
A´ Jonah and Nineveh: God's "vengeance" against Assyria	Jonah–Habbakuk

3rd Level Menorah: Fall of Jerusalem—Israel and the Nations	*Jer–Ezek*
A Jerusalem judged—restoration promised in a new covenant (Jer 30–31)	Jer 1:1—36:32
B Jeremiah and the fall of Jerusalem; first return of exiles; flight to Egypt	Jer 37:1—45:5
C Jeremiah and the nations—oracles against foreign nations	Jer 46:1—51:64
X **Fall of Jerusalem and the destruction of the First Temple**	Jer 52:1–34
C´ God's glory departs from Jerusalem—Israel and the nations	Ezek 1:1—32:32
B´ Ezekiel and the fall of Jerusalem—Israel among the nations	Ezek 33:1—39:29
A´ Jerusalem restored—vision of last days: God's glory returns (43:1-12)	Ezek 40:1—48:35

4th Level Menorah: Destruction of Jerusalem and the Temple	*Jer 52*
A Zedekiah rebels against Babylon	52:1-3
B Nebuchadnezzar captures Jerusalem and Zedekiah flees to Jericho	52:4-8
C Zedekiah brought to Riblah—he is blinded and imprisoned in Babylon	52:9-11
X **Destruction of Jerusalem and the First Temple**	52:12-23
C´ Rebel leaders brought to Riblah (in Hamath)—they are executed	52:24-27
B´ Three deportations listed (with surrender of Jehoiachin, 2 Kgs 24:12-16)	52:28-30
A´ Jehoiachin released from prison and made a ward of Babylonian court	52:31-34

The nesting of parallel texts within successive menorah patterns in the
Latter Prophets as a whole illustrates the literary unity of Jeremiah and
Ezekiel and the close relationship between the Former Prophets and
the Latter Prophets within the canonical process. The structure focuses
on Jeremiah 52, which is quoted with minor changes from 2 Kings
24:18—25:30. The center of this unit is the depiction of the destruction of Jerusalem by Nebuchadnezzar of Babylon (Jer 52:12–23).
According to the biblical text, "Nebuzaradan... *burned the house of
Yahweh*, and the king's house and all the houses of Jerusalem; every

great house he burned down" (Jer 52:12–13). This took place in August 587 B.C.E., and is commemorated to the present day in Judaism (along with the destruction of Herod's Temple in 70 C.E.) on the Ninth of Av (July–August) with the reading of the scroll of Lamentations.

The innermost frame in the menorah pattern for Jeremiah 52 opens with the blinding at Riblah (in Hamath) of King Zedekiah, who is imprisoned in Babylon "until the day of his death" (Jer 52:11). It continues with the execution of the priests Seraiah and Zephaniah, along with others of the rebels in Jerusalem, by Neb-uchadnezzar "at Riblah in the land of Hamath" (52:24–27). The second frame moves from the capture of Jerusalem by Nebuchadnezzar and the flight of Zedekiah from the city (52:4–8) to the list of three deportations by the Babylonians from Jerusalem (52:28–30). The outermost frame moves from the rebellion of Zedekiah against Babylon (52:1–3) to the release of Jehoiachin from prison in Baby-lon where is made a ward of the court (52:31–34).

With the fall of Jerusalem and the destruction of Solomon's Temple as the center (Jer 52), the menorah pattern for the books of Jeremiah and Ezekiel reveals the concentric structural design of these two books as a literary entity. The outermost frame opens with the presentation of Jerusalem judged, with restoration promised in a new covenant (Jer 1:1—36:32). It continues, in sharp contrast, with Ezekiel's marvelous vision of the restoration of Jerusalem in the last days, when God's glory returns (Ezek 40:1—48:35). The second frame presents the fall of Jerusalem and Israel among the nations as seen by both prophets (Jer 37:1—45:5 and Ezek 33:1—39:29). And the innermost frame includes oracles against foreign nations (Jer 46:1—51:64 and Ezekiel 25—32), in a context where God's glory leaves Jerusalem (Ezek 10).

The second-level menorah pattern of Isaiah 36 through Hab-bakuk (which corresponds to 2 Kings 14—25) reveals much about the relationship between the Former Prophets and the Latter Prophets. The framework (A, X, A′) moves from lengthy quotations from 2 Kings 18:13—20:19 (= Isa 36—39) and 2 Kings 24:18—25:30 (= Jer 52) to the reference to the prophet Jonah in 2 Kings 14:25. In the Former Prophets, the prophet Jonah is paired with King

Jeroboam II (2 Kgs 14:23–29) and the prophet Isaiah with King
Hezekiah (2 Kgs 18:13—20:21). The structural design suggests that
Jeremiah is paired with King Zedekiah and Ezekiel with King
Jehoiachin (2 Kgs 24:18—25:30). From the deuteronomic point of
view, neither of these kings is a "good" king along the lines of
David, Hezekiah, and Josiah (who is paired with the prophetess Huldah). In other words, they do not listen to the prophet God raises up
in their time—and they suffer the consequences. The transition from
the Former Prophets to the Latter Prophets is seen in the sequence of
prophets from Elijah to Elisha to Jonah. Though Jonah is mentioned
by name only once in the Former Prophets (2 Kgs 14:25), he is also
the unnamed disciple of Elisha who anoints Jehu to be king in Israel
(2 Kgs 9:1–13). And he makes quite a name for himself in the
delightful story of "Jonah son of Amittai, the prophet who was from
Gath-hepher" in the structural center of the Book of the Twelve (2
Kgs 14:25 and Jonah 1:1).

Isaiah and The Twelve (Lesser Prophets) are to be read over
against each other. Both are concerned with events that span the
same period of time—from the destruction of the Northern Kingdom by the Assyrians to the destruction of Jerusalem and the Babylonian Exile. In like manner, Jeremiah and Ezekiel are to be read
over against each other. Both contain lengthy oracles against foreign nations (Jer 46—51 and Ezek 25—32), presented within the
context of judgment speeches against the people of Judah. Jeremiah's message to the people of Judah, and Jerusalem in particular,
is primarily one of judgment in the face of impending disaster.
Though different in literary style, the message of Ezekiel is much
the same. Both are concerned with the preservation of the people of
Israel in the midst of the greatest crisis the nation has experienced
to that point in time.

The Book of the Prophet Isaiah

The books of Jeremiah and Ezekiel are framed by a carefully balanced arrangement of the books of Isaiah and The Twelve (Lesser

Prophets). The book of Isaiah may also be outlined in a nested series of menorah patterns:

The Book of Isaiah in a Menorah Pattern	Isa 1—66
A Isaiah's memoirs and the Day of Yahweh	1:1—10:23
B Yahweh's march of conquest—a new Exodus and Eisodus	10:24—12:6
C Oracles against foreign nations	13:1—23:18
X **Yahweh and the nations**	24:1—53:12
C´ The New Jerusalem and invitation to the messianic banquet	54:1—55:13
B´ Yahweh's future day of salvation	56:1—59:21
A´ Zion's day dawns: Day of Yahweh—the New Jerusalem	60:1—66:24

2nd Level Menorah: Yahweh and the Nations	Isa 24—53
A Day of Yahweh—the "Isaiah Apocalypse"	24:1—26:21
B Apocalyptic poem of deliverance—defeat of Yahweh's foe	27:1-13
C Oracles concerning Judah and Ephraim	28:1—33:24
X **Yahweh's "vengeance" against Assyria**	34:1—40:31
C´ Israel as God's servant and messenger in the world	41:1—44:23
B´ Cyrus as Yahweh's anointed one	44:24—48:22
A´ Yahweh's suffering and triumphant servant	49:1—53:12

3rd Level Menorah: Yahweh's "Vengeance" on Assyria	Isa 34—40
A Yahweh's "vengeance"—Edom's curse and Judah's renewal	34:1—35:10
B The Rabshakeh's speech: Yahweh will not deliver Jerusalem	36:1-22
C Hezekiah consults the prophet Isaiah	37:1-20
X **Day of Yahweh—against Sennacherib of Assyria**	37:21-38
C´ Hezekiah's illness and recovery	38:1-22
B´ Hezekiah's mistake with Merodach-baladan's embassy	39:1-8
A´ Prophetic all and proclamation of God's saving power	40:1-31

In the structural center of the book of Isaiah, we find a lengthy quotation from the book of 2 Kings concerning Isaiah and King Hezekiah during the invasion of Sennacherib (Isa 36—39 = 2 Kgs 18:13—20:19). In the face of the Assyrian threat, Hezekiah consults with the prophet Isaiah. Hezekiah spreads the letter from Sennacherib "before the Lord" and offers a prayer that God will "hear all the words of Sennacherib, which he has sent to mock the living God" (Isa 37:17). God responds through the prophet Isaiah, who declares that God will silence Sennacherib's arrogance (Isa 37: 21–35). God takes "vengeance" on Sennacherib by destroying his army and having the king assassinated (Isa 37:36–38).

Hezekiah is to be punished for the mistake of showing Merodach-baladan's envoys "his treasure house" and "his whole armory" (Isa 39:2). The judgment announced, however, appears to refer to the later events of 597 B.C.E.: "All that is in your house, and that which your ancestors have stored up until this day, shall be carried to Babylon; nothing shall be left, says Yahweh. Some of your own sons who are born to you shall be taken away; they shall be eunuchs in the palace of the king of Babylon" (Isa 39:6–8). At this point, the content of the book of Isaiah shifts two hundred years—to the time of the Neo-Babylonian Empire (612–539 B.C.E.) and its successor the Persian Empire, established by Cyrus when he conquers Babylon in 539 B.C.E. It is Cyrus who frees the exiled Jews from Babylon, and Isaiah speaks of him as the anointed ("messiah") of Yahweh who is destined to subdue all nations before him (Isa 45:1–3).

In the second-level menorah pattern (Isa 24—53), the focus shifts from Yahweh's "vengeance" against Assyria (Isa 36—39), to the larger issue of Yahweh and the nations. The focus here is on universal judgment in the so-called "Isaiah Apocalypse" (Isa 24—27), which is set over against the corresponding sections on Persia (Isa 44:24—48:22), with Cyrus as God's "shepherd" (44:28) and "anointed one" (i.e., God's messiah, 45:1), and Yahweh's suffering and triumphant servant (49:1—53:12). In this marvelous poem, it is possible to interpret the prophetic figure of God's "Suffering Servant" in the so-called Servant Songs (42:1–4; 49:1–6; 50:4–11; and 52:13—53:12) in a collective role. The people of Israel take their place alongside an "enlightened" Persian ruler on a global stage in an extension of the earlier relationship between prophet and king in Israel (i.e., the Samuel Compromise).

The Book of the Prophet Jeremiah

The book of Jeremiah may be outlined in a nested menorah pattern:

The Book of Jeremiah in a Menorah Pattern	Jer 1—52
A Historical note: The superscription	1:1-3
B Jeremiah introduced as a "prophet to the nations"	1:4-10
C Jeremiah prophesies doom for Israel	1:11–10:25
X **The prophet Jeremiah as a suffering servant**	11:1–45:5
C′ Jeremiah prophesies doom for the nations	46:1–49:39
B′ Culmination of the theme "prophet to the nations"	50:1–51:64
A′ Historical appendix (taken from 2 Kgs 24:18–25:30)	52:1-34

The second frame within this concentric structural pattern highlights the fact that Jeremiah functions as a "prophet to the nations" in the city of Jerusalem before and after the conquest of Nebuchadnezzar of Babylon. His prophecies of doom are directed against Israel as well as the neighboring peoples. The central section, which deals with matters of political leadership with regard to both kingship and prophecy in ancient Israel, may be expanded in another menorah pattern:

2nd Level Menorah: Jeremiah Is a Suffering Servant	Jer 11—45
A Prophet cut off from Anathoth–focus on prophetic conflict	11:1–19:15
B Jeremiah's first imprisonment recounted	20:1-18
C Jeremiah and Zedekiah–prediction of destruction and exile	21:1–25:38
X **Jeremiah's preaching ministry–a writing prophet**	26:1–36:32
C′ Jeremiah and Zedekiah–siege and fall of Jerusalem	37:1–39:18
B′ Jeremiah's final release from prison recounted	40:1-5
A′ Assassination of Gedaliah–Jeremiah taken to Egypt	40:6–45:5

The increasing isolation of the prophet Jeremiah is highlighted in the outermost frame, as the prophet is cut off from his own family (Jer 11:21), and ultimately from the land of Israel itself as he is taken in exile to the land of Egypt (40:6—45:5). The account of his first

imprisonment (Jer 20) is set over against an account of his final
release from prison (40:1–5). The two halves of the innermost frame
open with parallel accounts of events involving Jeremiah and
Zedekiah (21:1–7 and 37:1–10). They continue with predictions of
the coming destruction of Jerusalem and the Babylonian Exile
(21:8—25:38) and the account of the siege and fall of the city of
Jerusalem in particular (37:11—39:18).

The central section on Jeremiah's preaching ministry (Jer 25—
36) is expanded in another menorah pattern:

3rd Level Menorah: Jeremiah Is a Writing Prophet	Jer 25—36
A Jeremiah summarizes orally 23 years of preaching	25:1-14
B Cup of wine ("wrath") forced on neighboring peoples	25:15-38
C Temple sermon: Prediction that Babylon will enslave nations	26:1–27:22
X **Jeremiah, true prophet, envisions a new covenant**	28:1–33:26
C´ Owners renege on releasing their slaves	34:1-22
B´ Cup of wine refused by the Rechabites	35:1-19
A´ Jeremiah summarizes in writing 23 years of preaching	36:1-32

The outer frame in this concentric structure moves from an oral
account of twenty-three years of Jeremiah's preaching in Jerusalem
(25:1–14) to a written summary of the same in Jeremiah 36. Within
this framework, we find parallel passages on the general theme of
the "cup of wine." On the one hand, the cup is a symbol of Yahweh's
wrath that is forced on the nations by wicked Babylon (25:15–38).
On the other hand, we find a curious account of the Rechabites who
refuse to partake of the cup of wine in their abstinence from alco-
holic beverages (Jer 35). The innermost frame in this concentric
structure opens with an account of Jeremiah's "temple sermon," in
which he predicts that Babylon will enslave the people of Israel (Jer
26—27). It continues with an account of the perfidy of the slave
owners in Jerusalem who renege on their promise to free their slaves
(Jer 34). At the center of this structure, we find a section that deals
with prophetic conflict and future hope, which can be expanded in
another menorah pattern.

4th Level Menorah: Jeremiah Is the True Prophet	Jer 28—33
A Hananiah predicts short-term vindication of the nation	28:1-17
B Jeremiah tells exiles to settle permanently in Babylon	29:1-32
C Restoration promised for Israel and Judah	30:1–31:28
X **A new covenant—written on their hearts**	31:29-37
C´ Future rebuilding and enlarging of the city of Jerusalem	31:38-40
B´ Yahweh tells Jeremiah to settle permanently in Anathoth	32:1-44
A´ Jeremiah predicts long-term vindication of the nation	33:1-26

The focus of attention here narrows to the subject of future vindication of the nation, and to a new covenant written on the hearts of individual believers. This section opens with the classic account of prophetic conflict in which Hananiah predicts short-term vindication "within two years" (28:3). Jeremiah's prediction of vindication in "seventy years" (29:10) prevails. At a later point in time, the angel Gabriel reveals that Daniel's seventy years are really "seventy weeks of years"—i.e., 70 x 7 = 490 years, after which the messianic kingdom will come (Dan 9:24). The first half of the second frame finds Jeremiah telling the exiles in Babylon to settle there for a lengthy stay (Jer 29); this is set over against an account in which Yahweh instructs Jeremiah to settle down permanently in Anathoth by purchasing land there (Jer 32).

The center of the book of Jeremiah is found in the conclusion of the "Book of Consolation" (Jer 30—31). Here the prophet looks into the distant future when the kingdoms of Israel and Judah will be restored. He describes the future rebuilding and enlarging of the city of Jerusalem (31:38–40), a topic that Ezekiel will subsequently elaborate in vivid detail (Ezek 40—48). And in the very center of the book of Jeremiah we find a most remarkable text (Jer 31:31–34):

> The days are coming, says Yahweh,
>> when I will make a new covenant with the house of Israel
>> and the house of Judah.
> It will not be like the covenant that I made with their ancestors—

> when I took them by the hand to bring them out of the land of
>   Egypt—
> a covenant that they broke, though I was their husband, says
>   Yahweh.
> But this is the covenant that I will make with the house of Israel
>   after those days, says Yahweh:
> *"I will put my Torah within them,*
> *and I will write it on their hearts;*
> *and I will be their God, and they shall be my people.'"*
> No longer shall they teach one another,
>   or say to each other, "Know Yahweh,"
>   for they shall all know me,
>   from the least of them to the greatest, says Yahweh;
>   for I will forgive their iniquity and remember their sin no
>   more.

This text foreshadows what will take place in the distant future as
the canon of the Tanakh is completed with the addition of "The New
Covenant" in Jesus Christ.

The Book of the Prophet Ezekiel

The book of Ezekiel may be outlined in a three-level nested menorah pattern as follows:

The Book of Ezekiel in a Menorah Pattern	Ezek 1—48
A [July 31, 593] Ezekiel's vision of God and call to be a watchman	1:1—3:21
B Yahweh's glory departs from the Temple in Jerusalem	3:22—14:23
C Israel's continuing rebellion	15:1—23:49
X Fall and destruction of Jerusalem—Ezekiel's dumbness	24:1—39:24
C´ Israel will be restored to the land	39:25—29
B´ Yahweh's glory returns to a visionary new Temple in Jerusalem	40:1—46:24
A´ Ezekiel's vision of renewal—water flowing from the Temple	47:1—48:35

2nd Level Menorah: Fall and Destruction of Jerusalem—Ezekiel's Dumbness Ezek 24:1–39:24	
A Jan. 15, 588 Jerusalem besieged and Ezekiel struck with dumbness	24:1-27
B Oracles against former members of the Davidic Empire	25:1–28:23
C Oracles against Egypt	29:1–32:32
X **Ezekiel, as Israel's sentinel, is released from dumbness**	33:1–33
C´ Oracles against Edom's mountains	34:1–35:15
B´ Restoration of Israel and the valley of dry bones	36:1–37:28
A´ Discourse against Gog and Magog—the "Day of Yahweh has come"	38:1–39:24

3rd Level Menorah: Ezekiel Is Released from Dumbness	Ezek 33
A The word of Yahweh came to the prophet Ezekiel	33:1
B Ezekiel as Israel's sentinel (watchman)	33:2–9
C Yahweh's "vengeance"—justice and mercy	33:10–20
X Jan. 19, 586 **Ezekiel is released from dumbness**	33:21–22
C´ Yahweh's judgment has fallen on the survivors in Judah	33:23–29
B´ The Judahites in exile hear what they want to hear	33:30–33a
A´ When this comes, they will know a prophet has been among them	33:33b

The book of Ezekiel is unique among the Latter Prophets in that it includes a series of specific dates that are useful in determining the literary structure of the book. These dates are indicated in the outlines presented here (in superscript) at the beginning of each section marked in this manner. The dates are B.C.E.

The focus of attention in reading Ezekiel from the center is on the destruction of Jerusalem in the context of the prophet's "dumbness." This dumbness is announced at the outset (3:26), implemented at the time of his wife's death (24:15–27), and removed when the messenger arrives with news of the fall of Jerusalem (33:22). In short, the book of Ezekiel as a whole has a "riddle in the middle," in the sense that the precise meaning of Ezekiel's "dumbness" is not explained. Since the prophet is speaking what God instructs him to say throughout the seven years in question, some scholars interpret his "dumbness" to mean his inability to speak of anything but the coming destruction of Judah and Jerusalem for more than seven years. And when the event takes place, he is then able to speak a new message. This interpretation is possible, but not at all certain.

In terms of literary structure, the concept of Ezekiel's dumbness may be a marker, or signal, to designate the division of the text into three levels in its nested menorah pattern. It is important to note that the news of the destruction of Jerusalem stands at the structural center of Ezekiel. It is when the messenger arrives bearing the news that "the city has fallen" that the spell is broken. In fact, the prophet is prepared for this message the evening before the messenger arrives. Ezekiel already knows—and his mouth is opened, and he is no longer dumb (33:22).

Another way of looking at the concentric structure of Ezekiel is to outline the book in five parts—in the pattern of "four wheels of the same likeness" with a fifth "wheel within the wheels" in the center—as follows:

Four Wheels of the Same Likeness with a Wheel within the Wheels	*Ezek 1—48*
A Yahweh's glory departs from Jerusalem	1:1—24:27
B Israel among the nations	25:1—32:32
X **Ezekiel and the destruction of Jerusalem**	33:1-33
B´ Israel among the nations	34:1—39:29
A´ Yahweh's glory returns to Jerusalem	40:1—48:35

When each of these four "wheels" is explored further to find "wheels within the wheels," in terms of menorah patterns, the central teaching of the prophet Ezekiel is highlighted.

The "first wheel" (Ezekiel 1—24) may be outlined in a nested menorah pattern as follows:

Yahweh's Glory Departs from Jerusalem	*Ezek 1—24*
A [July 31, 593] Ezekiel's vision of God and fivefold commission	1:1—3:27
B Ezekiel's message—the coming siege of Jerusalem	4:1—5:17
C Oracle against the mountains—death upon the mountains	6:1-14
X **Yahweh's glory is replaced with exile and death**	7:1—14:23
C´ Allegories and metaphors of judgment	15:1—19:14
B´ [Aug. 14, 593] Final indictment and condemnation	20:1—23:49
A´ [Jan. 15, 588] Oracle of the cauldron and death of Ezekiel's wife	24:1-27

2nd Level Menorah: Yahweh's Glory Replaced with Exile and Death	Ezek 7—14
A Word of Yahweh: The bitter day of Yahweh's "vengeance"	7:1-27
B Sept. 17, 592 Ezekiel's vision of idolatry	8:1-18
C Punishment of the guilty	9:1-11
X **Departure of Yahweh's glory from the Temple in Jerusalem**	10:1—11:25
C´ Symbolic portrayal of the exile	12:1-20
B´ False prophets condemned	13:1-23
A´ God's judgments justified—four deadly acts of punishment	14:1-23

3rd Level Menorah: Departure of Yahweh's Glory from Jerusalem	Ezek 10—11
A Yahweh's glory departs from his Temple in Jerusalem	10:1-22
B Ezekiel's visionary journey to Jerusalem to prophesy	11:1-4
C Ezekiel prophesies against Jaazaniah and Pelatiah	11:5-11
X **Yahweh's word: "You shall know that I am Yahweh"**	11:12
C´ Pelatiah dies while Ezekiel is prophesying	11:13
B´ Yahweh is with his exiled people and will restore them	11:14-21
A´ Yahweh's glory departs from his Temple in Jerusalem	11:22-25

The focus of attention here is on the departure of Yahweh's glory from the Temple in Jerusalem, which makes up the outermost frame of the third-level menorah pattern (10:1–22 and 11:22–25). At the same time, it should be noted that the concentric structure here in chapters 10—11 narrows to highlight the words of Yahweh in 11:12—"and you shall know that I am Yahweh." This same statement appears elsewhere in Ezekiel as a repeated refrain to mark the boundaries of literary sub-units (see 6:7, 10, 13, 14; 7:4, 27). When Yahweh's glory actually returns to the Temple in Jerusalem, the name of the city itself is changed: "And the name of the city henceforth shall be, Yahweh is there" (48:35).

The two central "wheels," which take up the topic of Israel among the nations (chaps. 25—32 and 34—39), may be outlined in menorah patterns as well:

Israel among the Nations—Oracles against Foreign Nations	Ezek 25—32
A Oracles against Ammon, Moab, Edom, and Philistia	25:1-17
B March 587 Oracles against Tyre and Sidon (Phoenicia)	26:1—28:19

C	Oracle against Sidon	28:20-23
X	**Future blessing for Israel**	28:24-26
C´	Jan. 7, 587 Oracle against Pharaoh, king of Egypt	29:1–30:26
B´	June 21, 587 Oracle against Pharaoh: Allegory of the cedar	31:1-18
A´	Mar. 3, 585 Egypt joins Assyria, Elam... Edom and Sidon	32:17-32

Israel among the Nations in a Menorah Pattern		*Ezek 34—39*
A	Israel's false shepherds and Yahweh the true shepherd	34:1-31
B	Oracles against Edom's mountains	35:1-15
C	Discourse on salvation for Israel's mountains	36:1-15
X	**Cursory theological summary of Israel's history**	36:16-21
C´	Discourse on the restoration of Israel	36:22-38
B´	Valley of the bones and vision of the sticks	37:1-28
A´	Gog and Magog; and Israel restored to the land	38:1–39:29

In both instances, the menorah patterns converge in a positive note so far as Israel is concerned. The collection of oracles against foreign nations has in its center a brief note on future blessing for Israel (28:24–26). In the case of Ezekiel 34—39, the salvation and restoration of Israel constitute the innermost framework around a brief passage justifying Yahweh's action in "scattering them among the nations" (36:19). God's intended purposes with his people Israel include the nations. The menorah pattern concludes with the familiar picture of the "valley of dry bones" (chap. 37) and the apocalyptic imagery of the Gog and Magog oracles (chaps. 38—39), where God will ultimately be acknowledged by all nations as the undisputed victor (38:23 and 39:21–29).

The concluding section of the book of Ezekiel, which presents the return of Yahweh's glory to the Temple in Jerusalem (43:1–12), may also be outlined in a nested menorah pattern:

Yahweh's Glory Returns to the Temple in Jerusalem		*Ezek 40—48*
A	Apr. 28, 573 Ezekiel's visionary journey to Jerusalem	40:1-4
B	The temple area, gates, outer and inner courts	40:5-49
C	Inside the Temple—the vestibule, nave, and inner room	41:1-26
X	**Renewal of worship in Jerusalem**	42:1—46:24

C´	Water flows from the Temple, restoring life to a new Israel	47:1–23
B´	The new Jerusalem with 12 gates named after the 12 tribes	48:1–35a
A´	Conclusion: The name of the city shall be, "Yahweh is there"	48:35b

Renewal of Worship in the Temple in Jerusalem		*Ezek 42—46*
A	Inside the inner court—the priests' chambers	42:1–14
B	Going out the eastern gate—measuring the total temple area	42:15–20
C	The eastern gate and the return of Yahweh's glory	43:1–12
X	**The altar of burnt offering—dedicated by Zadokite priests**	43:13–27
C´	The eastern gate to remain shut—Yahweh's glory fills the Temple	44:1–4
B´	Temple ordinances and worship at the east gate of the inner court	44:5—46:18
A´	Inside the inner court—priests's chambers [+ outer court vv. 21–24]	46:19–24

The focus of attention here is on the renewal of worship in Jerusalem (chaps. 42—46), and specifically the dedication of the Zadokite priests to perform sacrifices on the altar of burnt offering in the court-yard of the rebuilt Temple in Jerusalem (43:13–27). Yahweh's glory will return to a new Temple in the visionary New Jerusalem (40:1—46:24). In that city, life-giving water flows forth from the Temple in Jerusalem such that even the Dead Sea becomes fresh. "And fisher-men will stand beside the sea; from Engedi to En-eglaim it will be a place for the spreading of nets; its fish will be of very many kinds, like the fish of the Great Sea [the Mediterranean]" (47:10).

Other menorah patterns appear throughout the book of Ezekiel to highlight important concerns. Ezekiel's "chariot vision" of the four wheels of the same likeness, with a wheel within the wheels, may be outlined in the following menorah pattern:

The Vision of Four Wheels of the Same Likeness with a Wheel Inside		*Ezek 1*
A	July 31, 593 In Babylon ($7^1/_2$ years before the fall of Jerusalem)	1:1–3
B	Vision of a great cloud and flashing fire out of the north	1:4
C	Vision of "four living creature" darting to and from	1:5–14
X	**Vision of the four wheels and a wheel within a wheel**	1:15–21
C´	Vision of the dome "over the heads of the living creatures"	1:22–25
B´	The glory of Yahweh enthroned above the dome	1:26–28a
A´	Ezekiel's response: "I fell upon my face, and I heard the voice"	1:28b

The so-called "throne chariot vision" stands in the structural center of this menorah pattern. The prophet describes "a wheel upon the earth beside the living creatures, one for each of the four of them ...and the four had the same likeness, their construction being as it were a wheel within a wheel" (1:15–16, RSV). He may be saying more than he knew, for these also describe the literary structure of the book of Ezekiel itself—and the Bible as a whole.

Ezekiel's "throne chariot vision" is also the first part of a larger menorah pattern that embraces the first three chapters of the book:

Ezekiel's Call Vision and His Fivefold Commission	Ezek 1—3
A Ezekiel's vision—4 wheels of the same likeness with a 5th wheel inside	1:1–28
B 1st Commission: "Son of man, stand ... and I will speak with you"	2:1–8a
C Symbolic action—eating a scroll filled with words of woe	2:8b–3:3
X **2nd Commission: His determination to prophesy must be strong**	3:4–9
C´ 3rd Commission: Emphasizing his mission to the exiles	3:10–15
B´ 4th Commission: "I have made you a *watchman* for...Israel"	3:16–21
A´ 5th Commission: Beginning of Ezekiel's "dumbness"	3:22–27

In this opening section of the book of Ezekiel, we find a word picture of "five wheels" and a fivefold delineation of what God has called the prophet to do. The remaining section of the menorah pattern makes specific reference to "a written *scroll*," which "had writing on the front and on the back" (2:10, RSV). This is a curious statement, because scrolls do not normally have writing on both sides. These words foreshadow the appearance of the "codex" centuries later, the first true "book" in the modern sense of that word, which emerged during the time of the Apostle Paul, as we will see in chapter 7.

Ezekiel's message about the coming siege and destruction of Jerusalem in chapters 4—6 may also be outlined in a menorah pattern:

Ezekiel's Message—The Coming Siege of Jerusalem	Ezek 4—6
A Sun-dried brick with a relief drawing of Jerusalem under siege	4:1–3
B Ezekiel must lie on his left side and eat bread for 390 days	4:4–17
C Shorn hair is a symbol of the fate awaiting people in Jerusalem	5:1–4

X	Threefold oracle of doom—corresponding to the symbolic acts	5:5-17
C´	Your cities shall be waste and your high places ruined	6:1-7
B´	Those who survive will be scattered through the countries	6:8-10
A´	They shall fall by the sword, by famine, and by pestilence	6:11-14

Ezekiel's message of judgment on Jerusalem is a carefully balanced presentation of symbolic acts and oracles of doom that focuses on the three standard themes of human suffering in antiquity: the sword, famine, and disease.

Two other menorah patterns of note are found in the first "wheel" of the book of Ezekiel (chaps. 1—24) as follows:

Allegories and Metaphors of Judgment		*Ezek 15—19*
A	Allegory of the vine	15:1-8
B	Allegory of the unfaithful wife	16:1-63
C	Allegory of the two eagles	17:1-21
X	**Allegory of the cedar—a messianic vision: future hope**	17:22-24
C´	A case for individual responsibility	18:1-32
B´	The lioness in Judah	19:1-9
A´	The vine in Judah	19:10-14

Final Indictment and Condemnation		*Ezek 20—24*
A	Israel's history of infidelity	20:1-44
B	Oracle against the south	20:45-49
C	Oracles on the sword	21:1-32
X	**The blood guilt of Jerusalem**	22:1-31
C´	Allegory of the two sisters	23:1-49
B´	Allegory of the cauldron	24:1-14
A´	Oracle at the death of Ezekiel's wife—Ezekiel's "dumbness" begins	24:15-27

In the center of the series of allegories and metaphors of judgment on Jerusalem, which the prophet interprets in terms of specific historical incidents, we find an allegory of hope in a messianic vision (17:22–24). Yahweh declares that he "will take a sprig from the lofty top of the cedar, and...plant it, that it may bring forth boughs and bear fruit." God's judgment is with a purpose. He has not given up on his people Israel, for they will yet become a light to the nations in spite of themselves. The people of Israel will become "a noble cedar" and "every bird of every feather shall take shelter under it, shelter in the shade of its boughs" (17:23, JPS Tanakh).

Within the oracles against foreign nations in Ezekiel 25—32, we find a series of six dated oracles against Egypt carefully arranged in a menorah pattern as follows:

Oracles against Egypt	Ezek 29–32
A Jan. 7, 587 Against Pharaoh (Hophra)	29:1–16
B Apr. 26, 571 Egypt as "wages" for Nebuchadnezzar	29:17–21
C The doom of Egypt—the "Day of Yahweh" is near	30:1–19
X Apr. 29, 587 **Breaking Hophra's other arm**	30:20–26
C´ June 21, 587 Allegory of the cedar—to be hewed down	31:1–18
B´ Mar. 3, 585 Lament over Pharaoh who thought himself a lion	32:1–16
A´ Apr. 27, 586 Pharaoh and his multitude in the netherworld	32:17–32

The series opens with an oracle directed against Pharaoh Hophra, whose attack against Nebuchadnezzar in the spring of 588 had failed to relieve the situation in Jerusalem (29:6–9). The oracle in the center of this menorah pattern continues with the same theme involving the same individual. Nebuchadnezzar had broken one arm of Pharaoh four months earlier. He will now break both of Pharaoh Hophra's arms—"both the strong arm and the one that was broken" (30:22). The series concludes with a picture of Egypt going down to the netherworld to join the others—Assyria, Elam, Meshech and Tubal, Edom, and the "princes of the north" (32:17–32).

The Book of the Twelve Lesser Prophets

Though the Book of the Twelve (so-called Minor Prophets) is seldom read as a single literary unit, it may be outlined as such in a menorah pattern within a menorah pattern:

The Book of the Twelve in a Menorah Pattern	*Hosea–Malachi*
A Israel's unfaithfulness and God's judgment	Hosea
B Day of Yahweh–the enemy from the north	Joel
C Israel and the nations–judgment and hope	Amos
X **Yahweh's "vengeance": Destruction and salvation**	Obadiah–Zephaniah
C´ Rebuilding the Temple in Jerusalem	Haggai
B´ Day of Yahweh and the restoration of Judah	Zechariah
A´ Day of Yahweh–against Judah and the nations	Malachi

The attribution of "vengeance" to the character of Yahweh has been a source of misunderstanding. As G. E. Mendenhall has shown (*The Tenth Generation*, Baltimore: Johns Hopkins University Press, 1973, pp. 69–104), the Hebrew root *nqm* is properly translated in terms that designate punitive vindication in a judicial sense and should not be construed as involving "malicious retaliation for inflicted wrongs." As a result, Yahweh is depicted in Nahum as a suzerain, one who demands the exclusive devotion of his vassals, for he is utterly intolerant of rivals. Nahum 1:2 is set over against 1:9–10, both of which focus on "the dark side" of Yahweh, namely, his jealous anger that leads to punishment. Nahum 1:3 and 1:7–8 present the other side of Yahweh, one who is "slow to anger" (cf. Exod 34:6–7). In biblical usage, God's "vengeance" has a redemptive quality. His punishment often takes the form of discipline, however harsh it may appear to the recipient at the outset.

The outer frame in the above menorah pattern begins with the powerful imagery of redeeming love in the account of the prophet Hosea and his faithless wife Gomer (Hos 1—3). It continues with a message of judgment against Israel for her perfidy, with the hope of ultimate restoration (Hos 4—14). This same dual theme is taken up in the book of Malachi, in the other half of the outermost frame. The book of Malachi begins with the words, "'I have loved you,' says Yahweh" (Mal 1:2). The ensuing words about the coming day of judgment in Malachi are climaxed with a remarkable vision of hope. "Behold, I will send you Elijah the prophet before the great and terrible Day of Yahweh comes. And he will turn the hearts of fathers to

their children and the hearts of children to their fathers, lest I come
and smite the land with a curse" (Mal 4:5–6). The second frame in
this menorah pattern presents Joel and Zechariah as a literary pair.
Both focus on the destructive aspects of the Day of Yahweh. Once
again we find hope within the context of gloom, for both books
include words of hope and restoration. God's promise of restoration
occupies the structural center and the conclusion of Joel's depiction
of the Day of Yahweh as a time of devastation for Judah and the
nations (see Joel 2:18–29 and Joel 3:18–21). The book of Zechariah
also has at its center words of hope that focus on the rebuilding of
the Temple in Jerusalem by "the man whose name is the Branch"
(Zech 6:9–15). The innermost frame in this menorah pattern sets the
book of Amos over against that of Haggai. The book of Amos ends
with specific prophecies of the restoration of the Davidic dynasty
and the glorious age to come (Amos 9:11–15). The book of Haggai,
which focuses on the building of the Second Temple in Jerusalem
more than two hundred years after the time of Amos, concludes with
a promise to Zerubbabel, governor of Judah (and a descendant of
David), that God will again redeem his people. Like Amos, Zechariah links Israel's earlier traditions with the coming messianic age
(Hag 2:20–23). The remaining six books in the Book of the Twelve
constitute the center of this menorah pattern, which is essentially an
expansion of the great confession of faith in Exodus 34:6–7 to show
the two sides of Yahweh—his anger (Exod 34:7) and his steadfast
love (Exod 34:6).

The center of the above menorah pattern may be expanded in its
own menorah pattern as follows:

2nd Level Menorah: The "Vengeance" of Yahweh	*Obadiah–Zephaniah*
A Day of Yahweh–against Edom and Judah	Obadiah
B Salvation of Nineveh	Jonah
C Salvation of Israel	Micah
X **Confession of faith (cf. Exod 34:6–7)**	Mic 7:18–20
C´ Destruction of Nineveh	Nahum
B´ Destruction of Judah	Habakkuk
A´ Day of Yahweh–against Judah and the nations	Zephaniah

The Day of Yahweh is a central theme in the Book of the Twelve (Lesser Prophets); and that theme is central in Obadiah and Zephaniah, which constitute the outer frame in this menorah pattern. In the structural center of the Book of the Twelve as a whole, we find a confession of faith that echoes Exodus 34:6–7. In the second frame, the book of Jonah is set over against the book of Habakkuk. The message of the book of Jonah focuses on the salvation of Israel's most repugnant enemy. The book of Habakkuk, on the other hand, deals with the issue of theodicy in an explicit manner. After raising his complaint, the prophet asks God how long he can look on faithless men and do nothing "when the wicked swallows up the man more righteous than he" (Hab 1:13). In the third frame, the book of Micah is set over against Nahum. Most of the central part of the book of Micah focuses on Zion's glorious future and the restoration of the Davidic kingdom (Micah 4—5). In contrast to this focus on the salvation of Israel, the book of Nahum presents a moving picture of the destruction of Nineveh.

Jonah and Nahum may be read in relation to the two aspects of God's nature, his mercy and his anger, with Jonah focusing on God's compassion and Nahum on God's wrath. Jonah presents God as one who is "compassionate, gracious . . . (and) abounding in steadfast love" (Exod 34:6–7a), whereas Nahum presents God as the "one who punishes sons and grandsons to the third and fourth generations for the iniquity of their fathers" (Exod 34:7b). In short, Nahum focuses on the "dark side" of God, while Jonah portrays God's mercy and compassion toward the same wicked city of Nineveh.

The books of Jonah and Nahum are the only two books in the Bible that end in a question. They both have the city of Nineveh as their subject. This is remarkable in the case of Jonah, since we know from 2 Kings 14:25 that the prophet ministered in the days of Jeroboam II against the Aramean threat centered in the cities of Damascus and Hamath (2 Kgs 14:28). These events occurred before the time of Tiglath-pileser III ("King Pul" of 2 Kgs 15:19) and the expansion of the Assyrian Empire in Palestine. Nineveh was the capital of Assyria at its height from the time of Sennacherib, who assumed the throne in 705 B.C.E., to its destruction in 612 B.C.E. It was not the capital of Assyria in the days of Jeroboam II (786–746 B.C.E). Moreover, there was never a time when it was appropriate to speak of the "king of Nineveh" (Jonah 3:6) outside the book of Jonah. Nineveh is mentioned in Isaiah 37:37 (= 2 Kgs 19:36) as the home of Sennacherib and the place where he was assassinated and succeeded by his son Esarhaddon.

The name Nineveh was chosen in the book of Jonah because of its symbolic value. The word *Ninuwa* and the alternate form *Nina* in the cuneiform sources refer to an enclosure with a fish inside. The letter *nun* actually means "fish" in the Hebrew language. The word "Nineveh" in Hebrew would be written NYNWH. If the initial *nun* ("fish") is removed, the letters that remain are YNWH. All one needs to do to get the word YWNH ("Jonah") is a simple metathesis of the two central letters. In other words, Jonah is already in Nineveh—if you remove the "fish"! It is important to note the fact that the word YWNH ("Jonah") in Hebrew means "dove," a primary symbol for the nation of Israel.

We are now in a position to understand the significance of the phrase "king of Nineveh" in relation to the prophet "Jonah." From a historical point of view, the king in question was not the "king of Nineveh" but rather the "king of Assyria." Nowhere else do we find a reference to the "king of Nineveh" outside the book of Jonah. The city of Nineveh was the capital of Assyria. Its symbolic value is of primary importance here.

Though Jonah contains only forty-eight verses, this remarkable work of art may be outlined in a three-part nested series of menorah patterns:

The Book of Jonah in a Menorah Pattern		Jonah 1—4
a	Jonah's commission to go to Nineveh	1:1–2
A	Jonah vs. Yahweh: Jonah's flight and Yahweh's storm ("anger")	1:3–4
B	Dialogue between sailors and Jonah: "Fear" motif	1:5–13
C	Sailors' prayer: "Hold us not responsible for this man's death"	1:14a
X	**Freedom, anger, and fear**	1:14b—4:2
C´	Jonah's prayer: "I am better off dead than alive"	4:3

| B´ | Dialogue between Yahweh/God and Jonah: "Anger" motif | 4:4–9 |
| A´ | Yahweh vs. Jonah: Yahweh justifies compassion for Nineveh | 4:10–11 |

2nd Level Menorah: Freedom, Anger, and Fear		*Jonah 1:14b—4:2*
A	Yahweh's freedom: "What pleases you is what you have done"	1:14b
B	The sea ceases its raging ("anger")	1:15
C	The men fear Yahweh with a Great Fear	1:16
X	**Conversion is changing one's mind**	1:17—3:10
C´	A Great Evil came upon Jonah	4:1a
B´	Jonah becomes angry	4:1b
A´	Yahweh's freedom: "I knew you would repent from the evil"	4:2

3rd Level Menorah: God Wants Conversion		*Jonah 2—3*
A	Yahweh appoints a Great Fish to change Jonah's mind	1:17—2:1
B	Song of Jonah: A "proclamation" of deliverance	2:2–9
C	Jonah's deliverance from the fish	2:10
X	**Jonah's commission renewed—with enigmatic message**	3:1–4
C´	Nineveh's repentance	3:5–7a
B´	Decree of king of Nineveh: Proclamation to turn from evil	3:7b–9
A´	God changes his mind	3:10
a´	Jonah's/Israel's commission/response: An oracle of salvation	implied

The relationship between the prophet Isaiah and King Hezekiah illustrates the proper relationship between the offices of prophet and king in terms of political leadership in ancient Israel. In like manner, the prophet "Jonah" (Israel) and the "king of Nineveh" illustrate the proper relationship between prophet and king in a symbolic sense, on a much broader stage. To those who shaped the canon of the Tanakh, as we now know it, Israel is called to be a "light to the nations" (Isa 42:6). This theme is explored in various ways within the Writings of the Tanakh and in the book of Daniel in particular.

4

The Writings
The People of God among the Nations

After the Torah and the Prophets *(Nevi'im)* came the Writings *(Kethubim)* to complete the Tanakh. As we have already seen, the Prophets are in two parts—the Former Prophets (Joshua through 2 Kings), and the Latter Prophets (Isaiah, Jeremiah, Ezekiel, and The Twelve). In an ultimate sense, the Writings are also in two parts— the Hebrew Writings of the Tanakh and the Apostolic Writings (i.e., the New Testament) of the Completed Tanakh. Our concern in this chapter is to describe the structure and content of the nine books that make up the Hebrew Writings.

THE "HAGIOGRAPHA":
PSALMS, JOB, PROVERBS, AND THE FESTAL SCROLLS

In the first chapter of this book we called the fourth of the primary sections of the Tanakh the "Hagiographa," which originally was made up of four parts: Psalms, Job, Proverbs, and the *Megilloth* (Festal Scrolls). To these four were added five others: Daniel and the four segments in the "The Chronicler's History"—Ezra, Nehemiah, 1 and 2 Chronicles. The formation and structure of these books is explored here in that order.

The Book of Psalms

Martin Luther once described the book of Psalms as "the Bible in miniature," arguing that the content of the whole can be found here. The subject of the creation of the world is taken up in the psalms, as is the history of ancient Israel from the patriarchs and matriarchs of Genesis to the Babylonian Exile. The Torah itself is a subject of praise (Pss 19, 119). And the book of Psalms moves beyond the Law and the Prophets with its primary focus on worship, for, in many respects, the book of Psalms is aptly described as the "hymnbook of the Second Temple."

The fact that the book of Psalms has a long and complex history is obvious to any reader who takes the time and effort to look closely at the facts. Though the psalms are frequently referred to as the "Psalms of David," David is actually designated the author in less than half of the 150 psalms in the Psalter. Other designated authors in the collection include Moses (Ps 90), Solomon (Pss 72, 127), the "sons of Korah" (Pss 42—49, 84—85, 87—88), Asaph (Pss 50, 73—83), Heman the Ezrahite (Ps 88), and Ethan the Ezrahite (Ps 89). Moreover, many of the psalms are without any designation so far as authorship is concerned. And some, like Psalm 137, clearly presuppose the destruction of the Temple of Solomon in Jerusalem and are written from the perspective of the Babylonian Exile, which took place centuries after the time of David. Thus, though David plays a significant role in the development of the Psalter and perhaps may even still be seen—at least in the broadest sense—as the "author" of the psalms we have in the Bible, the psalms enjoy a life of their own.

The collection of the psalms within the life of ancient Israel, in the canonical process that produced the Tanakh as we now have it, began as early as the time of Moses (Ps 90) and continued to grow long after the death of David.

Davidic Psalter ⟶ *Deuteronomic Psalter* ⟶ *Pentateuchal Psalter*

Ca. 1000–700 B.C.E.   Ca. 500 B.C.E.   Ca. 400 B.C.E.

Through the centuries most students of the Bible have noted that the book of Psalms is "pentateuchal" in structure. Like the Pentateuch (the five books of Moses), the psalms are divided into five books: book 1 contains Psalms 1—41; book 2, Psalms 42—72; book 3, Psalms 73—89; book 4, Psalms 90—106; and book 5, Psalms 107—150. In each case, the book is concluded by a benediction that is expanded in the case of book 5 into five separate psalms (Pss 146—150). The presence of the five-part structural design is marked in Codex Leningrad B[19], the oldest complete manuscript we have of the Hebrew Bible (1008 C.E.). But attempts to explain this phenomenon in relation to the structure and content of the Torah (the Pentateuch) have not convinced most scholars. Moreover, specific data in the biblical text sometimes remain to be explained. For instance, why should book 2 end with the statement, "The prayers of David, the son of Jesse, are ended," when at least eighteen more psalms of David are to be found in books 3–5?

Book 2 of the Psalter is commonly called the Elohistic Psalter because of its preference for the divine name '*Elohim* rather than *Yahweh*. When book 2 is removed, all of the "doublets" noted by scholars disappear (i.e., Ps 14 = Ps 53; Ps 70 = Ps 40:13–17; Ps 108 = Ps 57:7–11 and Ps 60:5–12). A reasonable working hypothesis posits the insertion of book 2 as the final addition to the Psalter, when the seventeen books of the deuteronomic canon were expanded to make the twenty-two books of the pentateuchal canon in the time of Ezra. It appears that an original collection of the psalms of David, preserved in books 1 and 5 of the Psalms as we now have them, was edited into a Deuteronomic Psalter. The Pentateuchal Psalter of mainstream Jewish tradition appeared with the formation of the twenty-two-book canon of the Tanakh in the time of Ezra (ca. 400 B.C.E.), when book 2 (Pss 42—72) was inserted into an existing collection.

We have already observed the fact that the original deuteronomic canon, which determines the ultimate shape of the Tanakh, contains seventeen books, arranged in four groups of four with the book of Deuteronomy in the center. The number seventeen is also significant in the structure of the book of Psalms. Within the Psalter, books 3 and 4 each contain 17 psalms. If the thirty-one psalms of book 2 are excluded in counting the psalms, an interesting picture emerges so far as the number 17 is concerned. The deuteronomic Psalter (with book 2 omitted) is made up of 119 psalms, which is 17 x 7. Two collections of 17 psalms each (books 3 and 4) are thus framed by inserting them into an original Davidic Psalter (books 1 and 5) made up of 85 psalms (= 17 x 5). Of these 85 psalms, 51 (= 17 x 3) belong to David and 34 (= 17 x 2) to other authors.

The overall structure of the book of Psalms may be outlined as follows:

The Book of Psalms in Five Parts		*Pss 1—150*
A Psalms of David—on the Torah and Temple	Book 1	1—41
B Psalms of David and Solomon—Kingdom of Israel	Book 2	42—72
X **Israel and the nations—a liturgy**	Book 3	73—89
B´ Psalms on kingship of God—from Moses to the Exile	Book 4	90—106
A´ Psalms of David—on the Torah and the Temple	Book 5	107—150

In this reading of the book of Psalms, the focus of attention is on the place of Israel among the nations. At the structural center of the Psalter as a whole we find Psalm 81—a psalm of Asaph, which is the liturgy for a festival in ancient Israel. Here the poet reviews the course of sacred history from the time of the patriarch Jacob (v. 4), to Joseph (v. 5a), and on to the Exodus from Egypt under Moses (vv. 5b–10). Particular emphasis is placed on the First Commandment: "There shall be no strange god among you; you shall not bow down to a foreign god" (v. 9). The poet then reflects on the stubbornness of Israel, who would not listen to God's voice (vv. 11–16). Psalm 82, another "psalm of Asaph," carries that thought a significant step further in its call for God's rule over the nations to ensure justice for the weak: "Rise up, O God, judge the earth; for all the nations belong to you!" (Ps 82:8). As we will see in the discussion below, this is a central theme throughout the Writings of the Tanakh.

The Content of the Book of Psalms

Each of the five books in the Psalter may in turn be analyzed in terms of concentric structural patterns that highlight the theology of the collection as a whole and help to explain the relation of the separate parts to each other.

Book 1: Psalms of David on the Torah and the Temple	Pss 1—41
A Joy of Torah and contrasting fate of the righteous and wicked	Ps 1
B Prayers for deliverance and healing	Pss 2—6
C Prayers and praise for Yahweh's power and justice	Pss 7—11
D Inner frame: Who shall abide in Yahweh's sanctuary?	Pss 12—18
X **Yahweh's glory in creation and the Torah**	Ps 19
D´ Inner frame: The divine shepherd and access to his sanctuary	Pss 20—26
C´ Yahweh speaks in the storm, bringing deliverance and healing	Pss 27—31
B´ Praise and prayer for deliverance	Pss 32—36
A´ Prayers and thanksgiving for healing, wisdom, and deliverance	Pss 37—41

Psalm 1 is a wisdom psalm that functions as an introduction to the Psalter as a whole. The theme is the joy of the Torah, anticipating Psalm 19 at the center of this concentric structure, which extols the glory of God as revealed in creation (19:1–6) and in Yahweh's Torah (19:7–10). The capacity of the Torah to bring joy and delight (19:8, 10) is reminiscent of Psalm 1 and anticipates the great meditation on the Torah in Psalm 119. Psalm 1 exalts the way of the righteous, who are devoted to Yahweh's instructions (Torah), and acknowledges the ultimate downfall of the wicked, who do not attend to God and his ways.

Psalm 2 introduces the theme of God as ruler over the nations, which dominates book 3 (Pss 73—89). Psalm 2 is also part of a much larger design of the Psalter as a whole, as Hempel has observed (*The Interpreter's Dictionary of the Bible*, vol. 3 [Nashville: Abingdon Press, 1962], p. 943). As Psalm 1 forms an inclusion with Psalms 146—150, so Psalm 2 is parallel to Psalm 110, which stands at the center of a group of five psalms (Pss 108—112) in book 5 (Pss 107—150).

Book 2: Psalms on the Kingdom of Israel   *Pss 42—72*

A   Korahite Psalms—longing for God's help in times of distress   Pss 42—44

B   Korahite Psalms on defense of Zion and God's rule over the nations   Pss 45—49

X   **Psalm of Asaph—a liturgy of divine judgment**   Ps 50

B´   Psalms of David—comfort in God's guidance and triumph   Pss 51—70

A´ Prayers for protection and guidance for the king   Pss 71—72

The original collection of the psalms of David in book 1 (Pss 1—41) and book 5 (Pss 107—150) are here augmented with another collection of twenty psalms of David (Pss 51—70), which is set over against a collection of Korahite psalms (Pss 42—49). The psalm of Asaph in the structural center of book 2 anticipates the larger collection of eleven psalms of Asaph that follow in book 3 (Pss 73—83).

The Psalms in Books 3 and 4   *Pss 73—106*

A   Israel in time of national troubles—Part One   Pss 73—79

B   Prayer for deliverance from national enemies   Ps 80

X   **Liturgy for a festival—God's appeal to stubborn Israel**   Ps 81

B´   Vision of Yahweh's judgment on pagan gods   Ps 82

A´ Israel in time of national troubles—Part Two   Pss 83—89

A   Moses and the kingship of God   Pss 90—96

B   Hymn celebrating God's kingship   Ps 97

X   **Hymn on the future establishment of God's kingship**   Ps 98

B´   Hymn celebrating God's kingship   Ps 99

A´ The kingship of David [Moses named in Pss 105—106]   Pss 100—106

Books 3 and 4 in the Psalter each contain seventeen psalms arranged in parallel concentric structures (in a pattern of 7 + 3 + 7 = 17). In content, these thirty-four psalms focus attention on Israel and the nations (book 3) and on the kingship of God (book 4) from the time of Moses (Ps 90) to the eschatological kingdom of God (Ps 98). Books 1 and 5 of the Psalter, which form the outer frame in the concentric structural design of the book of Psalms as a whole, are similar in detail in that both focus attention on the Torah at their centers (in Pss 19 and 119).

In Psalms 73—79 (within book 3), we find a carefully balanced arrangement in the titles ascribed to the seven psalms. The outer frame is made up of two psalms of Asaph. The first is a meditation on the justice of God (Ps 73) that reminds the reader of the book of Job and the book of the prophet Habakkuk. The second is a prayer for deliverance from national enemies in the form of a lamentation over the havoc wrought by foreign invaders of Jerusalem (Ps 79). The historical occasion for the composition of Psalm 79 is probably the same as that for Psalm 74, which is also a national lament describing the destruction of the Temple in Jerusalem by the Babylonians in 586 B.C.E. In the second frame of this concentric structure, both Psalm 74 and Psalm 78 are designated a "*maskil* of Asaph." Psalm 74 is a didactic psalm drawing lessons from Israel's past—with specific historical references that place its composition between the death of Solomon (922 B.C.E.) and the destruction of the Northern Kingdom (Israel) by the Assyrians in 721 B.C.E. These two *maskilim* (plural of *maskil*) serve as a frame around three psalms of Asaph in the center (Pss 75—77). It is interesting to note the reversal in the titles of the inner frame from "a psalm of Asaph" *(mizmor la'asap)* in Psalm 75 to "of Asaph, a psalm" *(la'asap mizmor)* in Psalm 77 on either side of the central psalm in the concentric structure. Psalm 75 is difficult to classify in terms of standard types of psalms. In Psalm 75:7–9 the psalmist describes God's supreme dominion, and depicts a scene of final judgment in imagery reminiscent of Jeremiah 25 (and the "cup of Yahweh's wrath" proffered to the nations). In its counterpart (Ps 77), which is also of mixed type, the psalmist laments the abandonment of his nation by God. Psalm 77:14–20 is in the form of a hymn of praise recounting God's glorious deeds of the past as motivation for his intervention again in the present (cf. Ps 74:13). The center of this menorah pattern contains another psalm of Asaph, in the form of a song of Zion (resembling Pss 46 and 48), that celebrates God's victory over the nations.

The second of the menorah patterns in book 3 (Pss 83—89) is introduced by another psalm of Asaph (Ps 83), which is the last of the twelve "psalms of Asaph" in the Psalter. Psalm 83 is a national lament in which the psalmist prays on behalf of the nation for deliverance from the surrounding enemies who threaten its existence.

Within this frame we find three psalms ascribed to the "Korahites" (Pss 84, 85, and 87) and a "*Maskil* of Heman the Ezrahite" (Ps 88). The central "prayer of David" in Psalm 86, which is the only psalm ascribed to David in book 3, is in the form of a royal letter addressed to God in which the psalmist asks for deliverance from enemies (see Ps 86:14). This single psalm of David in the center of this assemblage of psalms dealing with the subject of Israel in times of national troubles functions as a reminder to the reader (hearer) that God is not yet through with the Davidic kingdom and his chosen people Israel.

Book 5: Psalms of David on the Torah and the Temple	*Pss 107—150*
A The Song of the Redeemed	Ps 107
B Davidic Psalms—Part One	*Pss* 108—112
C Egyptian Hallel (Pss 113—114 and 115—118 sung after Passover)	*Pss* 113—118
X **Meditation on the Torah [an acrostic poem]**	*Ps* 119
C´ Songs of Ascent (Pilgrimage to the Temple in Jerusalem)	*Pss* 120—134
B´ Davidic Psalms—Part Two	*Pss* 135—145
A´ Hallelujah Psalms—the Great Doxology	*Pss* 146—150

Like book 1, the content of book 5 has as its theme the Torah and the Temple. The outer frame in this structure moves from an opening hymn of national thanksgiving (Ps 107), to the concluding "Great Doxology" of Hallelujah Psalms (Pss 146—150). Within this framework stands a collection of Davidic Psalms in two parts (Pss 108—112 and 135—145), which in turn frame two groups of "festival psalms" (Pss 113—118 and 120—134). And in the center we find the lengthy meditation on the Torah in the form of an elaborate acrostic (with eight lines beginning with each letter of the alphabet) in Psalm 119.

The Relation of the Psalter to the Torah

More than a hundred years ago, a German scholar by the name of Adolf Büchler called attention to a triennial system of reading the Torah within Palestinian Judaism in antiquity. A few years later, Eduard King examined the book of Psalms in light of Büchler's thesis with fascinating results (see the diagrams on pages 57 and 58 of my earlier book, *Bible 101: God's Story in Human History* [BIBAL Press, 1996]).

In the Triennial Lectionary Cycle of ancient Palestinian Judaism, which was generally replaced after the second century C.E. by the annual Babylonian cycle, the entire Pentateuch was read in public worship in a period of three years. Assuming four Sabbaths per lunar month and following Büchler's analysis of the use of the Torah in this three-year cycle, the reading of Genesis began on the first Sabbath, Exodus on the forty-second, Leviticus on the seventy-third, Numbers on the ninetieth and Deuteronomy on the one hundred and seventeenth. The similarity of this scheme to the divisions of the five books of psalms is striking. Except in the case of Deuteronomy, the Sabbath on which a new book in the Torah was begun is numerically equivalent to the opening psalm of each of the first four books (Pss 1, 42, 73, and 90). Allowing four psalms per lunar month, to parallel the four readings from the Torah per month, would mean that the public reading of the first four books of the Psalter would have begun on the same Sabbaths as the corresponding books of the Pentateuch. Norman Snaith subsequently argued that Psalm 119 should be seen as the psalm that originally opened the fifth book of psalms. This psalm was read on the first of the month Elul in the third year of the triennial cycle—on the 117th Sabbath, at the time when the reading of Deuteronomy began. Psalm 119, with its focus on the Torah in every single one of its 176 verses, forms an excellent companion to the commencement of the reading of the book of Deuteronomy. Moreover, in the midrash on Psalm 119 (*Midrash Tehillim*) there are twenty-one quotations from Deuteronomy.

Other scholars have long noted numerous relationships between the order of the psalms and the reading of the Torah in the triennial cycle, as well as the interplay and the relationship with the festival calendar in the placement of numerous psalms. Moreover, this interplay of readings from the Psalms, Torah lections, and the festival cycle can be seen in numerous instances in the rabbinical Midrash on the book of Psalms (*Midrash Tehillim*). For example, the midrash on Psalms 17 and 18 contains homiletical material that is almost impossible to explain apart from the association of these psalms with the triennial cycle. Psalms 17 and 18 were read early in the month of Ab. In the Jewish liturgical calendar, mourning over the destruction of the First Temple by the Babylonians (and later of the Second Temple by the Romans) took place during the weeks extending from the seventeenth day of the fourth month (Tammuz) until the ninth of the following month (Ab). The Temple was burned at this time (2 Kgs 25:8 = Jer 52:12), and a fast mourning its destruction developed at the time of the Babylonian Exile (Zech 7:1–5). In the midrash on Psalm 17, there is a long homily that concludes with a warning regarding the necessity to mourn for the Temple and the possible punishment for failure to mourn (see W. G. Braude, The Midrash on Psalms, vol. 2 [New Haven: Yale Uiversity Press, 1959], pp. 204 –29). Moreover, the midrashic exposition on verse 11 interprets the text in terms of Nebuchadnezzar, his successors, and the Babylonian looting of the Temple. The interpretation is then extended in the following section (17:12) and is related to Esau, because of the participation of Edom (= Esau) in the destruction of Solomon's Temple, and to Remus and Romulus as representatives of wicked Rome who, of course, burned the Second Temple in 70 C.E. In similar fashion, the midrash on Psalm 18 contains long discourses on the destruction of Jerusalem and the city's fate. The midrashic discussion on 18:11 refers specifically to the burning of the Temple and its subsequent fate. Numerous other close parallels between the content of individual psalms and the corresponding Torah reading of the triennial cycle of Palestinian Judaism have been noted.

One further illustration merits comment here. E. G. King says: "In the first year of the cycle the readings from Genesis would have reached chap. xi, i.e. the Story of Babel and the *Confusion of Tongues,* at the season of Pentecost. Now it is certain that the writer of Acts ii associated the Confusion of Tongues with the Day of Pentecost, the Gift of the Spirit being a reversal of the curse of Babel" ("The Influence of the Triennial Cycle upon the Psalter," *Journal of Theological Studies* 5 [1904], p. 205). In the second year of the cycle, the Ten Commandments were read on Pentecost, which explains the traditional association of Pentecost with the giving of the Torah. Exodus 34 was read near the 29th of Ab, eighty days after Pentecost, and the eighty days are accounted for by the two periods of forty days before and after the sin of the golden calf. In Exodus 34:28 we find specific reference to the Ten Commandments. Moreover, in the third year of the cycle, the reading of Deuteronomy in which the Ten Commandments are given began on that very day.

Job—A "Crypto-Patriarch"

Within the legends of the Jews, as preserved in the Talmud, the relationship between Job and Abraham is not consistent. On the one hand, Job is identified as a grandson of Jacob's brother Esau (Edom)—and thus a great-great-grandson of Abraham. At the same time, he is also described as the brother of Buz, who is a nephew of Abraham (Gen 22:21), which would make Job the nephew of Abraham as well. Moreover, Job is also identified as a worthy addition to the familiar triad of Abraham, Isaac, and Jacob (Israel)—the "patriarchs" of Jewish tradition. If Job had not murmured against God during his great trial, the distinction would have been conferred upon him of having his name joined to the name of God in prayer. People would have called upon the God of Job as they have called upon the God of Abraham, Isaac, and Jacob. But he was not found steadfast like the three Fathers, and he forfeited the honor God had intended for him by remonstrating against God.

In Jewish tradition, Job was the most pious Gentile who ever lived. He was king of Edom, the land wherein wicked plans were concocted against God, wherefore his home was also known as the land of Uz, which means "counsel." Job's four friends were related to each other, and each one was related to Job as well. Eliphaz, who was king of Teman, was a son of Esau. Bildad and Zophar were also identified as kings. Bildad, Zophar, and Elihu were cousins and their fathers, Shuah, Naamat, and Barachael, were brothers—the sons of Buz, the nephew of Abraham (Gen 22:21).

Job's first wife, who was named Zitidos, died during the years of his trials before the restoration of Job. Job subsequently married a second wife, Dinah, the daughter of Jacob, who bore him seven sons and three daughters. Thus Job was also the son-in-law of Jacob and brother-in-law of the twelve sons of Jacob who make up the twelve tribes of Israel.

In the book of Genesis, Jacob and Esau are presented as twin brothers and the eponymous ancestors of Israel and Edom, respectively:

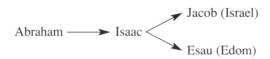

Job belongs within this ancient tradition as a sort of "crypto-patriarch" (hidden or secret patriarch), a model of righteousness comparable to and complimentary to Abraham. The 140 years allotted to Job after his restoration (Job 42:16) is part of a larger pattern that associates that number with the patriarchs. Abraham was 140 years old when his son Isaac married Rebekah; Isaac and Rebekah were married for 140 years; and Jacob was 140 years old at the time of his wrestling match at the Jabbok River when his name was changed to Israel (Gen 32). And, of course, Jacob's twin brother Esau (Edom) was also 140 years old at the decisive reunion of the estranged brothers. Placing Job within this schema makes him the literary counterpart of Abraham, as suggested in the following diagram:

Job		Jacob (Israel)
	Isaac and Rebekah	
Abra(ha)m		Esau (Edom)

The fact that the home of Job and his three friends is strongly associated with Edom takes on deeper meaning, for Edom is thus potentially included within the "New Israel" of prophetic vision, much like Moab in the story of Ruth. In short, from a canonical point of view, Job is the oldest of the patriarchs in the book of Genesis, one who lives long enough to see his "children's children to the fourth generation" (Job 42:16). His three daughters are named, while his seven sons are left anonymous. Though the father of Abraham in the Genesis narrative is Terah (Gen 11:31), it is possible to see here a parallel of sorts to the statement of Jesus: "I tell you God is able from these stones to raise up children of Abraham" (Matt 3:9). God is also able to provide a new kinsman for Abra(ha)m, out of the dust of the past, in the person of the legendary figure of Job—this foreigner, whose name has been explained by W. F. Albright to mean, "Where is (my) father?" (Nashville: Abingdon, *Interpreter's Dictionary of the Bible* [1962], vol. 2, p. 911).

The content of the book of Job may be outlined in a menorah pattern within a menorah pattern as follows:

The Book of Job in a Menorah Pattern	*Job 1—42*
A Introduction: Job in his original happiness	1:1–5
B Two conversations of Yahweh with Satan	1:6–2:13
C Discourse among Job and his three friends	3:1–27:23
X **Wisdom interlude and Job's final defense**	28:1–31:40
C´ Four discourses of Elihu–he proclaims God's majesty	32:1–37:24
B´ Two conversations of Yahweh with Job from the whirlwind	38:1–42:6
A´ Conclusion: Job's final contentment	42:7–17

2nd Level Menorah: Wisdom Interlude and Job's Final Defense	*Job 28—31*
A Wisdom interlude: God alone knows the way to wisdom	28:1–28
B Job's former estate: He remembers his happy past	29:1–25
C Job's present humiliation: My former friends "make sport of me"	30:1–15
X **Job describes his plight: "I have become like dust and ashes"**	30:16–23
C´ Job's self-lament: "I go about in sunless gloom" (v. 28)	30:24–31
B´ Job's innocence reiterated in the form of a negative confession	31:1–40b
A´ The words of Job are ended	31:40c

In the structural center of the book of Job we find an interlude on wisdom that raises the question: "Where then does wisdom come from?" (Job 28:20). Its value is beyond price (Job 28:12–19), much like the kingdom of heaven in Jesus' parable of the pearl of great price (Matt 13:45–46). God alone "understands the way of it, and he [alone] knows its place" (Job 28:23). The matter is summed up as follows: "Truly, the fear of Yahweh, that is wisdom; and to depart from evil is understanding" (Job 28:28). For his final defense, Job continues to maintain his innocence (Job 29—31), which he has done from the outset. He accuses his former friends of making sport of him (30:1–15), lamenting the fact that he goes about in sunless gloom (30:24–31). And in the center of the book he says he has "become like dust and ashes" (30:19), which anticipates his final words at the end of the book. When God speaks from the whirlwind, Job responds with the words: "I despise myself and repent in dust and ashes" (42:6).

It was Yahweh himself who handed Job over to Satan for two series of testings, in which everything he valued was taken from him. At the outset, we learn that Job was a "blameless and upright" man (1:1–5); and he did not change his ways—"in all this Job did not sin with his lips" (2:10). The opening section on the testing of Job may be outlined as follows:

Testing of Job by Satan—on "Blessing" and "Cursing"	*Job 1:1—2:13*
A Job introduced as the main figure	1:1–3
B Job and his children—theme of "blessing" God	1:4–5
C First episode in heaven: Will Job "bless" God?	1:6–12
X The series of disasters	1:13–22
C´ Second episode in heaven: Will Job "bless" God?	2:1–8
B´ Job and his wife—theme of "blessing" God	2:9–10
A´ Job's three friends are introduced as supporting actors	2:11–13

On four occasions here (1:5, 11; 2:5, 9) we find an interesting literary device in the Hebrew language called amphibology, in which the words used ("to bless") are to be understood with the opposite intent (i.e., "to curse"). The usage comes from the fact that it is considered inappropriate to "curse God" in the language of ancient Israel. To express this idea, the euphemism "to bless" is used instead (cf. also the two examples in the story of Naboth's vineyard in 1 Kgs 21:10–13, where two scoundrels are hired by Jezebel to accuse Naboth in court of having "cursed" God and king). The

Hebrew word here is *berak*, which means, "to bless." In the text of Job, the usage appears four times: once on the lips of Job himself (1:5), twice on the lips of Satan (1:11 and 2:5), and once more on the lips of Job's wife (2:9). Within the larger design of the book of Job as a whole, we find a note of irony here; Elihu later urges Job to give praise to God (36:24), as does Bildad by way of example in his hymn of praise in Job 25. Job's wife, in particular, speaks more than she knows when she says, "*curse (barek)* God and die" (2:9). When these words are taken at face value, they provide the way through Job's suffering. When Job finally chooses to "bless God" by means of praise, God intervenes to give life and the restoration of his fortunes.

The series of discourses between Job and his three friends makes up more than half of the entire book. Together with the introductory chapter, in which Job curses "his day" (i.e., the day of his birth and the day of trouble), this section may be outlined as follows:

Discourse Among Job and His Three Friends in a Menorah Pattern	Job 3—27
A Job curses "his day" (day of his birth and day of troubles)	3:1-26
B 1st speech of Eliphaz: Job has sinned, so God has disciplined him	4:1—5:27
C Job's 1st response: My complaints are just	6:1—7:21
X **Job is accused by his friends who insist he should repent**	8:1—22:30
C´ Job's 7th response: He renews his search for God's presence	23:1—24:25
B´ Bildad's praise and question with God's response	25:1—26:14
A´ Job continues to insist on his own righteousness	27:1-23

2nd Level Menorah: Job Is Accused by His Friends	Job 8—22
A 1st speech of Bildad: Job should repent	8:1-22
B Job's 2nd response: There is no mediator/I loathe my life	9:1—10:22
C 1st speech of Zophar: God is lenient	11:1-20
X **Job's 3rd, 4th, and 5th responses—reaffirms his innocence**	12:1—19:29
C´ 2nd speech of Zophar: Wickedness receives retribution	20:1-29
B´ Job's 6th response: The wicked remain unpunished	21:1-34
A´ 3rd speech of Eliphaz: Job's wickedness is great	22:1-30

3rd Level Menorah: Job Reaffirms His Innocence	*Job 12—19*
A Job's 3rd response (in sarcasm): I am a laughing stock	12:1–14:22
B 2nd speech of Eliphaz: Job undermines religion	15:1–35
C Job's personal lament: he complains against God	16:1–17
X **Job's 4th response: He appeals to earth and sky as witnesses**	16:18–22
C´ Job's personal lament—he describes his piteous condition	17:1–16
B´ 2nd speech of Bildad: God punishes the wicked	18:1–21
A´ Job's 5th response: "I know that my redeemer lives" (v. 25)	19:1–29

In the detail of this concentric structure, it becomes clear that the primary structuring device in the series of discourses between Job and his friends is the sequence of seven responses on Job's part. Within the larger concentric design, the two speeches of Zophar occupy corresponding positions (Job 11 and 20), as a frame around Job's third, fourth, and fifth responses. Moreover, the three speeches of Eliphaz and Bildad are arranged to balance each other in each instance: Job 4—5 (Eliphaz) and 25 (Bildad), Job 8 (Bildad) and 22 (Eliphaz), and Job 15 (Eliphaz) and 18 (Bildad). Job's fourth response (the center of the structure), in which he continues to reaffirm his innocence (Job 16—17), anticipates both the concluding chapter in the rounds of discourse presented here (Job 27) and Job's final defense (Job 29—31).

Like the prophet Elijah in 1 Kings 17, the figure of Elihu appears out of nowhere. Suddenly, without warning or announcement of any sort, he is simply there on the scene with a God-given calling that plays an essential role in the larger story as it unfolds. The four speeches of Elihu may be outlined as follows:

The Four Speeches of Elihu	*Job 32—37*
A When Elihu saw there was no answer, he became angry	32:1–5
B 1st speech: His *apologia* and point-by-point refutation of Job	32:6–33:33
C 2nd speech: Presentation of Job's complaint against God	34:1–9
X **Elihu's thesis: The ways of God are ultimately just**	34:10–37
C´ 3rd speech: He answers Job's arguments to be in the right	35:1–16
B´ 4th speech: He defends justice and offers praise to God	36:1–37:13
A´ Elihu speaks personally to Job—anticipation of Yahweh's speeches	37:14–24

When Elihu steps on stage, he is an angry young man (32:1–5); but as he delivers his lengthy fourth address, Elihu's demeanor softens and his words contain the message Job needs to hear: namely, to praise God instead of continuing to bemoan his sorry fate (36:17–23).

Robert Gordis observes in the name of Elihu a play on the name of Eliyahu (Elijah) and a reflection on the theme of the return of the prophet Elijah as a forerunner of the Messiah in "the great and terrible day of Yahweh" of Malachi 4:5–6 (*The Book of Job* [New York: Jewish Theological Seminary of America, 1978]). The appearance of Elihu just before the great theophany in which Yahweh speaks from the whirlwind in Job 38—41 evokes for Gordis the theme of Elijah's experience when he ascends in a whirlwind into heaven (2 Kgs 2:11).

Yahweh's two speeches, which are filled with sarcasm, and the subsequent restoration of Job's fortunes in Job 38—42 may be outlined in a menorah pattern:

Yahweh's Two Speeches and the Restoration of Job	*Job 38—42*
A Opening challenge: "Who is this that darkens counsel?"	38:1–3
B 1st speech from whirlwind: Questions about created order	38:4–39:30
C Yahweh invites Job to respond	40:1–2
X **Job wisely chooses silence: "I will not answer"**	40:3–5
C´ Yahweh answers Job out of the whirlwind	40:6
B´ 2nd speech from whirlwind: Questions about Job's power	40:6—41:34
A´ Restoration of Job: Fortunes restored twofold, his three daughters	42:1–17

The revelation of God's glory is associated with thick darkness in the Torah, when "Moses drew near to the thick darkness where God was" (Exod 20:21), and the awesome silence in the Former Prophets, when God appeared to Elijah in "a sound of sheer silence" (1 Kgs 19:12). These two images are brought together here: Job is responsible for the "darkness" by uttering "words without knowledge" (38:1). By choosing silence (40:3–5), Job finally finds the way through the darkness "to the dwelling of light" where God is (38:19–24)—for, in the fullness of time, it becomes increasingly clear that "God is light and in him is no darkness at all" (1 John 1:5).

The idea of suffering as discipline is introduced earlier in the book of Job by Eliphaz, in his first speech (5:17–27), which forms an inclusion with the extended speeches of Elihu. As Marvin Pope notes, "It is hard to find anything new in Elihu's bombast" (*Job*, Anchor Bible 15 [1973], p. lxxix). It is in the two speeches of Yahweh out of the whirlwind that we find the climax to the book as a whole. The content of God's answer to Job's affirmation of innocence and his challenge to God to explain his ways comes as a surprise ending to this marvelous epic poem. The issue as Job poses it is completely ignored. Instead, God turns the tables and subjects Job to questioning. Job has already expressed his awe and wonder at God's power, a wonder that is presented in exquisite hymns on human finitude and divine majesty. Job does not question God's omnipotence, however, but rather his justice and mercy.

In short, the book of Job is a profound theological treatise on the Torah and the Prophets within the canon of the Tanakh. Job takes his place in terms of sacred history as an elder "kinsman" of Abraham, and thus the book of Job forms a grand inclusion with Genesis 11:29 and 22:20–21. Abram and Nahor are brothers, the sons of Terah. "Abram and Nahor took wives; the name of Abram's wife was Sarai, and the name of Nahor's wife was Milcah" (Gen 11:29). "Now after these things it was told Abraham, "Milcah has borne children to your brother Nahor: Uz the firstborn, Buz his brother" (Gen 22:20–21). And Job is the brother of Buz. Placing Job in the land of Uz makes him "firstborn" in a theological sense, namely that he is "prior to Abraham" and contemporary with Abram. Moreover, among the grandsons of Buz, at least in Jewish tradition, are three of Job's colleagues: Bildad, Zophar, and Elihu. Eliphaz is the eldest son of Esau and his Hittite wife Adah (Gen 36:4, 10–11, 15; 1 Chron 1:35–36; cf. Job 2:11; 4:1; 15:1; 22:1; 42:7, 9). Bildad is the son of Shuah, a son of Abraham by Keturah (Gen 25:2). Zophar is the son of Naamat (Job 2:11; 11:1; 20:1; 42:9), who according to Jewish tradition is Shuah's brother. And Elihu is the "son of Barachel the Buzite, of the family of Ram" (Job 32:2). Is it mere coincidence that Ram is listed as an ancestor of David in Ruth 4:19 and 1 Chronicles 2:9; and as an ancestor of Jesus, according to Matthew 1:3–4 (who is given the name of Arni in Luke 3:33)?

The Book of Proverbs

In the remarkable figure of Lady Wisdom, the author of the book of
Proverbs takes the reader beyond the pages of the Torah to a point in
time before the words recorded in the first words of Genesis:

> Yahweh created me at the beginning of his work, the first of his
>   acts of old—
>   ages ago I was set up, at the first, before the beginning of the
>   earth . . .
> When he established the heavens, I was there,
>   when he drew a circle on the face of the deep,
>   when he made firm the skies above,
>   when he established the fountains of the deep,
>   when he assigned to the sea its limits,
>   so that the waters might not transgress his command,
>   when he marked out the foundations of the earth—
> Then I was beside him, like a master workman, and I was daily his
>   delight,
>   rejoicing before him always,
>   rejoicing in his inhabited world and delighting in the sons of
>   men. (Prov 8:22–31)

In some respects, the situation is comparable to the book of Job,
which explores the world of the patriarchs and matriarchs of Genesis
on a larger scale—among the nations of the world. And thus the land
of Edom takes its place as part of the "extended family" of God's
chosen people. But the author of Proverbs goes much further by
choosing an adaptation of the wisdom literature of ancient Egypt as
the structural center of a collection of proverbs traditionally associated with the person of Solomon.

The "thirty sayings" within the "words of the wise" in Proverbs
22:17—24:34 are of the same format as "The Instruction of Amenemope" in the wisdom literature of ancient Egypt. It is possible to
explain this borrowing of a foreign collection of proverbs in terms of
the cultural tradition Pharaoh's daughter brought with her to Jerusalem when she became Solomon's wife (1 Kgs 3:1). On the other

hand, the phenomenon may simply be part of the larger canonical process that places the whole of the sacred traditions of ancient Israel among the nations—with a mission to those nations. The "foreign" material becomes the focus of interest. In short, the book of Proverbs is a conscious literary link intended to bridge the world of the Torah and the Former Prophets (through the figure of Solomon) with that of the wisdom tradition in Israel.

The book of Proverbs is divided into five parts according to the headings in the Hebrew text to give a structure somewhat like that of the book of Psalms, which may be outlined as follows:

Proverbs in a Five-Part Concentric Structure		*Prov 1–31*
A Wisdom discourses—personification as Lady Wisdom	Book 1	1:1–9:18
B Proverbs of Solomon—original Solomonic collection	Book 2	10:1–22:16
X **Words of the wise [cf. "Instruction of Amenemope"]**	Book 3	22:17–24:34
B´ Proverbs of Solomon—copied by Hezekiah's officials	Book 4	25:1–29:27
A´ Words of Agur and Lemuel/Ode to a Virtuous Woman	Book 5	30:1–31:31

The center of this structure, which is identified as "the words of the wise" (22:17) or "the sayings of the wise" (24:23), contains "thirty sayings of admonition and knowledge" (22:20), the content of which is dependent on the "thirty chapters" of the Egyptian "Instructions of Amenemope." Both works follow the same format, with a general introduction followed by thirty "chapters" of surprisingly similar advice on specific topics.

In Proverbs 1—9 we find a coherent picture of a "father's instruction" (1:8) to his son, which is set over against the personification of "Lady Wisdom" (1:20–33 and 8:1—9:6) whose teaching is the same as that of the "father."

Wisdom Discourses—Personification as Lady Wisdom	*Prov 1—9*
A Warning against men whose greed breeds violence	1:1–19
B Personification of Lady Wisdom—the value of wisdom	1:20–2:22
C Rewards of a disciplined life—"wisdom's way"(3:17; 4:11)	3:1–4:27
X **Avoid the "loose woman"—her ways lead to death**	5:1–23
C´ Warnings against vices, especially the folly of adultery	6:1–7:27
B´ Personification of Lady Wisdom	8:1–9:12
A´ Enticements of Lady Stupidity	9:13–18

This section of poems on Lady Wisdom, and her counterpart "Lady Stupidity" (9:13–18), is set over against another collection of wisdom poems in what we have called "book 5" (Prov 30—31). The "words of Agur son of Jakeh" (30:1) suggest that we have here what was originally non-Israelite wisdom, adapted to a new purpose. The concluding "Ode to a Virtuous Woman" (31:10–31) suggests that this entire block of material is to be read over against the figure of "Lady Wisdom" in Proverbs 1—9.

Half a century ago, Patrick Skehan observed that the total number of proverbs in the biblical collection was announced at the outset, in coded form, within the opening verse of the book. This observation grew out of the fact that there were 375 proverbs in book 2 (the original Solomonic collection) and that this is also the numerical value of Solomon's name in the Hebrew language. The title in the opening verse of the book of Proverbs is "Proverbs of *Solomon,* son of David, king of *Israel.* The numerical value of the word *Solomon* in Hebrew is 375; and the numerical value of the word *Israel* is 541. The sum of these two numbers is 916, which is the number of proverbs (or versets) in the standard critical edition of the text of the book, if 24:12 is counted as two versets, since it contains two poetic "lines."

The conclusion that "book 3" is a later insertion into an already existing collection of proverbs associated with Solomon (the "deuteronomic" collection) is based on the observation that when these proverbs are removed, the number of proverbs remaining is 833 (= 17 x 7 x 7).

Book 1	256 lines (or verses in BHS = *Biblia Hebraica Stuttgartensia)*
Book 2	375 lines (= numerical value of the name "Solomon")
Book 4	138 lines (= numerical value of the name "Hezekiah")
Book 5	64 lines (= 256 divided by 4)

Total	833 lines (or verses in BHS) [= 17 x 7 x 7]

An original Solomonic collection of proverbs was in use in ancient Israel before 700 B.C.E. To this collection "officials of King Hezekiah of Judah" added other "proverbs of Solomon" (Prov 25:1). The first canonical edition of the book of Proverbs appeared in the deutero-nomic canon (ca. 500 B.C.E.) with a collection of 833 proverbs (= 17 x 7 x 7). The canonical process was completed with the formation of the Tanakh in the time of Ezra (ca. 400 B.C.E.), when "book 3" (Prov 22:17—24:34) was inserted to form the book as we now have it.

Solomonic Collection →	*Deuteronomic Collection* →	*Pentateuchal Collection*
Books 2 and 4	Addition of Books 1 and 5	Addition of Book 3
Ca. 700 B.C.E.	Ca. 500 B.C.E.	Ca. 400 B.C.E.

The Festal Scrolls *(Megilloth)*:
Ruth, Song of Songs, Ecclesiastes, Lamentations, Esther

Lamentations, which commemorates the fall of Jerusalem in August 586 B.C.E. marks the beginning of the canonical process that pro-duced the Festal Scrolls. The second step was apparently the writing of the book of Ruth, which is closely tied to both the ending of the book of Proverbs and the book of Jonah. The book of Ruth is associ-ated with Pentecost Sunday (the Feast of Weeks) in the third month (Sivan) and the book of Jonah with the Day of Atonement in the sev-enth month (10 Tishri).

Scroll:	*Ruth* ⟶	*Lamentations* ⟶	*Jonah*
Feast/Fast:	Pentecost	9th of Ab	Day of Atonement
	3rd month	5th month	7th month (10 Tishri)

The book of Ruth anticipates Lamentations in that the conclusion reached in the center of the book of Lamentations that God will not reject his people forever (Lam 3:31–33) is essentially the message of Naomi when she blesses her daughter-in-law Ruth. Naomi declares: "Blessed be (Boaz) by Yahweh, whose kindness has not forsaken the living or the dead!" (Ruth 2:20). At the same time, Ruth is explicitly described in terms of the "virtuous woman" (*'eshet hayil*) of Proverbs 31:10–31. "She rises while it is still night and provides food for her household...Her lamp does not go out at night. She puts her hand to the distaff, and her hands hold the spindle" (Prov 31:15, 18–19). Boaz observes that quality in Ruth and describes her as a "virtuous woman" ('*eshet hayil*) in Ruth 3:11. It should be noted that this particular phrase in the Hebrew Bible appears only in Proverbs and Ruth, and that the reader needs to turn only a single page in *The Leningrad Codex* to get from Proverbs 31:10 to this statement on the part of Boaz.

The next step in the growth of the Festal Scrolls was the addition of Song of Songs and Ecclesiastes as the scrolls for the Festival of Passover and the Festival of Booths respectively. Within the canonical process in ancient Israel, the book of Jonah subsequently took its place among the Latter Prophets within the Book of the Twelve (Lesser Prophets). The book of Esther became the fifth Festal scroll in the time of Ezra during the establishment of the twenty-two-book "pentateuchal" canon of the Tanakh.

Esther is used in the Festival of Purim, which was never considered to be on the same level as the three pilgrimage festivals of earlier times. Consequently, Esther was not always considered fully canonical in ancient Judaism. The end result was that the concept of the five Festal Scrolls as a single canonical category disappeared in the course of events in the centuries between the time of Ezra (ca. 400 B.C.E.) and the compilation of the Mishna (ca. 200 C.E.)—the section of the Talmud consisting of oral laws edited by Rabbi Judah ha-Nasi. The translation of the Hebrew Bible into Greek (the Septuagint), which took place from ca. 300 to ca. 100 B.C.E., played a role in this process as the individual Festal Scrolls were distributed in various ways within the canon itself in this new translation. In short, the original structure of the twenty-two-book "pentateuchal" canon known as the Tanakh [= Torah + Prophets + Writings] was displaced by other ways of thinking about the nature and structure of the Bible as a whole.

Just as the destruction of the Temple in Jerusalem plays a decisive role in the shaping of the Latter Prophets, that tragic event marks the beginning of the historical process that produced the five Festal Scrolls as a canonical category. By the end of the sixth century B.C.E., the four Festal Scrolls in the seventeen-book deutero-nomic canon were apparently structured in a simple chiasm as fol-lows: /Ruth / Song of Songs / / Ecclesiastes / Lamentations /. A cen-tury later, in the time of Ezra and Nehemiah, the book of Esther took its place as the fifth of the Festal Scrolls.

The Growth of the Festal Scrolls (Megilloth)

Destruction of Jerusalem	→	Deuteronomic Collection	→	Pentateuchal Collection
Lamentations		Ruth, Song of Songs, and Ecclesiastes		Addition of Esther
Ca. 586 B.C.E.		Ca. 500 B.C.E.		Ca. 400 B.C.E.

It is useful to keep in the mind the order of the various feasts and fasts within the Jewish calendar and the specific biblical texts asso-ciated with each of these events.

Feasts/Fasts in Judaism	Calendar Date	Month	Biblical Text
Passover and Unleavened Bread	14–21 Nissan	1st [Mar–Apr]	Song of Songs
Weeks (Pentecost)	Sunday in Sivan	3rd [May–June]	Ruth
Destruction of the Temple	9 Ab	5th [July–Aug]	Lamentations
Day of Atonement (*Yom Kippur*)	10 Tishri	7th [Sept–Oct]	Jonah
Booths/Tabernacles (*Succoth*)	15–22 Tishri	7th	Ecclesiastes
Simchat Torah (end of Torah cycle)	23 Tishri	7th	
Hanukkah (cleansing of Temple)	25 Kislev	9th [Nov–Dec]	Daniel?
Purim	14–15 Adar	12th [Feb–Mar]	Esther

Though there is no clear evidence that the book of Daniel was ever used as the Festal Scroll for the Feast of Dedication (Hanukkah), it is treated as though it were a sequel to the other five in the editorial arrangement of these texts in *The Leningrad Codex*. Moreover, the cleansing of the Temple in the time of Judas Maccabee is occasioned by "the abomination that makes desolate" (Dan 12:11), which is a primary theme of this book.

The concentric structural relationship between the four Festal Scrolls of the seventeen-book deuteronomic canon is evident in the following outline, which follows the order of these four books in *The Leningrad Codex* (and *Biblia Hebraica Stuttgartensia*):

"The Lord has not forsaken the living or the dead" (2:20)   *Ruth 1–4*

A   Ruth chooses to leave Moab and go to Bethlehem in Judah   1:1–22

B   Ruth seeks favor with Boaz as a "virtuous woman"   2:1–16

X   **Yahweh's blessing—not forsaking the living or the dead**   2:17—3:5

B´   Ruth finds favor with Boaz as a "virtuous woman"   3:6–18

A´ Ruth becomes the great-grandmother of David   4:1–22

"Eat, companions... become drunk, O lovers" (5:1)   *Song 1–8*

A   Opening dialogue: A woman and a man long for each other   1:1—2:7

B   A man and a woman extol each other's beauty   2:8–5:1a

X   **Coda: "Eat, companions, drink and become drunk, O lovers"**   5:1b

B´   A man and a woman extol each other's beauty   5:2—8:4

A´ Closing dialogue: A woman and a man long for each other   8:5–14

"Be satisfied with what you have" (6:9)   *Eccl 1–12*

A   Opening poem on vanity of toil with double introduction   1:1–18

B   Investigation of life: All is vanity and a chasing after wind   2:1—6:8

X   **Proverb: "Be satisfied with what you have"**   6:9—7:14

B´   Conclusion: Rejoice in what you have and fear God   7:15—9:12

A´ Concluding poem on old age and death (+ epilogue)   9:13—12:14

"The Lord will not abandon you forever" (3:31)   *Lam 1–5*

A   The desolation of Zion   1:1–22

B   Yahweh has done what he purposed   2:1–22

X   **Yahweh will not reject forever**   3:1–66

B´   Zion's children are ravaged by Yahweh's own wrath   4:1–22

A´ Remember us and restore us, O Yahweh!   5:1–22

The outside pair in this structure presents a common theme at the
center of Ruth and Lamentations: Yahweh has not forsaken the living or the dead (Ruth 2:17—3:5); indeed, he will not reject forever
(Lam 3:1–66). In like manner, the inner pair also has essentially the
same theme in the two centers: "Eat, companions, drink and become
drunk, O lovers" (Song 5:1b), and "Be satisfied with what you have"
(Eccl 6:9—7:14).

The Book of Ruth

Stephen Bertman explored the concentric structure of the book of Ruth in 1965 (*Journal of Biblical Literature* 84 [1965], pp. 165–68). Since then numerous other scholars have carried the discussion further. For our purposes here, the concentric design of the book as a whole may be outlined in a menorah pattern as follows:

Ruth in a Menorah Pattern—Story of a "Virtuous Woman"	Ruth 1—4
A Naomi leaves Bethlehem in time of famine—family tragedy in Moab	1:1–5
B Ruth goes with Naomi to Bethlehem	1:6–21
C Naomi and Ruth arrive in Bethlehem at time of barley harvest	1:22
X **Ruth the "virtuous woman" becomes a blessing in Israel**	2:1–3:18
C´ Boaz "redeems" Ruth at the gate of the town of Bethlehem	4:1–10
B´ The elders at the gate of the town of Bethlehem bless Ruth	4:11–16
A´ The "son of Naomi" (4:17) becomes the great-grandfather of David	4:17–22

2nd Level Menorah: Ruth—A "Virtuous Woman" Is a Blessing	Ruth 2—3
A Ruth seeks favor with Boaz by showing that she is a "virtuous woman"	2:1–16
B God blesses Ruth through Boaz—an ephah of barley	2:17–18
C Naomi asks Ruth: "Where did you glean today?"	2:19
X **Blessing: "Yahweh has not forsaken the living or the dead"**	2:20
C´ Ruth reports the words of Boaz: "[Glean] close by my servants"	2:21–23
B´ Ruth's future blessing by God through Boaz anticipated	3:1–5
A´ Ruth finds favor with Boaz by showing she is a "virtuous woman"	3:6–18

As this outline suggests, the story of Ruth is integrally related to the acrostic poem on the "virtuous woman" in Proverbs 31:10–31. That poem begins with the question, "A 'virtuous woman' (אשת־חיל) who can find?" The Hebrew phrase אשת־חיל appears only three times in the Bible—in Proverbs 12:4, 31:10, and Ruth 3:11. On the one hand, Boaz asks the question, "Who is this woman (הנערה הזאת מי)" (2:5). The corresponding phrase in Proverbs 31:10 is "who can find (מי ימצא)" a "virtuous woman"? When Boaz awakes on the threshing floor, he finds Ruth "lying at his feet" and he says, "Who are you? (מִי־אָתְּ)" (Ruth 3:9). Boaz then adds these words, "all the assembly of my people know that you are a 'virtuous woman'" (3:11).

The structure of the acrostic poem in Proverbs 31:10–31 may be outlined in a menorah pattern as follows:

Poem on the "Virtuous Woman" in a Menorah Pattern	Prov 31:10–31
A Who can find a "virtuous woman"?	31:10
B Her husband trusts her; she does him good all the days of her life	31:11–12
C She makes provision for her household—with no idleness	31:13–19
X **The "virtuous woman" is a blessing to others**	31:20–26
C´ She makes provision for her household—with no idleness	31:27
B´ Her husband praises her: "You surpass them all"	31:28–29
A´ Conclusion: "Let her works praise her in the city gates"	31:30–31

2nd Level Menorah: The "Virtuous Woman" Is a Blessing	Prov 31:20–26
A She shows generosity to those in need	31:20
B She does not fear the future—her household are clothed in crimson	31:21
C She makes herself clothing of fine linen and purple	31:22
X **Her husband is known in the city gates among the elders**	31:23
C´ She makes linen garments and sells them	31:24
B´ She prepares for the future—"strength and dignity are her clothing"	31:25
A´ She speaks wisdom and teaches kindness	31:26

By means of an extension of the law of the levirate marriage in Deuteronomy 25:5–10, Ruth provides a "son" to Naomi (see Ruth 4:17) and her son Mahlon, the deceased husband of Ruth. This son becomes the grandfather of David. As the "virtuous woman" of Proverbs 31, Ruth brings honor to her husband Boaz and a blessing to all the people. As Naomi foresaw, Yahweh "has not forsaken the living or the dead" (Ruth 2:20).

The Song of Songs (or Song of Solomon)

William Shea explored the concentric structural design of the Song of Songs in 1980 (*Zeitschrift für die alttestamentliche Wissenschaft* 92 [1980], pp. 378–96). Nonetheless, most critical scholars continue to deny that the book has any discernible structure. It is generally assumed that the book is an anthology of love poems, made up of from seven to forty-four discrete literary units or individual songs. The analysis presented here stands in sharp contrast with that majority view, holding that the Song of Songs is unified structurally. The Song of Songs displays an elaborate concentric structural pattern, which may be outlined in a menorah pattern:

Song of Songs in a Menorah Pattern: A Dramatic Love Poem	*Song 1—8*
A Introduction: The maiden longs for her lover	1:1–4
B Maiden: My own vineyard I have not kept	1:5–8
C Dialogue: Lovers express their desire for each other	1:9–2:17
X **Lovers express their desire for each other**	3:1–6:12
C´ Dialogue: Lovers express their desire for each other	7:1–8:10
B´ Youth: Not even Solomon's vineyard can compare to my vineyard	8:11–12
A´ The lover calls and the maiden answers	8:13–14

2nd Level Menorah: Lovers Express Desire for Each Other	*Song 3—6*
A Nighttime search by the woman and Solomon's wedding procession	3:1–11
B The man praises her matchless beauty	4:1–7
C The man urges his beloved to come away with him	4:8
X **Dialogue on lovemaking**	4:9–5:7
C´ Colloquy of women: "What makes your lover so special?"	5:8–10
B´ The woman praises her lover and the man praises his beloved	5:11–6:9
A´ The woman describes a journey in chariots with the prince	6:10–12

3rd Level Menorah: Dialogue on Lovemaking	*Song 4:9—5:7*
A The man praises his beloved: "How beautiful is your lovemaking"	4:9–11
B The man speaks: "A garden locked is my sister, my bride"	4:12–14
C The woman speaks: "Let my lover come to his garden"	4:15–5:1a

X	Riddle: "Eat, companions, drink and become drunk, O lovers	5:1b
C´	The man speaks: "Open to me, my sister, my companion"	5:2-3
B´	The woman speaks: "I myself arose to open to my lover"	5:4-5
A´	The man withdraws and the woman searches for him	5:6-7

The woman's lover in the Song of Songs is described in the term *dôd* (דוד), which may be interpreted symbolically as "David" (דוד), written in Hebrew with the same consonants. In this regard, one should note the Shulamite's description of her lover in response to the question asked by the daughters of Jerusalem: "My lover is radiant and ruddy/distinguished among ten thousand" (5:10). When the young David is first brought before the prophet Samuel, he is described as "ruddy," with a fine appearance and handsome features (1 Sam 16:12). And, after David has slain Goliath (1 Sam 18:7–8), the women dance and sing: "Saul has slain his thousands/and David his tens of thousands." This same refrain is repeated on the lips of the servants of Achish, king of Gath, after David flees from Saul (1 Sam 21:11). It appears a third time on the lips of the Philistine commanders shortly before the fateful battle on Mount Gilboa in which Saul and Jonathan are killed.

It is interesting to note that a medieval Jewish text represents Zerubbabel, a descendant of David, as God's herald in the messianic Garden of Eden (*Yalquty Shimon'oni* [thirteenth century C.E.]). Another striking passage is the Hanukkah hymn, "Mo'oztzur," attributed to Mordecai ben Isaac of the thirteenth century C.E., which recounts God's redemptive acts towards Israel with these words:

> Torn from all I cherished, almost had I perished;
> Babylon fell; Zerubbabel bad'st thou to restore me!

The seventeen-book deuteronomic canon of the Tanakh appeared in the time of Zerubbabel (ca. 550–500 B.C.E.). The Song of Songs was composed as the Festal Scroll for Passover within this historical setting—not to displace the traditional Passover tradition in Exodus 1—15, but to supplement it. The words of Song of Songs 3:6 thus take on double meaning: "Who is this going up from the wilderness like columns of smoke?" Taken in isolation, these words recall the ancient ritual of traditions about the "Wars of Yahweh," as remembered at Gilgal in the Passover ceremony of premonarchic Israel. But the words quickly shift their meaning within their own literary context.

> What is that coming up from the wilderness, like a column of
>   smoke,
>   perfumed with myrrh and frankincense,
>   with all the fragrant powders of the merchant?
> Behold, it is the litter of Solomon!
> About it are sixty warriors
>   of the warriors of Israel—
>   all girt with swords and expert in war,
>   each with his sword at his thigh against alarms by night.

The ancient Exodus-Eisodus tradition is linked to the Davidic dynasty and to Solomon in particular.

It is possible to see the woman (the Shulamite) in the Song of Songs as standing for Israel in a dramatic ritual of some sort. The shepherd/king imagery applies to both David and Solomon, and perhaps to some later king as well (i.e., Zerubbabel), who is joined with the Shulamite's little sister (8:8). The poem was composed for the Sabbath of the Passover celebration, which is its present canonical function within Judaism. The references to the "one going up from the wilderness like columns of smoke" (3:6) and the "one leaning on her lover" (8:5) refer to the celebration of the Exodus-Eisodus in the Passover tradition of premonarchic Israel. This is now linked to the institution of the kingship of David and Solomon, and perhaps Zerubbabel. The Song of Songs may then be the text for a specified "musical playlet" in ancient Israel, as surmised by Max Pusin (cited by Marvin Pope, *Song of Songs*, Anchor Bible, vol. 7C [Doubleday, 1977], pp. 133–34). The text became so fixed in actual worship in postexilic Judaism that misuse of it in the time of the so-called Council of Jamnia was not sufficient cause to abrogate its canonicity.

The Book of Ecclesiastes

In 1968, Addison Wright demonstrated that the structure of the book of Ecclesiastes is worked out mathematically in terms of the key word "vanity" (הבל in Hebrew), which has the numerical value of 37 and which appears 37 times in the book (*Catholic Biblical Quarterly* 42 [1980], pp. 313–33). There are 222 verses in the book—and the number 222 = 37 x 6. In the motto, as it appears in Ecclesiastes 1:2, the term "vanity" appears three times in the singular and twice in the plural within the space of eight words in the Hebrew text. Adding up the numerical value of each letter in the motto produces the number 216, the number of verses in the book without the epilogue of 12:9–14. The first word in the book, "words" (דברי in Hebrew) also has the numerical value of 216. Moreover, as Wright has suggested, the word ויתר, which introduces each of the two paragraphs in the epilogue (12:9, 12), may be translated "six additional . . . six additional," since the letter *waw* has the value of six. It is the author's way of indicating the addition of six additional verses, and 216 + 6 = 222 verses for the entire book. It should be also be noted that the numerical value of the five occurrences of the root "vanity" (הבל) in Ecclesiastes 1:2 is 185 (= 37 x 5), which corresponds to the number of verses in the so-called inner frame when the book is outlined in a five-part concentric structure.

Ecclesiastes in Five Parts: Six "Vanities" (6 x 37 = 222)		*Eccl 1—12*
A Outer frame (18 verses)	Poem on toil with double introduction	1:1–18
B Inner frame (92 verses)	Qoheleth's investigation of life	2:1–6:8
X Proverb (1 verse)	"Be satisfied with what you have"	6:9
B´ Inner frame (93 verses)	Qoheleth's conclusions	6:10–11:6
A´ Outer frame (18 verses)	Poem on youth and old age, with epilogue	11:7–12:14

The total number of verses in the outer frame plus the single verse in the center of this structure is 37 (= 18 + 1 + 18); and the number of verses in the inner frame is 185 (= 5 x 37). In content, the outer frame moves from a poem on the vanity of all human endeavors

(1:2–18) to a remarkable poem on old age that ends with repetition of the opening motto: "Vanity of vanities, says Qoheleth, all is vanity" (12:8, cf. 1:2). The inner frame presents a detailed investigation of life in terms of the futility of human toil (2:1—6:8), which is set over against the conclusions reached by Qoheleth that God's ways are inscrutable (6:10—11:6). And in the center we find a proverb: "Better is the sight of the eyes than the wandering of desire"—followed by the words: "This also is vanity and a chasing after wind" (6:9). In short, the reader is told to find satisfaction in what he or she already has.

Careful attention to mathematical detail allows the reader to discern another theme that is often missed by the average reader, that of joy. There are 111 verses in each half of the book. When the middle verse in each half of the book (the 56th verse) is located, we find the following:

> Thus I realized that the only worthwhile thing there is for them to *enjoy themselves* and do what is good in their lifetime; also, that whenever a man does eat and drink and *get enjoyment* out of all his wealth, it is a gift of God. (Eccl 3:12–13, *Tanakh*)

> Go, eat your bread in gladness, and drink your wine *in joy*; for your action was long ago approved by God. Let your clothes always be freshly washed, and your head never lack ointment. *Enjoy happiness* with a woman you love all the fleeting days of life that have been granted to you under the sun—all your fleeting days. For that alone is what you can get out of life and out of the means you acquire under the sun. (Eccl 9:7–9, *Tanakh*)

This theme of enjoying life by rejoicing in whatever blessings God has given is essentially the same message as that found in the proverb in the structural center of the book of Ecclesiastes (6:9). Moreover, this theme appears in four other places in the book, carefully positioned in terms of the overall structure.

The book of Ecclesiastes may be outlined in a menorah pattern:

Ecclesiastes in a Menorah Pattern: "All Is Vanity"	*Eccl 1—12*
A Prologue: Poem on toil—"all is vanity"	1:1–11
B All is vanity and a chasing after wind	1:12–3:22
C In the face of vanity remember to fear God	4:1–5:17
X **Be satisfied with what you have**	5:18–7:29
C´ Fear God despite the prosperity of the wicked	8:1–9:12
B´ Embrace the good, fear God, and keep his commandments	9:13–12:8
A´ Epilogue: "Fear God, and keep his commandments"	12:9–14

2nd Level Menorah: Be Satisfied with What You Have	*Eccl 5:18–12:14*
A It is fitting to find enjoyment in toil—this is the gift of God	5:18–20
B If one does not enjoy what he has, this is vanity	6:1–6
C The human condition: Toil does not satisfy the appetite	6:7–8
X **"Better is the sight of the eyes than the wandering of desire"**	6:9
C´ The human condition: Things are determined by God	6:10–12
B´ Critique of traditional wisdom on day of prosperity and adversity	7:1–14
A´ Critique of traditional wisdom on retribution ("Fear God" [7:18])	7:15–29

The proverb at the center of the book of Ecclesiastes is expanded in a menorah pattern within the larger menorah pattern of the book as a whole to express the primary theme of the book: Be satisfied with what you have. Since all is vanity and chasing after wind, what really matters is that we remember to fear God and keep his commandments.

There is a total of 18 verses in the prologue (1:1–12) plus the epilogue (12:9–14). When this number is subtracted from the total of 222 verses in the book as a whole, there are 204 (= 17 x 12) verses in the heart of the book. As a multiple of 17, the number 204 is similar to the totals for the book of Psalms and the book of Proverbs in the seventeen-book deuteronomic canon of sacred scripture, namely (119 = 17 x 7) psalms and 833 (= 17 x 7 x 7) proverbs.

One reading of Ecclesiastes suggested by the above outline is to take the prologue (1:1–12) and epilogue (12:9–14) in relation to the structural center (6:1—7:14). Toil alone accomplishes nothing, for all is vanity (1:2–3). Indeed, toil does not satisfy the appetite (6:7); and this is why the author exhorts us to be satisfied with what we have (6:9). In short, the whole duty demanded of us is summed up in the command to "Fear God, and keep his commandments" (12:13).

Since all is vanity and a chasing after wind (Eccl 1—3), the reasonable response for us is to embrace the good, fear God, and keep his commandments (9:13—12:8). And even though our toil is vain, we are to find enjoyment in that toil (2:24); for everything has its own place in time, as determined by God (3:1–22). In the face of the fact that all is vanity, we are admonished to fear God (Eccl 4—5) despite the fact that the wicked appear to prosper (7:15—9:12). And though one cannot discern between love and hate on the part of God, we are to "eat [our] bread with enjoyment, and drink [our] wine with a merry heart; for God has already approved what [we] do" (9:7).

The Book of Lamentations

The book of Lamentations consists of five poems patterned after the form of the laments in the book of Psalms. Norman Gottwald (*The Interpreter's Dictionary of the Bible,* vol. 3 [Nashville, Abingdon, 1962], p. 62) described its concentric literary structure as follows:

> Chaps. 1 and 5 are summaries of the disaster, chaps. 2 and 4 more explicit recitals of the details of death and devastation, while chap. 3 occupies the pivotal position in form (intensified acrostic) and content (trust in the goodness of God toward Israel). The strophes which are important from the standpoint of theology are central in the poem's structure and, consequently, the crux of the entire collection (3:31–36). The effect of the compilation has been to make everything lead up to the third poem and then flow away from it, thereby putting climax in the middle.

These poems were composed for an annual commemoration of the fall of Jerusalem. Events are seen through the eyes of Palestinian Jews who lived in the economically and spiritually depleted homeland between 586 and 538 B.C.E. In spite of the rather artificial form, the book of Lamentations attains remarkable emotional vitality. Though the form of the acrostic may have been chosen to facilitate memory, it also serves a psychological function in expressing the completeness of grief and despair—by exhausting the entire alphabet, it symbolically says all that can be said.

The content of the book of Lamentations may be outlined in a menorah pattern within a menorah pattern:

Lamentations in a Menorah Pattern: God's "Vengeance"	*Lam 1—5*
A Jerusalem remembers her days of misery	1:1–11
B A cry for help even though the punishment is justified	1:12–22
C Yahweh as enemy has destroyed land, city, and Temple	2:1–11
X **Yahweh's "vengeance"—he destroys but remains faithful**	2:12–4:11
C´ There is no one to turn to for help	4:12–22
B´ Remember us, O Yahweh, we are weary with hard labor	5:1–10
A´ Our dancing has been turned to mourning—renew our days as of old	5:11–22

2nd Level Menorah: Yahweh's "Vengeance" Includes Mercy	*Lam 2:12—4:11*
A Dying children, horror, jeers, and prayer	2:12–22
B Yahweh's anger: He lies in wait for me like a predatory animal	3:1–15
C Lament: "I say, 'Gone is my glory, and all that I hoped for'"	3:16–18
X **Yahweh's *hesed*: "Yahweh will not reject forever" (3:31)**	3:19–39
C´ Lament: "My eyes flow without ceasing…until Yahweh sees"	3:40–51
B´ We have sinned, but so have our enemies—pay them back	3:52–66
A´ Jerusalem has suffered a fate worse than that of Sodom	4:1–11

Reading from the outermost frame to the center we find that Jerusalem remembers her days of misery (1:1–11); for indeed, her dancing has been turned to mourning. And so she pleads with Yahweh to "renew our days as of old" (5:11–22). The cry for help is uttered even though she knows full well that the punishment is justified (1:12–22); and so she asks Yahweh to remember his people who are weary with hard labor (5:1–10). Yahweh himself is the one who has chosen to destroy Israel (2:1–11); and that is why there is no one to turn to for help (4:12–22). Violence and terror are present everywhere (2:12–22), for Jerusalem has suffered a fate worse than that of Sodom (4:1–11). Nonetheless, even though it was Yahweh who brought this great suffering on his people, the poet declares, "I still place my trust in him" (3:1–24). The suffering is justified, and so the poet admonishes, "Let us test and examine our ways, and return to

Yahweh. Let us lift up our hearts as well as our hands to God in heaven" (3:40–41). He then reflects on what the enemies have done and on God's response to his prayer (3:46–57), and he concludes with a surprising word of hope. The poet insists that, "The steadfast love of Yahweh never ceases, his mercies never come to an end; they are new every morning; *great is your faithfulness*" (3:22). For indeed "Yahweh will not cast off for ever, but, though he cause grief, he will have compassion according to the abundance of his steadfast love; for he does not willingly afflict or grieve the sons of men" (3:31–33).

The Book of Esther

The concentric structural design of the book of Esther is evident even to the cursory reader and has been explored through the years in different ways. In 1973, Yehudah Radday offered the following menorah pattern for the book of Esther as a whole (*Linguistica Biblica* 3 [1973], pp. 6–13):

Radday's Outline of the Book of Esther	Esth 1—10
A Opening and background	1:1–22
B The king's first decree	2:1–3:15
C The clash between Haman and Mordecai	4:1–5:14
X **Center: "On that night, the king could not sleep"**	6:1
C´ Mordecai's triumph over Haman	6:2–7:10
B´ The king's second decree	8:1–9:32
A´ Epilogue	10:1–3

It is also possible to see Esther's oft-quoted decision in 4:15–17 as the center in a three-level nested menorah pattern:

Purim: Esther and Mordecai Remember to "Hate the Amalekites"	Esth 1—10
A Setting: When Ahasuerus ruled in Susa over 127 provinces	1:1
B Feasts of Ahasuerus and Vashti, who is deposed	1:2–22
C Esther becomes queen—she and Mordecai save Ahasuerus's life	2:1–23
X **Mordecai and Esther turn the tables on Haman**	3:1–7:10

C´	Mordecai replaces Haman as vizier	8:1–2
B´	Purim is established in the 127 provinces of Ahasuerus' kingdom	8:3–9:32
A´	Epilogue: Mordecai continues in power under King Ahasuerus	8:9–10:3

2nd Level Menorah: The Tables Are Turned on Haman		**Esth 3—7**
A	Ahasuerus establishes Haman the Agagite as vizier	3:1
B	Mordecai refuses to do obeisance to Haman	3:2–5
C	Haman plots to destroy the Jews—"they cast Pur" to fix the date	3:6–15
X	**Esther risks her life to save the Jews from Haman**	4:1–5:14
C´	Haman honors Mordecai and is brought in haste to 2nd banquet	6:1–14
B´	Esther pleads for her people	7:1–6
A´	Haman pleads for his life and is impaled on his own execution "tree"	7:7–10

3rd Level Menorah: Esther Risks Her Life to Save the Jews		**Esth 4—5**
A	Mordecai learns of the plot against the Jews and informs Esther	4:1–3
B	Esther agrees to help the Jews	4:4–11
C	Mordecai asks Esther to go to the king	4:12–14
X	**Esther's decision: "Hold a fast ... If I perish, I perish"**	4:15–17
C´	Esther goes to the king and makes her request	5:1–4
B´	Esther prepares a banquet for King Ahasuerus and Haman	5:5–8
A´	Haman plans to have Mordecai impaled for all to see	5:9–14

In this reading, Esther's decision to risk her life to save her people becomes the center of the story as a whole. She tells her uncle Mordecai to "hold a fast on my behalf, and neither eat nor drink for three days, night or day... Then I will go to the king, though it is against the law; and if I perish, I perish" (4:16).

The innermost menorah pattern concludes with Haman's plan to have Mordecai impaled high on an execution "tree" for all to see (5:9–14). The second-level menorah pattern concludes with the execution of Haman on that very "tree" he prepared for Mordecai (7:7–10). The conclusion of the book of Esther in the first level menorah pattern is the establishment of the Festival of Purim in Persia (8:3—9:32), which is set over against three feasts on the part of Ahasuerus and his queen Vashti at the beginning of the story (1:2–9).

An important key to interpreting the meaning of the story of Esther is the reference to Haman as an Agagite, that is, a descendant of Agag, king of the Amalekites whom Saul was instructed to kill (1 Sam 15:7–9). Mordecai is presented as a descendant of Saul who completes the task his ancestor failed to accomplish. Behind this curious story lies the concluding law in the Central Core of the book of Deuteronomy—to remember to hate the Amalekites (Deut 25:17–19). The Amalekites are presented in the Torah as the paradigm of the enemy of the Jews, opposing the people of Israel from the very beginning of their journey in the Exodus from Egypt (Exod 17:8–16).

DANIEL:
BRIDGE CONNECTING PROPHECY, WISDOM, AND HISTORY

The book of Daniel is unique in two respects with regard to the canon of the Tanakh. In the first place, most of the book (2:4b—7:28) is written in Aramaic rather than in Hebrew.

Desecration of the Temple—Present and Future	*Dan 1—12*
A Hebrew: Desecration of Temple; Daniel and his three friends	1:1–2:4a
B Aramaic: Daniel, his three friends, and Nebuchadnezzar	2:4b–4:37
X **Aramaic core: Belshazzar desecrates the Temple vessels**	5:1–4
B´ Aramaic: Daniel, Belshazzar, and Darius—visions of four beasts	5:5–7:28
A´ Hebrew: Daniel's visions—to the final desecration of the Temple	8—12

The second feature that makes the book unique is the fact that it includes Daniel's visions of the future (Dan 7—12), which constitute the only example of the apocalypse as a literary genre in the First Testament. Like the book of Revelation, Daniel 7—12 contains a series of visions received through an angelic mediator. The content of these visions concerns future judgment and salvation, particularly "at the time of the end" (8:17, 19; 11:27, 35, 40; 12:4, 9). The apocalypse in the book of Daniel may be outlined in a menorah pattern:

The Apocalypse of Daniel in a Menorah Pattern	*Dan 7—12*
A Daniel's dream of four beasts (3¹/₂ years "given into his power")	7:1-28
B Daniel's vision of the ram and he-goat [= Alexander the Great]	8:1-27
C As Jeremiah predicted, desolation of Jerusalem will last 70 years	9:1-2
X **Prayer: "Look with favor on your desolated sanctuary"**	9:3-19
C´ Angel Gabriel reveals the desolation will last 70 "sevens"	9:20-27
B´ Daniel's vision of a man [= angel Gabriel] and the last days	10:1—12:4
A´ The end will come 3¹/₂ years after final desecration of the Temple	12:5-13

Daniel's prayer at the center of the book may be summarized as follows: "Though the disaster is deserved, turn from your wrath and look with favor on your desolated sanctuary" (9:3–19). The two references to "3¹/₂ years" (7:25; 12:7) refer to the time remaining after the final desecration of the Temple ("the abomination that makes desolate"—9:27; 11:31; 12:11; cf. 8:11–13) until the end comes.

1 Maccabees 1:41–59 describes the desolation of the Temple in Jerusalem by Antiochus IV Epiphanes that precipitated the Maccabean rebellion in 167 B.C.E. The cleansing of the Temple in 164 B.C.E. by Judas Maccabee "3¹/₂ years" after this defilement (see 1 Macc 4:36–61) is celebrated in the Jewish Festival of Hanukkah ("dedication"). The defilement of the Temple by Antiochus took place halfway through the "seventieth week" in the "seventy weeks of years" in Jeremiah's prophecy, as reinterpreted by the angel Gabriel.

Though the book of Daniel, as we now have it, was apparently intended to be read in conjunction with the Festival of Hanukkah, it seems likely that the stories contained in Daniel 1—6 are much older. In short, the book of Daniel emerged within the canonical process in three stages:

- Original wisdom stories about Daniel and his three friends were included in the Writings of the twenty-two-book "pentateuchal" canon from the time of Ezra.

- The "apocalypse of Daniel" was added to make the scroll correspond to the five Festal Scrolls—to be read in conjunction with the Festival of Hanukkah in the time of the Maccabees (ca. 164 B.C.E.).

- Four other additions are found in the Greek book of Daniel of the second century B.C.E.: the Story of Suzanna, the Prayer of Azariah, the Hymn of the Three Young Men, and the Story of Bel and the Dragon.

The concentric structure of the book of Daniel as a whole may be outlined in a menorah pattern within a menorah pattern:

The Book of Daniel in a Menorah Pattern	*Dan 1—12*
A Nebuchadnezzar's initial desecration of the Temple in Jerusalem	1:1-2
B Daniel and his three friends faithfully observe the Torah	1:3-21
C Nebuchadnezzar's dream—the statue and four kingdoms	2:1-49
X **Stories of Daniel and his three friends in Babylon**	3:1—6:28
C´ Daniel's dream—the four beasts and four kingdoms	7:1-28
B´ Daniel's visions ["abomination that makes desolate" (9:27)]	8:1—12:4
A´ Final desecration of the Temple ["abomination that makes desolate"]	12:5-13

2nd Level Menorah: Stories of Daniel and His Three Friends	*Dan 3—6*
A Daniel's three friends in the fiery furnace	3:1-30
B Nebuchadnezzar's dream of the tree; his madness and restoration	4:1-37
C Belshazzar's great feast for a thousand of his lords	5:1
X **Belshazzar desecrates the Temple vessels**	5:2-4
C´ The handwriting on the wall, which Daniel agrees to interpret	5:5-17
B´ Nebuchadnezzar's madness and restoration retold—Belshazzar slain	5:18-30
A´ Daniel in the lion's den for disobeying the decree of Darius	6:1-28

In this reading of the book of Daniel, the central theme is the desecration of the Temple in Jerusalem and its results in the episode of the handwriting on the wall. The book opens with a brief account of Nebuchadnezzar acquiring the Temple vessels in "the third year of the reign of King Jehoiakim of Judah" (1:1) and placing those vessels "in the treasury of his gods" in Babylon (1:2). The book concludes with an account of the final desecration of the Temple (the "abomination that makes desolate") in the days of Antiochus IV Epiphanes (12:5–13). Nebuchadnezzar's successor, King Belshazzar, brings those same vessels out for use by "his lords, his wives, and his concubines" in a pagan festival (5:1–4). This action causes the "hand of God" to write an ominous inscription "on the plaster of the wall of the royal palace, next to the lamp-stand" (5:5). Daniel interprets the words of this inscription as follows: "*Mene*, God has numbered the days of your kingdom and brought it to an end; *tekel*, you have been weighed on the scales and found wanting; *peres*, your kingdom is divided and given to the Medes and the Persians" (5:26–27).

THE CHRONICLER'S HISTORY: JUDAISM OF THE SECOND TEMPLE

From the time of the Greek translation of the Hebrew Bible in antiquity (ca. 300–100 B.C.E.), scholars have rearranged the books of Ezra, Nehemiah, 1 Chronicles and 2 Chronicles in what they consider to be a more logical order by placing Chronicles before Ezra and Nehemiah. The Masoretes went even further in *The Leningrad Codex* (ca. 1008 C.E.) by moving Chronicles to the beginning of the Writings, with Ezra and Nehemiah as the concluding books of the Tanakh.

The books of Ezra, Nehemiah, and 1 and 2 Chronicles (i.e., the Chronicler's History) were not part of the seventeen-book deuteronomic canon of sacred scripture in the sixth century B.C.E. Consequently, they did not go through the developmental process we have traced for Psalms, Proverbs, and the Festal Scrolls. Rather, the Chronicler's History was the final stage in the composition of the nine books that make up the Writings in the Tanakh, the twenty-two-book pentateuchal canon, as follows:

Psalms	Job		Ezra	Nehemiah
		Daniel		
Proverbs	*Megilloth*		1 Chronicles	2 Chronicles

As the first four books in this structure, the "Hagiographa" (Psalms, Job, Proverbs, and the *Megilloth* [Festal Scrolls]), are made up of "four wheels of the same likeness" in their canonical structure, so too is the Chronicler's History [Ezra, Nehemiah, 1 Chronicles, and 2 Chronicles]). The book of Daniel functions as a "bridge" connecting these two groups of four books.

The Chronicler's History (Ezra, Nehemiah, 1 and 2 Chronicles) is structured in relation to the reestablishment of worship in Jerusalem after the Babylonian Exile and the renewal of the covenant and keeping of the Torah in particular during the period of the Second Temple. In this regard, the following menorah pattern within a menorah pattern is instructive:

The Chonicler's History in a Menorah Pattern	*Ezra–2 Chr*
A Edict of Cyrus to rebuild the Temple in Jerusalem	Ezra 1:1–4
B Building and dedication of the Second Temple in Jerusalem	Ezra 1:5–10:44
C Rebuilding Jerusalem and keeping the Torah	Neh 1–13
X **From Adam to Temple worship after the Exile**	1 Chr 1–10
C´ Establishing Jerusalem as the location of the Temple	1 Chr 11–29
B´ From the building to the destruction of the First Temple	2 Chr 1:1–36:21
A´ Edict of Cyrus to rebuild the Temple in Jerusalem	2 Chr 36:22–23

2nd Level Menorah: From Creation to Temple Worship	*1 Chr 1–10*
A Genealogies from Adam to descendants of Benjamin in Jerusalem	1:1–8:28
B Genealogy of the family of Saul	8:29–40
C Genealogies of families in Jerusalem after the Exile	9:1–21
X **David and Samuel established the priests in the Temple**	9:22
C´ Duties of the priests described—including the Levites as singers	9:23–34
B´ Genealogy of the family of Saul	9:35–44
A´ Saul (a Benjaminite) as the unfaithful predecessor of David	10:1–14

In this reading, the focus of interest is on Jerusalem and its successive temples—the First Temple of Solomon and the Second Temple of the postexilic period. Proper worship, which is centered in the Second Temple, and proper observance of the Torah as a way of life (Neh 9—13) establish the parameters of Judaism for centuries to come. They also set the stage for another reform movement that was to originate in Jerusalem four centuries later, in the time of Herod's Temple (20 B.C.E.–70 C.E.; sometimes referred to as the "Third Temple"). In this new movement within Judaism, Yeshua (Jesus) the Messiah speaks of a "fourth Temple" in the New Jerusalem—"but he was speaking of the temple of his body. After he was raised from the dead, his disciples remembered that he had said this, and they believed the scripture and the word that Jesus had spoken" (John 2:21–22).

It is not surprising that the Jewish historian Josephus and the followers of Jesus Christ in the first century C.E., thought of the Chronicler's History in relation to the Prophets (Former and Latter Prophets) of the Tanakh, along with the book of Daniel. In this way of thinking, the Chronicler's History takes its place as a third section of the "Prophets," with Daniel as a bridge, connecting three groups of four books:

Joshua	Judges		Isaiah	Jeremiah
Samuel	Kings		Ezekiel	The Twelve
		Daniel		
	Ezra		Nehemiah	
	1 Chronicles		2 Chronicles	

Though the order of material presented in the Chroniclers' History is not arranged chronologically, the principle of chiasm in its structure is evident. At the outset, in the book of Ezra, the work focuses attention on the building and dedication of the Second Temple in Jerusalem. This work is set over against the book of 2 Chronicles, with its history of the First Temple, from its construction by Solomon to its destruction by Nebuchadnezzar and the seventy years of desolation (2 Chron 36:21). The book of Nehemiah focuses on the rebuilding of the city of Jerusalem and the keeping of the Torah. Its counterpart, the book of 1 Chronicles, focuses on the establishment of Jerusalem as the "City of David" and carries the story forward to David's elaborate preparations for building the First Temple in Jerusalem.

The Book of Ezra

The book of Ezra may be outlined in a menorah pattern:

The Book of Ezra in a Menorah Pattern	Ezra 1—10
A Decree of Cyrus and the census of the first return	1:1—2:70
B Building the Second Temple in the face of opposition	3:1—5:7a
C Second Temple built as decreed by Darius	5:7b—6:15
X **Dedication of the Second Temple [515 B.C.E.]**	6:16-18
C´ Passover celebrated in Jerusalem—at the rebuilt Temple	6:19-22
B´ Return and work of Ezra in Jerusalem	7:1—8:36
A´ Ezra deals with the problem of mixed marriages	9:1—10:44

The book of Ezra focuses on the building and dedication of the Second Temple (ca. 515 B.C.E.), as decreed by Darius, and the subsequent return and work of Ezra in Jerusalem (ca. 458 B.C.E.). Ezra arrived with an official letter of authorization from Artaxerxes (written in Aramaic, Ezra 7:12–26). The highlight of Ezra's ministry in Jerusalem is his prayer of confession (9:5–15), which was occasioned by the problem of mixed marriages of the returnees with foreign women.

The Book of Nehemiah

The book of Nehemiah may also be outlined in a menorah pattern:

The Book of Nehemiah in a Menorah Pattern	Neh 1—13
A Nehemiah's memoirs: Rebuilding the walls of Jerusalem	1:1—6:19
B Ezra reads the Torah at the Festival of Booths	7:1—8:18
C Day of penitence and prayer of the Levites	9:1-5
X **Ezra and the national confession of sin**	9:6-15
C´ Ezra's appeal for deliverance from foreign domination	9:32-37
B´ People covenant to keep the Torah as interpreted by Ezra	10:1—11:36
A´ Nehemiah's memoirs: Dedication of city walls and reforms	12:1—13:31

The book of Nehemiah focuses renewal of the covenant under Ezra and Nehemiah, with particular emphasis on Ezra's national confession of sin (9:6–15). In this recital, Ezra reviews the mighty acts of God from the time that God "chose Abram and brought him out of Ur of the Chaldeans and gave him the name Abraham" (9:7). He relates the experiences of the "Wars of Yahweh" (cf. Num 21:14) in the Exodus from Egypt (9:9–15), the rebellions in the wilderness in the time of Moses (9:16–22), and the entrance into the Promised Land in the days of Joshua (9:23–25). God's blessing on his people continued despite repeated rebellions (9:26–31). Against this background, Ezra appeals for God's deliverance of his people from foreign domination (9:32–37).

The outermost frame in the concentric structure of the book of Nehemiah is made up the "Memoirs of Nehemiah," which focus on the rebuilding of the walls of Jerusalem (Neh 1—6) and the dedication of those rebuilt walls (Neh 12—13). Nehemiah speaks in the first person throughout both of these sections.

The second frame opens with the account of Ezra reading the Torah at the Festival of Booths in Jerusalem (Ezra 7—8), and concludes with the covenant on the part of the people to keep the Torah as interpreted by Ezra (Ezra 10—11).

Though Nehemiah 8—9 is often called the "Ezra story," it should be noted that the first person plural "we" begins in 9:9 (in Ezra's public confession) and continues through 10:39 (10:40 in the Hebrew text). Both Nehemiah and Ezra are present throughout this section, which moves from a brief continuation of the so-called Memoirs of Nehemiah that break off in 7:5b and resumes in 11:1. In between we find Ezra reading the book of the Torah to the people (8:1–8), followed by Nehemiah and Ezra addressing the people together in 8:9. In 9:6–37, Ezra leads the people in a national confession of sin.

It is easy to understand why the books of Ezra and Nehemiah are often considered to be a single literary work, Ezra-Nehemiah. The book of Ezra is concerned primarily with the building of the Second Temple in Jerusalem (Ezra 1:1—6:18) and the subsequent return and work of Ezra in Jerusalem (Ezra 6:19—10:44). The book of Nehemiah is concerned with the rebuilding of the city wall in Jerusalem under the leadership of Nehemiah (Neh 1—6 and 12—

13). It also includes the account of the public reading of the Torah by Ezra (Neh 8:1–12) and Ezra's national confession of sin (Neh 9:6–37). The overlap between the books of Ezra and Nehemiah is considerable.

The Book of 1 Chronicles

Unlike the books of 1 and 2 Kings in the Former Prophets, which are considered to be a single book from a canonical point of view, the books of 1 and 2 Chronicles (like Ezra and Nehemiah) are separate books. The book of 1 Chronicles may be outlined in a menorah pattern as follows:

The Book of 1 Chronicles in a Menorah Pattern	*1 Chr 1—29*
A From Adam to David by way of genealogies	1:1–9:44
B Jerusalem established as the "City of David"	10:1–12:40
C The ark is brought from Kiriath-jearim	13:1–14
X **David brings the Ark of the Covenant to Jerusalem**	14:1–15:29
C´ The ark is placed in the Tent—David's psalm	16:1–43
B´ The reign of David in Jerusalem	17:1–21:30
A´ David makes preparation for the building of the Temple	22:1–29:30

The book of 1 Chronicles is primarily the story of David and the city of Jerusalem as the center of worship in ancient Israel, with particular focus on the transfer of the Ark of the Covenant from the house of Obed-edom (15:25) to the city of David. The collection of genealogies (1 Chr 1—9) and the brief account of Saul, the unfaithful predecessor of David (1 Chr 10) may be considered separately as the structural center of the Chronicler's History (Ezra through 2 Chronicles). That section consists of a series of genealogies, which converge on the house of David and Solomon (1 Chr 1—3) and the Levites and musicians appointed by David (1 Chr 6). On either side of this pivotal chapter we find the genealogies of the remaining eleven tribes of ancient Israel (1 Chr 4—5 and 7—8). The concluding chapter (1 Chr 9) presents the genealogies of families in Jerusalem after the Babylonian Exile.

The second frame moves from the capture of Jerusalem, which becomes the city of David (1 Chr 10—12), to the account of David's reign as king in Jerusalem (1 Chr 17—21). Within this latter section, we find another concentric structure in which the outer frame concerns why David does not build the First Temple in Jerusalem (1 Chr 17), and the acquisition of the threshing floor or Ornan (Araunah) the Jebusite on which the Temple will be constructed (21:18—22:1).

The innermost frame moves from the transfer of the Ark of the Covenant from Kiriath-jearim to the house of Obed-edom (1 Chr 13), to the placing of the ark "inside the tent which David had pitched for it" (16:1). The account of the subsequent service of celebration includes a composite psalm (16:8–36). The structural center of 1 Chronicles presents David as an ecclesiastical figure who brings the Ark of the Covenant from the house of Obed-edom to Jerusalem (1 Chr 15).

The Book of 2 Chronicles

Though the content of 2 Chronicles continues to focus on the First Temple in Jerusalem, it also deals with the subject of the Torah of Moses. This subject is taken up in three places: the teaching of the Torah by the Levites (2 Chr 17), certain legal reforms based on the Torah (2 Chr 19), and the place of the Torah in Josiah's reforms (2 Chr 34). The book of 2 Chronicles may be outlined in a menorah pattern as follows:

The Book of 2 Chronicles in a Menorah Pattern	*2 Chr 1—36*
A Reign of Solomon: Building of the First Temple in Jerusalem	1:1–9:31
B From Solomon to Asa: Kingdom divided, civil war, and reform	10:1–16:14
C Reign of Jehoshaphat—Levites teach the Torah	17:1–18:34
X **Jehu ben Hanani rebukes Jehoshaphat who rules wisely**	19:1–11
C´ Jehoshaphat's victory over enemies of the true faith	20:1–37
B´ From Jehoshaphat to Hezekiah: Joash repairs the Temple	21:1–28:27
A´ Temple cleansed (Hezekiah), rebuilt (Josiah), and destroyed	29:1–36:23

The outermost frame opens with a discussion of Solomon and the building of the First Temple in Jerusalem (1:1—9:31). It continues with an account of the cleansing of the Temple by Hezekiah (2 Chr 29—31), the repairing of the Temple by Josiah (2 Chr 34), and the destruction of the First Temple (2 Chr 36). The second frame focuses on the matter of war and reform, with particular interest in the reign of Asa and the reforms he carries out in conjunction with the prophecy of Azariah (2 Chr 14—15). It continues with the repair of the Temple by King Joash and the high priest Jehoiada (2 Chr 23—24).

The central section in the book of 2 Chronicles focuses on the reign of King Jehoshaphat (2 Chr 17—20). Though this section includes the account of Jehoshaphat's ill-fated alliance with Ahab and the prophetic conflict between Micaiah and Zedekiah (2 Chr 18, cf. 1 Kgs 22), the focus of attention is quite different from the parallel account in the Former Prophets. Here the innermost frame presents the Levites as teachers of the Torah "through all the cities of Judah" (17:8–9), and a remarkable story about Jehoshaphat's great victory over the enemies of the true faith (2 Chr 20). In the structural center of 2 Chronicles, we find the account of the prophet Jehu the son of Hanani who rebukes King Jehoshaphat. Like the "good kings" in the Former Prophets, Jehoshaphat listens to the prophet and rules wisely (2 Chr 19).

5

Ezra and the Completion of the Tanakh

Though Ezra is a towering figure within the canonical process in ancient Israel, second only to Moses, surprisingly little is known about him and the nature of his work in relation to that of his contemporary Nehemiah with any degree of certainty. Even the dates of Ezra's ministry in Jerusalem remain a matter of scholarly dispute. All that we know for certain is that "Ezra had set his heart to study the Torah of Yahweh, and to do it, and to teach the statutes and ordinances in Israel" (Ezra 7:10). He is called a scribe who brought with him "the book of the Torah of Moses that Yahweh had given to Israel" (Neh 8:1), which he read to the people in Jerusalem at the time of the fall Festival of Booths.

EZRA AND THE TWENTY-TWO-BOOK CANON OF THE TANAKH

According to 2 Maccabees 2:13–15, Ezra's contemporary Nehemiah "founded a library and collected the books about the kings and prophets, and the writings of David, and letters of kings about votive offerings." In the Talmudic booklet (tractate) Avoth 1:1–2, we read that "Moses received the Torah from Sinai and delivered it to Joshua, and Joshua to the Elders, and the Elders to the Prophets, and the Prophets delivered it to the Men of the Great Synagogue (or Assembly)." The "Men of the Great Synagogue" in the time of Ezra and Nehemiah were presumably some sort of special guild, who continued to function in the preservation and transmission of the Tanakh from ca. 400 to 200 B.C.E. By the time of the writing of the prologue of Sirach (or Ecclesiasticus, or the Wisdom of Jesus ben Sirach) in ca. 132 B.C.E, "the Torah and the Prophets and the other books of our ancestors" were reckoned as 'the Scriptures.'"

Though the historical details cannot be recovered, it appears that Ezra was responsible for determining the content of the Tanakh as we now have it, though some additions were subsequently made to the book of Daniel. Other additions to Daniel and Esther failed to achieve canonicity in the Tanakh. In short, Ezra marks the end of the first major stage in the canonical process that produced the Tanakh in a twenty-two-book canon, a process that began in the reforms of Hezekiah (ca. 725–700 B.C.E.) and Josiah (ca. 630–610 B.C.E.). Ezra's canon survived well into the Christian era. In fact, that canon survives to the present day, though Jewish tradition chooses to count those books as numbering twenty-four rather than twenty-two, from the time of the Mishna (ca. 200 C.E.), and perhaps a hundred years earlier, as witnessed by the text of 2 Esdras 14:1–48.

According to Jewish tradition, Ezra is a second Moses: "On the third day...a voice came out of a bush opposite me and said, 'Ezra, Ezra!' And I answered, 'Here I am, Lord.'...Then [Ezra] answered ...'For your Torah has been burned, and so...send the Holy Spirit into me, and I will write...all things that were written in your Torah, so that people may be able to find the path, and that those who want to live in the last days may do so" (2 Esdr 14:1–22). During a period of forty days, Ezra is reputed to have written ninety-four books. God instructed him to "make public the twenty-four books that you wrote first [namely, the books of the Tanakh], and let the worthy read them; but keep the seventy that were written last, in order to give them to the wise among the people" (2 Esdr 14:44–48). This tradition was set in writing some time after the time of Josephus in Jewish circles that already anticipated the twenty-four-book structure of the Tanakh as subsequently reported in the Mishna. By that time, the books of the Tanakh had been supplemented by many other sacred writings among the Jews. These books fall into two general categories: the Apocrypha and the Pseudepigrapha. Among these writings, however, none achieved the level of authority ascribed to the ancient Torah, Prophets, and Writings (i.e., the Tanakh) from the time of Ezra.

APOCRYPHA AND PSEUDEPIGRAPHA

The term "Apocrypha" refers to certain Jewish religious writings dating from approximately 300 B.C.E. to 70 C.E. Among these many works, thirteen were included in the old Greek codices of the Bible—in Codex Vaticanus, Codex Sinaiticus, and Codex Alexandrinus—as part of the First Testament. These include:

1 and 2 Esdras

Tobit

Judith

Additions to Esther (six expansions to the Greek translation of Esther)

The Wisdom of Solomon

Ecclesiasticus (or the Wisdom of Jesus the Son of Sirach)

Baruch

The Letter of Jeremiah

Additions to Daniel (three documents added to Daniel)

    The Prayer of Azariah and the Song of the Three Young Men

    Susanna

    Bel and the Dragon

The Prayer of Manasseh

1 and 2 Maccabees

The term "Pseudepigrapha" refers to a modern collection of ancient writings from ca. 250 B.C.E. to 200 C.E that are essential for understanding early Judaism. This collection of sixty-five documents, published in *The Old Testament Pseudepigrapha*, 2 vols. (Doubleday, 1983–85) is neither closed nor canonical. The most familiar among these include Jubilees, 1–3 Enoch, 3 and 4 Maccabees, the Sibylline Oracles, and Testaments of the Twelve Patriarchs. From a technical point of view, the term "Pseudepigrapha" means "falsely attributed" to another person—such as Adam, Enoch, Noah, Abraham, Moses, David, Solomon, Ezra, and others who lived before prophecy was considered to have ended (ca. 400 B.C.E.). It should be noted, however, that a number of documents included in modern collections of the Pseudepigrapha do not fit this definition, such as the Letter of Aristeas, Ahiqar, and others.

When Jerome translated the First Testament into Latin, he worked directly from the Hebrew text of the Tanakh and so he limited the text to the Hebrew canon. He considered the additional documents in the Greek canon to be "apocryphal." The Western church, however, added these works to the Vulgate, some of which appear to have been hastily, if not reluctantly, translated by Jerome himself. In the Protestant Reformation, the Apocrypha was rejected as not canonical. At the Council of Trent (1586), however, the Roman Catholic Church reacted by declaring these works to be part of the Christian canon. Hence, Roman Catholics continue to consider these works as "deuterocanonical" and inspired.

TARGUMS—THE EARLIEST TRANSLATION OF THE TANAKH

As early as the time of Ezra (see Neh 8:1–8), ancient Jewish scribes were making oral paraphrases of the Tanakh into Aramaic. Though these Targums were not intended to be translations as such, but rather aids in understanding the archaic language of the Bible, the work took on a life of its own. Gradually these Targums were committed to writing and an official text emerged. The earliest Aramaic Targums were probably put in writing in Palestine during the second century C.E., although there is some evidence of Aramaic Targums from the pre-Christian period. The official Targums contained only the Torah and the Prophets, although unofficial Targums of later times also included the Writings. A number of unofficial Targums were found among the Dead Sea Scrolls at Qumran. In the third century C.E., the official Palestinian Targums of the Torah and the Prophets were displaced by another family of paraphrases, the Babylonian Targums. A convenient edition of the Babylonian Targums was edited by Alexander Sperber under the title, *The Bible in Aramaic* (4 vols., Leiden: Brill: 1959–1973). A new edition in twenty volumes, *The Aramaic Bible* (Liturgical Press, 1987–present), is in progress.

Targums are extant for all the books of the Hebrew Bible except for Ezra, Nehemiah, and Daniel. The most important texts are Targum Onkelos (the Pentateuch) and Targum Jonathan ben Uzziel (the Prophets). Though Onkelos was known in Babylonia in the Talmudic period, there is good reason to believe that it originated in Palestine in the first or early second century C.E. Also Targum Jonathan originated in Palestine in the fourth century C.E. It is a freer rendering of the text than Onkelos. Both Targums were read in synagogues along with the regular readings from the Torah and the Prophets in Hebrew. Since the Writings were not read in regular synagogue worship, no official copies were made.

SEPTUAGINT—THE STANDARD GREEK TRANSLATION OF THE TANAKH

When Alexander the Great conquered the ancient world, he showed considerable favor to the Jews. Many of the centers of population he established to administer his empire were named Alexandria, and they subsequently became centers of Jewish culture. Just as the Jews had abandoned their native Hebrew tongue for Aramaic in the Persian period, they abandoned Aramaic in favor of Greek in the Hellenistic era.

When Alexander's empire was divided after his death in 323 B.C.E., the Ptolemies controlled Egypt, the Seleucids took charge in Asia Minor, and the Antigonids ruled Macedonia. During the reign of Ptolemy II Philadelphus in Egypt (285–246 B.C.E.), the Jews in Alexandria shared in the great cultural and educational programs, including the founding of a museum and the translation of great literary works into Greek. Among the works selected for translation was the Hebrew Bible. This was indeed the first time that the Tanakh was extensively translated into any language.

The Jewish leaders in Alexandria produced a standard Greek version of the Tanakh that is commonly known as the Septuagint (LXX). According to legend (in the Letter to Aristeas), the librarian at Alexandria persuaded Ptolemy to translate the Torah into Greek. Six translators from each of the twelve tribes of Israel were selected and their work was completed in only seventy-two days, hence the name

Septuagint ("seventy"). Though the term originally was applied to the Greek translation of only the Pentateuch, it subsequently came to designate the Greek translation of the entire Tanakh. The work of translating was done during the third and second centuries B.C.E. and must have been completed by 150 B.C.E., since it is discussed in the Letter of Aristeas to Philocrates (ca. 130–100 B.C.E.).

When the early Christian movement spread throughout the Roman Empire, the Septuagint was already established as an authoritative translation of the Tanakh within Judaism. From at least the time of the destruction of Jerusalem in 70 C.E., this text emerged as the First Testament of the Bible of the early Christian Church. As that movement spread, particularly in the western part of the Roman Empire, the origins of the text in the Tanakh (Hebrew Bible) were forgotten. Consequently, the original order of the books in the First Testament within the ancient categories of Torah, Prophets, and Writings was lost. As the transition from individual scrolls to the great uncial codices of the fourth and fifth centuries C.E. took place, the books of the Bible were generally placed in a presumed chronological order in both Testaments. The books were also arranged according to literary genre—i.e., law, history, and poetry. This "Septuagint order" of the books of the First Testament survives in the Christian Church to the present time, in spite of the fact that from the time of Jerome's translation of the Latin Vulgate in antiquity, the text of the Tanakh (Hebrew Bible) emerged as the "canonical" text. In short, the Christian Church enjoys the anomaly of having the Jewish Tanakh as an essential part of its sacred scripture, but in the order arranged by Gentiles in the Greek speaking world of antiquity.

6

The Apostolic Writings
A New Ending to an Old Story

The primary narrative structure of the national epic story in ancient Israel before the monarchy emerged under David and Solomon may be diagrammed as follows:

BONDAGE ⟶ WATERS ⟶ MOUNTAIN OF GOD
Egypt   Re(e)d Sea   Sinai/Horeb

The people of God were delivered from slavery in Egypt under Moses, who led them through the waters of *Yam Suf* (the Red Sea or "Sea of Reeds") to the holy mountain. God revealed his presence there—and his will in the Ten Commandments, which were written on tablets of stone.

FORMATION OF THE EPIC STORY—"WARS OF YAHWEH"

The ancient epic story was extended in the generation after the Exodus from Egypt as the people of God moved from their wilderness home at Kadesh-barnea in the Negev of southern Judah to the plains of Moab where leadership was transferred from Moses to Joshua. The ancient story of deliverance from slavery in Egypt (the Exodus) under Moses was augmented with the story of the Eisodus (Entry) into the Promised Land under Joshua, which was understood in terms of what the people of Israel called the "Wars of Yahweh."

The *Book of the Wars of Yahweh*, which is cited only once in the Bible (Num 21:14), was apparently an epic account of God's "Holy War" directed against Israel's enemies in the time of Moses and Joshua. Though many have assumed it to be a lost anthology of ancient war poems dealing with the conflict between the invading Israelites and the original inhabitants of Canaan, it is more likely that this "book" was an epic poem that was eminently familiar to all. The situation is similar to that of the *Iliad* and the *Odyssey* of Homer, which were well known in ancient Greece long before these epic poems were written down in the form we know today.

The brief quotation from the *Book of the Wars of Yahweh* in Numbers 21:14 was cited by the narrator so as to place the boundary of Moab at the Arnon Valley. Though the Hebrew text is difficult, it may be rendered as follows:

> The Benefactor (i.e., Yahweh) has come in a storm;
> Yea, he has come to the wadis of the Arnon.
> He marched through the wadis;
> He marched, he turned aside—to the seat of Ar;
> He leaned toward the border of Moab.

Because of archaic features, this text was subsequently misread with resultant confusion in the ancient versions and experienced some textual corruption in the received masoretic tradition as well. The picture presented is that of the Divine Warrior poised on the edge of the Promised Land, before the most celebrated battles of the Exodus-Eisodus. He has come in a whirlwind with his hosts to the sources of the Arnon River in Transjordan. He marches through the wadis, turning aside to settle affairs with the two Amorite kings, Sihon and Og, and then across the Jordan River to the battlecamp at Gilgal and the conquest of Canaan. This epic story may be diagrammed as follows:

LAND ⟶ BONDAGE ⟶ WATERS ⟶ BATTLE CAMP
[Promised   (Jordan River)   Land Regained]

FIRST TRANSFORMATION OF THE EPIC STORY

With the advent of the monarchy of David and Solomon, the ancient epic narrative was extended and given a new ending that focuses on the kingdom of David as God's new creation. The new pattern was achieved by moving from the mountain of God's revelation at Sinai to the mountain of God's abiding presence on Mount Zion in Jerusalem as follows:

CREATION/   BONDAGE   WATERS/   TEMPLE/
LAND   →   →   MOUNTAIN → NEW CREATION
                                [Mount Sinai]   [Mount Zion]

This diagram summarizes the content of the Primary History as discussed above in chapter 2. At the same time, it anticipates a second transformation of the ancient epic story that culminates in the formation of the Second Testament with its focus on the person of Jesus Christ.

SECOND TRANSFORMATION OF THE EPIC STORY

In John's Gospel, we read that Jesus said, "Destroy this temple, and in three days I will raise it up" (John 2:19). Those who heard him at the time thought that he was referring to Herod's Temple in Jerusalem, which had taken forty-six years to build (John 2:20); but, after the resurrection of Jesus, "his disciples remembered that he had said this" (John 2:22), and now they understood. In some mysterious way, Jesus himself is the Temple in Jerusalem; and the ancient epic story now has a new and deeper meaning.

The epic pattern for this interpretation of the New Israel, as the people of God in Jesus Christ, may be diagrammed as follows:

CREATION/   KINGDOM   BONDAGE/WATERS/   KINGDOM
LAND   →   →   WILDERNESS → OF GOD
Exile/New Exodus (Israel)   Present Church Age   New Jerusalem

Transformation of the ancient epic narrative was achieved by elaborating the kingdom of David into a messianic kingdom with the anticipation of a new theophany in which the mountain of God's revelation and abiding presence in ancient Israel is extended in an eschatological vision.

The Gospel of Luke is a good illustration of how this transformation becomes the structuring principle for an altogether new reading of the ancient epic narrative. In the center of Luke stands an account of the transfiguration of Jesus. After quoting Jesus' enigmatic statement that "there are some standing here who will not taste death before they see the kingdom of God" (Luke 9:27), Luke describes a mysterious experience on a certain mountain, where Moses and Elijah appear together with Jesus. There the three of them discuss "his *exodus*, which he was about to accomplish at Jerusalem" (Luke 9:31). The Greek Orthodox tradition, which places this event in the vicinity of Mount Sinai where both Moses (Exod 33) and Elijah (1 Kgs 19) had their great encounters with God in times past, is surely correct, at least symbolically. Jesus the Messiah appears on the mountain of God, which combines the experience of Moses and Elijah on Mount Sinai/Horeb with the anticipation of what God will achieve on Mount Golgotha not many days hence in Luke's narrative account.

At the end of his gospel, Luke tells the story of another mysterious experience in which Jesus appears to two of his disciples on the road to Emmaus, after his resurrection from the dead (Luke 24:13–35). As he explains the Tanakh to them, "beginning with Moses and all the prophets, he interprets to them the things about himself in all the scriptures" (v. 27). In recounting this event later, they said: "Were not our hearts burning within us on the road, while he opened the scriptures to us?" (v. 32). Though the details of that conversation are not given, it is safe to conclude that Jesus spoke of the "prophet like Moses" in Deuteronomy 18:18 (and 34:10), of the Suffering Servant in Isaiah 53, and of Psalm 22 with its vivid details of his crucifixion and death. He told them that the Messiah they were expecting had indeed come, though not in the manner expected. The "kingdom of God," which he taught his disciples in the form of parables, in so many different ways, was the ultimate ending of that sacred story.

During the first generation of the followers of Jesus, the old story with its new ending was told throughout the Roman world with a sense of great urgency. People believed they would live to see the establishment of the kingdom of God in their own lifetime, as Jesus had promised. Because of this belief, there was little felt need to add anything to the Tanakh of ancient Judaism, other than the correct reading of that text, which was now their Bible—the sacred scriptures of the early Christian Church as a movement.

The situation changed in the fateful decade prior to the destruction of Jerusalem and the Third Temple in 70 C.E. by the Romans. Beginning with Paul's arrest in Jerusalem and his transfer to prison in Caesarea (ca. 58–60 C.E.), and then in Rome (ca. 60–62 C.E.), we see significant developments in the canonical process. The death of James, the brother of Jesus and head of the church in Jerusalem (ca. 62 C.E.), added momentum as tension mounted in Palestine. The course of events was moving to the great Jewish Revolt against Rome (ca. 63–73 C.E.) and its culmination in the destruction of Jerusalem (70 C.E.) and the fall of Masada (73 C.E.). It is against the unfolding of these events that it becomes evident to the leaders in the early Christian movement that they have misinterpreted the words of Jesus. Gradually their understanding of eschatology shifts and soon the need for a "New Testament" is widely felt. Jewish leaders like Paul, Peter, and John begin to think in terms of an expanded canon of sacred scripture—in the form of the Apostolic Writings. The second major stage in the canonical process has begun, a stage that culminates in the formation of the Completed Tanakh.

7

The New Torah
Four Gospels and the Book of Acts

In the first generation of the followers of Jesus Christ, there was no felt need for a New Testament as such. The Church was made up almost entirely of Jewish believers who continued to worship as Jews in the Temple of Jerusalem, in the synagogues throughout the Roman world, and in "home churches." The pattern of missionary outreach was to the Jews first—primarily "in Jerusalem, in all Judea and Samaria" (Acts 1:8). Though the Christian faith soon spread throughout the Roman world by means of merchants and other travelers going to and from Jerusalem, it was some time before the early Christians intentionally set out to take the gospel message "to the ends of the earth." And even then the first missionaries focused their attention on the Jews. Paul set the pattern on his missionary journeys by entering the synagogues in each place that he went, where he interpreted the Tanakh in the light of Jesus Christ—the fullness and the completion of God's revelation.

From Apostolic Writings to the New Testament

The Bible of the early Christian movement was the Tanakh. At first, all that was needed beyond the traditional scripture of ancient Judaism was the preached "gospel" to explain the life and teaching of Jesus in relation to the Tanakh. In the course of time, however, the Apostolic Writings emerged as the fifth and final segment of the canon in the Completed Tanakh.

Torah:	Five books of Moses (the Pentateuch)
Former Prophets:	Joshua, Judges, Samuel, Kings
Latter Prophets:	Isaiah, Jeremiah, Ezekiel, The Twelve
Hebrew Writings:	"Hagiographa," Daniel, and Chronicler's History
Apostolic Writings:	The New Testament

Though the gospels, as a form of didactic literature for the purpose of instructing believers, appear early in the life of the emerging Christian Church, these documents are not integrated at the outset into the developing concept of completing the Tanakh. It is not until Paul's second missionary journey, when he joins forces with Luke in Macedonia, that the idea of the Apostolic Writings as the fifth section of the Completed Tanakh first emerges.

Luke begins his gospel with the acknowledgement that "many have undertaken to set down an orderly account of the events that have been fulfilled among us" (Luke 1:1). His particular work is different from these other works in that it has a sequel in the book of Acts and is integrally connected with the Letters of Paul. A strong case can be made that Luke and Paul were working on a first edition of the "Apostolic Writings," as a canonical entity, before they made that fateful journey to Jerusalem in 58 C.E. that led to Paul's arrest and eventually to his imprisonment in Rome (ca. 60–62).

When Paul writes his second letter to Timothy from prison in Rome, he asks Timothy to bring Mark with him to Rome, saying, "he is very useful in my ministry." Paul goes on to say, "When you come, bring the *book-carrier* (φαιλόνην) that I left in Troas, also the *scrolls* (βιβλία), and above all the *parchments* (μεμβράνα)" (2 Tim 4:11–13). Paul is here referring to the ministry of canonical activity, in which he is already engaged in the task of editing his own letters as part of the "Apostolic Writings." The βιβλία are papyrus scrolls ("books"), and the μεμβράνα are expensive parchment leaves on which the final copies of Paul's works are written. This reference to parchment "leaves," with writing on both sides, is probably the first

historical reference we have to a codex—a quire of manuscript
pages held together by stitching to make the earliest form of a book,
replacing the scrolls of earlier times. It is interesting to note that
Peter subsequently makes specific reference to the letters of Paul,
which he acknowledges to be scripture (2 Pet 3:15–16). It is also
possible that the apostle John had a codex in mind in his description
of a βιβλίον that is "written on the inside and the back, sealed with
seven seals" (Rev 5:1). Scrolls were not normally written on both
sides. When the angel brought John "the little scroll" that he was
instructed to eat, the word used is the term βιβλαρίδιον. This word
is sometimes translated as "little book" and may refer to a letter or a
shorter treatise on a single leaf of papyrus that would be rolled into a
small scroll and sealed. It should be noted in passing, however, that
all the earliest copies of Christian Scriptures that have survived,
including a fragment of the Gospel of John dated to ca. 125 C.E., are
in codex form.

The first edition of the "Apostolic Writings," as conceived by
Paul and Luke, may have been arranged as a conscious imitation of
the form of the Hebrew Writings of the Tanakh, as follows:

Romans	1 Corinthians		1 Thessalonians	2 Thessalonians
		Luke		
2 Corinthians	Galatians		Timothy	Titus

Psalms	Job		Ezra	Nehemiah
		Daniel		
Proverbs	Festal Scrolls		1 Chronicles	2 Chronicles

In the first edition of the "Apostolic Writings," eight of the Letters of
Paul, together with the Gospel of Luke, were intended to be "canonical scripture" from the outset by Paul and Luke, as the completion of
the Tanakh (ca. 55–58 C.E.).

THE SYNOPTIC GOSPELS: MATTHEW, MARK, AND LUKE

The second step in the canonical process, so far as the "Apostolic Writings" are concerned, is an extension of this conceptual design of nine books (in a 4+1+4 pattern) into a twenty-two-book canon as a structural counterpart to the twenty-two-book canon of the Tanakh.

Canon of Josephus (22 Books)		Canon of "Apostolic Writings" (22 Books)	
5 Books of Moses	Torah	New Torah	5 books (4 Gospels + Acts)
13 Prophets/Writings	Prophets	Paul as Prophet	13 Letters of Paul
4 Hagiographa	Writings	Other Writings	4 "pillars" of the Church

When Mark joins Paul and Luke in Rome, their ministry appears to be quite different from what is often assumed. Mark brings his own gospel with him, while Timothy brings the manuscripts Paul left in Troas. Luke's use of Mark in the editorial shaping of his own gospel at this time is easy to understand, as is the use of Mark in the editing of the Gospel of Matthew, which is the gospel to Jews as preached and taught in Jerusalem. It could be called the "Gospel according to James," the brother of Jesus who was martyred in 62 C.E., in the same way that Mark's Gospel is the "Gospel according to Peter," and Luke's Gospel the "Gospel according to Paul." In short, the Gospel of Mark is of central importance in the canonical activity that takes place in Rome (ca. 62 C.E.)—for indeed, Paul said, "Mark is very useful in my ministry" (2 Tim 4:11). Working together with Paul, Luke, Timothy, and others in Rome, Mark plays a significant role in the canonical activity that produces a twenty-two-book coun- terpart to the Tanakh of Jewish tradition.

The death of James, Jesus' brother and leader of the Jerusalem Church, leads to the decision to include an authoritative version of the Letter of James and the Gospel of Matthew in the canon of the "Apostolic Writings." As the sayings (*logia*) of Jesus taught in Jerusalem under the authority of James, Matthew was written as a gospel to the Jews. It was edited as the first of the Four Gospels, using Mark as a primary source. The canonical relationship between the Four Gospels may be outlined as follows:

Four Gospels	Four "Pillars"	Primary Intended Audience/Constituency
Matthew	James, brother of Jesus	Gospel to the Jews (Jerusalem)
Mark	Peter	Peter's Gospel—the Church in Rome
Luke	Paul	Paul's Gospel—Churches in Greece and Asia
John	John	Universal Gospel (Jerusalem → Ephesus)

Within the Four Gospels of the Completed Tanakh, the Gospel of Mark (as the "Gospel of Peter") is the structural counterpart to the Gospel of Luke, which reflects the teaching of Paul. Matthew is the structural counterpart to the Gospel of John, which John wrote in Asia Minor (modern Turkey). John takes refuge there from the chaos in Palestine on the eve of the Jewish Wars with Rome (66–73 C.E.) that culminate in the destruction of the Temple in Jerusalem (70 C.E.) and the fall of Masada (73 C.E.).

When Luke completes Acts and adds it to the Four Gospels to form a "New Torah" in the Completed Tanakh, the Gospel of Mark becomes the counterpart to the Gospel of John, as the following outline suggests:

The New Torah: Four Gospels and Acts of the Apostles

A	Matthew	Gospel to Jews (probably associated with James, brother of Jesus)
B	Mark	Peter's Gospel—narrative of what Jesus said and did
X	Luke	Paul's Gospel, Part I—to the Gentiles
B´	John	John's Gospel—treatise on what Jesus meant (universal Gospel)
A´	Acts	Paul's Gospel, Part II—to the Gentiles

This new pairing of Mark and John is strengthened by the fact that the Gospel of Mark is associated with Peter. Since Peter and John are the two surviving apostles among the three whom Jesus took with him on the Mount of Transfiguration, it is easy to think of them as a pair.

The Gospel of Mark is more action oriented and presents a narrative drama that focuses on what Jesus said and did. The Gospel of John, however, is more reflective and even contemplative in nature, focusing on what Jesus meant. Some in the early Christian Church, who lost sight of the canonical structure of the Four Gospels and read them independently, felt that the original ending of Mark's Gospel was too abrupt. Consequently, a longer ending (16:9–20) that includes the account of various post-resurrection appearances of Jesus was added.

The Gospel of Matthew opens with "an account of the genealogy of Jesus, the Messiah, the son of David, the son of Abraham" (Matt 1:1). It concludes with Jesus' command: "Go therefore and make disciples of all nations... and remember, I am with you always, to the end of the age" (Matt 28:19–20). The Acts of the Apostles opens with the promise that "you will be baptized with the Holy Spirit not many days from now" (Acts 1:5). It continues with a brief outline of the book itself: "You will receive power when the Holy Spirit has come upon you; and you will be my witnesses in Jerusalem, in all Judea and Samaria, and to the ends of the earth" (Acts 1:8). It concludes with Paul in Rome: "He lived there two whole years at his own expense and welcomed all who came to him, proclaiming the kingdom of God and teaching about the Lord Jesus Christ with all boldness and without hindrance" (Acts 28:30–31). The structural center of this "New Torah" is the Gospel of Luke (Paul's gospel), which was written by a Gentile on behalf of the Apostle to the Gentiles. The inner frame in the above structure moves from Peter's Gospel (the Gospel of Mark), with its focus in Galilee and Jerusalem, to the universal Gospel of John. These five books were edited in ca. 62–63 C.E. to constitute a "New Torah" within a twenty-two-book canon of the "New Testament."

Paul, Luke, and Mark play a dominant role at this stage of the canonical process. After the martyrdom of Paul and Peter in Rome (ca. 66–67 C.E.), the apostle John continues the canonical process as the only surviving member of the original four "pillars" of the Church. That process culminates in a forty-nine-book canon of the Completed Tanakh (ca. 96 C.E.), which includes the Revelation to

John, along with five General Epistles (2 Peter, 1–3 John, and Jude). This matter is discussed below in chapter 9.

The fact that the Gospels of Matthew, Mark, and Luke are closely related is evident to any observant reader. The very term "Synoptic Gospels" bears witness to the fact that the first three gospels have a common perspective in which they view the career and teaching of Jesus, a perspective that is sharply different from that of the Gospel of John. Scholars have demonstrated that approximately 91 percent of Mark is paralleled in one of the other two gospels or in both of them. The same is true of about 50 percent of Matthew and about 41 percent of Luke. Moreover, it is commonly assumed by the majority of New Testament scholars that Mark's Gospel is the earliest of the three, and that it is used as a source in the composition of both Matthew and Luke. This is what is meant when biblical scholars speak of the "priority of Mark."

Augustine and others among the church fathers consider Matthew to be the original gospel, Mark a condensed version of it, and Luke dependent upon both Mark and Matthew. This is still the official position of Roman Catholic scholars and is espoused by an occasional Protestant scholar as well. It remained the orthodox position until the nineteenth century, when the priority of Mark took center stage among most biblical scholars.

Despite the common characteristics of the first three gospels, which justify their being grouped as a literary unit over against the Fourth Gospel, their relationship each to the other poses problems of another sort—often referred to as the "Synoptic Problem." When the content is arranged in parallel columns in the various "Harmonies of the Gospels," curious differences are evident at many points. A number of theories have been advanced to explain the data.

Even though scholars often speak of the Synoptic Gospels as a literary entity, few attempt to analyze the content of these three books as a single literary unit. Such an exercise throws surprising light on some of the similarities and differences that produced the "Synoptic Problem" in the first place. The content of the three Synoptic Gospels may be outlined in a menorah pattern:

The Synoptic Gospels in a Menorah Pattern   Matt–Luke

A   From Judea to Galilee—kingdom announced by John and Jesus   Matt 1–13

B   From Galilee to Jerusalem—kingdom established by Jesus   Matt 14–28

C   Galilee: Jesus as Messiah healing and teaching with the Twelve Mark 1:1–8:21

X   **Jesus' teaching on discipleship—giving sight to the blind**   Mark 8:22–10:52

C′   Jerusalem: Jesus as Servant-Messiah with the Twelve   11:1–16:8

B′   From Galilee to Jerusalem—way of kingdom taught by Jesus   Luke 1:1–19:44

A′ In Jerusalem—the king enters the city to die and be resurrected   Luke 19:45–24:53

The geographical movement of Jesus is carefully balanced in this reading of the Synoptic Gospels. After the story of Jesus' birth, which takes him from Bethlehem (Judea) to Egypt and then to Nazareth in Galilee (Matt 1:1—2:23), the story of Jesus' public ministry begins in Judea with the baptism and temptation of Jesus (Matt 3:1—4:11) and moves quickly to Galilee (Matt 4:12—13:58). This is set over against the final ministry of Jesus in the Temple in Jerusalem, which leads to his redemptive suffering, death, resurrection, and ascension (Luke 19:45—24:53). The movement in both halves of the second frame in this structure is the same—from Galilee to Jerusalem (Matt 14—28 and Luke 1:1—19:44). Both of these sections concern the teaching and establishment of the kingdom by Jesus. The geographical movement in the innermost frame of this menorah pattern is also from Galilee (Mark 1:1—8:21), with its focus on Jesus as Messiah, to Jerusalem (Mark 11:1—16:8), with its focus on Jesus as Suffering Servant. The center of the Synoptic Gospels is the center of the Gospel of Mark—Jesus giving sight to the blind (Mark 8:22—10:52).

An even more interesting structure emerges if one takes a close look at the place and function of the three accounts of the transfiguration of Jesus and the structural centers of the larger literary units on either side of these parallel units within a menorah pattern:

Three Accounts of the Transfiguration in a Menorah Pattern

A   Ministry of Jesus in Galilee—Sermon on the Mount   Matt 4:23–7:29

B   Transfiguration of Jesus—conversation with Moses and Elijah   Matt 17:1–13

C   Death of John the Baptist reported   Mark 6:14–29

X   **Transfiguration linked to resurrection and opening blind eyes** Mark 9:2–13

C´   Death of Jesus interpreted—institution of Lord's Supper   Mark 14:12–25

B´   Transfiguration of Jesus and his "Exodus" as Servant-Messiah   Luke 9:1–50

A´ Ministry in Jerusalem—Jesus cleanses Temple and teaches there   Luke 19:45–21:38

The outermost frame in the above concentric structure indicates the center" of the first half of Matthew's Gospel (4:23—7:29), and the second half of Luke's Gospel (19:45—21:38). The story of the transfiguration of Jesus is in the structural center of the second half of Matthew and the first half of Luke. It also appears in the structural center of Mark. In the first telling of this story, the focus is on the fact that Moses and Elijah were "talking with him" on the mountain (Matt 17:3). In the second half of this frame, Luke tells us what they were talking about, namely his "*exodus,* which he was about to accomplish at Jerusalem" (Luke 9:31). In Mark's version of the transfiguration of Jesus, the focus of attention shifts to the conversation between Jesus and his disciples on the way down the mountain. Jesus "ordered them to tell no one about what they had seen, until after the Son of Man had risen from the dead. So they kept the matter to themselves, questioning what this rising from the dead could mean" (Mark 9:9–10). This is the "riddle in the middle" of the Synoptic Gospels. It is also Mark's way of saying that the theme of "blindness" includes the closest of Jesus' disciples—and Jesus has come to open their blind eyes (cf. also Luke 4:18 where Jesus describes his ministry as one sent to proclaim "recovery of sight to the blind").

The innermost frame in this menorah pattern of the Synoptic Gospels as a literary unit sets the report of the death of John the Baptist (Mark 6:14–29) over against the interpretation of the death of Jesus in the institution of the Lord's Supper (Mark 14:12–25). The outermost frame moves from the teachings of Jesus in the Sermon on the Mount in Galilee (Matt 4:23—7:29), to the moment when Jesus enters the Temple and drives out those who are selling things there in Jerusalem (Luke 19:45–48). Jesus continues to teach in the Temple daily until Passover, when the Lord's Supper is instituted (Luke 22:7–38), and the events unfold that lead to his death on

Good Friday (23:44–49), and his resurrection on Easter Sunday (24:1–12).

The Gospel of Matthew

We know little about Matthew beyond the fact that he is one of the twelve disciples of Jesus (see Matt 10:3; Mark 3:18; Luke 6:15; Acts 1:13). Apart from the four lists of Jesus' disciples, Matthew's name appears only once in the New Testament—in Matthew 9:9, as a tax collector who follows Jesus. The parallel accounts in Mark 2:14 and Luke 5:27–29, however, identify him as Levi, the son of Alphaeus (Mark 2:14), and thus Matthew is probably the brother of the apostle James "the less" who is also called the "son of Alphaeus" (Mark 3:18, cf. 15:40). This would mean that there are three pairs of brothers among the Twelve: Peter and Andrew, James and John (sons of Zebedee), and Matthew and James (sons of Alphaeus).

The Gospel of Matthew is of primary importance in early Christianity to the extent that it all but eclipses the other Synoptic Gospels (Mark and Luke). The fact that Matthew's actual name is Levi suggests that he is of Levitical descent, which would accord him a position of authority among ordinary Jews. Moreover, it is readily apparent that his gospel is oriented to Jewish readers, not to the Gentile world. It is quite possible that the Gospel of Matthew is included in the canon as representative of the teachings of Jesus as remembered and used among the Christians in Jerusalem during the ministry of James, the brother of Jesus.

The church fathers cite Matthew far more than Mark and Luke, and Matthew is also more prominent in liturgical usage. The earliest historical information about Matthew comes from Papias, bishop of Hierapolis in Asia Minor (ca. 100–125 C.E.), who says that "Matthew composed the *logia* in the Hebrew tongue and everyone interpreted them as he was able" (Eusebius, *Church History* iii.39.16). Immediately before this passage, Eusebius quotes Papias who cites "the Lord's oracles (*logia*)" in reference to the Gospel of Mark (iii.39.15). Moreover, Papias is the author of a five-volume commentary, *Exegesis of the Oracles* (logia) *of the Lord* (iii.39.1).

Among the Four Gospels, Matthew is the most Jewish in flavor. Its birth narratives are centered on the Davidic descent of Jesus and the kingdom is called the kingdom of heaven. The Sermon on the Mount (Matt 5—7) and chapter 23, with its "seven woes to the scribes and the Pharisees," focus attention on the Jewish religious leaders of Jesus' time. Matthew retains the command to the disciples "not to go to the Gentiles" (10:5; cf. 7:6; 15:26). At the same time, Matthew's Gospel ends on a universalistic note—"to make disciples of all nations" (28:18–20; cf. 24:14), and the author sees the Jews as having forfeited their right to the kingdom (8:11; 22:8).

The Gospel of Matthew is closely related to Judaism. It presents Christian faith and life within the context of a messianic community that is the true heir to the Tanakh. It argues for the right to be understood over against the Jewish synagogue with which it is in constant dialogue, as K. Stendahl notes ("Matthew," *Peake's Commentary on the Bible* [Edinburgh: Thomas Nelson and Sons, 1962], p. 770). In fact, according to Stendahl, Matthew follows the same rules of interpretation found in the Dead Sea Scrolls. For Matthew, the question is who will inherit the kingdom? The answer is clear: the church, that is those who recognize Jesus as the Messiah. In this church, the Gospel of Matthew serves as a manual in which the teachings of Jesus are assembled in five discourses, each of which ends with the same formula: "When Jesus had finished (saying these things)" (7:28; 11:1; 13:53; 19:1; 26:1). These five discourses may be outlined within a framework to give a menorah pattern:

Matthew's Gospel in Terms of the Five Discourses	*Matt 1—28*
A Birth, baptism, testing, and preparation of Jesus for ministry	1:1—4:11
B 1st discourse (Galilee): Sermon on the Mount (ethics of the kingdom)	4:12—7:29
C 2nd discourse: Mission of the disciples and their martyrdom	8:1—11:1
X 3rd discourse: Coming kingdom of heaven (with 7 parables)	11:2—13:53
C´ 4th discourse: Relations among the disciples and church discipline	13:54—19:1
B´ 5th discourse (Jerusalem): The *Eschaton* and the *Parousia* (2nd coming)	19:2—26:1
A´ Suffering, death, and resurrection of Jesus; charge to the 11 disciples	26:2—28:20

The outer frame in this concentric structure moves from the account of the birth, baptism, testing, and preparation for Jesus' ministry

(1:1—4:11) to his suffering, death, and resurrection (26:2—28:20). Each of these two sections has its setting in the geographical region of Judea. The center of this structure focuses attention on the kingdom of heaven, which is introduced by an account of John the Baptist in prison, who is likened to the prophet Elijah (11:2–15). It concludes with a series of parables where Jesus continues to communicate the nature of his kingdom (11:2—13:53). The second frame opens with the first discourse in Galilee (4:12—7:29), most of which is known as the Sermon on the Mount (Matt 5—7). It concludes with the fifth discourse, in which Jesus travels from Galilee to Jerusalem by way of Perea (east of the Jordan River). The first discourse presents the ethics of the kingdom (4:12—7:29). The fifth discourse (19:2—26:1) continues the use of parables to communicate the nature of the kingdom of heaven (20:1–16 and 21:28—22:14), but shifts attention to the coming events of Jesus' suffering and death in Jerusalem (20:17–19)—and the more distant future. Its teaching concerns the end of the age (24:4–35), the Second Coming of Jesus (the *Parousia*, 24:36—25:30), and the great Day of Judgment for the nations (25:31–46).

Another way of looking at the concentric structure of the Gospel of Matthew is to outline the book on the basis of geographical location and the specific nature of Jesus' ministry within a menorah pattern:

The Gospel of Matthew in a Menorah Pattern	Matt 1—28
A Genealogy, birth, and the infancy narrative of Jesus	1:1–2:23
B Jesus in Judea—baptism, testing, and preparation	3:1–4:17
C Public ministry in and around Galilee; preparing the disciples	4:18–10:42
X **Response to Jesus' public ministry—*teaching in parables***	11:1–16:20
C´ Private ministry in Galilee; preparing the disciples	16:21–18:35
B´ Jesus in Judea—from Palm Sunday to Passover	19:1–25:46
A´ Death and resurrection of Jesus	26:1–28:20

In this reading, the focus of interest is on the message that Jesus taught and proclaimed in the cities of Galilee (11:1). Essential elements of that message include the identification of John the Baptist as "Elijah, who is to come" (11:7–15). The central core in this structure includes the third discourse (11:2—13:53) and seven parables on the kingdom in Matthew 13.

The center of the above concentric structure (11:1—16:20), which is also the structural center of the Gospel of Matthew as a whole, may be expanded in a similar menorah pattern:

2nd Level Menorah: Response to Jesus' Public Ministry	*Matt 11:1–16:20*
A John the Baptist as Elijah and Jesus as wisdom's spokesperson	11:1–30
B Plucking grain on the Sabbath–"his disciples were hungry"	12:1–8
C Responses to Jesus' healing ministry–Pharisees plan to kill him	12:9–32
X **Hidden treasure and seven parables on the kingdom**	12:33–13:53
C´ Responses to Jesus' teaching ministry–rejection in Nazareth	13:54–14:12
B´ From feeding the 5000 to feeding 4000–the people are hungry	14:13–15:39
A´ The sign of Jonah and Peter's declaration	16:1–20

The focus of attention in this reading narrows to a section on hidden treasure and the presentation of a series of seven parables on the kingdom of heaven (12:33—13:53). The innermost frame in this concentric structure moves from the attempt of the Pharisees to destroy Jesus (12:9–32), to the rejection of Jesus in his hometown of Nazareth (13:54—14:12). The second frame opens with an account of the disciples plucking grain on the Sabbath because they were hungry (12:1–8) and continues with parallel accounts of Jesus feeding multitudes (14:13—15:39). The outermost frame moves from an account on John the Baptist and a self-revelation on the part of Jesus (11:1–30) to a specific reference to the sign of Jonah (cf. 12:38–50) and Peter's declaration that Jesus is the Messiah (16:13–20).

Once again, the center of this concentric structure may be expanded in a menorah pattern:

3rd Level Menorah: Hidden Treasure and Seven Parables	*Matt 12:33–13:52*
A A tree and its fruit–good things out of a good treasure and vice versa	12:33–50
B Parable of the soils given and explained	13:1–23
C Parables of the weeds among the wheat	13:24–30

At the center of this concentric structure we find the characteristic "riddle in the middle." Here the eleventh of the fourteen formula quotations quotes Psalm 78:2, in which Asaph is considered a prophet when he said, "I will open my mouth in parables; I will utter what has been hidden from the foundation of the world" (Matt 13:35). In particular, it is the parables of the mustard seed (13:31–32) and the leaven (13:33) in which the key to the mystery of the kingdom of heaven is to be found. The innermost frame in this structure presents the parable of the weeds among the wheat (13:24–30), which is set over against an explanation of the meaning of that parable (13:36–43). The second frame presents the parable of the soils, together with its explanation (13:1–23), which is set over against a group of three parables: on hidden treasure, fine pearls, and a fishing net (13:44–50). The outermost frame opens with an enigmatic presentation of a tree and its fruit (12:33–37), which has in its center another riddle of sorts: "The good person brings good things out of a good treasure (θησαυροῦ), and the evil person brings evil out of an evil treasure (θησαυροῦ)" (12:35). It concludes with a repetition of this same Greek word in a parallel context: "Therefore every scribe who has been trained for the kingdom of heaven is like the master of a household who brings out of his treasure (θησαυροῦ) what is new and what is old" (13:52). The point is that Jesus taught in parables—"without a parable he told them nothing" (13:34). In this reading of the Gospel of Matthew we find a striking example of the principle of the "riddle in the middle" in the composition of the biblical text.

The Gospel of Mark

All of the earliest witnesses (including Papias, Irenaeus, Clement of Alexandria, Origen, and Jerome) associate the second gospel with

Mark and link it to the authority of Peter. Papias says, "The Elder said this also; Mark who had been Peter's interpreter (*hermeneutes*), wrote down carefully as much as he remembered, recording both sayings and doings of Christ, not however in order. For he was not a hearer of the Lord, nor a follower, but later a follower of Peter, as I said. And he [Peter or Mark] adapted his teachings to the needs of his hearers... as one who is engaged in making a compendium of the Lord's precepts" (Eusebius, *Church History* iii.39). The key term in understanding the relationship between Mark and Peter is the word *hermeneutes* (ἑρμηνευτῆς) as used by Papias, which is rendered both "translator" and "interpreter." Whatever the precise nuance may be, Mark became Peter's ἑρμηνευτῆς by publishing a gospel in which he recorded Peter's teaching, modified by his own knowledge of Paul's teaching as well.

John Mark is known from references in Acts (12:12, 25; 13:5, 13; 15:37–39), the Letters of Paul (Col 4:10; 2 Tim 4:11; Phlm 24), and Peter (1 Pet 5:13). Mark's mother is a member of the Jerusalem Church, and her home is a regular place of Christian assembly and the place to which Peter came after his escape from prison (Acts 12:12). Mark accompanies Paul on his first missionary journey but leaves him in Pamphylia and returns to Jerusalem (Acts 13:13). Paul interprets this decision on Mark's part as desertion (Acts 15:38). Mark is the cousin of Barnabas, whom he accompanies on a mission to Cyprus. Some years later, Mark and Paul are reconciled, for Paul recommends him to the church at Colossae (Col 4:10). Still later, Paul asks Timothy to bring Mark to him at Rome, saying, "He is very useful to me in my ministry" (2 Tim 4:11). It may be in conjunction with that ministry in Rome that Mark rejoins Peter who refers to him as "my son" in a letter from Rome (1 Pet 5:13).

The Gospel of Mark is best understood as a religious proclamation based on historical events, not as a dispassionate chronicle of Jesus' life. Mark stresses the suffering and death of Jesus, with one-third of the text given to the events of the final week of Jesus' earthly life (the Passion narrative in chaps. 11—16). The concentric structure of the whole may be outlined in a menorah pattern:

The Gospel of Mark in a Menorah Pattern	Mark 1—16
A Proclamation of John: "One who is more powerful than I is coming"	1:1–8
B Beginning of Jesus' ministry—baptism, temptation, first disciples	1:9–3:6
C Jesus' ministry in Galilee—healing and teaching with the Twelve	3:7–8:21
X **Jesus' teaching on discipleship—giving sight to the blind**	8:22–10:52
C´ Jesus' ministry and teaching in Jerusalem with the Twelve	11:1–13:37
B´ End of Jesus' earthly ministry—death and burial of Jesus	14:1–15:47
A´ Proclamation of angel at the empty tomb: "He is risen; he is not here"	16:1–8

In this menorah pattern, the outermost frame moves from the proclamation of John the Baptist (1:1–8) to the proclamation of an angel at
the empty tomb (16:1–8). On the one hand, John declares that, "The
one who is more powerful than I is coming after me; I am not worthy to stoop down and untie the thong of his sandals. I have baptized
you with water; but he will baptize you with the Holy Spirit." On the
other hand, the angel tells the frightened women, "Do not be
alarmed; you are looking for Jesus of Nazareth, who was crucified.
He has been raised; he is not here. Look, there is the place they laid
him. But go, tell his disciples and Peter that he is going ahead of you
to Galilee; there you will see him, just as he told you." The second
frame opens with a section on the beginning of Jesus' earthly ministry, on his baptism and temptation, and on the calling of the first
disciples (1:9—3:6). It continues with a section on the end of Jesus'
earthly ministry, from the plot to kill him (14:1–11), to his trial, crucifixion, and burial (15:1–47). The third frame presents parallel
accounts of Jesus' ministry and teaching in Galilee (3:7—8:21) and
Jerusalem (chaps. 11—13). The latter moves from the triumphal
entry into Jerusalem on Palm Sunday (11:1–11) to a discourse on
eschatology (13:1–37).

Jesus' teaching on discipleship in the central section of the
above structure (8:22—10:52), which is considered pivotal even by
interpreters who refuse to acknowledge the concentric structure of
the whole of the Gospel of Mark, may in turn be expanded in
another menorah pattern:

2nd Level Menorah: Jesus Gives Sight to the Blind	*Mark 8:22—11:10*
A They came to Bethsaida	8:22a
B Healing of the blind man at Bethsaida	8:22b–26
C Peter's declaration: "You are the Messiah!"	8:27–30
X **Jesus foretells his death and resurrection three times**	8:31–10:34
C´ Request of James and John—Jesus models a servant ministry	10:35–45
B´ Healing of blind Bartimaeus at Jericho	10:46–52
A´ They came to Jerusalem—the triumphal entry on Palm Sunday	11:1–10

The theme of blindness sets the stage for a closer look within the center of this structure, which may be expanded once again in a menorah pattern:

3rd Level Menorah: The Transfiguration of Jesus	*Mark 8:31—10:34*
A Jesus foretells his death and resurrection	8:31–38
B An unusual teaching: "some standing here will not taste of death"	9:1
C Transfiguration of Jesus—Jesus, Moses, and Elijah on the mountain	9:2–8
X **The disciples do not see the meaning of "rising from the dead"**	9:9–10
C´ The coming of Elijah: "I tell you Elijah has come"	9:11–13
B´ An unusual healing: "Why could we not cast it out?"	9:14–29
A´ Jesus foretells his death and resurrection (twice)	9:30–10:34

The framework in this concentric structure includes the pairing of three specific prophecies on Jesus' part on his coming death and resurrection (8:31–33; 9:30–32; 10:32–34). In the center we find the fourth reference to the same topic as Jesus orders the disciples "to tell no one about what they had seen (on the Mount of Transfiguration) until after the Son of man had risen from the dead" (9:9). The next verse indicates that the disciples too are "blind," like Bartimaeus; for they cannot see what Jesus means by "this rising from the dead" (9:10). The inner frame in this structure moves from the appearance of Moses and Elijah with Jesus on the Mount of Transfiguration (9:2–8) to Jesus' teaching about Elijah (9:11–13). Jesus tells them, "I tell you that Elijah has come, and they did to him whatever they pleased." Jesus was referring to John the Baptist.

Numerous scholars have observed that the account of the transfiguration of Jesus (9:2–13) is in the structural center of Mark's Gospel. It is more important to note that this literary unit itself may be divided into two parts to constitute a frame around the true center in 9:9–10, which has the character of a "riddle in the middle." Here the apostles Peter, James and John are puzzled—"So they kept the matter to themselves, questioning what this rising from the dead could mean" (9:10). The meaning of these words does not become clear until after Jesus has actually risen from the dead, as reported at the conclusion of the book in 16:5–8. The fact that these three disciples are unable to see what Jesus means suggests that they are "blind," at least symbolically. The verse thus forms a connecting bridge with the parallel accounts of Jesus healing a blind man that function as the structural frame around the central section of the Gospel of Mark (8:22—10:52). This concentrically structured subunit (8:22—10:52), which occupies the larger structural center of Mark, moves from the healing of the blind man at Bethsaida (8:22–26) to that of the blind Bartimaeus (10:46–52). The innermost frame opens with a description of the transfiguration, in which the prophet Elijah appears with Jesus and Moses on the mountain (9:2–8). It continues with a discussion on the coming of Elijah in which the prophet is identified with John the Baptist (9:11–13). Some of the more persuasive examples of parallel features within the Gospel of Mark as a whole include: the baptism of Jesus (1:9–11) and the burial of Jesus (15:42–47); the beginning of Jesus' ministry in Galilee (1:14–15) and the end of Jesus' earthly ministry in Jerusalem (15:1–32); the calling of Peter and three other disciples (1:16–20) and Peter's three denials of Jesus (14:66–72); Jesus' healing and teaching ministry in Galilee (1:29—2:12) and his final ministry on the Mount of Olives (14:26–52); Jesus eating with tax collectors and the call of Levi (2:13–17) and Jesus' eating with the twelve disciples at the institution of the Lord's Supper (14:22–25); and the death of John the Baptist reported (6:14–29) and the plot to kill Jesus (14:1–2).

As with other great works of literary art, proper interpretation of the Gospel of Mark focuses on the plot, characterization, use of symbols, and function of theme. James Williams has shown that Mark emphasizes plot from the very beginning, developing it in a manner that connects all the individual scenes (*Gospel against Parable: Mark's Language of Mystery* [Sheffield: Almond Press, 1985], p. 28). The story Mark tells us is intended to be a model for living. In the first encounter with Jesus within the narrative, we are essentially observers of the action described. Gradually, however, the situation changes as the reader/hearer is invited to identify with the struggles of Jesus' disiciples and so to be drawn into the action itself. At the conclusion of the book, both the disciples and the reader/hearer are required to go again to Galilee and to reenact the plot of Mark's Gospel. But this second time they and we are empowered by the presence of the living Christ in the task of mimesis, or imitation.

In 1991, the American Bible Society released a remarkable video presentation of the Gospel of Mark performed by Alec McCowen. Anyone who takes the time to watch this performance, which takes 105 minutes (with one intermission), cannot help but be moved by the power of the message communicated in this action-packed drama. The entire text of the Gospel of Mark (in the King James version) is presented from memory with the simplest of props. The performance raises intriguing questions about how this book was first used in the life of the early church.

The Gospel of Luke

As most readers know, the Gospel of Luke is closely connected with the Acts of the Apostles, for both of these books were written by the same author and addressed to the same man—a certain Theophilus (cf. Luke 1:1–4 and Acts 1:1), about whom we know nothing. It seems best to simply translate the name Theophilus directly as "lover of God" and to understand these two books as intended for the general reader, for the Gospel of Luke appears to be intended for general circulation among Gentiles. It should be noted, however, that Luke's name is nowhere mentioned in either of these books. The name "Luke" (Λουκᾶς) occurs only three times in the entire New

Testament (Col 4:14; 2 Tim 4:11; Phlm 24). Though some scholars
believe that "Lucius (of Cyrene)," who is mentioned in Acts 13:1
and Rom 16:21, is to be identified with Luke, this is not probable. At
the same time, it should also be noted that the text of Luke's Gospel
emphasizes the fulfillment of the Tanakh with frequent allusions to
passages in Deuteronomy and Isaiah, in particular, to legitimate
Jesus as the Messiah and Savior promised in times past by God.

All we know about Luke from the Bible itself is the fact that he
was a physician beloved by Paul (Col 4:14); a co-worker with Paul
during his imprisonment in Rome (Phlm 24); and a Gentile by birth.
The latter conclusion is drawn from the fact that Paul does not group
him among the "men of the circumcision" in Colossians 4:10–14.
Luke's native country is uncertain. Eusebius and Jerome, among
others in early church tradition, claimed that Luke was from Antioch
in Syria. On the other hand, certain data in Acts suggest that Luke
lived in Philippi. The "we" passages, which begin in Acts 16:10,
suggest that the author of the book is himself the "man of Macedonia" and that he joins Paul and his party in Troas for the journey to
Philippi, his home town. He apparently remains in Philippi while
Paul journeys on in Achaea, and he rejoins Paul some years later
when Paul again comes through Philippi (Acts 20:5–6). It has been
suggested that Luke's reason for remaining in Philippi is that he
married Lydia, Paul's first convert in Philippi (see Acts 16:11–15).
Luke accompanies Paul on his fateful journey to Jerusalem, and two
years later on the ocean voyage that takes Paul from Caesarea to
Rome. On the basis of 2 Corinthians 8:18 and 12:18, Origen and
Jerome conclude that Luke and Titus were brothers. According to
Eusebius (*Church History* vi.14), Clement of Alexandra (d. 220 C.E.)
believed that Luke translated the Epistle of Hebrews into Greek
from the Hebrew language (see chapter 9 below).

As a working hypothesis, we posit three primary steps in the
second major stage of the canonical process that produced the Completed Tanakh. The Gospel of Luke is part of that process from the
beginning, as a definitive presentation of the person and work of
Jesus the Messiah who is seen as the completion, or fulfillment, of
the Tanakh (Hebrew Bible). The first step in this process is the com-

pilation of the initial edition of the "Apostolic Writings"—in a collection of nine books, as a counterpart to the Hebrew Writings, and the concluding fifth section of the Tanakh (ca. 55–58 C.E.).

In the second step in this historical process, which takes place during Paul's imprisonment in Rome (ca. 62 C.E.), the "Apostolic Writings" are expanded into a twenty-two-book canon as a reflection of the twenty-two-book canon of the Tanakh. At this time, the Gospel of Luke plays a central role in the formation of a "New Torah." Paul is joined by Luke, who apparently sent a Greek manuscript of the Epistle to the Hebrews on ahead to Rome while he waited for Timothy to join him (Heb 13:22–23). Timothy does not come in time and Luke goes on to Rome without him—to continue his work with Paul on the "Apostolic Writings." In the meantime, Paul invites Timothy to join the two of them in Rome and to bring with him the manuscripts Paul left in Troas—and, perhaps more important, to bring Mark with him (2 Tim 4:11–13).

When Mark and Timothy arrive in Rome to work with Paul and Luke, the Gospel of Mark becomes the center around which the Gospel of Matthew and the Gospel of Luke are edited in what we now call the Synoptic Gospels. This three-part literary work is conceived from the outset as an integral part of a "New Torah," which is made up of Four Gospels (including that of John) and the Acts of the Apostles (written by Luke). It is possible that Paul sent Tychicus to Ephesus (2 Tim 4:12) to obtain a copy of the Gospel of John, or perhaps the First Letter of John, for inclusion in this twenty-two-book canon of the "New Testament."

The martyrdom of James, the brother of Jesus and head of the church in Jerusalem, in the spring of 62 C.E., serves as a catalyst to speed up the canonical activity in Rome. The subsequent martyrdom of both Paul and Peter sometime after the great fire of 64 C.E. in Rome leaves only the apostle John among the original "pillars" of the Christian Church. John lives on through the Jewish Revolt, with its climax in the destruction of Jerusalem (ca. 66–70 C.E.) and the fall of Masada (73 C.E.) and beyond—to the reign of Domitian (81–96 C.E.). It is John and his followers who produce a forty-nine-book canon, in which the Four Gospels and the Acts of the Apostles function as a "New Torah" connecting the two testaments, each of which is made up of twenty-two books. Though the nature of the conceptual design of forty-nine books structured around a "New Torah" is forgotten in the subsequent life of the expanding Christian Church in the larger Roman world, the design itself survives in popular tradition. It is seen in the traditional order of the twenty-two (twenty-four) books in the Tanakh within Judaism and in the popular order of the twenty-seven books of the New Testament as we now have it in Christianity. It should be noted that this is also what we have chosen to call here the "correct order" of the books of the Bible.

The content of the Gospel of Luke, like that of Matthew and Mark, may be outlined in a menorah pattern:

The Gospel of Luke in a Menorah Pattern	Luke 1—24
A Birth and childhood of Jesus	1:1–3:38
B Temptation of Jesus in the wilderness and ministry in Galilee	4:1–8:56
C Transfiguration of Jesus and discussion of his "Exodus"	9:1-50
X **Jesus' journey to Jerusalem**	9:51–19:35
C´ Triumphal entry into Jerusalem and cleansing of the Temple	19:36–48
B´ Teaching and ministry of Jesus in Jerusalem	20:1–21:38
A´ Death and resurrection of Jesus	22:1–24:53

The focus of attention in this structure is on the lengthy section dealing with the journey to Jerusalem that ends in the events of the final week of Jesus' life and his ministry in Jerusalem (9:51—19:35). The innermost frame opens with the transfiguration of Jesus on the mountain with Moses and Elijah, in which the three of them discuss Jesus' coming "exodus" (ἔξοδον). It continues with the triumphal entry into Jerusalem and the cleansing of the Temple that sets in motion the flow of events leading to "his departure (ἔξοδον), which he was about to accomplish at Jerusalem" (9:31). The second frame moves from the temptation of Jesus in the wilderness "for forty days" (4:2) at the outset of his public ministry to the advent of his public teaching ministry in the Temple at Jerusalem that culminates in the plot to kill him (20:1—21:38). The unfolding of that plot in the events of Jesus' betrayal, arrest, trial, death by crucifixion, resurrection, and ascension (22:1—24:53) is set over against the opening account of Jesus' birth and childhood (1:1—3:38).

The journey to Jerusalem, as presented in the center of the above concentric structure, may in turn be expanded in another menorah pattern as well:

2nd Level Menorah: Jesus' Journey to Jerusalem	*Luke 9:51—19:35*
A Jesus sets his face to go to Jerusalem and sends messengers ahead	9:51-56
B On the way to Jerusalem Jesus teaches the way of the kingdom	9:57—11:13
C Teaching on discipleship	11:14—13:9
X **Journey ends in Jerusalem—Sabbath controversy**	13:10—14:6
C´ Teaching on discipleship	14:7—17:10
B´ On the way to Jerusalem Jesus teaches the way of the kingdom	17:11—19:27
A´ Jesus goes on toward Jerusalem and sends two disciples ahead	19:28-35

As one moves more deeply into the central section of Luke's Gospel, the focus of interest narrows to the controversy over Jesus' teaching and healing in the synagogues on the Sabbath (13:10—14:6). The larger literary unit in this structure opens with Jesus setting his face to go to Jerusalem and sending messengers ahead (9:51–56). It concludes with a parallel passage as Jesus leaves Jericho and journeys to Jerusalem by way of Bethany, on the Mount of Olives (19:28–29). Jesus sends two of his disciples ahead to get the colt on which he will ride for his entry into the city of Jerusalem.

We can move more deeply into the center of the Gospel of Luke by expanding the central section (13:10—14:6) in another menorah pattern:

3rd Level Menorah: The Journey Ends in Jerusalem	*Luke 13:10—14:6*
A Jesus heals a crippled woman—third Sabbath controversy	13:10-17
B Parable of the mustard seed—image of remarkable growth	13:18-19
C Parable of yeast—positive metaphor for hidden growth	13:20-21
X **Narrow door: "Eat in the kingdom of God" (i.e., salvation)**	13:22-30
C´ Jesus links his fate with that of the prophets, foretelling his resurrection	13:31-33

B´   Jerusalem is the focus of the impending confrontation   13:34–35
A´   Jesus heals a man with dropsy—fourth Sabbath controversy   14:1–6

In this reading, the center of Luke's Gospel has the quality of a "riddle in the middle" in the teaching on the narrow door (13:22–30), which is introduced by a resumption in the narrative account of the journey to Jerusalem introduced in 9:51 (see also 17:11 and 19:28). The reference to people coming from afar to "eat in the kingdom of God" (13:29) is a common image for salvation (see 14:15; 22:16, 29–30; and cf. Isa 25:6–8; 65:13–14; Rev 3:20; 19:9). The outer frame is made up of two parallel stories of healing miracles by Jesus, both of which are part of the sequence of texts dealing with the matter of controversy over the Sabbath (13:10–17 and 14:1–6). Controversy on observing the Sabbath provides the occasion for the impending confrontation between Jesus and the religious leaders of the Jews in Jerusalem (13:10—14:6). The conflict itself is played out within the context of an extended account of the journey to Jerusalem during which Jesus teaches the way of the kingdom (9:51—19:35).

It is interesting to note the fact that the parables in the center of Luke on the mustard seed (13:18–19) and yeast (13:20–21) appear also in the structural center of the Gospel of Matthew, where they also function as a "riddle in the middle" (Matt 13:24–33). In Matthew, these two short parables are used to explain why Jesus taught in parables. Here in Luke they are used to introduce a remarkable passage about the narrow door to salvation and the end of the age. The Messiah, as "the owner of the house" (13:25), serves as host to peoples who have come from the farthest reaches of the globe. "Then people will come from east and west, from north and south, and will eat in the kingdom of God. Indeed, some are last who will be first, and some are first who will be last" (13:29–30). This story, and the lament over Jerusalem that follows (13:31–35), in which Jesus once again alludes to his resurrection in the words "on the third day I finish my work" (13:32–33), is framed by the accounts of the third and fourth Sabbath controversies (13:10–17 and 14:1–6). The confrontation with the Jewish religious leaders over the issue sets the stage for the events that follow in Jerusalem and the death and resurrection of Jesus.

THE GOSPEL OF JOHN AND THE SECOND TESTAMENT

From a structural point of view, the Gospel of John is the most carefully constructed work of literary art in the Bible. Though there are parallels to the concentric structures we have observed elsewhere in both testaments, there is also much here that is quite different. In his penetrating study of the concentric structure of the Fourth Gospel, Bruno Barnhart discusses what he calls "The Chiastic Mandala of John's Gospel." Moreover, as Barnhart observes, "Suddenly the stunning possibility emerges that John's narrative has been composed according to a quaternary figure, centered in the episode of the night sea-crossing [6:16–21], in such a way as to retrace the scheme of the *seven days of creation!*" (*The Good Wine: Reading John from the Center* [New York, Mahwah: Paulist Press, 1993], p. 37).

Though the Gospel of John was included in the twenty-two-book canon, as part of the "New Torah" as conceived by Paul, Luke, Mark, and the others in Rome (ca. 62 C.E.), it was probably in a somewhat different form than what we have in our Bibles today. John outlived Paul, Peter, and the others who had contributed to this particular canon of the "New Testament" by some thirty years. During this time, John and his followers were responsible for the third and final step in the canonical process that produced the Completed Tanakh.

In this final stage of the canonical process, John and his followers produce the book of Revelation and a revised edition of John's Gospel. Moreover, the Second and Third Letters of John are added, along with a second Letter of Peter and the Letter of Jude, to produce a twenty-seven-book canon of the New Testament. In this new understanding of the structure of the canon, the Four Gospels and Acts are separated out as a "New Torah" that forms a bridge connecting the First Testament and the Second Testament, each of which is made up of twenty-two books. The Bible as a whole, the Completed Tanakh, is thus made up of forty-nine books.

Though the Gospel of John is included in the canonical process at the time of Paul's ministry in Rome, there is no evidence that John himself works directly with the others there who are gathered as a sort of "editorial board." Mark joins them, as does Peter who subsequently experiences martyrdom in Rome, like Paul. James, the brother of Jesus and head of the church in Jerusalem, is martyred while Paul is still a prisoner in Rome (ca. 62 C.E.). A copy of John's Gospel is probably brought to Rome at this time, perhaps by Tychicus (2 Tim 4:12). John seems to have remained in Ephesus, or its vicinity in Asia Minor, and so escapes persecution and death in the days of the Emperor Nero. John lives on, continuing his ministry and canonical activity for another thirty years.

Three Steps in the Canonical Process to Complete the Tanakh

1st Step	2nd Step	3rd Step
[Ca. 55–58 C.E.]	[Ca. 58–64 C.E.]	[Ca. 96 C.E.]
Apostolic Writings	*"New Testament"*	*Completed Tanakh*
[As a 5th section in the Tanakh]	[22 books in each Testament]	[22 + 5 + 22 = 49 books]
Paul and Luke	Paul, Luke, Mark, etc.	John
Greece & Asia Minor	Rome	Ephesus & Palestine

Bruno Barnhart outlines the Gospel of John "into five great parts," each of which is governed by an overall theme. When these five sections are enclosed within the framework of the prologue and epilogue of the book, we have the following menorah pattern:

The Gospel of John: Unfolding of the New Creation	John 1—21
A Johannine prologue: The Word became flesh	1:1–18
B Part One: Witness and discipleship	1:19–4:3
C Part Two: Response to Jesus–positive and negative	4:4–6:15
X **Part Three: New Creation/Exodus—Jesus walks on the sea**	6:16–21
C´ Part Four: Response to Jesus–positive and negative	6:22–12:11
B´ Part Five: Witness and discipleship	12:12–20:31
A´ Petrine epilogue: On the seashore	21:1–25

In this reading, we find a five-part concentric pattern set within the framework of a carefully crafted prologue (1:1–18) and epilogue (21:1–25). The prologue presents Jesus as the Word of God incarnate in human flesh, with John the Baptist as a primary witness. Here we find the familiar pairing of Jesus as the king and John the Baptist as the prophet anticipated in the structure and content of the First Testament. The epilogue presents Peter and the beloved disciple (John) in a final scene with overtones for understanding the canonical process itself. Jesus said to Peter, "If it is my will that he [John] remain until I come, what is that to you?" (21:22). There were many who believed "that this disciple would not die." But that is not what Jesus said, as John himself bears witness. John outlives Peter and the other disciples by thirty years and is used of God to bring the canonical process to its conclusion—with the completion of the Revelation to John (ca. 94 C.E.).

The focus of attention in the above structure is on what Barnhart calls "The New Exodus" as portrayed in 6:16–21. In reaching this conclusion, Barnhart is following the earlier work of Peter Ellis (*The Genius of John: A Composition-Critical Commentary on the Fourth Gospel* [Liturgical Press, 1984], pp. 14–15). Barnhart finds within this imagery of Jesus walking upon the dark waters a reflection of "*the first moment of creation*, as recounted in Genesis 1:2. This is the center of the book, from whence Barnhart reads the "mandala" of the whole through the seven days of "The Unfolding of the New Creation."

The Unfolding of the New Creation

1. **First Day**: Light in Darkness
       The Sea-Crossing (6:16–21)
2. **Second Day**: Bread from Heaven
       The Sign of Bread (6:1–15)
       The Bread Discourse (6:22–71)
3. **Third Day**: His Glory Fills the Earth
       John the Baptist and Jesus (3:22—4:3)
       Witnesses to Jesus: Several to One (5:31–47)
       The Festival of Booths (7:1–53)
       The Festival of Booths (8:12–59)
       Final Passover Approaches: Jesus Enters Jerusalem (12:12–50)

4. **Fourth Day**: You Are the Light of the World
    Nicodemus (3:1–21)
    The Paralytic (5:1–30)
    The Man Born Blind (9:1–41)
    The Lord's Supper (chapters 13—17)
5. **Fifth Day**: The Living Temple is the Lamb
    Jesus Cleanses the Temple (2:13–25)
    The Royal Official's Son (4:43–54)
    The Gate: Lazarus (chapters 10—11)
6. **Sixth Day**: In the Image of God He Created Them
    The Wedding at Cana (2:1–12)
    The Woman at the Well (4:4–42)
    The Anointing at Bethany (12:1–11)
    In the Garden of Gethsemane (20:1–18)
        The Disciples at the Tomb (20:1–10)
        Jesus and Mary Magdalene (20:11–18)
7. **Seventh Day**: Into the Place of His Rest
    John the Baptist and the First Disciples of Jesus (1:19–51)
    Jesus Appears to the Gathered Disciples (20:19–31)
8. The Continuing Day [an 8th Day—"active life of the church in history"]
    On the Seashore (chapter 21)
    Prologue (1:1–18)—synthetic perspective from which to view the whole

When the Gospel of John is outlined in a series of "wheels within wheels," the process begins with the following menorah pattern:

The Gospel of John in a Menorah Pattern	John 1–21
A Prologue: Focus on Jesus and John the Baptist at the Jordan River	1:19–51
B Mary at Cana–Jesus' first sign, turning water to wine at a wedding	2:1–12
C Jesus cleansing the Temple at Passover	2:13–25
X **From discourse to Nicodemus to that of the Lord's Supper**	3:1–17:26
C´ Jesus' passion displayed in Jerusalem at Passover	18:1–19:42
B´ Mary at the tomb–Jesus' seventh sign, the resurrection	20:1–18
A´ Epilogue: Focus on Peter and John at the Sea of Galilee	20:19–21:25

The innermost frame in this concentric structure opens with the account of Jesus cleansing the Temple in Jerusalem by "making a whip of cords" and driving out the merchants and money-changers (2:13–25). It continues with the account of the arrest, trial, crucifixion, and burial of Jesus (18:1—19:42). John informs us that both of these events take place at the time of Passover—one at the beginning of Jesus' public ministry in Jerusalem and the other at the end. The second frame opens with the story of the wedding at Cana of Galilee and the role of Jesus' mother Mary in the presentation of the first sign of Jesus, that of turning water to wine (2:1–12). This story is set over against that of Jesus' seventh sign—his resurrection, in which Mary Magdalene plays a significant role (20:1–18).

The center in John 3:1—17:26, which is bounded by the first and the last of Jesus' seven discourses, may be outlined in another menorah pattern:

2nd Level Menorah: Seven Discourses of Jesus	John 3–17
A Discourse to Nicodemus—necessity of the new birth	3:1–21
B Witness of John the Baptist	3:22—4:3
C Jesus and the woman at the well in Samaria—"living water"	4:4–42
X **From Galilee to Jerusalem—"New Exodus" on Sea of Galilee**	4:43—10:39
C´ Jesus and women at Bethany (Mary and Martha), raising of Lazarus	11:1–12:11
B´ Witness of the Jerusalem crowd	12:12–50
A´ Discourse at the Last Supper—meaning of Jesus' death	13:1—17:26

John's Gospel moves back and forth from discourse to narrative throughout this section, beginning with Jesus' discourse to Nicodemus on the necessity of the new birth (3:1–21) and ending with his farewell discourse at the Last Supper (14:1—17:26). The second frame opens with an account of further testimony on the part of John the Baptist (3:22–36, cf. 1:19–34). It concludes with the events of Palm Sunday, as the crowd comes to the festival in Jerusalem "continuing to testify" (12:12–50). The innermost frame presents parallel accounts of Jesus with women—at the well in Samaria with the woman who draws water for him and learns from him about "living water" (4:4–42) and at Bethany with Mary and Martha when Jesus raises their brother Lazarus from the dead (11:1—12:11).

The central section in the above concentric structure may be expanded into a menorah pattern of its own:

3rd Level Menorah: From Galilee to Jerusalem	*John 4:43—10:39*
A Jesus teaching in Galilee and healing a pagan official's son	4:43–54
B Feast of Passover (?)—Jesus cures a paralytic	5:1–47
C Bread multiplied—feeding the five thousand	6:1–15
X **The New Creation/Exodus—Jesus walks on the sea**	6:16–21
C´ Bread discourse: "I am the bread that came down from heaven"	6:22–71
B´ Feast of Booths—Jesus cures a man born blind	7:1–10:21
A´ Jesus teaching in Jerusalem at the festival of Dedication	10:22–39

The outermost frame in this concentric structure moves from an account of Jesus' ministry in Galilee (4:43–54) to his teaching in the Temple at Jerusalem during the festival of Dedication (Hanukkah) and a brief journey "across the Jordan to the place where John had been baptizing earlier" (10:22–39). The second frame opens with Jesus traveling from Galilee to Jerusalem for the observance of "a festival of the Jews" (which may have been Passover) where he healed a paralytic (5:1–47). It continues with Jesus in Jerusalem for the observance of the festival of Booths where he healed a man born blind (7:1—10:21). The innermost frame moves from the miracle of the feeding of five thousand in Galilee, where bread was multiplied (6:1–15) to Jesus' discourse on bread in which he declares, "I am the bread that came down from heaven" (6:22–71). And in the structural center we find the account of Jesus walking on the waters of the Sea of Galilee (6:16–21).

Ellis argues convincingly that the narrative of the sea crossing (6:16–21) is the center of the Gospel of John as a whole, and that it signifies theologically a *new exodus* (*The Genius of John*, p. 111).

Only when the reader recognizes the episode as the turning point of the Gospel and as the dramatization of a new exodus constitut-

ing a new people of God does it dawn upon him or her that respon-
sive Israel (the disciples and Christians in general) is about to
replace unresponsive Israel (the synagogue) as the true Israel of
God—the Christian Church.

Building on the work of Ellis, Barnhart proposes a quaternary development of these structures. He also divides the Gospel of John into a
series of twenty-one narrative sections, which are analyzed in terms
of the seven days of creation in Genesis 1—2, and the details of the
prologue in John 1:1–18. The end result is a journey into the hidden
meaning of the text.

The obvious question that emerges from the study of John's role
in the canonical process of early Christianity, and the concept of a
forty-nine-book "Completed Tanakh" in particular, is why this particular concept of sacred scripture was not preserved in the life of the
early church after John's death. Though evidence is lacking for a decisive answer to this question, a number of observations can be made.

The fact that John left Palestine prior to the Jewish Revolt against
Rome (ca. 66–73 C.E.) and that he lived and worked in the vicinity of
Ephesus in Asia Minor is well attested. After the destruction of
Jerusalem in 70 C.E., a Christian presence was reestablished there, but
John does not appear to be among those particular leaders. He appar-
ently continues his work in western Asia Minor, for Irenaeus said that
John wrote his Gospel in Ephesus (*Against Heresies* 3.1.1).

By the time of John's death (ca. 96 C.E.), the center of the church
had moved westward to the city of Rome. Moreover, the church
itself had become independent from Judaism and was already primarily Gentile in its constituency. The Septuagint translation of the
Tanakh became the Bible of the early church, along with the twenty-
seven books of what became known as the "New Testament" as well
as certain other books that were sometimes included as part of the
sacred literary tradition in both testaments. In short, the ancient Jewish principle of "Tanakh" in the sense of the Bible in three major
divisions—Torah, Prophets, and Writings—was no longer the common way of thinking about the the Bible. Instead, the individual

books of the Bible were arranged according to ideas about their content and genre.

The use of the codex in the early church played a significant role in the loss of the idea of a "Completed Tanakh" in early Christianity; for increasingly those who produced these texts were cut off from their Jewish roots. According to Roberts and Skeat, the codex as a form of book originated in the first century C.E. (*The Birth of the Codex* [London: Oxford University Press, 1983], pp. 45–53). The earliest known example of a codex is a portion of the New Testament. In fact, it has been argued that the codex itself was invented to disseminate the New Testament. There were obvious advantages to the codex, as opposed to scrolls of papyrus or leather, for sacred literature of earlier times. The use of the codex allowed the whole of the New Testament to be written on both sides of parchment leaves, which were placed between the covers of a single book. Not only did this provide a more compact source for purposes of reference and study, it also maintained a fixed order of the twenty-seven books in question. Unfortunately, however, it appears that those responsible for producing copies of the Bible in these codices were no longer cognizant of the Tanakh as the organizing principle of sacred scripture. Instead, a more logical arrangement of the individual books of the Bible in terms of a presumed chronological order of their composition or content replaced the three-part structure of the Completed Tanakh as envisioned by the apostle John and others before him.

By the time of Constantine, the two testaments had already been put together in single uncial codices for use as pulpit Bibles in churches throughout the Roman Empire. When the emperor Constantine needed fifty copies of the Bible for use in churches of his newly established capital, Constantinople, he called on Eusebius in Caesarea to make these copies. In spite of the fact that the work of copying these Greek texts of the Bible took place in Palestine, the church leaders in this setting were increasingly separated from their Jewish forebears in modes of thought and customs. Consequently, the books of both testaments were arranged in a more logical order from their point of view and the very idea of the Tanakh as a structuring principle was lost in Christian circles. With that loss came a new arrangement of the books of the New Testament as well, as the books were placed in assumed chronological order, much like what had already taken place in Alexandria with the Septuagint translation of the Tanakh (and related sacred writings).

The curious thing to note is the fact that the correct order of the books of the New Testament, as envisioned by the apostle John, managed to survive in popular usage within church tradition. The situation is much the same as the survival of the correct order of the books of the Tanakh within Judaism. Even the authority of the masoretic tradition in Tiberias, which produced the Leningrad Codex and the Aleppo Codex, could not change the popular tradition as witnessed by the refusal to place the books of Chronicles at the beginning of the Writings in the Tanakh within worship tradition in the synagogues. Though the masoretic scribes of antiquity moved 1 and 2 Chronicles to the beginning of the Writings, popular tradition in synagogue usage continued to place them at the end of the Writings as the last books in the Bible. In like manner, the decision to place the seven "General Epistles," which were associated with the apostles Peter, John, James, and Jude (brother of James and Jesus) before the Letters of Paul did not affect the popular usage of the order of the books in the Second Testament. John's concept of the "Completed Tanakh" never died, even though countless scribes in antiquity and in modern times have rearranged the books of the Bible to fit their own understanding of a more correct order.

ACTS OF THE APOSTLES AS A LITERARY BRIDGE

The opening verse in the book of Acts calls attention to "the first book" that the author has already written to a certain person by the name of Theophilus, namely the Gospel of Luke (see Luke 1:1–4). The abrupt ending to the book of Acts, with its brief note on Paul's two years as a prisoner in Rome awaiting trial, suggests that the written composition of this book was completed at this point in time (ca. 62 C.E.).

The "we" passages, which begin in Acts 16:10 immediately after Timothy is introduced (16:1) along with a certain "man of Macedonia"

(16:9), break off when Paul leaves Philippi in 17:1. The "we" sections resume in Acts 20, when Paul returns to Philippi to begin his final journey to Jerusalem. The "we" sections continue in the journey to Jerusalem and commence again when Paul sails from Caesarea for Rome (Acts 27:1—28:16). If we conclude that the "we" sections are the contribution of Luke, as author of the book of Acts, to indicate those sections of the story in which he is personally involved, the historical situation may be reconstructed in unusual detail.

Paul and Luke were already engaged in theological reflection on canonical activity before Paul's fateful journey to Jerusalem (ca. 58 C.E.). That activity includes writing the Gospel of Luke and editing eight of the Letters of Paul, as a fifth segment of the Tanakh, corresponding to the Hebrew Writings. These documents were left in a "book-carrier" (φαιλόνης) in Troas, where Paul and Luke "stayed for seven days" (Acts 20:6, cf. 2 Tim 4:13). The purpose of the trip to Troas was to join other members of their party there, including Timothy (Acts 20:4–5).

During his two years in Palestine (ca. 58–60 C.E.), while Paul was under arrest in Caesarea, Luke was probably working with James, Peter, John, and others in Jerusalem. In particular, he learned of other writings, which would eventually become part of the emerging New Testament, including the content of the "Epistle to the Hebrews," which Luke himself subsequently either rewrote in its entirety or edited in the Greek language. After the assassination of James, the brother of Jesus and head of the Church in Jerusalem (ca. 62 C.E.), two other documents made their way from Palestine to Rome—the Gospel of Matthew and the Letter of James.

After their arrival in Rome, Luke left Paul and made his way to some unspecified location, perhaps to his own home in Philippi or perhaps to Ephesus to consult with John. At this point in time, Luke's primary tasks were to complete the book of Acts and to arrange for the inclusion of the Epistle to the Hebrews, which plays a central role in the structure and content of the second half of the emerging "New Testament." He may also have taken this opportunity to consult with the apostle John so as to include his writings in the proposed "canon of the New Testament."

In characteristic fashion, Luke tells us nothing about himself in the brief note he appends to a manuscript of the Epistle to the Hebrews (13:22–25). He sends that Greek manuscript to Paul in Rome, informing him that Timothy "has been released" from his other duties so that he is now free to join the team in their work. Luke is waiting for Timothy's arrival and plans to bring him to Rome, if he arrives in time. For some reason, Timothy's arrival is delayed, so Luke goes on without him. There in Rome, Paul writes his second letter to Timothy in which he informs him that "Luke alone is with me" (2 Tim 4:11). By this time, Paul has already sent Tychicus to Ephesus (2 Tim 4:12), perhaps to bring a completed copy of John's Gospel for inclusion in their canonical project. He now urges Timothy to bring Mark with him, "for he is very useful in my ministry" (2 Tim 4:11). But, most important of all, Timothy is instructed to bring the "book-carrier" that Paul "left with Carpus at Troas, and also the books, and above all the parchments" (2 Tim 4:13). As Skeat has argued, these parchments were not scrolls, but parchment leaves—to be sewn in the form of a codex (T. C. Skeat, "'Especially the Parchments': A Note on 2 Timothy IV.13." *JTS* n.s. 30 [1979], pp. 173–77).

Luke was already at work on the book of Acts as a sequel to his gospel. That story of the expansion of the early church is carried to the point in time when Luke leaves Paul in Rome at the end of their perilous journey by sea from Palestine. It is likely that the book of Acts is intended from the outset to serve as an introduction to the collection of the Letters of Paul, with the Letter to the Romans appearing as its sequel in the "Completed Tanakh" envisioned by Paul and Luke. In one sense, then, the book of Acts functions for the "New Testament" like the book of Deuteronomy in the Tanakh, which serves a double role—as the conclusion to the Torah (the five books of Moses) and the introduction to the Prophets (Former Prophets and Latter Prophets). Acts completes the collection of five books in the "New Torah" and serves as a bridge to connect the Four Gospels with the "Ecclesiastical Letters" of Paul to the seven churches that follow. The first four of these letters (Romans, 1 and 2 Corinthians, and Galatians) correspond to the Former Prophets in the

First Testament. The book of Acts connects them with the Four Gospels so as to continue the story of Jesus Christ and the establishment of early Christianity through his disciples—from the beginning to the imprisonment of the apostle Paul in Rome. That is when the second step in this stage of the canonical process itself is undertaken, in which the book of Acts plays such a central role.

The Four Gospels and Acts constitute a "New Torah," which is augmented by a collection of thirteen letters of Paul and four works associated with "James [the brother of Jesus] and Cephas [Peter], and John, who were reputed to be pillars" (Gal 2:9). At the completion of this phase in the canonical process, these four books are the Epistle to the Hebrews (associated with Paul), the Letter of James (the brother of Jesus and head of the Jerusalem Church), the First Letter of Peter, and the First Letter of John. This canon of twenty-two-books was intended to be the counterpart to the twenty-two-book canon of the Tanakh, as described by Josephus. The structure of each of these collections is the same: five books in the Torah, thirteen prophets (or Letters of Paul), and four writings (associated with the four "pillars"—with Paul taking his place alongside James, Peter, and John). In the Tanakh, the four writings ("Hagiographa") are Psalms, Job, Proverbs, and the "Megilloth" (five Festal Scrolls: Ruth, Song of Songs, Ecclesiastes, Lamentations, and Esther).

Since the book of Acts is a continuation of the Gospel of Luke, it shares much in common with that book in terms of its concentric design. The book as a whole can be outlined in a menorah pattern:

The Acts of the Apostles in a Menorah Pattern	Acts 1—28
A The apostles in Jerusalem—the Church from Pentecost to Gamaliel	1:1—5:42
B Ministry of Stephen and Philip—the first Christian martyr	6:1—8:40
C Saul's conversion; "conversion" of Peter and Cornelius	9:1—11:25
X **Herod kills James and imprisons Peter**	12:1–25
C´ Missionary journeys of Paul and Barnabas; Council at Jerusalem	13:1—15:41
B´ Ministry of Paul as prophet and leader in Greece and Ephesus	16:1—20:38
A´ Paul's journey to Jerusalem—arrest and prison in Caesarea and Rome	21:1—28:31

The narrative opens with the apostles in Jerusalem at the moment of Jesus' ascension into heaven (Acts 1:1–11, cf. Luke 24:50–53). In this reading of Acts, the first half of the outer frame concludes with an account of the persecution of the apostles who are arrested and put in prison. The second frame in the concentric design of the book of Acts opens with the ministry of Stephen and Philip, with particular interest in the remarkable sermon of Stephen at the time of his martyrdom in Acts 7. The second frame continues with the ministry of Paul as prophet and leader of the churches in Greece and Ephesus (Acts 16—20). The innermost frame opens with the conversion of Saul (who is renamed Paul) and the "conversion" of Peter who learns to accept Gentiles in the person of the Roman centurion Cornelius (Acts 9—11). It continues in the account of the missionary journeys of Paul and Barnabas that result in the great Council at Jerusalem (Acts 13—15), which also opens the door to Gentile believers.

The center of the above concentric structure may be expanded in a menorah pattern of its own:

2nd Level Menorah: Herod Kills James and Imprisons Peter	Acts 12
A Herod kills James and imprisons Peter (at Passover)	12:1–3
B Herod appoints four squads of soldiers to guard Peter in prison	12:4
C The church prays fervently to God for Peter in prison	12:5
X **Peter is delivered from prison**	12:6–11
C′ Peter goes to the place where the church is praying for him	12:12–17
B′ Herod examines the guards and orders them to be put to death	12:18–19
A′ Death of Herod—"an angel of the Lord struck him down"	12:20–25

The outer frame in this concentric structure moves from the account of the martyrdom of James at the hand of Herod (12:1–3), to the death of Herod (12:20–25). In the middle we find a detailed account of Herod's imprisonment of Peter and his deliverance by the angel of the Lord in the night. The second frame opens with Herod's appointment of four squads of soldiers to guard Peter (12:4) and concludes with Herod's order that those guards be put to death (12:18–19). The innermost frame moves from an account of the church praying fervently to God for Peter who is in prison (12:5) to the portrayal of Peter himself showing up at the door of that church body as they are praying for him (23:12–17).

In the structural center of the above menorah pattern, we find the account of Peter's deliverance, which may be outlined in a similar manner:

3rd Level Menorah: Peter Delivered from Prison	*Acts 12:6–11*
A Peter asleep inside the prison between two soldiers with guards posted	12:6
B An angel of the Lord appears and wakes him, saying, "Get up quickly!"	12:7
C Peter followed the angel—"he thought he was seeing a vision"	12:8–9
X **They passed two guards and the gate opened "of its own accord"**	12:10a
C´ Peter and the angel "went outside and walked along a lane"	12:10b
B´ Outside the prison—"suddenly the angel left him"	12:10c
A´ Peter awake outside the prison—"He came to himself and said..."	12:11

As we move more deeply into the center of Acts, the concentric structure becomes tighter, much the same as in the Gospel of Luke. The outer frame opens with Peter asleep inside the prison (12:6) and concludes with Peter awake outside the prison (12:11); for an angel appears to him in the prison and wakes him saying, "Get up quickly!" (12:7). The angel leaves Peter suddenly, as soon as they are safely outside the prison (12:10c). The innermost frame has Peter following the angel, thinking it is all a dream (12:8–9 and 10b). And in the center we find the miraculous deliverance from prison as Peter and the angel pass by the guards and through the prison gate that opens "of its own accord" (12:10a).

Like the story of the narrow door at the center of the Gospel of Luke, the account of Peter's deliverance from prison has symbolic value. The story speaks to the heart of the gospel, for each one of us is a bit like Peter—chained in a dark prison, with the forces of evil assembled against us. But in the midst of the darkness, the angel of the Lord appears to guide us out of our prison to take us to others of like mind who serve the same risen and ascended Jesus Christ.

Delbert Wiens argues that Stephen's sermon in Acts 7 is pivotal to understanding the structure and meaning of the book of Acts in relation to the Torah and Prophets of the Tanakh (*Stephen's Sermon and the Structure of Luke–Acts* [BIBAL Press, 1995]). It should be noted that when Luke records the experience of the two disciples on the road to Emmaus, he highlights the fact that even though the disciples are able to tell their unrecognized companion about the empty tomb and Jesus' reported resurrection, they remain puzzled and disheartened. As Wiens puts it (p. 4), "Only after Jesus shows them from 'Moses and all the prophets' that these confusing events are wholly appropriate, even necessary, within the larger story of God's actions are they able to believe (Luke 24:13–35)." Luke 16:31 states plainly that Moses and the prophets must be understood before a resurrected one can be recognized. The "New Torah" of the Four Gospels and Acts presumes knowledge of the original Torah in the five books of Moses.

8

The New Prophet to the Nations
Thirteen Letters of Paul

The apostle Paul plays a central role in the formation of the canonical structure of the Completed Tanakh. In the previous chapter, we suggested three primary steps in the canonical process that added the "Apostolic Writings" to the Tanakh of ancient Judaism. In the first, which is completed prior to the fateful journey to Jerusalem that results in Paul's arrest (ca. 58 C.E.), Paul's letters to seven churches are arranged together with the Gospel of Luke on folio pages (*membrana*). These documents, and the papyrus letters (*biblia*) on which they are based, are left with Carpus in Troas for safekeeping before Paul and Luke embark for Rome (cf. 2 Tim 4:13 and Acts 20:1–6). Luke, who travels with Paul to Jerusalem, spends the two years of Paul's imprisonment in Caesarea in Palestine working on his second volume, the Acts of the Apostles, in consultation with the leaders of the Jerusalem Church (ca. 58–60 C.E.).

The next step in the canonical process that produces the Completed Tanakh is carried out in Rome, following the harrowing sea journey from Caesarea on which Luke accompanies Paul. This is the point at which Luke ends the book of Acts, as he turns his attention to the task of gathering the remaining documents he and Paul envision as the Greek "New Testament." The end result is a collection of twenty-two books arranged to mirror an understanding of the twenty-two books in the canon of the Tanakh. The structure of this canon of the "Apostolic Writings" is parallel to the structure of the Tanakh as subsequently described by the Jewish historian Josephus: five books of the Torah, thirteen "prophets," and four "Hagiographa."

Thirteen of Paul's letters are arranged to form a structural counterpart to the thirteen "prophets" in the Tanakh, with three groups of four letters arranged around the Letter to the Ephesians.

Romans		1 Corinthians	
2 Corinthians		Galatians	
	Ephesians		
Philippians	Colossians	1 Timothy	2 Timothy
1 Thessalonians	2 Thessalonians	Titus	Philemon

NINE ECCLESIASTICAL LETTERS OF PAUL TO SEVEN CHURCHES

Nine letters of Paul to seven churches in Rome, Greece (Corinth, Philippi, and Thessalonica), and Asia Minor (Galatia, Colossae) are arranged in two groups, the first of which is made up of four letters, arranged in the form of a simple chiasm: Romans / 1 Corinthians // 2 Corinthians / Galatians. The inner pair in this structure is addressed to the same church in Greece; and the other pair is addressed to churches in Europe (Rome) and Asia Minor (Galatia). Romans and Galatians are similar in theological content, since both are concerned primarily with the meaning of the gospel and the matter of Christian liberty from the demands of Jewish law.

The narrative in Acts ends with Paul under house arrest in Rome prior to his trial and death. The concluding events in Acts, with Paul appearing before Festus in Caesarea (Acts 25:6—26:32) followed by his imprisonment in Rome take place from 58 to 62 C.E. Paul's martyrdom in Rome falls within the persecution of the Emperor Nero, presumably after the great fire in Rome (64 C.E.). The story of the "New Torah" (the Four Gospels and Acts) takes us from the birth of Jesus to Paul's imminent trial in Rome. At this point, the first four of Paul's nine letters to the seven churches highlight his missionary activity in reverse order: the Letter to the Romans (ca. 56–57 C.E.), two letters to the Corinthians (ca. 54–56 C.E.), and the Letter to the Galatians (ca. 52–54 C.E.).

The Letter of Paul to the Romans

Paul's Letter to the Romans may be outlined in a menorah pattern:

Paul's Letter to the Romans in a Menorah Pattern	*Rom 1—16*
a Salutation: "Gospel of God...through his prophets in the scriptures"	1:1–7
A True Jews are those who have the Torah written on their hearts	1:8–4:25
B The Messiah's death and resurrection triumphs over sin and death	5:1–7:25
C Those who have the Spirit of God are children of God	8:1–30
X **God's love is revealed in Christ Jesus**	8:31–39
C´ God chooses those who are the true descendants of Abraham	9:1–29
B´ Salvation in Jesus Christ is for all—including faithless Israel	9:30–11:36
A´ Put on the Lord Jesus Christ, for love fulfills the Torah	12:1–16:24
a´ Benediction: "My gospel...through the prophetic writings"	16:25–27

The focus of attention in this reading of Romans is on the love of God as expressed in Christ Jesus (8:31–39). God "did not withhold his own Son, but gave him up for all of us" (v. 32; cf. John 3:16). "It is Christ Jesus who died, yes, who was raised, who is at the right hand of God, who indeed intercedes for us" (8:34); and nothing in the whole of creation "will be able to separate us from the love of God in Christ Jesus our Lord" (v. 39). The outermost frame in this structure moves from a section on the devastating problem of sin (1:18—3:20) and the way of faith in dealing with this problem (3:21—4:25), to ethical instructions related to transformed living (12:1—16:24). Here Paul exhorts his hearers to present their bodies as a living sacrifice to God, a vehicle of God's transforming power (12:1–2). They are to affirm humbly their spiritual gifts from God, to treat one another with genuine love, and to avoid the ways of evil (12:3–21).

Paul's self-giving spirit is modeled on the spirit of Christ (15:1–6); and his hope is that all people will praise God and be filled with joy and peace (15:7–13). In the concluding portion of this section, Paul expresses his commitment to carry the gospel to the Gentiles with the ultimate goal of extending that mission to Spain and, on his way, to visit the church in Rome (15:14–33). The second and third frames in this structure move from an account of the gospel as the power of God for salvation (5:1—8:30) to the salvation of Israel, which rejects the gospel at the outset (9:1—11:36). The latter section concludes with reflection on the inscrutable "depth of the riches and wisdom and knowledge of God" (11:33) that elicits a doxology on Paul's part (11:36).

The Letter of Paul to the Romans opens with a penetrating analysis of the devastating and universal problem of sin: "For all have sinned and fall short of the glory of God" (1:18—3:31). The problem is not that people do not know God's general revelation of his will in the world; it is instead that people refuse to acknowledge him and worship things in the created order rather than the Creator (1:18–23). Therefore, God delivers every aspect of their being (heart, passions, and mind) to unholy activity; and they not only practice evil but conspire in such practices (1:24–32). Paul then turns his attention to the moralistic Jews who condemn pagan immorality and think that they are superior in God's sight—reminding them that God judges not merely by what one thinks or says one is, but by what one does (2:1–16). Paul concludes that real Jewishness is not a matter of externals such as bloodline or physical circumcision (2:17–29). Jews have the advantage of their history and the fact that they have been given the word of God; but because of their refusal to obey, the Jews also stand under judgment like everyone else (3:1–20). True righteousness, which is revealed in Christ, rests not upon obedience to the law, but on faith in God's act of redemption and all boasting is excluded (3:21–31). God is one, and he has chosen to deal with Jews and Gentiles on the same basis. To show the centrality of faith in the continuing saving activities of God from the beginning, Paul presents the example of Abraham. His faith in receiving both circumcision and the promise that he would be the father of a multitude of peoples illustrates for Paul how faith has always been regarded as a basis for righteousness (4:1–22). In like manner, placing our trust in the effectiveness of the death and resurrection of Jesus Christ is basic to our forgiveness of sins and justification before God (4:23–25).

There is a major change in focus in chapter 5, as Paul turns his attention to what is sometimes called "sanctification"—the way of growing in holiness. Since we are justified by faith, we are in harmony with God and will be saved in the final judgment (5:1–11). Sin and death entered this world through Adam's disobedience; but acquittal and life for all followed upon Christ's perfect obedience (5:12–21). Salvation is an undeserved gift from God that sets us free from the power of sin and death and we are no longer sin's slaves but God's slaves. "For the wages of sin is death, but the free gift of God is eternal life in Christ Jesus our Lord" (6:1–23). A person who has died to sin is no more bound to it than a woman is to her deceased husband. This does not mean, however, that there is no longer an inner struggle, for sin is personified as an evil power entrenched within our very souls, forcing us to cast ourselves upon God's mercy in Christ (7:1–25).

In the central section of Paul's Letter to the Romans, we find the principle stated clearly that to be in Christ is to belong to a new order in which we know the Spirit, who is the actual presence of God in our midst and in our hearts. Only through the power of the Spirit can we hope for the righteousness that the law requires but cannot attain because of our weakness in the flesh (8:1–17). Though the Christian life involves sufferings, Paul rejoices in the sure hope of future glory when we will share in the resurrected life of Christ (8:18–30). At the structural center of Paul's letter we find a concise summation of the "good news" as Paul sees it: "In all these things we are more than conquerors through him who loved us. For I am sure that neither death, nor life, nor angels, nor principalities, nor things present, nor things to come, nor powers, nor height, nor depth, nor anything in all creation, will be able to separate us from the love of God in Christ Jesus our Lord" (8:37–39).

At this point, Paul turns his attention to the problem of Israel's unbelief, which was one of the most difficult problems for Paul. Though he senses that God's promise to the Jews has failed, he also knows that not all descendants of Abraham are in fact children of that promise. Like a potter with clay, God is in control of the history of Israel and only a remnant will be saved (9:14–29). True righteousness is attained through faith, and the nation of Israel stands responsible for its failure. Moreover, it cannot claim that it has not had the opportunity of hearing the gospel that proclaims salvation for all (9:30—10:21). Nonetheless, Israel's rejection is not final. As was the case in the days of Elijah (1 Kgs 19:10, 18), there is a faithful remnant among the Jews. The resistance to the gospel on the part of the nation of Israel is providential; God has hardened their hearts for his own loving purpose, namely, that the Gentiles might have an opportunity to hear and receive the gospel (11:1–24). In God's own time, Israel as a whole will be saved (11:25–36).

Once again, there is an abrupt change in focus in the letter as Paul shifts his thoughts to a concluding section of ethical instructions related to transformed living (12:1—15:13). In short, Paul urges his readers to put on the Lord Jesus Christ, for love is the fulfillment of the Law of Moses (13:8–14). For those who would be led by the Spirit, Paul exhorts us to present our bodies as living sacrifices of God's transforming power (12:1–2). He urges us to affirm humbly our spiritual gifts from God, to treat one another with a genuine love, and to avoid the ways of evil (12:3–21). He reminds us to respect civil authority as a basis for law and order and to deal responsibly with such issues as taxes in the way Jesus instructed (13:1–7, cf. Mark 12:17). Paul opposes the establishment of new laws concerning proper food rules or ceremonial days (14:1–9). We ought not to pass judgment in such matters, for clean and unclean laws are meaningless to Paul, who declares: "I know and am persuaded in the Lord Jesus that nothing is unclean in itself; but it is unclean for anyone who thinks it unclean" (14:14). Paul refuses to condemn others on such matters or to force them into his way of thinking. Because his desire is the edification of others, he will not use his freedom to destroy their faith (14:10–23). Paul's self-giving spirit is modeled on the spirit of Christ (15:1–6), and his hope is that all people will give praise to God and that believers will be empowered by the Holy Spirit and be filled with joy and peace (15:7–13).

Paul concludes his Letter to the Romans with personal notes in which he apologizes for his apparent boldness in writing so long a

letter to a church with which he has had no earlier connections
(15:14–23). He then recounts his travel plans to visit the church in
Rome on route to Spain (15:24–29) and requests their support in
prayer (15:30–33). In the final chapter, Paul voices his concern for
the reception of Phoebe, a female deacon (16:1–2), and greets a long
list of colleagues—both male and female—in the work of Christ
(16:3–16). He then adds a warning to avoid persons who cause dissension (16:17–20) and extends greetings from Timothy and others
(16:21). Tertius, Paul's amanuensis, extends his greetings and that of
Erastus and Quartus (16:22–23). Finally, the letter closes with alternate benedictions (16:24 and 25–27).

Two Letters of Paul to the Corinthians

The Greek city of Corinth enjoyed a long and proud history until its
destruction by Mummius of Rome in 146 B.C.E. It lay in ruins for a
century until Julius Caesar made it the seat of the Roman governor
of the province of Achaea in 44 B.C.E. Paul reached Corinth in the
fall of 50 C.E. and worked there for eighteen months (Acts 18:1–11),
and visited a second time in what he calls a "painful visit" (2 Cor
2:1). Crispus, the leader of the Jewish synagogue in Corinth, was
among Paul's early converts (Acts 18:8; 1 Cor 1:14). After Paul's
departure, the work was continued under Apollos (1 Cor 3:6), an
able orator from Alexandria and more recently from Ephesus, where
he was instructed by Aquila and Priscilla (Acts 18:24–28), who had
been with Paul in Corinth from the founding of the church there
(Acts 18:2–3). It appears that Peter was also in Corinth (1 Cor 1:12).

First Corinthians

Paul's first letter to the church in Corinth is one of the most valuable
of his letters for the light it throws on the character and mind of the
apostle and its vigorous presentation of the gospel. Moreover, it provides vivid glimpses into the life of a local church in the middle of
the first century C.E. The content of the letter may be outlined in a
menorah pattern:

Paul's First Letter to the Corinthians in a Menorah Pattern	*1 Cor 1—16*
A Salutation and thanksgiving: "Gace from God…and the Lord Jesus Christ"	1:1-9
B Proclaiming Christ crucified in face of divisions in the church	1:10—4:21
C Glorify God in your body which is the temple of the Holy Spirit	5:1—7:40
X **Flee from idols: "Be imitators of me, as I am of Christ"**	8:1—11:1
C´ We are the body of Christ which is one body with many members	11:2—14:40
B´ Proclaiming the resurrection from the dead and other business	15:1—16:20
A´ Personal greeting and benediction: "Grace of the Lord Jesus Christ"	16:21-24

In this reading, the focus is on the matter of eating food offered to idols (8:1—11:1). Though we may have rights under the law, it is not always wise to exercise them. Paul urges us to follow his personal example in such matters (11:1). The second frame in this structure moves from an account of Paul's decision to keep himself focused on proclaiming the gospel of Christ crucified in spite of the divisions in the church (1:10—4:21) to a discussion on proclaiming the resurrection of the dead (15:1–58). The innermost frame deals with the two aspects of the "body" in Paul's teaching. Paul urges us to glorify God in our bodies, which are the temple of the Holy Spirit (5:1—7:40); and he asserts that we are the body of Christ, which is one body with many members (11:2—14:40).

The center of the above concentric structure, which focuses on the matter of eating food offered to idols, may be opened up in another menorah pattern (8:1—11:1).

2nd Level Menorah: "Imitate Me as I Imitate Christ"	*1 Cor 8:1—11:1*
A May a Christian eat food consecrated to an idol?	8:1-13
B Paul's rights as an apostle, which he refrains from asserting	9:1-27
C Learn from our ancestors' errors—they perished in the wilderness	10:1-13
X **Flee from the worship of idols**	10:14
C´ Do not partake of the Lord's Supper with food sacrificed to idols	10:15-22
B´ Do not insist on doing what is lawful; do what is beneficial	10:23-24
A´ Whether you eat or drink, do it for the glory of God—as I [Paul] do	10:25—11:1

The question is raised concerning a Christian's right to eat food that has been consecrated to an idol (8:1–13). Paul concludes that whether one chooses to eat or drink anything is not the real issue. The second frame in this structure opens with Paul's statement of his rights as an apostle, which he has chosen not to exercise (9:1–27). It continues with practical advice: Do not insist on doing what is lawful; but rather choose to do what is beneficial (10:23–24). Paul cites scriptural examples to warn his readers against even unwitting participation in pagan worship (10:1–13), by eating food that has been sacrificed to idols (10:15–22). The central point is clear: "flee from the worship of idols" (10:14).

In the first major section of the letter, after a brief salutation (1:1–3) and a thanksgiving in which Paul touches on some of the themes he will take up in detail later (1:4–9), the issue of divisions in the church is raised at the very outset (1:10–17). In the first half of the outer frame of 1:1—4:21, four different factions are identified, namely those who "belong to" Paul, Apollos, Cephas (Peter), and Christ. These same parties are taken up again in the second half of the outer frame in this sub-section where the dissension over leaders is explored further (3:1–23). At that point Paul makes it clear that there should be no boasting over human leaders, for we all belong to Christ and thus to God (3:21–23). Moreover, since even the teachers themselves are "servants of Christ and stewards of God's mysteries, boasting and blaming are ruled out (4:1–7). The inner frame in the opening sub-section moves from a presentation of "Christ crucified," which demonstrates "the power of God and the wisdom of God" (1:18–31) to an expansion on spiritual wisdom (2:6–16). Paul declares that he did not come with lofty words of wisdom. In fact, he deliberately chose "to know nothing among you except Jesus Christ, and him crucified" (2:2). His speech and proclamation were not in "words of wisdom, but with a demonstration of the Spirit and of power, so that your faith might rest not on human wisdom but on the power of God" (2:4–5).

The structural center of the second major section of the letter (5:1—7:40) focuses attention on the need to glorify God in our bodies, particularly in the matter of sexual purity. The outer frame expands this theme as it opens with a section on the subject of sexual immorality with a call for church discipline: "Drive out the wicked person from among you" (6:1–13). This passage is set over against a more complex one on the subject of eschatology in relation to marital status (7:17–40). Because of his belief that the end of the world is fast approaching, Paul advises everyone to remain as they are and not seek to change their outward situation. He then applies this counsel to the subject of marriage with this conclusion: "So then, he who marries his fiancée does well; and he who refrains from marriage will do better" (7:38). The inner frame in this unit moves from a section on lawsuits in pagan courts, which Paul considers to be shameful (6:1–11) to another one on the subject of marriage. Here Paul spells out his convictions on the gift of singleness and options to take in marriages with an unbelieving spouse (7:1–16).

The third and central section in the letter addresses the question: "May a Christian eat food consecrated to an idol?" (8:1—11:1). The outer frame in this section explores the issue and its solution (8:1–13 and 10:25—11:1). On the one hand, Paul concludes: "We are no worse off if we do not eat, and no better off if we do" (8:8). On the other hand, he urges his readers: "Be imitators of me, as I am of Christ" (11:1). The example of Paul's personal conduct is explored further as Paul states that though he knows his rights as an apostle, he has chosen to refrain from exercising them (9:1–27). For Paul, the issue is not what is lawful but rather what is beneficial: "Do not seek your own advantage, but that of the other" (10:23–24). The dangers of idolatry are explored further in the structural center of this section, with specific warnings taken from the days of Israel's experience in the time of Moses (10:1–22).

The focus of interest in the fourth section (11:2—14:40) is on the concept of the body of Christ, which requires a variety of members (12:12–31). The outer frame here moves from a discussion of orderly worship in regards to propriety of dress and the abuse of the Lord's Supper (11:2–34) to disturbances in public worship by inappropriate use of spiritual gifts (14:1–40). The subject of spiritual gifts is taken up in detail in the inner frame, which moves from a presentation of the variety of spiritual gifts (12:1–11), to the lyric chapter on love as the greatest of all spiritual gifts (13:1–13). Among the other gifts, prophecy outranks that of tongues (14:1–19).

The concluding section (15:1—16:24), which deals primarily with the subject of resurrection, focuses on the fact that the resurrected body of an individual will be a new body (15:35–44). A discussion of the significance of the resurrection of the dead (15:12–34) is set over against a section on the profound mystery of the resurrection (15:45–57). Paul's understanding of eschatology leads him to the conclusion that, "We will not all die, but we will all be changed, in a moment, in the twinkling of an eye, at the last trumpet" (15:52). At the time this letter was written, Paul believed that the day of the Lord's return was near at hand. The letter concludes with a series of brief messages on various topics: a "collection for the saints" (16:1–4); Paul's plans to visit Corinth "after passing through Macedonia" and a stay at Ephesus (16:5–9); words about Timothy, Apollos, Stephanus, Fortunatus, and Achaicus (16:10–18); and greetings from the churches of Asia, and Aquila and Prisca in particular (16:19–20). The final benediction includes a note that Paul's personal greeting was written in his own hand (16:21–24).

Second Corinthians

After Paul establishes the church in Corinth (ca. 50 C.E.), he continues his relationship by writing at least four letters and visiting this church in person on at least one subsequent occasion. His first letter is mentioned in 1 Corinthians 5:9; the second is our 1 Corinthians, written from Ephesus (1 Cor 16:8). Paul sends Timothy to Corinth (1 Cor 4:17; 16:10–11), and shortly thereafter a group of Jewish-Christian missionaries arrive in Corinth and criticize the apostle. Timothy apparently returns to Ephesus with a troubling report about the church that prompts Paul to change his plans and to travel directly to Corinth. He later describes this second visit as "painful," because someone there wronged him (2 Cor 2:1–11, 7:12). Subsequent to this second visit, Paul writes a third letter, a "letter of tears" (2 Cor 1:23—2:4; 7:5–11), which is written from either Macedonia immediately after Paul's departure from Corinth (2 Cor 1:16) or upon his return to Ephesus.

Instead of sending Timothy back to Corinth, Paul apparently sends his "Second Letter to the Corinthians" (his fourth known correspondence to them) with Titus, another co-worker (ca. 54–56 C.E.). This places it between 1 Thessalonians and Romans in the most theologically productive period of Paul's ministry as a missionary.

The content of 2 Corinthians may be outlined in a menorah pattern:

Paul's Second Letter to the Corinthians in a Menorah Pattern   *2 Cor 1–13*

A   Paul urges forgiveness of an offender and life by faith in face of affliction 1:1–5:10

B   Apostolic existence as a ministry of reconciliation   5:11–6:10

C   Appeal to the heart–for the church to be reconciled with him   6:11-13

X   **As the temple of God, let us cleanse ourselves from defilement**   6:14–7:1

C´   Appeal resumed–Paul's joy at the church's repentance   7:2-16

B´   The matter of the collection for the church in Jerusalem   8:1–9:15

A´ Paul defends his ministry against false apostles–he asks forgiveness   10:1–13:14

The letter moves from the response on the part of Paul and the people at Corinth in a crisis in which Paul's integrity is challenged (1:1—5:10), to another crisis in which Paul defends his ministry against false apostles (10:1—13:14). The second frame within this structure moves from a portrayal of Paul's apostolic ministry of reconciliation (5:11—6:10) to the matter of the collection Paul is receiving for the Christians in Jerusalem that may be understood as another act of reconciliation (8:1—9:15). The two crises of the outermost frame in this concentric structure concern this very issue of reconciliation. The innermost frame presents an appeal for the church to be reconciled (6:11–13) and Paul's joy at the church's repentance (7:2–16). In the structural center, Paul declares: "We are the temple of the living God," and so, "let us cleanse ourselves from every defilement of body and spirit, making holiness perfect in the fear of God" (6:14—7:1).

Following an opening salutation and thanksgiving, which reflects the relief he felt as a result of the news Titus brought him from Corinth (1:1–11; cf. 2:12–13), Paul turns his attention to the apostolic ministry and the crisis in Corinth (1:12—7:16). In place of the usual thanksgiving, Paul presents a benediction derived from ancient Jewish liturgical practices (1:1–11). The content of the letter moves from an account of relations with the church in Corinth in which Paul says "I wanted to visit you on my way to Macedonia" (1:12—2:4) to a brief expression of Paul's anxiety in Troas (2:14–17). Here Paul writes, "I said farewell to them and went on to Macedonia" to meet Titus for news from Corinth (2:12–13). In the center of this section, Paul presents a major goal of the letter—reconciliation of the person who mistreated him during his second visit to Corinth (2:5–11).

The next major section of the letter (3:1—5:10) explores further the nature of ministry within the context of the new covenant (3:1–11) and of Paul's confidence in facing death (5:1–10). The inner frame in this concentric structure opens with a discussion of the freedom we experience when we are in the presence of the Spirit of the Lord (3:12–18). It concludes with a description of the weakness of the body ("we have this treasure in earthen vessels," 4:7–18). Within this framework we find an account of God's revelation in the apostolic proclamation of the gospel in which Paul declares: "We do not proclaim ourselves; we proclaim Jesus Christ as Lord and ourselves as your slaves for Jesus' sake" (4:1–6).

The next major section in the letter focuses attention on the ministry of reconciliation (5:11—9:15). Here Paul urges his readers to respond faithfully to God's grace in Christ (5:11—6:10). The people are urged to "open wide your hearts also" (6:13) and "make room in your hearts for us" (7:2). In the center of his appeal to the heart, Paul asserts that "we are the temple of the living God" (6:16) and as such we are called to "cleanse ourselves from every defilement of the body and of the spirit, making holiness perfect in the fear of God" (7:1). Paul then urges the people in Corinth to show proof of their love and of his reason for boasting about them (8:24) by giving generously to the collection he is receiving for the Christians in Jerusalem (9:1–15).

The final section (10:1—13:14) opens with Paul's defense of his ministry against false apostles within an appeal for true apostleship (10:1–18), which includes an ironic "fool's speech" in which his opponents are designated as Satan's agents (11:1—12:13). The speech concludes with an epilogue on "the signs of a true apostle" and the brief request: "Forgive me this wrong!" (12:11–13). Paul then shifts his attention to an expression of concern for the Corinthian church. He discusses preparations for a third visit (12:14–21) and ends with further warnings (13:1–10), final greetings (13:11–13), and a closing benediction (13:14).

The Letter of Paul to the Galatians

The first edition of Paul's letter to the Galatians was written about 55 C.E., or perhaps as early as 48–49 C.E., and contains many autobiographical details of the apostle's life and ministry. With impassioned eloquence, Paul sets forth the function of the Law of Moses in light of God's grace revealed in Christ. The importance of this letter is hard to overestimate. It has been called the Magna Charta of Christian liberty, for it deals with the question of whether Gentiles must become Jews before they can become Christians. Certain Judaizing teachers infiltrated the churches of Galatia in central Asia Minor that Paul had planted, declaring that in addition to having faith in Jesus Christ a Christian must observe Jewish law (see Acts 16:6). Arguing against them, Paul insists a person is made right with God by faith in Christ alone and not by performance of good works, ritual observances, and the like (2:16; 3:24–25; 5:1; 6:12–15).

The content of Paul's Letter to the Galatians may be outlined in a menorah pattern:

Paul's Letter to the Galatians in a Menorah Pattern	*Gal 1—6*
a Salutation: "Grace to you and peace from...the Lord Jesus Christ"	1:1-5
A Paul received the gospel of Christ's liberating death from God	1:6—2:14
B True descendants of Abraham are those who believe in Christ	2:15—3:18
C The Law's purpose: to be "our disciplinarian until Christ came"	3:19-25
X One in Christ: Jew or Greek, slave or free, and male or female	3:26-29
C´ Turning to the Law is slavery to "weak and beggarly elements"	4:1-11
B´ You are Isaac, children of Sarah, not children of Hagar	4:12—5:12
A´ We keep the law when we love our neighbor as ourselves	5:13—6:10
a´ Postscript: "Grace of our Lord Jesus Christ be with your spirit"	6:11-18

The essential message of Galatians may be summed up in one verse: "There is no longer Jew or Greek, there is no longer slave or free, there is no longer male or female; for all of you are one in Christ Jesus" (3:28). This verse stands in the structural center of the book, at the center of the central section (3:19—4:11). In the above concentric structure, the inner frame moves behind the laws of Moses to the narrative in Genesis to argue that the true descendants of Abraham are in fact those who believe in Christ (2:15—3:18). This section is set over against one in which Paul argues that the Galatians themselves are the true Isaac, children of the promise to Sarah and her husband Abraham, and that these Judaizers are in fact the children of Hagar, the "slave woman" (4:12—5:12). The outer frame in this structure opens with Paul's vindication of both his authority as an apostle and his message of Christ's death as an act of liberation (1:1—2:14). It continues with a summary section in which Paul concludes that we observe the law when we love our neighbor as ourselves (5:13—6:10).

In the opening section (1:1—2:14), Paul defends his apostolic authority against attacks by his opponents and he insists that there is no other gospel than what he has proclaimed in their midst; for his gospel was received from God himself (1:1–24). Moreover, the Jerusalem leaders recognized him as an apostle (2:1–10) and Paul had to correct Peter in Antioch on the same issue he was now defending with the Galatians (2:11–13).

The next section presents arguments from the stories of Abraham and Sarah in Genesis, which stress the fact that from the very beginning we learn in the example of Abraham that we are justified by faith and not by works of obedience to the laws of Moses (2:15—3:18). The argument continues in 4:1–31 where we learn that those who believe in Christ are in fact the true son of promise in the story of Abraham and Sarah and their promised son Isaac. It is the Judaizers who are the children of Hagar.

The third section, which is the center of the letter, contains the teaching that all are one in Christ so that all former social distinctions dissolve. Paul argues that the Law of Moses was "our disciplinarian until Christ came, so that we might be justified by faith" (3:19–25). In Christ Jesus we are all children of God through faith

(3:26) and there is no longer any distinction between Jew or Greek, slave or free, male or female (3:27–29). God sent his Son into the world that we might receive adoption as his children (4:1–7). To turn back to observing the law as a means of salvation is to become enslaved once again to "weak and beggarly elements."

The Letter to the Galatians concludes with a section that explores the true meaning of the laws of Moses (5:1—6:18). Paul quotes the words of Jesus to show that the essential meaning of the law is summed up in the command to "love your neighbor as yourself" (5:13–15). True Christian liberty means that we are governed by the Spirit, and not ruled by the law. We are to bear one another's burdens and so demonstrate our love for others. Paul's conclusion so far as the Judaizers are concerned is summed up in a single verse: "For neither circumcision nor uncircumcision is anything; but a new creation is everything" (6:15).

The Letter of Paul to the Ephesians

At the end of his second missionary journey (46–51 C.E.), Paul visited Ephesus on his way back to Syria where he "had a discussion with the Jews" in the synagogue and promised them that he would return, "if God wills" (Acts 18:18–21). Apollos, who "knew only the baptism of John," ministered there, and "began to speak boldly in the synagogue in Ephesus (Acts 18:25–26). When Paul returned to Ephesus on this third missionary journey, "he found some disciples" there, though Apollos had gone on to Corinth (Acts 19:1). Paul "entered the synagogue and for three months spoke out boldly and argued persuasively about the kingdom of God" (Acts 19:8). Paul made Ephesus the base of operations for his missionary activity for more than two years, during which time Christianity spread into the adjacent cities and regions of Asia Minor—to the seven churches of Asia (addressed in Revelation 1—3). Paul's letters to the church in Corinth were written from Ephesus during his ministry there, and the Letter to the Romans was written shortly thereafter.

The earliest and best manuscript witnesses of this letter and some commentators in the early church make no reference to Ephesus in 1:1, nor does the letter deal with the problems of a particular congregation. These early textual witnesses include the Chester Beatty Papyrus (ca. 200 C.E.) and the great uncials, Vaticanus and Sinaiticus (fourth–fifth centuries C.E.). The Gnostic Marcion (ca. 140 C.E.) included Ephesians in his canon under the title "to the Laodiceans." Ephesians is thus widely regarded as a "circular letter" that was distributed among the "seven churches" of Asia Minor (Rev 1—3). In terms of the larger canonical structure, Paul's Letter to the Ephesians functions as a literary bridge to link the seven churches, to which Paul sent "canonical" letters, with the seven churches of Asia that John addresses in the opening chapters of the Revelation to John. The church at Ephesus is the only church to appear in both groups, though Paul's Letter to the Colossians is for the Laodiceans as well (Col 4:16). In Paul's letters, the letter to the church at Ephesus is in the structural center of his nine ecclesiastical letters. In the Revelation to John, Ephesus heads the list of seven churches: Ephesus, Smyrna, Pergamum, Thyatira, Sardis, Philadelphia, and Laodicea.

The concentric structure of the letter of Paul to the church in Ephesus may be outlined in a menorah pattern:

Paul's Letter to the Ephesians in a Menorah Pattern	*Eph 1—6*
a Salutation: "Peace from God our Father and the Lord Jesus Christ"	1:1-2
A The seal of the Holy Spirit is the pledge of our inheritance in Christ	1:3-23
B Christ's benefits are for both Gentiles and Jews	2:1—3:21
C Lead a life worthy of your calling—seven elements of unity	4:1-6
X **God's gifts are intended to equip the saints for ministry**	4:7-13
C´ Speaking the truth in love, we must grow up into Christ the head	4:14-16
B´ Renounce pagan ways—"be imitators of God...and live in love"	4:17—5:17
A´ Be filled with the Spirit, subject to one another, "armed for warfare"	5:18—6:20
a´ Closing: "Peace from God the Father and the Lord Jesus Christ"	6:21-24

The first frame presents the Holy Spirit as the pledge of our inheritance in Christ (1:3–23). This section is set over against 5:18—6:20, with its opening injunction to "be filled with the Spirit" (5:18) and the subsequent command to "pray in the Spirit" (6:18), which form an envelope around the unit as a whole (5:18—6:20). The second frame moves from a section on Christ's benefits for both Gentiles and Jews (2:1—3:21) to an appeal to renounce the pagan ways of the Gentiles (4:17—5:17). The latter includes an injunction to "be imitators of God, as beloved children, and live in love, as Christ loved us and gave himself up for us" (5:1–2). The innermost frame opens with an appeal to maintain the unity of the faith that lists seven elements of unity: "There is one body and one Spirit...one hope of your calling, one Lord, one faith, one baptism, one God and Father of all" (4:4–16). The center of the structure focuses on the gifts God has given his people "to equip the saints for the work of ministry, for building up the body of Christ" (4:7–13).

The focus of attention in the first major section of Ephesians is on the seal of the Holy Spirit, which is a pledge of the inheritance God promised (1:1–23). Paul reminds his readers that, "In Christ we have also obtained an inheritance...so that we, who were the first to set our hope on Christ, might live for the praise of his glory" (1:3–12). God put his power to work in Christ as head of the church, "which is his body" (1:20–23).

In the second major section of the letter, the benefits of Christ are presented as available to all—both Gentiles and Jews; for "the dividing wall" between them has been broken down (2:1—3:21). Paul reminds his readers to "remember that you were at that time without Christ, being aliens from the commonwealth of Israel ...having no hope and without God in the world" (2:11–13). The purpose of Paul's imprisonment is "to bring to the Gentiles the news of the boundless riches of Christ, and to make everyone see what is the plan of the mystery hidden for ages in God who created all things" (3:1–13). Since we have passed from death to life, we are created in Christ Jesus for good works (2:1–10). And so Paul prays that Christ may dwell in our hearts through faith so that we "may be filled with all the fullness of God" (3:14–21).

The next major section of the letter continues with an appeal to maintain the unity of the faith (4:1–16) by putting away old pagan ways and clothing oneself "with the new self, created according to the likeness of God in true righteousness and holiness" (4:17–24).

Paul then spells out what this means in detail, with a list of pagan practices to be renounced, namely: falsehood, uncontrolled anger, theft, evil talk, bitterness, wrath, wrangling, slander, and malice. Instead we are to "be kind to one another, tenderhearted, forgiving one another, as God in Christ has forgiven you" (4:25–32). The whole matter is summed up in the command to "be imitators of God...and live in love, as Christ loved us" (5:1–2). Paul then resumes his account of pagan practices that must go, in terms of the specific matters of fornication and impurity, obscenity, and vulgar talk. Instead we are to "live as children of light...making the most of the time, because the days are evil" (5:3–17).

The final section opens with a command: "Be filled with the Spirit...giving thanks to God the Father at all times and for everything in the name of our Lord Jesus Christ" (5:18–20). The way to this end is presented first in principle: "Be subject to one another out of reverence to Christ" (5:21). The principle is then applied to practical situations—between wives and their husbands (5:22–23), children and parents (6:1–4), and slaves and masters (6:5–9). Since the power to achieve these ends comes from God, Paul urges us to "put on the whole armor of God"—truth, righteousness, readiness to proclaim the gospel of peace, faith, salvation, and "the sword of the Spirit, which is the word of God" (6:10–17). Armed for spiritual warfare, we are to "pray in the Spirit at all times" and "keep alert and always persevere in supplication for all saints" (6:18–20).

The central message of Ephesians is an appeal to maintain unity of faith (4:1–16). We are called to lead a life worthy of our calling in Christ Jesus—"with all humility and gentleness, with patience, bearing with one another in love, eager to maintain the unity of the Spirit" (4:1–3). Paul continues with a list of seven elements of unity: "one body and one Spirit...one hope of your calling, one Lord, one faith, one baptism, [and] one God and father of all" (4:4–6). God has given us a variety of gifts, so that some are called to "be apostles, some prophets, some evangelists, some pastors and teachers." The leaders' primary task is "to equip the saints for the work of ministry. It is 'the saints' who have the responsibility of building up the body of Christ, until all of us come to the unity of the faith and of the knowledge of the Son of God, to maturity, to the measure of the full stature of Christ" (4:7–16).

In the structural center of Ephesians we find a quotation from Psalm 68:18, which is applied here to Christ's victory over spiritual powers (cf. 1:20–21 and Col 2:15). The concluding line in this quotation reads "he gave gifts to his people" (4:8), which is probably the reason Paul remembers the verse. But his mind quickly turns to the preceding clause: "When he ascended on high he made captivity itself a captive." Here Paul's attention focuses on Christ's ascent: "He who descended is the same one who ascended far above all the heavens, so that he might fill all things" (4:10). We serve an exalted Lord, and in the body of Christ we find a unity that breaks down all dividing walls—between Gentiles and Jews and within the Christian household (wives and husbands, parents and children, masters and slaves). Moreover, the very distinction between male and female is dissolved so far as leadership roles are concerned in the body of Christ, as is spelled out so clearly in the parallel passage in Galatians 3:28.

The Letter of Paul to the Philippians

Of the nine letters of Paul that were addressed to seven churches, three were written from prison: Ephesians, Philippians, and Colossians. It is probable that all three of these letters were written in Rome, while Paul was in prison awaiting trial in ca. 60–62 C.E. Even if these "prison epistles" originated earlier—when Paul was a prisoner in Philippi (Acts 16:23–40), Caesarea (Acts 23:35), or perhaps even Ephesus—the three appear together as a group (to which we must also add Paul's letter to Philemon and 2 Timothy as well).

In response to a vision in Troas during his second missionary journey, Paul crosses over to Macedonia (Acts 16:9–12). The first church he establishes there is in Philippi (Acts 16:11–40), and the next is in Thessalonica (Acts 17:1–9). From there Paul goes on to Beroea (Acts 17:10–13), Athens (Acts 17:15–34), and then Corinth (Acts 18:1–18), which becomes the base of his operations in Greece for eighteen months. At the end of that second missionary journey, Paul visits Ephesus on route to Syria. He returns to Ephesus and ministers there for more than two years on his third missionary journey. Paul then travels to Jerusalem where he is arrested, imprisoned in Caesarea, and taken to Rome in the reign of the Emperor Nero (54–68 C.E.). Paul is a prisoner when he writes Philippians (see 1:7, 13, 14, and 16). The serious nature of this imprisonment (see 1:20–23, 30; 2:17; and 3:11) suggests that Paul's life is at stake and that he has no certainty of release. Nonetheless, he continues to hope that he will be spared (1:19); and the letter itself has the subject of joy as a primary motif.

The content of Paul's Letter to the Philippians may be outlined in a menorah pattern:

Paul's Letter to the Philippians in a Menorah Pattern	Phil 1—4
A Salutation and prayer that the Philippians' love may overflow	1:1-11
B Paul's joy in the fact that Christ is proclaimed through suffering	1:12-30
C Be like Christ—he humbled himself without complaint	2:1-16
X **Paul urges the Philippians to rejoice in the Lord with him**	2:17–3:1
C´ Be like Paul—press on; God transforms humiliation into glory	3:2-21
B´ Paul urges the Philippians to rejoice in the Lord always	4:1-9
A´ Paul's joy in the love expressed by the Philippians; benediction	4:10-23

In this reading, the dominant theme is that of joy and rejoicing without complaint. At the structural center of the letter as a whole, Paul urges the Philippians to be glad and to rejoice in the Lord with him (2:17—3:1). The innermost frame in this concentric structure moves from the example of Christ (2:1–16) to that of Paul (3:2–21). Christ "humbled himself and became obedient unto death" (2:8). Paul is blameless "under the law" and his "humble body" will one day be conformed to the glory of Jesus (3:21). The source of joy is found in the fact that Christ is proclaimed through Paul's imprisonment (1:12–30); and so, Paul urges the Philippians to rejoice in the Lord always (4:1–9). The outermost frame continues the same theme. On the one hand, Paul prays that the Philippians' "love may overflow more and more . . . so that in the day of Christ you may be pure and blameless" (1:9–10). And, by way of conclusion, Paul rejoices greatly in the fact that their love for him did overflow—"you were concerned for me . . . for no church shared with me in the matter of giving and receiving, except you alone" (4:10–15).

Philippians opens with a salutation and prayer that their love may overflow more and more (1:1–11), which is set over against the injunction to "live your life in a manner worthy of the gospel of Christ" (2:27–30). Though some are proclaiming Christ for the wrong reasons (1:12–17), Paul takes joy in the fact that the cause of Christ is advancing (1:18–19), and he declares that for him to live is Christ and to die is gain (1:20–26).

In the second major section of the letter (2:1–16), Paul urges his readers to imitate Christ's humility by regarding others better than themselves (2:1–4). These verses are set over against a parallel section in which Paul urges them to do all things without murmuring and disputing (2:14–16). Paul urges us to have the same mind that was in Christ Jesus (2:5) by working out our salvation with fear and trembling (2:12–13). The remarkable hymn at the center of this section portrays Christ as emptying himself of his divine prerogatives by taking the form of a servant, who "became obedient to the point of death." This suffering servant was then exalted "so that at the name of Jesus every knee should bow, in heaven and on earth" (2:6–11).

The central section of Philippians (2:17—3:6) starts with Paul's testimony that he takes joy in the fact that he is "being poured out as a libation over the sacrifice and the offering of (their) faith" (2:17–18). It is faith alone that God honors, and Paul has no confidence whatsoever "in the flesh"—that is, in physical observance of the terms of the Jewish law (3:3–6). Paul announces that he is sending Timothy and Epaphroditus to the Philippians (2:19–30), and he warns them once again of "the dogs"—those Judaizers "who mutilate the flesh," a harsh rejection of literal circumcision of Christians (cf. Gal 5:12). And in the very structural center of the letter, Paul once again reiterates his primary theme: "Finally, my brothers and sisters, rejoice in the Lord" (3:1a).

The example of Paul emerged in 3:4–6 in his account of the "reason for confidence in the flesh" he could make as a zealous Jew;

but all this he regards "as rubbish." In Christ he has found a right-eousness that does not come from observing the law, "but one that comes through faith in Christ, the righteousness from God." As Paul put it, he "suffers the loss of all things ... in order that [he] may gain Christ (3:7–9). In the concentric structure of the fourth major section in his letter to the Philippians (3:7–21), this opening unit is set over against Paul's conclusion that God "will transform the body of our humiliation that it may be conformed to the body of his glory" (3:21). In short, Paul sets himself up as an example for the believers in Philippi to follow: "Join in imitating me, and observe those who live according to the example you have in us" (3:17); for Paul has chosen to imitate Christ's humility as portrayed in 2:6–11.

The concluding section of this letter (4:1–21) returns once again to the theme of joy as Paul declares that the Philippians are his "joy and crown" and that they "should stand firm in the Lord" (4:1). Paul's joy in their concern for him is expressed again in the final section of the book (4:10–20), which begins with the words, "I rejoice in the Lord greatly that now at last you have revived your concern for me." The chapter concludes with reference to "the gifts you sent, a fragrant offering, a sacrifice acceptable and pleasing to God" (4:18). Paul urges the two women, Euodia and Syntyche, to settle their differences (4:2–3) by turning their attention to those things that are excellent and praiseworthy (4:8–9). The center of this concluding section reiterates once again the central theme: "Rejoice in the Lord always; again I will say, rejoice!" (4:4).

The Letter of Paul to the Colossians

Paul's thirteen letters are grouped in two categories: nine "Ecclesias-tical Letters" to seven churches and four "Personal Letters" to indi-viduals. Since the fourth century, church tradition has claimed that Paul's four "prison epistles" were written in Rome between 60 and 62 C.E., as the apostle waited trial as a result of his appeal to Caesar. Paul's Letter to the Colossians is one of these four "prison epistles," along with Ephesians, Philippians, and Philemon. There are close connections between Colossians and both Ephesians and Philemon. In the section on "The Letter of Paul to the Ephesians," we noted that that letter calls for unity of the faith (both Gentiles and Jews) in the body of Christ. The letter to the Colossians focuses on the sole lordship of Christ throughout the entire cosmos, and within the church in particular.

Colossians was written to a Gentile congregation (2:13), which was established by Epaphras (1:7–8, 2:1). In this letter, Paul deals with a theological and ethical issue that he designates as "philosophy and empty deceit" (2:8), and a personal issue on the circumstances of Onesimus and his owner Philemon. The theological issue is often described as "syncretism"—the tendency to introduce ideas from other philosophies and religions into the Christian faith. The dispute centers on what has already been accomplished in Christ and the specific question: Are believers actually liberated from spiritual powers and given proper access to God? Paul's opponents were urging asceticism and the observance of special holy times. They also taught the worship of celestial powers as the means of gaining wisdom and access to God. By appealing to the Christ hymn of 1:15–20 and to the readers' personal experience of a new and full life in Christ, Paul disputes the need for requirements beyond the "Christ in you" (1:27) that they already know. He calls on his readers to show endurance and steadfastness while they live in a manner appropriate to what they have already received. The theological content moves beyond that of Paul's earlier letters to the Romans, Corinthians, Galatians, and Thessalonians. The letter asserts that believers already share Christ's resurrection (2:12–13, 3:1), and that Christ is the head of the church, his body, in a manner that extends the metaphor beyond that of Romans 12:4–5 and 1 Corinthians 12:12–27. The personal issue concerns Onesimus, and one must read the companion letter to Philemon to see the whole situation. Paul is sending the runaway slave Onesimus back to his owner (Col 4:9), asking that he be forgiven and accepted as a brother (Phlm 8–20).

The content of Paul's Letter to the Colossians may be outlined in a menorah pattern:

Paul's Letter to the Colossians in a Menorah Pattern   *Col 1—4*

A   Salutation from Paul and Timothy: "Grace to you and peace from God"   1:1-2

B   Through Christ God has reconciled to himself all things   1:3-29

C   God made you alive in Christ—the fullness of God incarnate   2:1-15

X   **You are all one in Christ, so live as though you belong to him**   2:16—3:11

C´   Let the word of Christ control your thoughts and actions   3:12—4:1

B´   Make the most of the time—knowing how to answer everyone   4:2-6

A´ Final greetings and benediction in Paul's own hand: "Grace be with you!" 4:7-18

The focus of attention in this reading of Colossians is a warning against false teachers (2:16–23) that is coupled with instructions on what believers should do in light of their resurrection with Christ (3:1–11). Those who have been raised with Christ are told to seek those things that are above: "Set your minds on things that are above, not on things that are on the earth (3:2). In practical terms, this means that we are to turn from such things as impurity, greed, wrath, malice, slander, and all forms of evil speech (3:5–10). In the innermost frame of the above concentric structure, Paul reminds the Colossians that they have come to the fullness of life itself in Christ (2:1–15). In light of this fact, they are to let the word of Christ control their thoughts and actions by clothing themselves with compassion, kindness, humility, meekness, and patience in their household relationships (3:12—4:1). The outer frame develops the same theme. Since God has reconciled to himself all things through Christ (1:1–29), the Colossians are urged to make the most of the time— with a ready answer to everyone they meet (4:2–6). The final greetings include a note on the return of Onesimus, "the faithful and beloved brother," whom Paul is sending with Tychicus to "tell you about everything here" (4:7–9). Other greetings follow, with specific instructions that the letter be "read also in the church of the Laodiceans" (4:15–16).

When Colossians is divided into two equal parts, the focus of attention is on the fullness of life in Christ (2:6–15) and the command to put on the fivefold list of virtues of this new life in Christ (3:12–17). Through Christ, God has reconciled to himself all things (1:1–29); and so, make the most of your time, knowing how to answer everyone (4:2–18). By "erasing the record that stood against us with its legal demands, he set this aside, nailing it to the cross" (2:14). Since God has made you alive in Christ (2:1–19), let the word of Christ control your thoughts and actions (3:12—4:1). In short, put on the Lord Jesus Christ, and let the peace of Christ rule your hearts. "And be thankful. Let the word of Christ dwell in you richly; teach and admonish one another in all wisdom; and with gratitude in your hearts sing psalms, hymns, and spiritual songs to God. And whatever you do, in word and deed, do everything in the name of the Lord Jesus, giving thanks to God the Father through him" (3:15–17).

In the first chapter, Paul prays that the Colossians "may be filled with the knowledge of God's will in all spiritual wisdom and understanding, so that you may live lives worthy of the Lord, fully pleasing to him" (1:9–14). He argues that Christ has reconciled them to himself "in his fleshly body through death, so as to present you holy and blameless and irreproachable before him" (1:21–23). In short, Paul declares that his mission to the Gentiles is to make known the mystery of Christ in you, so as to "present everyone mature in Christ. For this I toil and struggle with all the energy that he powerfully inspires within me" (1:24–29).

The second chapter takes up the theological error of Paul's opponents with their "philosophy and empty deceit" and applies the message of the fullness of life in Christ in practical ways. Though absent in the body, Paul declares that he is with them in spirit (2:1–5). He urges them to live their lives in Christ—"rooted and built up in him and established in the faith, just as you were taught, abounding in thanksgiving" (2:6–7). They are not to let anyone rob them of their prize by their demands for false worship (2:16–19). In short, the legalism taught by Paul's opponents is "of no value in checking self-indulgence" (2:20–23). These thoughts are carried further in the third chapter in practical advice. The Colossians are to set their minds on things above, not on things on the earth (3:1–4). They are to put to death what is earthly, namely: impurity, greed, wrath, malice, and evil speech of all kinds (3:5–10). Instead, they are to clothe themselves with compassion, kindness, humility, patience, and love (3:12–17). These principles are then applied to practical human relations between wives and husbands, children and parents, and slaves and masters (3:18—4:1)—for all are one in Christ, and "Christ is all and in all!" (3:11).

In the fourth and final chapter, Paul turns his attention once again to prayer and thanksgiving (cf. 1:1–14). This time he requests prayer on his own behalf "that God will open to us a door for the word, that we may declare the mystery of Christ...so that I may reveal it clearly" (4:3–4). In his final greeting to the Colossians, Paul entrusts Tychicus and Onesimus to them with the words, "They will tell you everything here" (4:7–9). Personal greetings are extended from Aristarchus, Mark, Justus, Epaphras, Luke, Demas, and Paul himself (4:10–18).

Two Letters of Paul to the Thessalonians

The apostle Paul established the first Christian churches in Europe at Philippi and Thessalonica on his second missionary journey (46–51 C.E.). After being driven out of Philippi (1 Thess 2:2, Acts 16:11–40), Paul, Silvanus, and Timothy came to Thessalonica, the capital of the Roman province of Macedonia on the Via Egnatia. Intense opposition there forced them to move on to Beroea and from there to Athens (Acts 17:10–15). When Timothy joined Paul in Athens, Paul immediately sent him back to Thessalonica for information about the church (1 Thess 3:1–2) and Paul went on to Corinth, where Timothy and Silas met him later (Acts 18:1–5). Timothy brought a favorable report from Thessalonica, but he also brought news of their anxiety over Paul's failure to return to them. It was Timothy's report that stimulated Paul to write 1 Thessalonians from Corinth in 51 C.E., which makes it the oldest book in the New Testament. The different eschatological perspective in Paul's Second Letter to the Thessalonians suggests that he is clarifying what he meant in his earlier teaching on the imminent return of Jesus.

In light of the unfolding events in the opening years of that fateful decade from 60 to 70 C.E., Paul edits the earlier edition of his own letters and expands them into a larger collection of thirteen letters, which include his nine "Ecclesiastical Letters to the Seven

Churches." His intention is to leave behind a legacy of instruction for the early Christian Church. His letters take their place alongside the Four Gospels and Acts as the logical sequel to the "New Torah" as presented in the person and work of Jesus Christ.

The First Letter of Paul to the Thessalonians

In this letter, Paul responds to the anxiety of the Thessalonians about his failure to return to them by reviewing his initial reception there (1:2–10) and by expressing his ongoing concern for the church (2:1—3:13). He reinforces his original teaching by describing how they should live in the face of Jesus' imminent return (4:1—5:10) and how they should strengthen one another in their life together (5:11–22). The content of 1 Thessalonians may be outlined in a menorah pattern:

Paul's First Letter to the Thessalonians in a Menorah Pattern	*1 Thess 1—5*
a Salutation from Paul, Silvanus and Timothy: "Grace to you and peace"	1:1
A Word of your response to the gospel has spread far and wide	1:2–2:16
B You are our glory and joy and we long to see you face to face	2:17–3:11
C Continue to live lives that are pleasing to God more and more	3:12–4:2
X **God has called you to holiness—the way of sanctification**	4:3–8
C´ Continue to love one another more and more	4:9–12
B´ When Jesus returns, we will join the dead in Christ with him	4:13–5:10
A´ Continue in path of sanctification; be thankful in all circumstances	5:11–27
a´ Benediction: "The grace of our Lord Jesus Christ be with you"	5:28

Paul recounts the reception of his preaching by the Thessalonians, adding the remark that word of their response to the gospel has spread far and wide (1:2—2:13). Paul encourages the Thessalonians to continue in the path of sanctification by being thankful in all circumstances (5:11–27). The second frame in this structure begins with Paul's description of the Thessalonians as being his "glory and joy" and his strong desire to see them again "face to face and restore whatever is lacking in your faith" (2:17—3:11). It continues with a description of Jesus' imminent return in language that calls for vigilance for "the day of the Lord will come like a thief in the night" (4:13—5:10). It is clear that Paul does not expect to die before Jesus' coming, as seen by his remark that "we who are alive, who are left until the coming of the Lord" (4:15, cf. also 1 Cor 15:51–52). The Lord will descend from heaven "with a shout, with the archangel's call and with the sound of God's trumpet...and the dead in Christ will rise first. Then we who are alive, who are left, will be caught up in the clouds together with them to meet the Lord in the air; and so we will be with the Lord forever" (4:16–17). In the innermost frame, Paul enjoins his readers to continue to live lives that are pleasing to God (3:12—4:2), by loving one another more and more (4:9–12). In the center we find a call to holiness in living pure lives and abstaining from unchastity by the power of indwelling Holy Spirit (4:3–8).

The Second Letter of Paul to the Thessalonians

In 1 Thessalonians, Paul views the "second coming" of Jesus as imminent, and one of his concerns is to prepare the church for this approaching day of the Lord (1 Thess 4:13—5:10). In sharp contrast, the author in 2 Thessalonians is taking great pains to refute the idea that this return is near and to remind the church that a number of events must take place first (2:1–12). The situation faced here is one of keen apocalyptic expectations fueled by persecution (1:4). The author draws on a rich reservoir of apocalyptic tradition to show that the church's present affliction will be reversed on the day of the Lord (1:5–10). Since that climactic day has not yet arrived, actions in the present circumstances continue to be important (2:15—3:16).

The structure of 2 Thessalonians may be outlined in a menorah pattern:

Paul's Second Letter to the Thessalonians in a Menorah Pattern	*2 Thess 1—3*
a Salutation and thanksgiving for your faith, love, and steadfastness	1:1–4
A Judgment at Christ's coming will repay those who afflict you	1:5–10
B We pray that God will make you worthy of your call	1:11–12
C Do not be alarmed by thinking the Day of Yahweh is already here	2:1–2

The focus at the center of this construction is on the coming day of the Lord, when the lawless one will be removed in God's own time (2:3–10). Paul warns the people not to be alarmed by thinking that the day of Yahweh is already here 2:1–2), for God himself sends a delusion so that they believe what is false (2:11–12). The second frame moves from Paul's prayer that God will make the Thessalonians worthy of their call (1:11–12) to Paul's thanksgiving to God for calling them to salvation through sanctification (2:13–16). A time of judgment is coming, in which the fortunes of those who have afflicted the Thessalonians will be reversed (1:5–10). Paul warns against believers who are living in idleness because of the mistaken belief in the imminent return of Jesus (3:1–11).

The center of this structure, which concerns the Day of Yahweh and the destruction of the "man of lawlessness, the son of perdition" (2:3, RSV), may be expanded in a menorah pattern of its own:

2nd Level Menorah: The Final Day will Come in God's Own Time	*2 Thess 2:3–10*
A That day will not come until the lawless one is revealed	2:3
B The lawless one is seated in the Temple declaring himself to be God	2:4–5
C You know what is now restraining him	2:6a
X **The lawless one will be revealed when his time comes**	2:6b
C´ Lawlessness is at work until the one who restrains it is removed	2:7
B´ The lawless one will be revealed and Jesus will destroy him	2:8
A´ The coming of the lawless one is the working of Satan	2:9–10

In some respects, this entire literary unit has the quality of a "riddle in the middle" in that the identity of the lawless one remains enigmatic. The Day of Yahweh will not come until the lawless one is revealed (2:3); and the coming of the lawless one is the working of Satan (2:9–10). The lawless one "exalts himself above every so-called god or object of worship so that he takes his seat in the temple of God, declaring himself to be God" (2:4–5). That lawless one will be revealed and Jesus will destroy him at his coming (2:8). Paul reminds the Thessalonians that they already know what is restraining the lawless one (2:6a), for lawlessness is at work until the one who restrains it is removed (2:7). In short, the lawless one will be revealed and destroyed in God's own time.

The fact that 2 Thessalonians is a conscious clarification of Paul's eschatological teaching of 1 Thessalonians is shown by the fact that the two letters may be outlined together as a single literary entity, as follows:

A	Paul's gratitude for the Thessalonians' response to the gospel	1 Thess 1–3
B	Christ's coming–a time of reunion with dead in Christ	1 Thess 4–5
B´	Christ's coming–a time of judgment and vindication	2 Thess 1–2
A´	Paul's concern that the Thessalonians continue steadfast in Christ	2 Thess 3

In this reading, the two letters to the Thessalonians emerge as a single literary unit in the form of a simple chiasm. The first and fourth parts are concerned primarily with the conduct of both Paul and the Thessalonians; whereas the second and third parts are concerned with Paul's teaching on the coming of Jesus.

Paul's First Letter to the Thessalonians opens with a section on the Thessalonians' reception of Paul's gospel (1:2–10) and Paul's conduct among them, which was beyond reproach (2:1–12). It continues with a section on Paul's concern for the Thessalonians while absent from them (2:17–20), which is expressed concretely in his sending Timothy to encourage them (3:1–13).

Though the second section (1 Thess 4:1—5:28) has a section on the coming of Jesus in its center (4:13–18), it is also concerned with the doctrine of sanctification. It is God's will that his people live lives that are pleasing to him, and so the Thessalonians are urged to love one another and to practice good public morality toward outsiders (4:1–12). Moreover, in light of Paul's teaching on the coming of Jesus, they are to be vigilant, for the day of the Lord will come like a thief in the night—when least expected.

The Second Letter to the Thessalonians continues with both of these themes developed within an envelope of thanksgiving to God (1:3–4 and 2:13–16). It is God's will that the people be made worthy of the kingdom of God through suffering (1:5), and so Paul prays for them that "God will make you worthy of his call" (1:11–12). The central teaching on Christ's coming (1:6–10) is expanded in a detailed discussion of this coming day of the Lord (2:1–12).

The fourth section (2 Thess 3:1–17) of the two letters taken as a whole opens with a request for prayer "that the word of the Lord may spread rapidly" (3:1). It continues with Paul's prayer that the Lord may "direct your hearts to the love of God and to the steadfastness of Christ" (3:5). A further continuation of this prayer is implied as Paul turns his attention from the believers living in idleness (3:6–11) to his desire that God might strengthen the Thessalonians in every good work and that they not become weary in well-doing (3:12–15).

The fact that 1 and 2 Thessalonians form a single literary work, as outlined above, suggests that these two letters were edited by Paul himself as part of his Ecclesiastical Letters to the seven churches. It is difficult to imagine a third party editing two of Paul's letters in this manner. The editor has done his work with the freedom of an author—presumably because he is the author.

FOUR PERSONAL LETTERS OF PAUL: 1–2 TIMOTHY, TITUS, AND PHILEMON

The two letters to Timothy and the one to Titus are commonly called Paul's "Pastoral Epistles," and the letter to Philemon is usually grouped with Ephesians, Philippians, and Colossians as a fourth "prison epistle." As pointed out in the previous section, 2 Thessalonians is a "prison epistle" as well, in the sense that it was written in Rome at the end of Paul's missionary career and edited to be part of Paul's nine Ecclesiastical Letters to the "seven churches." Since Paul's second letter to Timothy is also a "prison epistle," and one of the last of Paul's thirteen canonical letters to be written, it seems best to arrange the four letters examined here under a more general title—the four "Personal Letters" of Paul.

It is important to note the fact that the four "Personal Letters" of Paul to Timothy, Titus, and Philemon may be read as a single literary unit—much like 1 and 2 Thessalonians. The content of these four books may be outlined in a menorah pattern:

Paul's Four Personal Letters in a Menorah Pattern	*1 Tim–Phlm*
a Salutation: "To Timothy, my true child in the faith"	1 Tim 1:1–2
A Paul and Timothy—a personal charge: "Fight the good fight"	1 Tim 1:3–20
B Practical instruction on prayer, worship, and leadership	1 Tim 2:1–5:25
C Instruction on false teaching and greed; "fight the good fight"	1 Tim 6:1–21
X **Warnings of problems to come and how to deal with them**	2 Tim 1–4
C´ Instruction on church governance; dealing with false teachers	Titus 1:1–16
B´ Practical instruction in church government	Titus 2:1–3:15
A´ Paul and Philemon: On social ethics (reinstatement of Onesimus)	Phlm 1–22
a´ Greetings from Epaphras, Mark, Aristarchus, Demas, and Luke	Phlm 23–25

The opening salutation (1 Tim 1:1–2) and the closing greeting from those who are working with Paul in Rome, including Mark and Luke (Phlm 23–25), take on fresh meaning when interpreted in terms of the center of this structure—the Second Letter of Paul to Timothy. That letter concerns problems to come in the life of the Christian Church and how to deal with them. Paul uses his personal example as an encouragement to endure suffering (2 Tim 3:10–15). He urges Timothy to make haste to join with him and his co-workers in Rome to work on the canonical activity at hand, and in particular to "get Mark and bring him with you, for he is useful in my ministry" (4:12). As the concluding verses of Paul's Letter to Philemon indicate (Phlm 23–25), Mark does join Paul, Luke, and the others, and presumably Timothy joins them as well.

The outer frame in this menorah pattern moves from a section on Paul and Timothy (1 Tim 1:3–20) to another on Paul and Philemon (Phlm 1–22). On the one hand, we have a personal charge from a spiritual father to his "child" to "fight the good fight" of faith (1 Tim 1:18). The phrase translated "divine training" (v. 4) actually pictures the Christian life as the discipline of servants in a large household. This imagery takes on concrete form in the corresponding Letter of Paul to Philemon, which concerns such a household servant by the name of Onesimus, who had emancipated himself and whom Paul is sending back to his master in Colossae (Phlm 1–22). The second frame consists of lengthy parallel passages that present practical instruction on proper conduct within the church and matters of church governance (1 Tim 2—5 and Titus 2—3). The innermost frame deals with further instruction, both parts of which take up the matter of false teachers (1 Tim 6:3–5 and Titus 1:10–16). In the former instance, this is within a context of exhortation and encouragement to "fight the good fight of faith" (1 Tim 6:12). In the center of this menorah pattern we find the entire book of 2 Timothy.

Paul's four "Personal Letters" include practical instructions on how to behave in church and the treatment of false teachers in particular. Paul's second letter to Timothy expands an earlier warning against false teachers (1 Tim 1:1–20). In a similar manner, the letter to Philemon functions as an addendum to Paul's letter to Titus—and, of course, to the earlier group of three of Paul's Ecclesiastical Letters (Ephesians, Philippians, and Colossians). Onesimus is identified as a Colossian in Colossians 4:9, where he is also called a "beloved brother" (cf. Phlm 16).

The subject of false teachers emerges as a primary issue. 1 Timothy opens with a warning against false teachers (1 Tim 1:3–11), and 2 Timothy picks up the same subject in its center (2 Tim 3:1–9). The subject is taken up a third time in 1 Timothy 4:1–5 and a fourth time in Titus 1:10–16.

Each of Paul's four "Personal Letters" may be outlined in a menorah pattern:

Paul's First Letter to Timothy in a Menorah Pattern		*1 Tim 1—6*
a	Salutation: "To Timothy, my true child in the faith" (v. 18)	1:1–2
A	Paul's personal charge to Timothy: "Fight the good fight"	1:3–20
B	Instruction on prayer and worship—godliness, women's behavior	2:1–15
C	Qualifications of bishops and deacons	3:1–13
X	**Administration is a spiritual task in the household of God**	3:14–16

C´ What it takes to be a good minister of Jesus Christ — 4:1–16

B´ Instruction on various groups—older men and women, widows, elders — 5:1—6:2

A´ Instruction on false teaching and greed: "Fight the good fight" (v. 12) — 6:3–21a

a´ Benediction — 6:21b

Paul's Second Letter to Timothy in a Menorah Pattern — 2 Tim 1—4

a Salutation — 1:1–2

A Thanksgiving and exhortation — 1:3–7

B Paul exhorts Timothy to join with him "in suffering for the gospel" (v. 8) — 1:8–18

C Paul's special appeal for Timothy to show courage — 2:1–26

X **Warning about the last days—immorality and false teaching** — 3:1–9

C´ Paul's further charges to Timothy — 3:10—4:8

B´ Paul exhorts Timothy and his associates to assist him in canonical endeavors — 4:9–18

A´ Concluding exhortations — 4:19–21

a´ Benediction — 4:22

Paul's Letter to Titus in a Menorah Pattern — Titus 1—3

a Salutation — 1:1–4

A Administration of churches in Crete: "Appoint elders in every town" — 1:5–9

B Description of false teachers — 1:10–16

C Instructions on various groups—based on God's grace — 2:1–10

X **Admonition: "Declare these things...Let no one look down on you"** — 2:11–15

C´ Instructions to Titus buttressed with a description of God's mercy — 3:1–8

B´ Final warning about false teachers, emphasizing their divisiveness — 3:9–11

A´ Final words: Meet me at Nicopolis; speed Zenas and Apollos on their way — 3:12–14

a´ Final greetings and benediction — 3:15

Paul's Letter to Philemon in a Menorah Pattern — Phlm 1–25

a Salutation — 1

A Other addressees: Apphia, Arichippus, and the church in your house — 2–3

B Paul's confidence in Philemon's love and faith — 4–7

C Paul's plea for Onesimus—"I am sending him back to you" — 8–14

X **Take him back "as a beloved brother...in the flesh and in the Lord"** — 15–16

C´ Paul's plea for Onesimus—"Receive him as you would receive me" — 17–20

B´ Paul's confidence in Philemon's obedience and support — 21–22

A´ Greetings from Epaphras, Mark, Aristarchus, Demas, and Luke — 23–24

a´ Benediction — 25

Paul's first letter to Timothy is primarily about proper conduct within the church in matters of prayer, worship, church regulation, and ethical morality. A secondary theme, which functions as a framework around the book as a whole, is a warning against false teachers and the personal injunction to Timothy to "fight the good fight" (1:18 and 6:12). The letter to Philemon picks up on some of the same themes in Paul's commendation of Philemon's love and faith and Paul's confidence of Philemon's continued obedience and support; but the primary focus here is that of a plea for the restoration of Onesimus. 1 Timothy concerns matters of corporate morality and ethics within the life of the church as a body of believers. Philemon concerns the matter of private ethical behavior within the context of a specific household in the church of Colossae (a "house church").

Though 2 Timothy is primarily about specific matters of encouragement and counsel on the part of a dying "patriarch" to his faithful child, it also contains in its structural center a prediction of false teachers that will arise in time to come and the advice to "avoid them!" (2 Tim 3:1–9). This same concern is picked up in the structural center of Paul's letter to Titus, with specific advice on how to deal with false teachers—"They must be silenced, since they are upsetting whole families by teaching for sordid gain what is not right to teach" (Titus 1:10–16). Like 2 Timothy, Paul's letter to Titus also contains specific advice and counsel, but primarily in matters of church life rather than the very personal instruction Paul gives his "beloved child" in 2 Timothy.

The outermost frame in the structure of 2 Timothy moves from a statement of thanksgiving and exhortation (1:3–7) to concluding exhortations urging Timothy to "come (to Rome) before winter" (4:19–21). The second frame opens with Paul exhorting Timothy to share in his suffering for the gospel, following the example of Onesiphorus (1:8–18). It continues with personal instructions urging Timothy to come soon and to bring with him Mark to work with Luke (4:11) and the "book-carrier" with its contents, which Paul left with Carpus in Troas (4:9–18). Paul is referring to the canonical activity in which he and Luke are already engaged. The innermost frame consists of a special appeal on Paul's part for Timothy to show courage (2:1–26), which is set over against further charges to Timothy that he "be prepared in season and out of season...with great patience and careful instruction" (4:2, NIV). And in the center of this structure we find warnings about the last days when "distressing times will come" with false teachers "of corrupt mind and counterfeit faith" (3:1–9).

In the larger structure of the four letters as a whole, Paul's instruction to Timothy on prayer, worship, and church regulations (1 Tim 1—3), is set over against his letter to Philemon on matters of social ethics. Here Paul argues from the personal example of his own life—"As an old man, and now also a prisoner of Christ Jesus, I am appealing to you for my child, Onesimus, whose father I have become during my imprisonment" (Phlm 9–10). Paul's personal example is also highlighted in 2 Timothy, where he instructs Timothy "to present himself to God as one approved by him, a worker who has no need to be ashamed, rightly explaining the word of truth" (2:15). Paul's charge for Timothy to "continue in what you have learned and firmly believed, knowing from whom you have learned it" (3:14) recalls his own steadfastness in persecutions and sufferings of times past in Antioch, Iconium, and Lystra (see Acts 13—14). His personal behavior stands in sharp contrast to that of the false teachers who will arise "in the last days" (2 Tim 3:1–9).

The matter of how to deal with these false teachers is taken up in detail in two parallel sections within this larger concentric design in 1 Timothy 4—6 and Titus 1—3. These two sections also contain parallel instructions on matters of church life and ethical morality (1 Tim 5:1–24 and Titus 1:5–9 and 2:1–15). Some scholars describe Paul's letter to Titus as almost a reduced version of 1 Timothy, since both take up the same themes—the threat of false teaching, the concern with church order, and the importance of personal example.

9

The Epistle to the Hebrews
and the Seven General Epistles

In the present arrangement of the canon, the Epistle to the Hebrews functions as a literary bridge to connect the thirteen Letters of Paul with the seven General Epistles of James, Peter (2), John (3), and Jude, as indicated in the following outline:

The Twenty-two Books of the Apostolic Writings

A   Nine Ecclesiastical Letters of Paul—to seven churches in Europe and Asia

B   Four Personal Letters of Paul—to Timothy (2), Titus, Philemon

X   **Hebrews—epistle of the four "pillars" (James/Jude, Peter, John, and Paul)**

B´   Seven General Epistles from four apostles—James, Peter (2), John (3), and Jude

A´ Revelation to John to the seven churches of Asia

The Epistle to the Hebrews is the focus of attention in this concentric structure, which is connected with Paul in its closing verses (13:22–25) and with the Letter of James in its title. James is addressed to "the twelve tribes [of Israel] in the Dispersion" (i.e., the "Hebrews"; James 1:1). The outer frame in this concentric structure moves from Paul's letters to seven churches to the Revelation to John, which is addressed to the seven churches of Asia Minor. The inner frame connects a group of four "Personal Letters" from Paul, the apostle to the Gentiles, with seven "General Epistles" associated with four apostles who preceded Paul, which are arranged by author in a simple chiasm as follows:

The Four Authors of the Seven General Epistles

A   James, the brother of Jesus and "bishop of Jerusalem"

B   Peter—surviving member of trio on Mount of Transfiguration

B´   John—surviving member of trio on Mount of Transfiguration

A´ Jude, the brother of James and Jesus (otherwise virtually unknown)

The outer pair in this chiastic structure is made up of letters ascribed to James and Jude—two of the brothers of Jesus. James, the head of the church in Jerusalem, was martyred at Passover in the spring of 62 C.E. Virtually nothing is known of Jude other than a story attributed by Eusebius to Hegesippus, who relates that there survived of the family of the Lord grandsons of Jude, who were accused before Domitian, but released by him because of their simple way of life (*Church History* iii.20). The inner pair consists of two of the three disciples Jesus took with him to the Mount of Transfiguration—Peter, James, and John. James, son of Zebedee and brother of John, is the only one of the twelve disciples of Jesus whose martyrdom is recorded in the New Testament. He died at the hands of Herod Agrippa I (42–44 C.E.) as part of a wider persecution that included the arrest of Peter (Acts 12:1–3). Within the canonical process, James the brother of Jesus replaced James the brother of John. Among the twelve disciples, Peter and John enjoyed unusually close relationships with Jesus. Moreover, these two men played major roles in the canonical process that produced the Completed Tanakh.

THE EPISTLE TO THE HEBREWS

The tradition that Paul wrote the Epistle to the Hebrews in the Hebrew language and that Luke translated it into Greek, as reported by Clement of Alexandria (ca. 200 C.E.), raises issues worth exploring. In the first place, Hebrews is included in the Pauline corpus and was part of that corpus from earliest times, even though Pauline authorship was questioned widely among the church fathers in antiquity. It is the association of Hebrews with Luke as well as with Paul that remains intriguing.

As already noted, Luke was with Paul when Paul's "prison epistles" were completed (2 Tim 4:11; Col 4:14; Phlm 24). Moreover, Luke plays a major role in the canonical process with the writing of the Gospel of Luke and Acts of the Apostles, which constitute two of the five books in the "New Torah" (the Four Gospels and Acts). The first step in the canonical process that eventually produced the Completed Tanakh is the editing of the Letters of Paul. Together with Luke's Gospel, these letters are intended to be a counterpart to the Hebrew Writings (*Kethuvim*) of the Tanakh, as a fifth section of the canon of sacred scripture. At the time that this initial step in the canonical process was taking shape, Luke had already written his gospel and was at work on its sequel, the Acts of the Apostles. When Paul sent his letter to Philemon, or shortly thereafter, the Gospel of Luke and the nine "Ecclesiastical Letters" of Paul to seven churches were apparently circulating in Ephesus. This would help to explain the nature of the canon advanced later by Marcion in the second century C.E. Before Marcion's excommunication by Rome (ca. 144 C.E.), he was active in Ephesus, where he encountered the Pauline corpus of nine "Ecclesiastical Letters" plus the Letter to Philemon. The earliest papyrus of the Pauline Letters (P46) contains only these ten letters of Paul; and Marcion's order of these letters, once thought to be unique, is now known in certain Syrian texts.

While Paul was a prisoner in Caesarea (ca. 58–60 C.E.), Luke was present in Jerusalem with ample opportunity to gather information about the Epistle to the Hebrews. Though Luke is probably not the author, as such, he may well be the editor of this important work by another gifted writer—perhaps Apollos, or even Priscilla. At any rate, it is the labors of Luke and Paul within the canonical process that make Hebrews the center around which the other seventeen books in the second half of the twenty-two-book canon of the Apostolic Writings of the Second Testament are structured. The canon in this conception includes a "New Torah" consisting of five books, thirteen Letters of Paul as the new prophet, and four "Hagiographa" associated with the four "pillars" of the church.

The editorial note at the end (Heb 13:22–25) appears to have been written by Luke as a colophon on the outside of the scroll of the Epistle to the Hebrews, which was sent ahead to Paul in Rome. The writer includes greetings from other Italians laboring with him. He mentions a brief note (the colophon itself) and the fact that Timothy is free to join them, adding the words, "if he comes in time, he will be with me when I see you" (13:23). Apparently Timothy did not arrive in time and Luke, the author of the note, went on to join Paul in Rome without him. Paul subsequently invited Timothy to bring Mark with him, along with the manuscripts that Paul and Luke had left behind at Troas on route to Jerusalem and Paul's arrest some years earlier (ca. 58 C.E.).

If Luke is not the actual author of the Epistle to the Hebrews, he is the one who secured this particular document, which plays a significant role in the formation of the canon of the New Testament. Hebrews appears to have been written in ca. 60–62 C.E., to judge from its teaching on eschatology, which reflects the belief in the imminent return of Jesus. Nothing is said explicitly in Hebrews about the persecution under Nero or about Paul's and Peter's martyrdom in Rome. It should be noted that Codex Alexandrinus includes in its superscription to Hebrews, "written from Rome." Whether or not Paul wrote the book, it is edited in a manner that associates it with Paul's letters and also with the Letter of James to "the twelve tribes (of Israel) in the Dispersion" (James 1:1).

The Epistle to the Hebrews argues forcefully that through Christ faithful Christians have direct access to God. The text urges the faithful to follow Christ's example—to be faithful, hopeful, loving and patient in suffering. The content of the letter as a whole may be outlined in the following menorah pattern:

The Epistle to the Hebrews in a Menorah Pattern	*Heb 1—13*
a Prologue: God has spoken in these last days by a Son	1:1–4
A God's eternal son (Jesus) is superior to angels and ever the same	1:5–14
B Warning not to neglect the Son's message	2:1–4
C The Son's humiliation and exaltation—tested by suffering	2:5–18
X **God's Son (Jesus) brings Moses' covenant to completion**	3:1–11:40
C´ Jesus endured the cross, disregarding its shame	12:1–13

B´	A final warning against rejecting God's grace	12:14–29
A´	Concluding admonitions: Jesus the same yesterday, today, and forever	13:1–19
a´	May God make you complete to do his will; exhortation and greetings	13:20–25

In place of the normal salutation, the Epistle to the Hebrews opens with a brief summation of what follows in the body of the book (cf. Acts 1:8 and Rev 1:1–2). While God has spoken in various ways by the prophets in times past, he has done something new in these last days—"he has spoken to us by a Son." That Son is the very fullness of God in human flesh, who "has become as much superior to the angels as the name he has inherited is more excellent than theirs."

In the concentric design of the whole, this brief introduction (1:1–4) is set over against a concluding benediction, exhortation, and greetings (13:20–21), in which the author prays that God who has so exalted his Son, our Lord Jesus, may perfect his work in us. Immediately after the benediction, we find a colophon by the editor of the book (13:22–25), which stands outside the literary structure of the work itself. This personal note from Luke to Paul in Rome suggests much in terms of the nature of the canonical process itself, which placed Hebrews in the center of the second half of the New Testament. In the second frame, a warning not to neglect the Son's message (2:1–4), is set over against a final warning against rejecting "the one who warns from heaven...for indeed our God is a consuming fire" (12:14–29). The innermost frame explores further the example of Jesus, God's Son, who was tested by suffering (2:1–13).

The extensive central section of the above structure (Heb 3—11), which shows how Jesus Christ, as God's Son, brings the covenant of Moses to its completion, may in turn be outlined in another menorah pattern:

2nd Level Menorah: Jesus Completes Moses' Covenant	*Heb 3—11*
A Moses a servant, Christ a son—warning against unbelief	3:1–19
B The "Sabbath rest" God promised to Joshua still remains for us	4:1–13
C Jesus is a merciful and faithful high priest	4:14–16
X **Jesus is high priest forever, after the order of Melchizedek**	5:1—7:28

C´	As our heavenly priest, Jesus is mediator of a better covenant	8:1–10:39
B´	The meaning of faith—from Abel to Jacob	11:1–22
A´	The faith of Moses and other Israelite heroes after him	11:23–40

The outermost frame takes up the person of Moses (3:1–19) and other Israelite heroes after him (11:23–40) to show that Jesus Christ is indeed superior to Moses. The second frame opens with a discussion of the "Sabbath rest" that God promised to Joshua, which remains for faithful Christians to inherit (4:1–11). It continues with a roll call of giants of the faith in times past—from Abel to Moses, which includes Enoch, Noah, Abraham and Sarah, Isaac, Jacob, and Joseph (11:1–22). The theme of Jesus Christ as our high priest is introduced in 4:14–16 and developed at length in a section on Christ's "heavenly" sacrifice, which inaugurates a new and better covenant with God (8:1—10:39). Christ is our sacrifice, as well as the high priest who offers that sacrifice once for all. Other priests stand day after day at their service, "offering again and again the same sacrifice that can never take away sins. But when Christ offered for all time a single sacrifice for sins, 'He sat down at the right hand of God'... for by a single offering He has perfected for all time those who are sanctified" (10:11–14).

In the center, we find a lengthy section on the theme of Jesus as our high priest forever (Heb 5—7), which may be outlined in another menorah pattern:

3rd Level Menorah: Jesus Is Our High Priest Forever	Heb 5–7
A Jesus was appointed a priest—according to the order of Melchizedek	5:1–6
B Jesus learned obedience; God made him our high priest forever	5:7–10
C Warning against falling away	5:11–14
X **Therefore let us go on toward perfection**	6:1–3
C´ The peril of falling away and God's fidelity to his promise	6:4–12
B´ God's promises are made certain in Jesus, our high priest forever	6:13–20
A´ As priest in the order of Melchizedek, Christ is our priest forever	7:1–28

The outermost frame here includes repetition of the verse: "You are a priest forever, according to the order of Melchizedek" in 5:6 and

7:17. That theme, which is introduced in 5:1–6, is developed at length in 7:1–28. The Levitical priesthood is inadequate, because of its provisional and temporary nature. The priesthood of Melchizedek is without end. The second frame of this menorah pattern expands this theme of the eternal nature of Christ's priesthood. We learn that Jesus learned obedience by what he suffered in human flesh (5:11–14). At the same time, God remains faithful and his promises are certain. If we choose to go our own way, having "tasted the heavenly gift," it will be at great peril (6:4–12).

The conclusion of the matter, and the central message of the Epistle to the Hebrews, is clear: "Therefore let us go on toward perfection, leaving behind the basic teaching about Christ, and not laying again the foundation" (6:1–3). Looking to Jesus, the author and finisher of our faith, we are to press on, for our calling is the same. His humiliation was transformed to exaltation; and the same holds true for us. Christ is our eternal high priest through whom we have access to God. Moreover, he himself is the perfect sacrifice for our sins. Let us then "show the same diligence so as to realize the full assurance of hope to the very end, so that [we] may not be sluggish, but imitators of those who through faith and patience inherit the promises" (6:11–12).

In the first major section (Heb 1—2), we learn that God has spoken in a special way by his Son, and we are to hold fast to him and to his message. The example of Jesus is explored further in the fourth major section of the epistle (Heb 11—13), where we see that he endured the cross, disregarding the shame. In like manner, we are to follow Jesus, realizing that even the great heroes of faith in ages past were justified by faith (11:1–40). Both the second major section (Heb 3—6) and the fourth (Heb 7—10) explore the meaning of Jesus Christ as our great high priest, "after the order of Melchizedek." The meaning of this reference to an incident in the life of Abraham (Gen 14) is spelled out in 7:1–28. The Hebrew name Melchizedek means "king of righteousness." Since he is also king of Salem, he is "king of peace"—"without father, without mother, without genealogy, having neither beginning of days nor end of life, but resembling the Son of God, he remains a priest forever" (7:2–3).

When the details of the structural center in Hebrews 5—6 are examined closely within the larger context, two very different pictures of Jesus emerge. On the one hand, we find the example of Jesus who learned obedience through suffering and who calls us to follow his example as we move on toward perfection in him (5:1—6:20). But, at the same time, we learn that this Jesus is our great high priest, "after the order of Melchizedek." He is our high priest forever, through whom we have access to God who will bring us to the promised "Sabbath rest" (3:1—4:16). Moreover, we learn that Christ is also the perfect sacrifice for sin—offered once for all, to provide a better covenant, for his sacrifice takes away sin itself (7:1—10:39). God has spoken by his Son and we are called to hold fast to him and to his message (1:1—2:18). We are to follow the example of Jesus, knowing that a "great cloud of witnesses" to his redemptive and intercessory work surrounds us in our behalf (11:1—13:25).

SEVEN GENERAL EPISTLES:
JAMES, 1–2 PETER, 1–3 JOHN, AND JUDE

The Letter of James

James is listed first among the brothers of Jesus in Matthew 13:55 and Mark 6:3. Paul met James, the Lord's brother, on his first visit to Jerusalem, three years after his conversion (Gal 1:19). Though he was not a disciple during the ministry of Jesus (Matt 12:46–50; Mark 3:31–35; Luke 8:19–21; John 7:5), James was a witness to the resurrection (1 Cor 15:7), and he emerged very early as an important leader in the Christian community in Jerusalem. In Galatians 2:1–10, Paul says that in a private conference at Jerusalem, the "pillars"—James, Peter, and John—accepted him and his ministry to the Gentiles.

By tradition, James is the first "bishop" of Jerusalem (according to Clement of Alexandria, quoted by Eusebius, *Church History* ii.1.3). According to the Jewish historian Josephus (*Antiquities* ix), James was stoned to death at the instigation of the Sadducee high priest Ananus, who held that office in Jerusalem for only three months following the death of Festus in 62 C.E. Eusebius places this

event at Passover in 62 C.E. (cf. Eusebius, *Church History* iii.23).
The martyrdom of James had a profound effect on Jewish Christians,
and on the canonical activity in process at this time in the city of
Rome.

The Letter of James is written to a church under pressure. Since
James dies before the outbreak of a systematic Roman persecution in
the years following the burning of Rome (64 C.E.), Christians are not
facing martyrdom as such. They are suffering economic persecution
and oppression and the church is breaking under the pressure. There
are two ways Christians respond to such extreme pressure. They
either choose to pull together and help one another through difficult
times or they compromise with the forces at work against them and
split into bickering factions. Unfortunately, the latter is the case in
Jerusalem.

Its lack of sophisticated theology, its practical "Old Testament"
morality (much like the book of Proverbs), and its echoes of the
teachings of Jesus, probably drawn from oral tradition, are all consistent with an early date near the time of the martyrdom of James
(62 C.E.). The content of the Letter of James may be outlined in a
menorah pattern:

The Letter of James in a Menorah Pattern	Jas 1—5
A Endure testing with joy; three themes: testing, wisdom, and wealth	1:1-25
B True religion is more than devotional exercises—it lies in what you do	1:26-27
C Love one another by showing no partiality in dealing with other	2:1-26
X **True wisdom is pure speech without arrogance and criticism**	3:1-18
C´ Love one another by speaking no evil against one another .	4:1-16
B´ Proverb: Those who fail to do what they know is right commit sin	4:17
A´ Endure testing with patience until Jesus returns; summary of three themes	5:1-20

The Letter of James opens with a section on perseverance under trial
(1:2–25), which is set over against the concluding chapter on enduring testing with patience until the Lord returns (5:1–20). Both of
these sections take up three themes: that of testing or trials and the
reasons why people fail when tested; the subject of wisdom and the

control of the tongue; and the subject of wealth and its use in acts of charity. The focus of attention in this reading of the Letter of James is on the subject of true wisdom, which is found in pure speech without arrogance and criticism (3:1–18). The innermost frame in this structure takes up the injunction to love one another in two complementary ways. On the one hand, we are not to show partiality in dealings with one another (2:1–26). On the other hand, we are not to speak evil against one another (4:1–16). A second frame is found that includes a brief summary of "true religion" as characterized by those who have learned to "bridle their tongues," who "care for orphans and widows in their distress," and who keep themselves unspotted by the world (1:26–27). This summary statement is set over against a concluding proverb: "Anyone, then, who knows the good he ought to do and doesn't do it, sins" (4:17). In short, true religion consists in observing the spirit of the Torah as expressed in the laws of the book of Deuteronomy. This means that we are to move past these traditional laws of Moses to observe the law of love written on the heart of the believer who would follow the ways of Jesus—to love one's neighbor as oneself.

The center of the above structure may be expanded in another menorah pattern:

2nd Level Menorah: True Wisdom is Pure Speech without Criticism	Jas 3
A Those who are teachers will be judged more strictly	3:1
B Perfection comes by keeping the body in check with a "bridle"	3:2–5a
C Evil of intemperate speech—the tongue is a "world of iniquity"	3:5b–12
X **The truly wise person is characterized by a good life**	3:13
C´ Earthly wisdom brings disorder and wickedness of every kind	3:14–16
B´ Wisdom from above is a gift of the Spirit without partiality or hypocrisy	3:17
A´ Proverb: Peacemakers who sow in peace reap a harvest of righteousness	3:18

The focus here is on the fact that true wisdom is characterized by living a good life. If you are wise and understanding, you will "show by your good life that your works are done with gentleness born of wisdom" (3:13). The evil of intemperate speech, which is likened to a fire that "stains the whole body" (3:5b–12), is set over against a description of the evil consequences of earthly wisdom (3:14–16). Perfection comes by controlling the tongue (3:2–5a); and so true wisdom is from above—"without a trace of partiality or hypocrisy" (3:17). The outermost frame moves from a statement that teachers "will be judged with greater strictness" (3:1) to a concluding proverb: "A harvest of righteousness is sown in peace for those who make peace" (3:18).

The focus of attention in the first chapter of James is on the promise that the one who perseveres under trial will be blessed (1:12). On one side of this central verse we find a statement on the themes of testing, prayer, and use of wealth in acts of charity (1:2–11). On the other side, we find the same themes (1:13–25). The chapter opens with a greeting addressed "to the twelve tribes in the Dispersion" (1:1) and concludes with a summary injunction to "bridle the tongue" and a description of "true religion" as caring for orphans and widows in their distress and remaining unspotted by the world (1:26–27).

The second chapter has in its center two proverbs on judgment and mercy (2:13), which are framed by a sermon on not showing partiality by loving your neighbor as yourself (2:2–12) and another on generosity and faith that presents the contrast between faith and works (2:14–25). The chapter opens with a statement on the principle that Jesus is our glorious Lord (2:1) and concludes with another declaring that faith apart from works of love is dead (2:26).

The third section (3:1—4:12) has a proverb in its center, which says that peacemakers who sow in peace will reap a harvest of righteousness (3:18). The framework here presents a contrast between the evil of arrogance, in which jealousy and selfish ambition breed contention (3:13–17), and a summons to humble ourselves before the Lord who will exalt us in due course (4:1–10). The section opens with a statement on the evils of intemperate speech where an uncontrolled tongue is presented as the source of great evil (3:1–12). It concludes with an appeal not to speak evil against one another (4:11–12).

The fourth and concluding section (4:13—5:20) picks up where the first chapter left off, with a summons to be patient until the coming of the Lord (5:7). We are urged not to boast about tomorrow, for we do not know what a day will bring forth (4:13–17). Rich oppressors are warned (5:1–6), and those who are oppressed are urged to be patient in their suffering (5:8–11). The book concludes with a prayer of faith envisioning a healthy, mutually supportive community (5:12–20).

James closes the letter by stating why he has written it (5:19–20). Some of the readers have wandered from the truth. If such are believers, it is the author's hope that someone will bring them back. Rather than condemnation, restoration is the goal. And that is what James hopes will happen. Such restoration has a wonderful result in that the person is saved from eternal death by the covering over of a multitude of sins. God will accept the repentance and forgive the sins of that person. Then the forgiven person will continue in the right way, rejoicing in trials and testing, knowing that the reward is coming in God's own time.

The First Letter of Peter

Like the Letter of James, 1 Peter is a general epistle "to the exiles of the Dispersion," in this instance to five of the Roman provinces in Asia Minor (1:1). Peter wrote the letter with the help of Silas (Silvanus) from a place he calls "Babylon," where his "son" Mark is with him (5:12–13). In Revelation 16:19 and 17:5, the term "Babylon" is a cryptic name for Rome (cf. also 2 Esdras 3:1–2, 28, 31). Moreover, we learn from Colossians 4:10 and Philemon 24 that Mark was in Rome with Paul (ca. 62 C.E.). In 2 Timothy 4:11, Mark was in Asia Minor, from whence Paul summoned him to come to Rome "for he is very useful to me in my ministry." As we have already seen, a major part of that ministry is canonical in nature—namely the editing of the "Apostolic Writings" that ultimately take their place in the Completed Tanakh, alongside the Torah, the Prophets (Former and Latter), and the "Hebrew" Writings. The fact that Peter is writing from Rome is supported by Tertullian (*Against Heresies*, 36) and Eusebius (*Church History* 2.25.8, 2.15.2 and 3.1.2–3). Since no reference is made to the martyrdom of Paul, the letter was written before ca. 64–66 C.E. (see also 2:13). Thus the letter was probably written ca. 63–64 C.E., with the assistance of Sylvanus and Mark, and edited to be part of the twenty-two-book canon of the "Apostolic Writings" that were associated with the "four pillars" of the early Christian Church (James, Peter, John, and Paul).

The First Letter of Peter offers encouragement to a beleaguered church facing persecution. As was the case with the Letter of James, Christians are not facing martyrdom as such. The social tensions and suffering reflected in 2:19–24; 3:14–15; 4:12–19; and 5:10 are best explained by the conversion of Gentiles to Christianity within a Greco-Roman society with its fear that conversion to Christianity would reverse established hierarchical relationships (cf. Cicero, *Laws* 2.14–15). The Romans believed that foreign religions would cause immorality (especially adultery), insubordination within the household, and sedition against the state. 1 Peter addresses each of these fears. The letter emphasizes that those who are converted are to imitate Christ (2:21–23) by doing good works (2:12, 15, 20; see Luke 6:27) and by not retaliating against those who slander their community (2:18, 20–23; 3:9, 14–16).

The concentric structure of 1 Peter may be outlined in a menorah pattern:

The First Letter of Peter in a Menorah Pattern	1 Pet 1—5
A Salutation—self-introduction, addressees, and prayer for grace and peace	1:1-2
B A blessing—our living hope in Christ	1:3-12
C On living holy lives—"You shall be holy, for I am holy"	1:13-25
X **Christian conduct among unbelievers**	2:1–4:11
C´ On suffering as a Christian—"sharing Christ's suffering"	4:12-19
B´ Exhortation—tending the flock of God in presence of the evil one	5:1-11
A´ Final exhortation to "stand fast," greetings and benediction—"peace to all"	5:12-14

The First Letter of Peter is addressed to "the exiles of the Dispersion in Pontus, Galatia, Cappadocia, Asia, and Bithynia"—five Roman provinces, which include the cities of Ephesus, Colossae, Laodicea (and the others of the "seven churches of Asia" in Rev 2—3), in what is today the country of Turkey (1:1). The letter is written to encourage these churches to stand fast (5:12) and to continue "to do what is good"—"For its is better to suffer for doing good, if suffering should be God's will, than to suffer for doing evil" (3:17). Christians are called to live holy lives on the basis of our hope in Christ (1:3–25). The leaders, in particular, are summoned to be vigilant shepherds of the flock of God, in full awareness of the wiles of the devil who prowls about in search of prey (5:1–11). The people are urged to live as God's people—as "living stones" in the construction of a spiritual house in a pagan world (2:1–25). They are to live as good stewards of God's grace, showing love one to another—"sharing Christ's sufferings . . . while continuing to do good" (4:1–19).

The center of the above structure, which concerns Christians among unbelievers, may be outlined in another menorah pattern:

2nd Level Menorah: Christian Conduct among Unbelievers	1 Pet 2—4
A Live as servants of God, for you are living stones and a chosen people	2:1-17
B The example of Christ's suffering—the Suffering Servant (Isa 53:5-12)	2:18-25
C On wives and husbands—the example of Abraham and Sarah	3:1-7
X **Love one another—"All of you, have unity of the Spirit"**	3:8
C´ Do not repay evil for evil, repay with a blessing—and be blessed	3:9-12
B´ Suffering for doing right—Christ suffered so as to bring us to God	3:13-22
A´ Live as good stewards of God's grace, for "the end of all things is near"	4:1-11

In this structure, the focus narrows to the injunction to love one another (3:8). The believers are commanded to live as servants of God (2:1–17), which is set over against a similar command to live as good stewards of God's grace, for "the end of all things is near" (4:1–11). The example of Christ's sufferings, as portrayed in the Suffering Servant of Isaiah 53:5–12 (2:18–25), is set over against another that calls attention to the fact that Christ suffered so as to bring us to God (3:13–22). The first half of the innermost frame exhorts wives to accept the authority of their husbands (3:1–6); and husbands are urged to "show consideration for your wives in your life together, paying honor to the woman as the weaker sex" (3:7).

The second half of this frame is more general in nature, with a quotation from Psalm 34:12–16, which includes terms and ideas central to 1 Peter, such as the warning against evil speech (3:10b, cf. 2:22–23) and the emphasis on doing good deeds (3:11a).

The First Letter of Peter opens with a salutation (1:1–2), which is similar to that of the Letter of James. In both cases, the "author" is identified in similar phrases followed by a designation of the addressees "in/of the Dispersion."

> **James**, a servant of God and of the Lord Jesus Christ,
>   to the twelve tribes *in the Dispersion*
> **Peter**, an apostle of Jesus Christ, to the exiles *of the Dispersion*
>   in Pontus, Galatia, Cappadocia, Asia, and Bithynia

The phrase "exiles of the Dispersion" calls to mind the experience of those in ancient Israel who were exiled from the land of Israel to Babylon. The author declares that God has given us a new birth into a living hope" (1:3). Our salvation was made known to us through prophets of old (1:10–12), but now it has come through "the precious blood of Christ" (1:19). In light of this fact, we are called to live holy lives (1:13–16). In short, we are to love one another, for we have been born anew through the living word of God (1:22–25).

In the second chapter, the author returns to imperatives once again, urging Christians to "grow into salvation" (2:1–3). We are to live as servants of God (2:11–12), with Christ the Suffering Servant as our example to imitate (2:18–25). As "living stones," we are to be built into a spiritual house to be a witness to the nations, for we are God's own people (2:4–10). Like Christ, we are to submit to government authorities—fearing God and giving honor to the Roman emperor (2:13–17).

The third chapter in 1 Peter focuses on the matter of doing good works and patiently enduring suffering in persecution (3:13–17). The author turns to stories in Genesis about Abraham and Sarah, on the one hand (3:1–7), and Noah, on the other (3:20) in order to communicate the nature of God's salvation "through water" and right conduct in relation to prescribed roles in the household of that day. Christians are urged to have the unity of the Spirit in their fellowship (3:8–12), for Christ suffered for sins in order to bring us to God (3:18–20).

Chapter 4 returns to the theme of chapter 2, urging Christians to live godly lives as good stewards of God's grace by showing love for one another. The chapter begins with exhortations to the moral life that distinguishes Christians from unbelievers (4:1–6). The focus of the exhortations shifts from relations with outsiders to the ways in which Christians are to treat each other (4:7–11). A concluding doxology (4:11) and the repetition of the address "beloved" (cf. 2:11) signal a new section (4:12) that restates the themes of 1:6–8 and 3:13–17 on doing good and enduring suffering patiently as Christians (4:12–19).

The final chapter in 1 Peter turns to matters of leadership in the churches. Peter speaks as a pastor exhorting "the elders among you to tend the flock of God that is in your charge ... [as] examples of the flock" (5:1–3). Younger leaders "must accept the authority of the elders," and all are to "clothe yourselves with humility in your dealings with one another" (5:5). God will exalt those who humble themselves "in due time" (5:6), so cast all your cares on him (5:7). The central issue in this concluding chapter is a warning to be alert, for "your adversary the devil prowls around, looking for someone to devour. Resist him, steadfast in your faith, for you know that your brothers and sisters in all the world are undergoing the same kinds of sufferings" (5:8–9). The book concludes with a summary encouragement to "stand fast" and final greetings from Peter, Silvanus, and Mark (5:12–13), followed by a brief benediction (5:14).

The Remaining Five Letters: 2 Peter, 1–3 John, and Jude

As was the case with Paul's four "Personal Letters" (1–2 Timothy, Titus, and Philemon), the remaining five General Epistles function as a single literary unit from a canonical perspective, which may be outlined as follows:

Structure of Five Remaining General Epistles: 2 Peter, 1–3 John, Jude

A	Peter's testament and a warning against false teachers	2 Peter
B	Children of God, it is the last hour! Love one another!	1 John
X	**Distinguish between those who have God and those who don't**	2 John
B´	The "brethren" testify "to your love before the church"	3 John
A´	A warning against false teachers	Jude

The close relationship between 2 Peter (esp. 2:1–18 and 3:1–3) and Jude have been noted by numerous scholars through the years. The close relationship between the remaining three epistles is obvious from the simple fact that all three are ascribed to John. The working hypothesis here is that these five General Epistles were edited, under the authority of John, to form the Completed Tanakh. It was John who transformed the twenty-two-book canon of the "New Testament" into the forty-nine-book canon of the Completed Tanakh, in which the Four Gospels and the book of Acts function as a "New Torah"—a New Testament "Pentateuch," which connects the two testaments and belongs to both of them.

The Second Letter of Peter

The concentric structure of the Second Letter of Peter may be outlined in a menorah pattern:

The Second Letter of Peter in a Menorah Pattern — 2 Pet 1–3

a	Salutation: Grace and peace in "knowledge of God and of Jesus our Lord"	1:1–2
	A	Peter's testament: Summary of his teaching stressing faith and works	1:3–15
	B	The grounds of Christian hope in Christ's future coming	1:16–21
	C	False teachers will arise and bring destructive heresies	2:1–3
	X	**False teachers and their punishment**	2:4–19
	C´	Their end worse than if they not known the way of righteousness	2:20–22
	B´	The promise of the Lord's coming—grounds for holy living	3:1–13
	A´	Paul's writings—he also saw hope as a motive for righteous living	3:14–17
a´	Benediction: Grow in grace and knowledge of our Lord … Jesus Christ	3:18

The focus of attention in this reading of 2 Peter is on the subject of false teachers and their punishment (2:1–22). The framework around this structure opens with a salutation that includes the words "grace and peace be yours...in the knowledge of God and of Jesus our Lord" (1:2). It concludes with a benediction that contains similar words: "Grow in grace and knowledge of our Lord and Savior Jesus Christ" (3:18). The letter itself opens with a section that summarizes Peter's teaching as it is to be remembered after his death, stressing both God's grace and the need for moral effort if Christians are to gain "entry into the eternal kingdom of our Lord and Savior Jesus Christ" (1:3–11). The other half of this frame makes reference to Paul's letters as scripture (3:14–16). The next frame moves from a section on the grounds of Christian hope in Christ's future coming (1:16–21) to another on the same subject (3:1–13). The innermost frame concerns false teachers. On the one hand, they bring destructive heresies (2:1–3), and on the other they will suffer the consequences (2:20–22). "For it would have been better for them never to have known the way of righteousness than after knowing it to turn back from the holy commandment delivered to them" (2:21). The structural center in 2:5–19, which deals with punishment God has in store for false teachers, is framed by repetition of the word ζόφος "nether gloom" (2:4, 17; cf. Jude 6, 13). As we will see in the discussion below, the subject of false teachers, and their punishment is of primary importance in the five remaining General Epistles taken as a whole, alongside that of showing love one to another (see 1 John and 3 John).

The Second Letter of Peter includes Peter's testament (1:3–15), which is set over against concluding exhortations that include a description of Paul's letters in which they are treated as scripture (i.e., read in Christian worship along with the Torah, the Prophets, and the Writings of the Tanakh). The letter contains two major themes: teaching on the Lord's coming (1:16–21 and 3:1–10), and false teachers who will be punished (2:1–22). The teaching in 3:3–4 seems to reflect a time when the early Christian expectation that Christ would appear in glory within the lifetime of the first Christian generation has been disappointed. As such, it stands in contrast to the earlier teaching of 1 Peter 4:7. Like Paul in his second letter to the church at Thessalonica, Peter, too, has come to grips with the fact that he and others have misread the words of Jesus in times past on matters of eschatology. God does not measure time as human beings do.

The First Letter of John

Though 1 John develops the subject of false teachers (called "antichrists") at some length in 2:18–27 and 4:1–6, it is primarily concerned with the matter of keeping the commandment to love one another (2:28—3:24). The author insists that one cannot truly believe in Jesus Christ without selflessly loving other believers. The outer frame in the concentric structure of this book moves from the opening section declaring that "God is light" (1:5—2:11) to a concluding section on the subject "God is love" (4:7—5:12).

The First Letter of John may be outlined in a menorah pattern as follows:

The First Letter of John in a Menorah Pattern	1 John 1—5
a Prologue: We declare "the word of life…that our joy may be complete	1:1-4
A *God is light*, so do not walk in darkness by loving the world	1:5–2:17
B Warning against antichrists who deny the Father and the Son	2:18–27
C Children of God—"little children, abide in him"	2:28–29
X **Love of God "the Father" empowers us to *love one another***	3:1-17
C´ Abiding in God—"by this we know that he abides in us"	3:18–24
B´ Testing the spirits: "Many false prophets have gone out into the world"	4:1–6
A´ *God is love*, so let us abide in him and conquer the world by faith	4:7–5:12
a´ Epilogue: We are in Christ—"He is the true God and eternal life"	5:13-21

In this structure, the central concern for the commandment to love one another is highlighted (3:1–17). The framework around the main body of the letter moves from a prologue on the topic of "the word of life" (1:1–4) to the concluding epilogue in which Jesus Christ is presented as "the true God and eternal life" (5:20). The outermost frame presents a rather complex section on the theme "God is light"

(1:5—2:17), which is set over against another on the theme "God is love" (4:7—5:12). Both of these sections take up the subject of "the world." On the one hand, the readers are commanded not to "love the world or the things of the world" (2:15). And, on the other hand, it is our faith "that conquers the world" (5:4–5). Within this framework, we find parallel sections on the subject of false teachers. On the one hand, the readers are warned against "antichrists" that have come in this "the last hour" (2:18–27). And, on the other hand, they are enjoined to "test the spirits to see whether they are from God, for many false prophets have gone out into the world" (4:1–6). The innermost frame in this structure focuses on the subject of "abiding in God" (2:28–29 and 3:18–24). "All who obey his commandments abide in him, and he abides in them. And by this we know that he abides in us, by the Spirit that he has given us" (3:24).

The Second Letter of John

The brief letter of 2 John has the quality of a "riddle in the middle" within the larger structural design of what we have called the five remaining general epistles (2 Peter, 1–3 John, and Jude). The structure of 2 John, which is addressed from the author as "the elder" to "the elect lady and her children, whom I love in the truth, and not only I but also all who know he truth" (v. 1), may be outlined in a menorah pattern:

The Second Letter of John in a Menorah Pattern	2 John 1–13
a Salutation: "The elder to the elect lady and her children"	1–2
A Blessing: "Grace, mercy, and peace will be with you"	3
B I rejoiced greatly to find some of you following the truth	4
C I ask you to love one another	5
X **This is love—to walk according to God's commandments**	6
C´ Distinguish those who have God from "antichrists"	7–9
B´ Do not receive those who come without this teaching	10–11
A´ Parting wish: I hope to come to you so that our joy may be complete	12
a´ Final greeting: "Children of your elect sister greet you"	13

The phrases "the elect lady" (v. 1) and the "children of your elect sister" (v. 13) appear to be used metaphorically to refer to the Christian Church itself—corporately as a body, and in terms of any specific congregation. The letter takes up the themes of loving one another (vv. 4–6) and distinguishing between true and false teachers (vv. 7–9). The readers are urged not to receive into the house (church) or welcome anyone who comes to you and does not bring this teaching; for to welcome is to participate in the evil deeds of such a person" (vv. 10–11). The author hopes to be with his readers "and talk with you face to face, so that our joy may be complete" (v. 12).

The Third Letter of John

The teaching on love in 1 John and 2 John continues in this letter as well. Here the conduct of Gaius is presented as an example of love in action, for John notes that others testify to his love before the church (v. 6). The letter may be outlined in a menorah pattern:

The Third Letter of John in a Menorah Pattern	*3 John 1–15*
a Salutation: "The elder to the beloved Gaius"	1
A Personal remark: "I pray that all may go well with you"	2
B Gaius commended for "walking in the truth"	3
C John's joy—"to hear that my children follow the truth	4
X **The "brethren" testify "to your love before the church"**	5–8
C´ Diotrephes condemned—"prating against me with evil words"	9–11
B´ Demetrius commended—"from the truth itself…my testimony is true"	12
A´ Personal remark: I have more to write; "we will talk face to face"	13–14
a´ Closing: "Peace be to you…Greet the friends, everyone of them"	15

The letter is addressed from "the elder to the beloved Gaius, whom I love in truth" (v. 1). Though the name Gaius appears in three other contexts (see Acts 19:29; 20:4; Rom 16:23; 1 Cor 1:14), it is not possible to identify either Gaius or Demetrius (v. 12) with any certainty. The two names appear in the same context in Luke's account of the riot in Ephesus that was provoked by Paul's preaching (Acts

19:23 and 20:4). According to a tradition reported by Origen (*Commentary on Romans* 10.41), Gaius became the first bishop of Thessalonica. Gaius is commended for "walking in the truth" (v. 4); and the "brethren" of John bear witness of his love "before the church" (v. 6). Gaius is praised for his hospitality and Diotrephes is criticized because he "likes to put himself first" (v. 9). The innermost frame in this structure presents the contrast between John's joy in hearing that his children follow the truth (v. 4) and the disappointment he finds in the prating of Diotrephes (vv. 9–10). John reminds Gaius that "he who does good is of God; he who does evil has not seen God" (v. 11). In the center of this concentric structure, John commends Gaius for his love of the brethren in the church (v. 6) and adds the comment that we should support such brethren who are "fellow workers in the truth" (v. 8).

The Letter of Jude

The content of the letter of Jude, which was written to warn its readers about the dangers posed by certain false teachers and to advise them on how to respond, may be outlined in a menorah pattern:

The Letter of Jude in a Menorah Pattern	*Jude 1–25*
a Salutation: "Jude, a servant of Jesus Christ and brother of James"	1–2
A Appeal to contend for the faith that was entrusted to you	3
B Intruders have come who "deny our only Master and Lord, Jesus"	4
C Illustrations from Israel's past of how God judges the disobedient	5–7
X **Unlike the angel Michael, these men "walk in the way of Cain"**	8–13
C´ Citation from the book of Enoch on how God judges the ungodly	14–16
B´ In "the last time" scoffers indulge "their own ungodly lusts"	17–19
A´ Resist the danger from false teaching and reclaim the false teachers	20–23
a´ Doxology: "To the only God our Savior, through Jesus Christ our Lord"	24–25

This brief letter opens with an "appeal to you to contend for the faith that was once for all entrusted to the saints" (vv. 3–4). It continues with an explanation on how the readers are to respond to that appeal: "But you, beloved, build yourselves up . . . [and] keep yourselves in the love of God...And have mercy on some who are wavering; save others by snatching them out of the fire" (vv. 20–23). The focus of attention in the center of the letter is on judgment on false teachers who have "indulged in sexual immorality" (vv. 5–16). These false teachers have claimed that the grace of God in Christ frees them to do as they please (v. 4), especially by sexual indulgence (v. 7). In response, Jude insists that faith in the Christian gospel cannot be separated from moral obedience to Christ. His advice on how to deal with the opponents and their followers (vv. 22–23) combines a realistic sense of the danger they pose with a pastoral concern for their salvation.

10

The Revelation to John
A Vision of the New Creation

After the martyrdom of Paul and Peter in Rome (ca. 65–67 C.E.), the authority for the canonical process was in the hands of the apostle John, the sole survivor among the four "pillars" of the early Christian Church. John and the "brothers" working under his authority continued their work on the "Apostolic Writings" within the canonical process until John's death (ca. 96 C.E.). The dominant church tradition states that the apostle John moved to Ephesus after years of leadership in Jerusalem, and there wrote the five writings known as Johannine. He is said to have lived to an old age and to have died a natural death at Ephesus. According to Eusebius (*Church History* iii.18.1, 20.9, 23.4), John lived until the time of Trajan (98–117 C.E.). Irenaeus claimed that when he was "still a boy" he learned about John's ministry in Ephesus from Polycarp (Eusebius, *Church History* v.20.5). The Muratorian Fragment (ii.9–23) states that John was with the rest of the apostles when he was led to write his gospel. This would require a date while the apostles Paul, James, and Peter were alive and would favor Palestine as the place of writing. As we will see in the discussion below, the first edition of the Revelation to John appeared before the destruction of Jerusalem in 70 C.E. It would appear that the apostle John played a singular role in the canonical process from the death of Peter (ca. 67 C.E.) until his own death, some thirty years later (ca. 96 C.E.).

THE PROBLEM IN DATING THE REVELATION TO JOHN

The date of Revelation is a matter of dispute in scholarly discussion. Though there is strong tradition that John lived until the last decade of the first century and that the book was written near the time of his death, numerous scholars have dated the book earlier—in the late fifties or early sixties C.E. A number of historical indications in the book support this conclusion. The most important argument is the eschatological perspective of the imminent return of Jesus, which is like that of Paul's earlier letters (1 Thess 4:16–17 and 1 Cor 15:23–28), Hebrews (1:2; 9:26; 10:25, 37), James (5:3–8), 1 Peter 4:7–11, and 1 John 2:18. The book opens with the statement, "The revelation of Jesus Christ, which God gave him to show his servants *what must soon take place*" (Rev 1:1). In the final chapter we read: "The Lord, the God of the spirits of the prophets, has sent his angel to show his servants *what must soon take place*" (22:6); "See, *I am coming soon! (22:7); for the time is near (22:10); See, I am coming soon* (22:12); *Surely, I am coming soon*" (22:20). This appeal to the soon coming advent of Jesus Christ is also found in the messages to the seven churches (2:5, 16, 25; 3:3, 11, 20). The author believes in the imminent return of Jesus.

Scholars cite other evidence supporting an early dating in Nero's reign (ca. 54–68 C.E.). In Revelation. 11:1–2, it appears that the Temple in Jerusalem is still standing; this would demand a date prior to 70 C.E.; and John's indication that Jerusalem had a population of seventy thousand persons (Rev 11:13) suggests a time before the devastating war of 66–70 C.E. Moreover, the code name of the beast in Revelation 13:18 is 666, widely thought to symbolize the name of Nero Caesar. The Tenth Legion of the Roman army occupied the central area of Jerusalem in the years following the war for some years after the fall of Masada in 73 C.E. Moreover, the statements in Revelation 2:9 and 3:9 suggest that some Christians wished they were Jewish. During and after the war, the Jewish people were held in such disdain throughout the Roman Empire that this was no longer likely, as E. L. Martin has noted (*Restoring the Original Bible*, ASK Publications, 1994), pp. 323–24).

At the same time, it should be noted that from antiquity scholars have dated the composition of Revelation to the last decade of the first century (Irenaeus, *Against Heresies* 5.30.3). Allusion to the legend of Nero's return in Revelation 13:3 and 17:9–11, which suggests a time in the decades after his suicide in 68 C.E., lends support to this later date of composition.

It appears that the book, as we now have it, was more than thirty years in the making and went through at least two editions. About halfway through Revelation we find John being informed by an angel that he would experience a second phase of understanding prophetic information at some undisclosed future time. He was told to take a small scroll from the hand of this angelic messenger and to eat it, and it would be sweet to his mouth but bitter to his stomach. When this happened, John would receive further instructions about a future revelation dealing with the end-times that would concern the nations. "Then they said to me, 'You must prophesy again about many peoples and nations and languages and kings'" (Rev 10:11). Martin says, "This new prophetic message that John was to receive in the future could have been his final visionary experience when he was taken by the Spirit to the Isle of Patmos and where he put the final touches on the complete Book of Revelation" (*Restoring the Original Bible*, p. 436).

We learn from Eusebius that some of the most prestigious of early Christians returned to Jerusalem after its destruction in 70 C.E. and established a congregation there, apparently located on the Mount of Olives (Eusebius, *Proof of the Gospel*, iii.5 ¶124d). There were fifteen Jewish overseers in succession in Jerusalem until the Romans once again destroyed the city in 135 C.E. After that, the Jerusalem congregation continued to exist until the time of Eusebius and Constantine; but it was made up of Gentiles, since the Roman Emperor Hadrian (117–138 C.E.) banned anyone of Jewish ancestry from Jerusalem and its environs.

Though the apostle John ministered in Asia Minor during the Jewish Revolt and afterward (ca. 66–96 C.E.), he continued to take seriously his commission to go to the Jews, while Paul and others had gone to the Gentiles (Gal 2:9–14). The last part of John's life continued to be within the Jewish environment, while the center of

Christendom had moved to the Gentile world—and to the city of Rome in particular. Martin argues that "John was consistently in contact with Ephesus in his last 30 years of life, but since he considered himself the remaining apostle commissioned to go to the Jews, he must have spent time among the Jews in Jerusalem, Jabneh, and in Palestine. In his old age when he could not travel himself, he sent his representatives whom he customarily called 'the brethren' to teach the Jewish people in the areas of his responsibility (III John 5,6)" (*Restoring the Original Bible*, p. 460).

THE CONCENTRIC STRUCTURE OF THE REVELATION TO JOHN

Like John's Gospel and the First Letter of John, the Revelation to John is structured concentrically in elaborate detail. The book contains frequent allusions to the Tanakh and to the books of Ezekiel and Daniel in particular. Semitic features in John's Greek style support our conclusion that the author was a Jewish Christian from Palestine who immigrated to Asia Minor (modern Turkey) after the martyrdom of James (spring of 62 C.E.). By calling his work a prophetic book (1:3; 22:7, 10, 18–19), John implies that he himself is a prophet. His familiarity with the seven Christian communities he addresses in Asia Minor suggests that John was well known as an itinerant Christian prophet (22:9).

The emperor at the time Revelation was written in the canonical form we now have was the widely hated Domitian (81–96 C.E.), who demanded worship while he was alive. Worshiping the image of the emperor in his temple was a test of loyalty to the state. Anyone refusing to participate in the official religion of the state was considered subversive, and Rome was brutally paranoid about subversive religions. Available sources indicate that Domitian repressed Judaism and Christianity. Evidence on the imperial cult in Asia Minor and outright persecution of Christians on the provincial level in the early second century suggests that Domitian's own claims and behavior stimulated the environment in which provincial persecution of Christians subsequently occurred.

The content of Revelation may be outlined in a menorah pattern:

The Revelation to John in a Menorah Pattern	Rev 1–22
a Introduction and salutation	1:1–2
A Prologue: Jesus described as the one who is and was and is to come	1:3–8
B Preparatory vision of Christ on the island of Patmos	1:9–20
C The letters to the seven churches of Asia	2:1–3:22
X **Opening of the scroll of God's revelation with seven seals**	4:1–17:18
C´ Fall of "Babylon" (Rome) and the millennial kingdom	18:1–20:15
B´ New heaven and new earth—vision of the New Jerusalem	21:1–27
A´ Epilogue: John records the words of Jesus—"I am coming soon!"	22:1–20
a´ Benediction	22:21

The Revelation to John opens with a brief prologue, which presents
the book as a revelation of Jesus Christ to John by an angel, followed by greetings to the seven churches of Asia and a doxology
affirming the fact that the time of Jesus' coming is near (1:1–8).
The outer frame concludes with an epilogue in which the angel
shows John a river of life within the New Jerusalem where "there
will be no more night" (22:5). The angel affirms the fact that "the
time is near" (22:10)—Jesus is coming soon!" (22:12–20). The second frame opens with a preparatory vision on the island of Patmos
in which John sees the exalted Jesus as someone "like a son of
man" (1:13), who instructs him to "Write, therefore, what you have
seen" (1:9–20). It concludes with John's climactic vision of "a new
heaven and a new earth," which includes "the Holy City, the New
Jerusalem, coming down out of heaven from God, prepared as a
bride beautifully dressed for her husband" (21:1–2). The next frame
opens with a series of seven letters to the seven churches of Asia
(Rev 2—3). It continues with the vision of the fall of "Babylon"
(Rev 18) and the great joy in heaven as the rider on the white horse
presents the "King of Kings and Lord of Lords" (19:11–16), who
establishes his millennial kingdom and rules until the final judgment
(Rev 18—20).

The center of this menorah pattern may be opened up in another
menorah pattern, which focuses on the opening of the seventh seal
on the scroll of God's revelation of things to come:

2nd Level Menorah: Opening the Scroll with Its Seven Seals	Rev 4—17
A Vision of God enthroned in heaven, a sealed scroll, and the Lamb	4:1–5:14
B The four horsemen and the opening of the first six seals	6:1–17
C The 144,000 of Israel and the multitude from every nation	7:1–17
X **Opening the seventh seal and the seven trumpets**	8:1–12:17
C´ The Lamb and the 144,000 redeemed from the earth	13:1–14:20
B´ The seven last plagues and the seven bowls of God's wrath	15:1–16:21
A´ Vision of the great whore (Rome) and the beast ("Neronic Antichrist")	17:1–18

John passes through a door "standing open in heaven," where he sees a throne surrounded by twenty-four other thrones, on which are seated twenty-four elders and four living creatures who offer continuous praise to God (Rev 4). The Lamb who is worthy to open the scroll takes a scroll sealed with seven seals from the right hand "of him who was seated on the throne" (Rev 5). The outer frame concludes with a vision in which an angel reveals the punishment of the great whore (Rome) and of the beast she rides (Rev 17). The second frame presents the opening of the first six seals on the scroll and the four horsemen associated with the first four of them (Rev 6). It concludes with a vision of seven angels with the seven last plagues, for "with them God's wrath is completed" (Rev 15—16). The innermost frame presents parallel accounts of the "144,000 from all the tribes of Israel" (7:4) and the "great multitude...from every nation, tribe, people and language (7:9) and the beast out of the sea who has authority over this very multitude (13:7). This sets the stage for the opening of the seventh and final seal.

The opening of the seventh seal, which is presented in central section of this concentric structure, may be outlined in another menorah pattern:

3rd Level Menorah: Opening the Seventh Seal—the Seven Trumpets	Rev 8—12
A The seventh seal is opened—with awesome silence (cf. 1 Kgs 19)	8:1–5
B The first six trumpets	8:6–9:21
C The angel with the little scroll that John eats	10:1–10
X **John is told to prophesy again**	10:11

The opening of the seventh seal is followed by "silence for about half an hour" and the appearance of seven angels with seven trumpets (8:1–2). The concluding reference to "peals of thunder, rumblings, flashes of lightning and an earthquake" (8:5) is repeated in 11:19 to introduce the second half of the outermost frame—a vision of the woman, the male child, and an enormous red dragon (Rev 12). Michael and his angels defeat the dragon and his angels and hurl them to the earth where they wreak havoc for a season ("for a time, times and half a time"—12:14). In the second frame, the first six trumpets announce cosmic judgment (8:6—9:21); and the seventh trumpet announces the consummation of God's kingdom (11:14–19). "The time has come for judging the dead . . . and for destroying those who destroy the earth" (11:18).

The center of Revelation focuses on the coming of another angel from heaven who holds "a little scroll, which lay open in his hand" (10:1–4). John is commanded to eat this scroll, which "tasted sweet as honey in (his) mouth," but turned his stomach sour (10:10). As the angel presented the scroll, "seven thunders sounded" (10:4), but John was instructed not to write down what he heard, for some divine secrets must not be disclosed (2 Cor 12:4). Then the angel with the scroll in his hand spoke clearly, "There will be no more delay, but in the day when the seventh angel is to blow his trumpet, the mystery of God will be fulfilled" (10:6–7).

John is also given "a reed like a measuring rod" and told to "measure the temple of God and the altar, and count the worshipers there" (11:1). Here we find two witnesses who "have the power to shut up the sky so that it will not rain . . . [and] power to turn the waters into blood and to strike the earth with every kind of plague as often as they want" (11:3–6). These two witnesses are then identified with "two olive trees and two lampstands" (11:4, cf. Zech 4:3–14 where these symbols are metaphors for Joshua the priest and Zerubbabel the royal heir). These witnesses are Elijah (cf. 1 Kgs 17—18) and Moses (cf. Exod 7—11), the same persons who appear together with Jesus on the Mount of Transfiguration in the Synoptic Gospels. In short, the little scroll is an addition to the Torah and the Prophets as a concluding section of the Tanakh, which is presented as a command to the apostle John: "You must prophesy again about many peoples, nations, languages and kings" (10:11). The concluding book in the Completed Tanakh is seen as a continuation of the ministry of the prophets of old.

READING THE REVELATION TO JOHN FROM ITS CENTER

As the rest of the Revelation to John unfolds, each section is carefully balanced with another in the first half of the book in a grand inversion. The seventh trumpet (11:15–19) introduces another throne room scene like that of 4:1–11, 7:9–17, and 8:1–5. At this point, John reports loud voices in heaven, saying, "The kingdom of the world has become the kingdom of our Lord and of his Messiah, and he will reign forever and ever" (11:15). Though the great portent of the woman, the child, and the dragon that follows in 12:1–17 is an adaptation of the vision of the birth of Apollo in Roman mythology, it speaks of both the Israel from whom the Messiah came (12:5) and the church (12:6, 14, 17). The twelve stars (12:1) represent the twelve tribes of Israel. And the great dragon, which is Satan, is also an allusion to Leviathan, the enemy of God (see Job 41:1; Ps 74:14; Isa 27:1). The "seven heads" symbolize seven "kings" (as in 17:9–10), and the "ten horns" represent ten subordinate kingdoms (17:12, cf. Dan 7:7, 20, 24). The "male child" is the Davidic Messiah, "who is to rule all the nations with a rod of iron," i.e., conquer the enemies of Israel (12:5, see Ps 2:8–9). John then presents an eschatological vision of the expulsion of Satan from heaven (see Luke 10:18; John 12:31), which is based on an ancient Jewish myth (see Isa 14:12–15; 2 Enoch 29:4–5). In the concentric structural design of the whole, the vision of the woman, the child, and the dragon is set over against another throne room scene that echoes the theophany of Elijah on Mount

Horeb in 1 Kings 19:11–13. "When the Lamb opened the seventh seal, there was silence in heaven for about half an hour. . . and there were peals of thunder, rumblings, flashes of lightning, and an earthquake" (8:1–5).

Reading Revelation 13—14 in Relation to Revelation 7

The vision of the two beasts that serve the dragon (12:18—13:18) is followed by a victory vision of the Lamb and the 144,000 (14:1–20). The dragon (Satan) "took his stand on the sand of the seashore" (12:18) to await the emergence of the beast. The "blasphemous names" refer to divine titles, such as "Lord," "Savior," and "Son of God," claimed by Roman emperors (13:1). The "second beast" (13:11–18) is the "Neronic Antichrist," whose number is 666 (13:18).

The subject of the corresponding section in the larger concentric structure of Revelation is the 144,000 of Israel "who were sealed" (7:1–17). The "seal of the living God" (7:2) refers to a signet ring used to indicate ownership and to provide protection (see Job 9:7). "Seal" was also a term for Christian baptism (see 2 Cor 1:21–22; Eph 1:13; 4:30). Those "with a seal on their foreheads" (7:3) were divinely protected. The number 144,000 in 7:4 refers to the people of God, calculated using twelve as a multiple of twelve—for the twelve tribes of Israel (7:5–8). In 14:1–5 this same number refers to the martyrs. The "great ordeal" (7:14) refers to the period of distress and suffering often called "the great tribulation," prior to God's eschatological triumph (cf. 3:10; 13:5–10; Dan 12:1; Matt 24:21; Mark 13:7–20; 1 Cor 7:26).

Reading Revelation 15—17 in Relation to Revelation 4—6

Another throne room scene introduces the vision of the seven last plagues and the great whore seated on the beast in Revelation 15—17. Those who conquered the beast "sing the song of Moses (cf. Exod 15:1–18 and Deut 32:1–47) and the song of the Lamb" (15:2–8). In the vision, seven angels appear with "seven golden bowls full of the wrath of God" (15:7, cf. Jer 25:15–29). One by one the seven angels pour out their bowls on the earth with awe-some results (16:1–21), a description that echoes language of the plagues against Egypt and the crossing of the Red Sea in Exodus 7—14. "When the sixth angel poured his bowl on the great river Euphrates, and its water was dried up" (16:12), "the kings of the whole world" assembled "for battle on the great day of God the Almighty...at the place that in Hebrew is called Armageddon" (16:14–16). The seventh angel then declared, "It is done!" (16:17), and the awesome display of God's theophany in 8:5 is repeated: "And there came flashes of lightning, rumblings, peals of thunder, and a violent earthquake, such as had not occurred since people were upon the earth" (16:18). The vision of the seven last plagues (15:1—16:21) marks the climax of the opening of the seventh seal in 8:1–5. In terms of the inverted structure of the book as a whole, this vision is set over against the account of the opening of the first six of the seven seals in 6:1–17.

One of the seven angels with the seven bowls then showed John a vision of "a woman sitting on a scarlet beast that was full of blas-phemous names and it had seven heads and ten horns" (17:3). The woman is later identified as "the great city [of Rome] that rules over the kings of the earth" (17:18). The image of "the great whore" (17:1) appears elsewhere as a metaphor for godless cities (see Isa 1:21; 23:16–17; Nah 3:4). The "blasphemous names" are the divine titles of the Roman emperor (see the "beast rising out of the sea" in 13:1). The "seven mountains" are the seven hills of Rome (17:9) and the "seven kings" are the seven emperors from Julius Caesar to Domitian. The "war on the Lamb" (17:14) is the final end-time bat-tle (see 16:12–16, 19:17–21).

In the concentric structural design of Revelation as a whole, this vision of the great whore and the beast (17:1–18) is set over against a marvelous vision of the glory of God and the Lamb (4:1—5:14). This vision of heavenly worship begins with the first of a series of heavenly throne room scenes in Revelation (see also 7:9–17; 8:1–5; 11:15–19; 14:2–3; 15:2–8; 19:1–10 and 21:3–8). The "door" is a metaphor for the entrance to heaven (4:1). The "throne" symbolizes God's sovereignty (4:2); and heaven is conceived as a throne room filled with angelic courtiers (cf. 1 Kgs 22:19). The "rainbow that looks like an emerald" (4:3) is an allusion to the throne vision in Ezek 1:27–28. The "flashes of lightning, and rumblings and peals of thunder" (4:5) draw our attention to the scene of God's appearance at Mount Sinai (Exod 19:16–19; see also Rev 8:5; 11:19; 16:18). The "seven spirits of God" (4:5) are the seven archangels who stand before God (see also 1:4; 3:1; 5:6; 8:2). The "four living creatures" (4:6) refer to the cherubim, angelic beings that guard and support the throne of God (see Exod 25:17–22; 1 Kgs 6:23–28; Ps 18:10; Isa 6:2; Ezek 10). They are "full of eyes in front and behind" (4:6), an allusion to Ezekiel 1:18 and 10:12. The image of the four creatures with animal forms, one of which has a human face (4:7), is a modification of Ezekiel's vision, where each creature has four faces (Ezek 1:10). The Trisagion (4:8—"Holy, holy, holy") occurs first in Isaiah 6:3 and elsewhere in Jewish and Christian liturgies. The focus of the vision then shifts to that of a scroll representing God's final plan for the world (5:1–14). The reference to "a scroll (*biblion*) written on the inside and the back, sealed with seven seals" (5:1) is interesting, for papyrus scrolls were used on one side only, though legal scrolls sometimes had a summary of the contents on the outside. The image is probably taken from the visionary description of the scroll presented to the prophet Ezekiel, which "had writing on the front and on the back" (Ezek 2:9–10, cf. also the "flying scroll" in Zech 5:1–3 with writing on both sides). At the same time, however, it is also possible to see here a reference to the concept of a codex that is "sealed with seven seals" such that it is virtually impossible for an unauthorized person to open it (5:3).

The "lion of the tribe of Judah, the Root of David" refers to the king or messiah expected to come from the tribe of Judah, a claim frequently made for Jesus (Heb 7:14). The image of Jesus as a "Lamb standing as if it had been slaughtered" (5:6) stands in sharp contrast to that of a lion (5:5) and suggests the Passover sacrifice (1 Cor 5:7). Revelation uses the term "Lamb" as a designation for the exalted Christ eighty-eight times, highlighting his sacrificial role (see 5:8; 7:14; 12:11; 13:8; 17:14; and cf. Isa 53:7). The term "slaughtered" appears in 5:9, 12 (cf. 13:8) where it suggests the

Jewish Passover (Exod 12:1–28, 1 Cor 5:7). The phrase "by your blood" alludes to the atoning death of Jesus using the metaphor of the twice-daily expiatory sacrifice of a lamb in the religion of ancient Israel (Exod 29:28–42; Num 28; see also Rev 1:5, 7:14, 12:11). The "myriads of myriads and thousands of thousands" (5:11) refer to the innumerable angelic beings (cf. Dan 7:10; see also Rev 7:9, Jude 14).

Reading Revelation 18—22 in Relation to Revelation 1—3

The vision of the fall of "Babylon" (Rome) and the millennial reign of Christ on earth (18:1—20:15) picks up the language and imagery of ancient prophetic oracles against Babylon (Jer 50—51, cf. Isa 23—24 and Ezek 26—27). The statement, "Come out of her, my people" (18:4) is in the form of a prophetic summons to flight (cf. Isa 48:20–22; Jer 50:8–10; 51:6–10). Three dirges in 18:9–20 are adapted from Ezekiel 27. The "great millstone" thrown into the sea (18:21) symbolizes Rome's downfall in language taken from Jeremiah 51:63–64. In 19:1–10, we find another throne room scene that reflects on Rome's fall (19:1–5) and anticipates "the marriage of the Lamb," a metaphor for the union of Christ as bridegroom and the church as "his bride" (19:6–10; cf. Isa 54:5; Hos 2:19–20).

In the following section on the defeat of God's adversaries (19:11—20:3), Christ rides forth as a divine warrior, leading the heavenly armies against God's foes (cf. 1:12–16). The "robe dipped in blood" (19:13) refers to the garment of a warrior stained with the blood of his enemies (see Isa 63:1–6). The statement, "his name is called The Word of God" (19:13) is a rare designation for Jesus (cf. John 1:1; 1 John 1:1). The statement, "Come, gather for the great supper of God, to eat the flesh of kings" (19:17), is an invitation to birds of prey intended as a parody of ancient cultic dinner invitations. The "lake of fire that burns with sulfur" (19:20) is a place of eternal punishment, located not in the netherworld but "in the presence of the Lamb" (14:10), and elsewhere called Gehenna (Matt 18:9). The "dragon, that ancient serpent" refers to Satan in the imagery of an ancient Jewish expulsion myth (20:2; see also Gen

3:1–7; Luke 10:18; John 12:31; 2 Cor 11:3). The reference to "a thousand years," i.e., the millennium, is without parallel in Jewish eschatology. The Christian martyrs ("those who had been beheaded for their testimony to Jesus") are raised for a thousand-year reign during Satan's imprisonment (20:2–6). The concept of "the first resurrection" as restricted to Christian martyrs appears only here in the writings of the Completed Tanakh (20:5–6). The "second death" refers to eternal punishment of the wicked following their physical death (20:6; see also 2:11; 20:14; 21:8). The release and second defeat of Satan are without parallels in Jewish eschatology (20:7–10). In Ezekiel 38—39, "Gog and Magog" were the names of a hostile northern king and his nation. Here these names have come to symbolize all of Israel's enemies (20:8). In rabbinical sources, the final eschatological war is referred to as "the war of Gog and Magog" (*Babylonian Talmud, Berakot* 7b; *Sanhedrin* 97b). The final judgment includes the rest of the dead (20:11–15). The statement "the books were opened" suggests two sets of books, "the book of life" for the righteous and the other for the wicked (20:12).

In the larger concentric structural design, this vision of the fall of "Babylon" and the teaching on the millennial kingdom in Revelation 18—20 are set over against the letters to the seven churches in Revelation 2—3. The messages "to the seven churches that are in Asia" (1:4) are written in the literary form of edicts or proclamations issued by Persian kings of old or by the Roman emperors of John's day. The structure and content of the seven letters may be outlined in a menorah pattern:

John's Letters to the Seven Churches of Asia in Revelation 2—3

A	Ephesus	"You have abandoned the love you had at first"	2:1–7
B	Smyrna	"Be faithful until death" in the face of affliction and poverty	2:8–11
C	Pergamum	"You did not deny your faith in me" except for some	2:12–17
X	**Thyatira**	**"I know your love" but you tolerate that woman Jezebel**	**2:18–29**
C´	Sardis	"You have a name of being alive but you are dead" except for some	3:1–6
B´	Philadelphia	"You kept my word of patient endurance" / an open door	3:7–13
A´	Laodicea	"You are neither cold nor hot" / I stand at the door and knock	3:14–22

The most negative judgments are rendered against Ephesus and Laodicea, the churches in the outermost frame of this concentric structure, and against Sardis and Pergamum, in the innermost frame. The church at Ephesus is commended for their "patient endurance (2:2–3); but they have fallen away from their first love and are called to "repent and do the works you did at first," or God declares that he will "remove your lampstand from its place" (2:5). In short, God will obliterate the church in Ephesus as a Christian community, "unless you repent."

Because the church in Laodicea is judged as being "neither cold nor hot," God declares that he is "about to spit [them] out of [his] mouth" (3:15–16). Nonetheless, God reminds them that, "Those whom I love, I reprove and chasten; so be zealous and repent. Behold, I stand at the door and knock; if any one hears my voice and opens the door, I will come in to him and eat with him, and he with me" (3:19–20).

The church at Pergamum is commended for "holding fast" and not denying their faith "in the days of Antipas my witness, my faithful one, who was killed among you, where Satan's throne is" (2:13). The enigmatic reference to "Satan's throne" probably means the proconsul's judgment seat in Pergamum, which was a center of the imperial cult. Or it may refer to the Great Altar of Zeus erected there after 230 B.C.E., for altars were often designated as thrones in antiquity. In spite of these words of commendation, God pronounces judgment. "I have a few things against you: you have some there who hold to the teaching of Balaam, who taught Balak to put a stumbling block before the people of Israel, so that they would eat food sacrificed to idols and practice fornication" (2:14). The term "witness" (*martus*), used here of an otherwise unknown Christian who was "martyred" marks the beginning of the change in the meaning of this Greek word as commonly used. Though based on the story in Numbers 22—24, the error of Balaam in post-biblical Jewish literature was expanded to involve idolatry and sexual immorality (see Num 31:16; 2 Pet 2:15–16; Jude 11). The reference to the "teaching of the Nicolaitans" refers to those who repeat the error of Balaam (see 2:6).

The church in Sardis is judged almost as harshly as the ones in Ephesus and Laodicea: "I know your works; you have a name of being alive, but you are dead. Wake up, and strengthen what remains and is on the point of death" (3:1–2). There are "still a few persons in Sardis who have not soiled their clothes" with evil deeds (3:4).

The churches in Smyrna and Philadelphia have the distinction of having nothing negative said about them in John's messages to the seven churches. Moreover, in both instances reference is made to the enigmatic "synagogue of Satan who say that they are Jews and are not" (2:9 and 3:9). The church in Smyrna is encouraged in the face of "what you are about to suffer. Beware, the devil is about to throw some of you in prison . . . and for ten days you shall have affliction" (2:10). The church in Philadelphia is commended for their "patient endurance" in the face of suffering, for which God declares: "I will keep you from the hour of trial that is coming on the whole world to test the inhabitants of the earth" (3:10). The message to the church in Philadelphia opens with the words, "Behold, I have set before you an open door, which no one is able to shut" (3:8). Elsewhere the "open door" is a metaphor for opportunities to evangelize (Acts 14:27; 1 Cor 16:9; 2 Cor 2:12) or for access to salvation (Luke 13:24). That the latter is the meaning here is suggested by the fact that the same imagery continues in the following message to the church in Laodicea: "Behold! I stand at the door and knock" (3:20).

The message to the church in Thyatira stands at the structural center of John's messages to the seven churches of Asia (2:18–29). John first commends the church for their "love, faith, service, and patient endurance" (2:19). He then turns his attention to a certain Christian prophetess there whom he designates as "that woman Jezebel, who calls herself a prophet and is teaching and beguiling my servants to practice fornication and to eat food sacrificed to idols" (2:20–23). The sin in question is the "teaching of Balaam" in the message to the church in Pergamum (2:14), which is also the "teaching of the Nicolaitans" (2:6, 15). The reference to "Jezebel" is to the Canaanite queen in Israel (1 Kings 18—19, 2 Kings 9), who induced her husband Ahab to worship Canaanite gods. The reference to "the deep things of Satan" (2:24) is probably a sarcastic revision of the prophetess's own motto—"the deep things of God." The message to the church at Thyatira concludes with a promise, "To the one who conquers I will also give the morning star"—an epithet of Christ (22:16) and a messianic symbol (Num 24:17, Matt 2:2, 10).

The Revelation to John begins with a remarkable vision of the exalted Christ from the Island of Patmos, which functions as an introduction to the messages to the seven churches and the book of Revelation as a whole (1:9–20). The description of the exalted Christ in 1:12–16 resembles other epiphanies of divine figures (19:11–16, Dan 10:5–9). The "seven golden lampstands," which represent the seven churches (1:12, 20), are menorahs intended to burn continually before God in the sanctuary (Exod 27:20–21, Lev 24:2–4). Standing "in the midst of the seven golden lampstands," John saw "one like the Son of Man"—an allusion to Daniel 7:13 (see also Rev 1:13; 14:14). The hair is described as "white as wool" (1:14), which characterizes the "Ancient of Days" in Daniel 7:9. Thus Christ is presented here as implicitly equal with God. The "sharp two-edged sword" proceeding from Christ's mouth is a metaphor for the word of God and for judgment (1:16; see Isa 49:2; 2 Thess 2:8; Heb 4:12). John "fell at his feet as though dead" in fright, but God "placed his right hand on [him]" and instructed him to "write what you have seen (1:9–20), what is (2:1—3:22), and what is to take place after this (4:1—22:5)"—a three-part outline of the book of Revelation.

Revelation concludes with a vision of the new heaven and the new earth (21:1–8) and a final vision of the New Jerusalem (21:9—22:7). In Jewish tradition, the renewal of creation constitutes the final eschatological event—the end is a return to the beginning. The "New Jerusalem" indicates belief in a heavenly counterpart to the earthly Jerusalem, "coming down out of heaven from God, prepared as a bride adorned for her husband...the wife of the Lamb" (21:2, 9). The "measuring rod of gold to measure the city and its gates and walls" (21:15) appears also in the structural center of Revelation, where it is used to "measure the temple of God and the altar and those who worship there" (11:1). "The city lies foursquare"—it forms a gigantic cube (cf. the vision of Ezek 40—48). In this instance, however, there is "no temple in the city, for its temple is the Lord God the Almighty and the Lamb" (21:22). Moreover, "nothing unclean will enter it, nor anyone who practices abominations or falsehood, but only those who are written in the Lamb's book of life"—a heavenly registry of the names of God's people, a metaphor for salvation and election (21:27; cf. 3:5). On the imagery of "the river of the water of life" (22:1), see Ezekiel 47:1–12 and Zechariah 14:8. John saw "the tree of life with its twelve kinds of fruit" on either side of the river (cf. Ezek 47:7–12 and Gen 2:9). The reference to "the leaves of the tree are for the healing of the nations" is to their conversion (22:2). The servants of God from all the nations "will see his face" in a reversal of the ancient tradition in which no one can see God's face (Exod 33:20; Deut 4:12; cf. John 1:18; 6:46; 1 John 4:12). The statement that "his name will be on their foreheads" indicates God's ownership and protection (see 7:2–3). "And there will be no more night; they need no light of lamp or sun, for the Lord God will be their light, and they will reign forever and ever" (22:5). The vision concludes with the words, "See, I am coming soon!" (22:7). The imminent eschatological return of Christ, as proclaimed by John and others in the days prior to the "great disappointment" of ca. 63 C.E., is restated here in keeping with the true meaning of the words of Jesus of earlier tradition (see Matt 24:3–8; Acts 1:6–11).

11

Completion of the Tanakh

THE CANONICAL PROCESS FROM PAUL TO JOHN

The apostle John, who survives the other three "pillars" of the early Christian Church (James [the brother of Jesus], Peter, and Paul) by thirty years, is responsible for five books commonly referred to as the Johannine literature: the Gospel of John, 1–3 John, and the Revelation to John. As we have already noted, he is also responsible for the expansion of the "Apostolic Writings" from a collection of twenty-two books in the original "New Testament" to the forty-nine-book canon of the Completed Tanakh. This is achieved by separating the Four Gospels and Acts as a "New Torah" to connect the First Testament with the Second Testament, each of which is made up of twenty-two books.

After the assassination of James, the brother of Jesus and head of the Jerusalem Church, in the spring of 62 C.E., chaos broke out in Jerusalem within both the Christian community and Judaism as events moved toward a political revolt against the Roman Empire. A mass exodus of people from Palestine takes place from 62 to 64 C.E. and large numbers of Jewish Christians abandon the Christian faith after the great disappointment in 63 C.E. in which the expected events of the final week in Daniel's "seventy weeks of years" fail to materialize. The apostle John is among the émigrés from Palestine, taking refuge in Ephesus in Asia Minor. When the last remnants of the Christian community in Jerusalem retreat to the city of Pella, some sixty miles northeast of Jerusalem, in the summer of 66 C.E., they number at best a thousand or so (Eusebius, *Church History* iii.5). Many of those who leave the Christian community join the ranks of the revolutionary forces when the Jewish Revolt against Rome breaks out in 66 C.E. By the year 70 C.E., Jerusalem is destroyed and the Third Temple (that of King Herod; ca. 20 B.C.E.—70 C.E.) is reduced to smoldering ruins. Three years later at Masada (73 C.E.), the last of the Jewish resistance choose suicide rather than surrender to Rome.

Meanwhile, in Rome, the great fire breaks out on July 19, in 64 C.E. and much of the magnificent city is destroyed. The repercussions of this event are felt throughout the whole Roman Empire. According to Suetonius (*Nero* 40), some of Nero's astrologers even suggest that he ought to move his capital to Jerusalem because in popular belief a new world empire is soon to appear on the scene in Palestine.

Though we cannot trace with any certainty the course of events within the early Christian Church from ca. 62 to 70 C.E., it appears that both Paul and Peter were victims of the persecution of Christians in Rome after the fire of 64 C.E. By this time, the earlier eschatological expectations in which Christians believed in the imminent return of Jesus had shifted a bit. James shared this belief, as witnessed by his comment, "for the coming of the Lord is near" (Jas 5:8). It was his martyrdom in 62 C.E., and the events that unfolded in the following months that led to widespread reassessment of this popular belief.

The shift in Paul's eschatological beliefs had already taken place some years earlier, as shown by careful study of 1 Thessalonians 4:16–17 and 2 Thessalonians 2:1–12 and the simple fact that Paul sees the necessity of leaving behind the Completed Tanakh as canonical scripture for subsequent generations. In 2 Thessalonians 2:1–12, Paul clarifies his earlier teaching, arguing that the day of the Lord's return will not come until the "lawless one" is revealed and destroyed by Jesus himself. It is Paul's belief in a delayed Second Coming of Jesus that leads him and Luke to undertake the task of completing the Tanakh with a collection of "Apostolic Writings." A similar shift in

Peter's teaching is seen by comparing 1 Peter 4:7 ("The end of all things is near") with 2 Peter 3:3–4, which says "that in the last days scoffers will come...saying, 'Where is the promise of the coming? For ever since our ancestors died, all things continue as they were from the beginning of creation!" The former expectation that Christ will come in glory within the lifetime of the first Christian generation is giving way to a new and deeper understanding of the climax of human history in relation to the work of Jesus Christ.

John carries the discussion further with his warning against antichrists. In 1 John 2:18–27, he declares, "Children, it is the last hour!" Like many other early Christians, John believes that he lives "in the last hour" and expects an enemy of God (see 2 Thess 2:3–12) or false messiahs (cf. Mark 13:5–6, 21–22) before the final end. John applies these teachings of an "antichrist" ("counter-Messiah") to the many false teachers within the Christian community that emerge in the months and years following the assassination of James in 62 C.E. In 2 John 7–9, John speaks of "many deceivers...who do not confess that Jesus Christ has come in the flesh." His use of the word "antichrist" here (v. 7) suggests that he has widened his understanding somewhat to include "everyone who does not abide in the teaching of Christ, but goes beyond it" (2 John 9).

Careful analysis of the opening verses of Hebrews, each of the seven General Epistles, and the Revelation to John suggests a deliberate editorial process in the canonical arrangement of these nine books. It also suggests that much of the canonical process, which produced the Completed Tanakh, took place before the destruction of Jerusalem in 70 C.E. It is useful to list and compare the introductory notes for the books associated with the "four pillars" of the church as follows:

Four Books Associated with the Four Pillars of the Early Christian Church

A   Paul/*Hebrews*   "Long ago God spoke by the prophets...but (now) by a Son"

B   James   "servant...of Jesus Christ, to *the twelve tribes in the Dispersion*"

B´   Peter   "an apostle of Jesus Christ, to *the exiles of the Dispersion*"

A´   John/*Revelation*   "The revelation of Jesus Christ...to his servant John"

The introductions to James and 1 Peter make specific reference to Jesus Christ and to "the Dispersion" of the "twelve tribes" or "the exiles" within the Roman Empire. The Epistle to the Hebrews picks up this same theme in its very title, which suggests that the author saw the early Christian Church as the "true Israel" of God. The introduction to Hebrews makes reference to God speaking "by the prophets" in times past, "but in these last days he has spoken to us by a Son" (Heb 1:1–2). The introduction to the Revelation of John continues the same thought with its reference to the "revelation of Jesus Christ," which God makes "known by sending his angel to his servant John" (Rev 1:1). It should be noted that the introduction to Hebrews also makes reference to God's Son as "having become as much superior to angels as the name he has inherited is more excellent than theirs" (Heb 1:4). In short, the wording of the introductions to the four major works associated with the "four pillars" of the early Christian Church is carefully structured in chiastic form—with Paul and John forming a framework around James and Peter. Moreover, the first three of these "pillars" (Paul, James, and Peter) are all addressing the "Hebrews" of "the Dispersion." John, on the other hand, is the channel of "the revelation of Jesus Christ" to "the seven churches that are in Asia" (Rev 1:4).

We have already observed that 2 Peter, 1–3 John, and Jude form a literary unit of their own within the canonical process. It is useful to place these five books within a larger literary context in terms of the editing process carried out by John at the final stage of the canonical process, which may be outlined as follows:

Nine Writings Associated with the Four Pillars of the Church

A	Hebrews	"in these last days (God) has spoken to us by a Son"
B	James	"servant of God and … Jesus Christ"—love one another (2:1–26; 4:1–16)
C	1 Peter	"an apostle of Jesus Christ"/ love one another (3:8)
D	2 Peter	"servant and apostle" / false teachers and their punishment (2:1–22)
X	**1 John**	**No title given—"love one another"**
D′	2 John	"the elder to the elect lady" / false teachers ("antichrists," vv. 7–9)
C′	3 John	"the elder to Gaius" / love to the brethren in the church
B′	Jude	"servant of Jesus Christ and brother of James"—false teachers (vv. 5–7)
A′	Revelation	"revelation of Jesus Christ, which God gave him to show his servants"

The focus of attention in this concentric structure is on 1 John and the command to love one another. Hebrews and 1 John are connected in that they are the only writings among these nine "apostolic writings" in this section of the canon without an editorial introduction that names the author and addressee. Moreover, the opening words of 1 John are intended to direct our attention to the opening words of the Gospel of John. "We declare to you what was from the beginning, what we have heard, what we have seen with our eyes, what we have looked at and touched with our hands, concerning the word of life" (1 John 1:1).

The introductions in the outermost frame of this structure (Hebrews and Revelation) are connected in another way. Hebrews begins with the words "in these last days [God] has spoken to us by a Son" (Heb 1:2). That Son is named in the opening words of the Revelation to John—"The revelation of Jesus Christ, which God gave him to show his servants what must soon take place" (Rev 1:1). The second frame pairs the letters of James, "servant of God and of the Lord Jesus Christ" (Jas 1:1), and Jude, "a servant of Jesus Christ and brother of James" (Jude 1). A further pairing of these two books is evident, by way of contrast, in terms of the subject that occupies the center of each of these two epistles. The injunction to love one another by showing no partiality in our dealings one with another (Jas 2), and by speaking no evil against one another (Jas 4) frame the structural center of James in chapter 3. For Jude the center of attention is on false teachers. The command to love one another occupies center place in 1 Peter and also in its structural counterpart 3 John. The warning about false teachers is in the structural center of 2 Peter and 2 John. These two books form the innermost frame around the book of 1 John, with its elaborate presentation of the command to love one another in 1 John 2:28—3:24. The two primary concerns of the apostle John are clear: We are called to love one another and to beware of false teaching in the church. It is not easy to maintain a proper balance between these two commands. All too often the zeal to protect the faith causes us to forget the command to love one another, or for that matter, to love our enemies as Jesus commanded in the Sermon on the Mount (Matt 5:44).

THREE STEPS IN THE CANONICAL PROCESS
OF EARLY CHRISTIANITY

The first step in the canonical process of early Christianity that produced the Completed Tanakh was the editorial arrangement of eight of Paul's Letters, together with the Gospel of Luke, as a counterpart to the Writings of the Tanakh of ancient Judaism.

In the second step, these "Apostolic Writings" were expanded to form a twenty-two-book canon of the "New Testament" in three parts. This canon included a New Torah consisting of five books (the Four Gospels and Acts), thirteen Letters of Paul as the new prophet, and four writings that were associated with the four "pillars" of the early Christian Church. The structure of this canon reflects the popular understanding of the structure of the twenty-two-book canon of the original Tanakh as described by Josephus at the end of the first century C.E. Josephus described that canon as consisting of five books of Moses (the Torah), thirteen books of the prophets from Moses to the time of Artaxerxes, and four other books that "contain hymns to God and rules of life for men" (the "Hagiographa").

The description of this second step in the canonical process is complicated by the fact that there was no longer a consensus within the Jewish community on how to count the books of the Tanakh. The addition of Esther and Daniel to that canon, both of which are closely associated with the older category of the Festal Scrolls (*Megilloth*) led to new ways of thinking about the structure of the Tanakh in Jewish circles. As a result, even the number of individual books became a matter of dispute. By the time the Mishna was compiled (ca. 200 C.E.), Jewish tradition reckoned the Tanakh as containing twenty-four books.

It was the apostle John who took the third step at this stage of the canonical process by envisioning the canon in terms of its concentric structural design with a "New Torah" at the center of a menorah pattern in a forty-nine-book canon:

The Forty-Nine Books of the Completed Tanakh in a Menorah Pattern

A   Genesis as introduction—from creation to Moses (the true prophet)

B   Twelve Writings—by Moses (4) and the Prophets (8)

C   Nine Writings of First Testament—on life and worship in Second Temple

X   **New Torah: Gospels and Acts—Jesus as the "Prophet like Moses"**

C´   Nine Writings of Second Testament—on life and worship in the church

B´   Twelve Writings—by Paul (4) and the four "pillars" (8)

A´   Revelation as conclusion—judgment and new creation (the final prophet)

In this way of thinking, the Four Gospels and Acts are seen as the center of the Completed Tanakh—forming a bridge to connect the First Testament and the Second Testament. The outermost frame in this concentric structure moves from the book of Genesis, as an introduction to the Bible as a whole, to the book of Revelation, as a grand conclusion that includes a new creation at the end of history. In the center of this structure, we find Jesus Christ as the "true prophet" like Moses, who is presented within the context of a "New Torah" (a Christian Pentateuch) in the structural center of the Bible as a whole. The first half of the second frame in this structure presents the epic story of ancient Israel in twelve books. The story begins with the Exodus from Egypt (Exodus through Deuteronomy). It continues with the Eisodus into the Promised Land, and moves on to the ultimate loss of that land (Former Prophets). It then shifts to a formulation of the messianic vision of God's work among the nations through the people of Israel in time to come (Latter Prophets). These twelve books of the First Testament, four by Moses and eight prophetic writings (the Former Prophets and the Latter Prophets) are set over against twelve apostolic writings in the Second Testament, extending from Paul's four "Personal Letters" to the eight "General Epistles" (Hebrews through Jude). The innermost frame opens with nine books in the Writings of the Tanakh, in which the book of Daniel connects the four books of the "Hagiographa" (Psalms, Job, Proverbs, and the Festal Scrolls) with the Chronicler's History (Ezra, Nehemiah, and 1 and 2 Chronicles). That frame concludes with Paul's nine letters to seven churches (Romans through 2 Thessalonians).

Three Steps in the Canonical Process to Complete the Tanakh

1st Step	2nd Step	3rd Step
[Ca. 55–58 C.E.]	[Ca. 58–64 C.E.]	[Ca. 96 C.E.]
Apostolic Writings	*"New Testament"*	*Completed Tanakh*
[As a 5th section in the Tanakh]	[22 books in each Testament]	[22 + 5 + 22 = 49 books]
Paul and Luke	Paul, Luke, Mark, etc.	John
Greece & Asia Minor	Rome	Ephesus & Palestine

Another way of looking at the structure of the Completed Tanakh (Torah + Prophets +.Writings) is to put the books of the Bible in their "correct" order in a linear outline, as follows:

Contents of the Completed Tanakh (49 books = 22 + 5 + 22 = 7²)

First Testament

    Torah (Genesis through Deuteronomy)

    Prophets (*Nevi'im*)—Former Prophets and Latter Prophets

    Writings (*Kethuvim*)—"Hagiographa," Daniel, and "Chronicler's History"

New Torah

    Four Gospels (Matthew, Mark, Luke, and John)

    Acts of the Apostles

Second Testament

    Letters of Paul—an apostolic prophet

    Other Apostolic Writings—associated with the four "pillars" of the Church

    Revelation to John—as the final prophet

For the First Testament, this order of the books in the Completed Tanakh is essentially that of the common practice in Judaism through the centuries. For the Second Testament, it is the order of books in the traditional "New Testament," as recognized in common practice in the Christian Church from the time Jerome published the Latin Vulgate (ca. 400 C.E.) to the present. We believe that this order of the books in the Bible as a whole is also that of the apostle John at the end of the first century C.E. John revised his own Gospel and the book of Revelation. But, of perhaps greater importance, he is responsible for adding five books (2 Peter, 2–3 John, Jude, and Revelation) so as to have twenty-seven books in the "New Testament" and forty-nine books in the Completed Tanakh.

For John and the followers of Jesus who come after him, the center of the canonical process is the person and work of God in Yeshua the Messiah (Jesus Christ) and the appearance of the Holy Spirit within the life-span of the original twelve apostles. The story of that work constitutes a New Torah, a canon within the canon that connects the twenty-two books of the First Testament with the twenty-two books of the Second Testament to form the official canon of God's revelation, the Completed Tanakh—the Bible as a whole.

Index